Essential Reading Skills

Third Edition

Kathleen T. McWhorter

Niagara County Community College

PEARSON
Longman

New York   San Francisco   Boston
London   Toronto   Sydney   Tokyo   Singapore   Madrid
Mexico City   Munich   Paris   Cape Town   Hong Kong   Montreal

Acquisitions Editor: Melanie Craig
Development Editor: Gillian Cook
Senior Supplements Editor: Donna Campion
Media Supplements Editor: Jenna Egan
Marketing Manager: Thomas DeMarco
Production Manager: Bob Ginsberg
Project Coordination, Text Design, and Electronic Page Makeup:
	Thompson Steele, Inc.
Cover Design Manager: Wendy Ann Fredericks
Cover Photos: *(top)* Tom Grill/AGE Fotostock America, Inc.; *(bottom left)*
	Martin Heitner/Stock Connection/Jupiter Images; *(bottom right)* Banana
	Stock/AGE Fotostock America, Inc.
Photo Researcher: Jody Potter
Manufacturing Buyer: Lucy Hebard
Printer and Binder: R.R. Donnelley & Sons, Inc. / Crawfordsville
Cover Printer: Coral Graphic Services, Inc.

For permission to use copyrighted material, grateful acknowledgment is made to the
copyright holders on pp. 489–491, which are hereby made part of this copyright page.

Visit us at www.ablongman.com

ISBN 0-321-42993-1   (Student Edition)
ISBN 0-321-43147-2   (Annotated Instructor's Edition)

7 8 9 10 11 12-DOC-10 11 12 13 14 15

Brief Contents

Detailed Contents

Directions for Accessing Online Chapter
1. Type in URL http://www.ablongman.com/mcwhorter
2. Click on cover of text
3. Click on link to Online Chapter

⁎ This chapter is available online at www.ablongman.com/mcwhorter

Preface

Essential Reading Skills is designed to improve students' reading and thinking skills through concise skill instruction, extensive guided practice, assessment, and feedback. It was written to provide students at both two- and four-year colleges with a foundation of reading and thinking skills that will enable them to successfully handle their college courses. The text offers brief strategies for and extensive application of the reading skills essential to college success: active reading and thinking, vocabulary development, literal and critical comprehension, and information organization.

Content Overview

The text is organized into eleven chapters, each focusing on a set of specific reading and thinking skills and each following a consistent format. Chapter 1 introduces students to active reading strategies and builds a positive attitude toward reading and learning in college. Students learn to build their concentration, preview before reading, and use guide questions to focus their reading. Chapters 2, 3, and 4 teach essential vocabulary skills: dictionary skills, contextual aids, and word parts, respectively. Chapters 5, 6, and 7 focus on literal comprehension skills: locating main ideas, identifying supporting details and transitions, and understanding implied main ideas. Chapter 8 identifies five ways of organizing information: highlighting, marking, outlining, mapping, and summarizing. Basic organizational patterns are introduced in Chapter 9, while Chapter 10 focuses on two specific patterns: comparison/contrast and cause/effect. Chapter 11 provides an introduction to critical thinking skills and explores two essential skills: making inferences and identifying the author's purpose.

Chapter Format

Each chapter follows a regular format and sequence, giving students the benefit of a predictable, consistent structure.

Read Me First!   The chapter opener begins with a striking visual (a photograph, cartoon, or drawing) to elicit student response. This section immediately engages the students, sparks their interest, demonstrates the relevance of chapter content, and motivates them to progress through the chapter.

Concise Skill Instruction.   Chapter skills are presented briefly and concisely, using frequent examples. This section tells students what they need to know in the simplest terms possible.

Practice Exercises.   Interspersed within the concise skill instruction section are numerous exercises that provide students with ample opportunity to develop and apply skills. The exercises usually involve small steps, leading students through skills gradually and sequentially.

Textbook Challenge.   Divided into two parts, this exercise encourages students to apply chapter skills to a textbook excerpt in the text and then to a chapter in one of their own textbooks.

What Have You Learned?   This self-test quiz reviews factual chapter content and enables students to determine whether they have understood and learned chapter concepts and ideas.

What Vocabulary Have You Learned?   Based on words used in the chapter, this exercise provides vocabulary enrichment and emphasizes the importance of ongoing vocabulary development.

Test-Taking Tips.   These tips provide students with strategies for approaching multiple choice items on reading vocabulary and comprehension tests.

Practice Tests.   Three review tests at the end of every chapter encourage students to synthesize the skills they have learned. Often, these tests are based on slightly longer material.

Mastery Tests.   Three mastery tests conclude each chapter. The first two tests require students to apply and integrate chapter-specific reading skills to paragraphs and short passages. The third mastery test, based on a full-length reading selection, includes general comprehension questions as well as questions on the specific skills taught within the chapter.

Special Features

The following features enhance the text's effectiveness and directly contribute to student success:

- **Emphasis on essential reading skills.** Because the instruction is brief and concise, students learn the most important college reading skills. The text does not contain extra material—often perceived by students as filler—that they have to pay for but do not use.

- **Visual elements.** Increasingly, college students have become visual learners as visual literacy has become critical to success in today's world. In addition, many students are more comfortable with images than with text. To facilitate visual learning and to accommodate students' visual learning preferences, this four-color book uses visual material to teach key concepts. Photographs, maps, diagrams, and charts are used to clarify relationships, depict sequences, and demonstrate paragraph organization.

- **Consistent format.** Both students and instructors will benefit from the consistent format followed in each chapter. Students will learn the value of consistency, and instructors will find it easy to structure class time, plan assignments, and develop a grading system.

- **Extensive practice.** Numerous exercises enable students to successfully apply their learning. The chapter tests provide students with observable, measurable evidence that they are learning and improving their skills. Students may use these exercises as practice tests—as the "test before the test."

- **Student Resource Guide A: Introduction to College Textbook Reading.** This section explains useful textbook features, how to read, study and learn from textbooks, and includes three textbook excerpts for application of skills.

- Online **Student Resource Guide: Test-Taking Strategies: A Review.** This guide shows students how to approach all types of exams, and how to apply thinking and reasoning skills to objective exams.

Changes to the Third Edition

The third edition of *Essential Reading Skills* contains numerous changes and additions that recognize and accommodate the needs and skill levels of students using the book.

- **NEW: Chapter 2, "Using Your Dictionary,"** shows students how to read dictionary entries, determine word meaning, and pronounce unfamiliar words.

- **NEW: Student Resource Guide B: A Guide for ESL Readers** begins with practical tips for ESL readers of English and is followed by instruction on sentence basics, using punctuation, recognizing word order, and understanding idioms. A glossary of Frequently Confused Words and Phrases is also included.

- **NEW: Multicultural Reader.** Replacing the Additional Readings in the previous edition, this collection of seven readings represents a wide range of racial and ethnic communities. The apparatus that follows each reading uses the same format as Mastery Test 3 Readings at the end of each chapter, allowing instructors to substitute readings as desired.

- **NEW full-length reading selections.** New topics include online dating, single parenting, the AIDS crisis, Native American mascots, and parental relationships (Amy Tan).

- **NEW: A Textbook Challenge exercise at the end of every chapter** provides students with practice using vocabulary words that appear in the chapter's examples and exercises. These exercises reinforce the importance of ongoing vocabulary development.

- **NEW: A "Studying Words" exercise has been added to each full-length reading and to the readings in the Multicultural Reader.** This exercise focuses on dictionary usage and word study, and includes items on word pronunciation, multiple meanings, parts of speech, etymology, and restrictive meanings.

Book-Specific Ancillary Materials

- **Annotated Instructor's Edition.** (ISBN 0-321-43147-2) This annotated edition is identical to the student text but includes all the answers printed directly on the pages where questions, exercises, or activities occur.

- **Instructor's Manual.** (ISBN 0-321-44579-1) This manual includes an answer key and describes in detail the basic features of the text. This manual also offers suggestions for structuring the course, teaching non-traditional students, and approaching each chapter of the text.

- **Test Bank (Printed and Electronic).** (ISBN 0-321-44580-5) This book-specific test bank contains additional practice material and mastery tests for each chapter. It is printed in an 8½-by-11-inch format that allows for easy photocopying and distribution.

- **Companion Website.** A complete Web site accompanies *Essential Reading Skills* with additional quizzes, readings, and Web-based activities for each chapter of the text. Stop by for extra practice at http://www.ablongman.com/mcwhorter

- **Reader's Journal.** Instructors may choose to shrink-wrap *Essential Reading Skills* with a copy of The Longman Reader's Journal at no additional cost. This innovative journal provides students with a place to record their questions about, reactions to, and summaries of what they've read. Also included is a personal vocabulary log and additional pages for reflection. To preview the journal, contact your Longman sales consultant.

- *Vocabulary Simplified.* Instructors may choose to shrink-wrap *Essential Reading Skills* with a copy of Kathleen McWhoter's *Vocabulary Simplified* (ISBN 0-3231-14256-X) for a significant discount. Students can work through the book independently or units may be incorporated into weekly lesson plans. Topics covered include methods of vocabulary learning, contextual aids, word parts, connotative meanings, idioms, euphemisms, and many more interesting and fun topics. The book concludes with vocabulary lists and exercises representative of eleven academic disciplines.

The Longman Developmental Reading Package

Longman is pleased to offer a variety of support materials to help make teaching developmental reading easier for teachers and to help students excel in their course work. Visit http://www.ablongman.com or contact your local Longman sales rep representative for a detailed listing of our supplements package or for more information on pricing and how to create a package.

Acknowledgments

I wish to express my gratitude to my reviewers for their excellent ideas, suggestions, and advice on the preparation of this text and its revision: Allison De Vaney, El Camino College; Vicki Fox, Pima Community College East; Jean Gammon, Chattanooga State Technical Community College; Richard D. Grossman, Tompkins Cortland Community College; Maureen E. Hoffman, Central Community College; Brenda Inglis Marks, Clackamas Community College; Joan Mauldin, San Jacinto College South; William McNeill, Robeson Community College; Susan Messina, Solano Community College; Susan Nnaji, Prairie View A [M University] Marcia Oppenheim, Pima Community College; Given Parsons, Howard College; Vonnye Rice-Gardner, Austin Community College; Florinda Rodriguez, South Texas Community College; Carol G. Shier, Fullerton College; Ellen Smith, Contra Costa College; Paula Therrell, Holmes Community College; Joy Wells, South Texas Community College; Pam Williamson, Odessa College.

I am particularly indebted to Gillian Cook, development editor, for overseeing this project and attending to the many details to ready the book for production, and to Melanie Craig, acquisitions editor, for her support and assistance in the revision of this book.

KATHLEEN T. MCWHORTER

READ ME FIRST!

Look at the two photographs below, which show people watching a sporting event. How do the fans in each photograph differ in their behavior? Which group seems interested and is actively participating in the game? Which group does not seem to be involved? These two photographs demonstrate the difference between active involvement and passive observation. The fans in only one photograph are responding and reacting—shouting, cheering, and interacting with the game they are watching. They feel and act as if it's their game, not just the players' game. In a similar way, active readers get involved with the material they are reading. They think, question, challenge, and criticize the author's ideas. They try to make the material *their* material. This chapter will give you some tips on how to become an active, successful reader.

CHAPTER 1

Reading Actively

Starting with a Positive Attitude

Just as active sports fans have a positive attitude about the games they watch, college students need to be positive about their courses and what they read. A positive attitude is a key to college success and to success on the job. Here are a few tips that will help you become a successful college student:

- **Be confident: Send yourself positive messages.** Tell yourself that college is something you want and can do. Negative thoughts such as "I might not be able to do this" or "What if I fail?" will only get in the way. Send yourself positive messages such as "I can do this," or "I've studied hard, and I'm going to pass this test."

- **Visualize success.** Close your eyes and imagine yourself completing a long or difficult assignment, or doing well on an upcoming exam.

- **Set long-term goals for yourself.** You will feel more like working on assignments if you have specific objectives you are working toward. Goals such as "To get my own apartment," "To be able to quit my low-paying job," or "To become a registered nurse" will help you stick with daily tasks.

- **Plan on spending time reading.** Reading is not something you can rush through. The time you invest will pay off in better understanding and better grades.

1

- **Actively search for key ideas as you read.** Think of reading as a way of sifting and sorting out what you need to learn from the less important information.

- **Think of reading as a way of unlocking the writer's message to you, the reader.** Look for clues about the writer's personality, attitudes, opinions, and beliefs. This will put you in touch with the writer as a person and help you understand his or her message.

- **Stick with a reading assignment.** If an assignment is troublesome, experiment with different methods for completing it. Try highlighting important ideas or taking notes, for example. (Several methods are discussed in Chapter 8.)

Improve Your Surroundings

Make sure you create a workable study environment.

- **Choose a place with a minimum of distractions.**
- **Establish a study area** with a table or desk that is yours alone for study.
- **Control noise levels.** Determine how much background noise, if any, you can tolerate and choose a place best suited to you.
- **Eliminate distracting clutter.** Get rid of photos, stacks of bills, mementos, and so forth.
- **Have necessary supplies at your fingertips**—for example, dictionaries, pens, calculator, calendar, clock.

Pay Attention

Once your study area is set up, use the following ideas to help you pay attention to what you are reading or studying:

- **Establish goals and time limits for each assignment.** Deadlines will keep you motivated and create a sense of urgency so you will be less likely to daydream or become distracted.
- **Reward yourself.** Use rewards such as phoning a friend or ordering a pizza when you complete an evening of study.
- **Use writing to keep mentally and physically active.** Highlighting or taking notes will force you to keep your mind on the material you are reading.
- **Vary your activities.** Alternate between writing, reading, reviewing, and solving math problems.

- **Keep a distractions list.** As distracting thoughts enter your mind, jot them on a notepad. You may, for example, think of your mother's upcoming birthday as you're reading psychology. Writing it down will help you remember it and will eliminate the distraction.

Exercise 1–1

Directions: Rate each of the following statements from students as either helpful (H) or not helpful (NH) in building a positive attitude toward college and improving concentration. Then discuss how each of the statements marked NH could be changed to be more helpful.

_____   1. This assignment is taking forever! My sister won't turn down her loud music, and I can't find my dictionary or notebook.

_____   2. Whenever I imagine myself taking a test, I see myself getting nervous and my mind going blank.

_____   3. If I do this reading assignment really fast, I'll get to watch my favorite TV show.

_____   4. This assignment is more difficult than I expected. I'll start over and try highlighting it.

_____   5. I plan to become an elementary school physical education teacher, so college is important to me.

_____   6. This assignment is boring; I don't know why we have to read about World War I.

_____   7. I worked really hard and finished all of my assignments tonight. I think I'll celebrate by meeting Janie for Chinese food.

_____   8. This writer seems opposed to high-protein diets. I wonder if she'll give her reasons later in the reading.

_____   9. I read and reviewed the assignment twice, and I feel like I understand the material, so I should be able to pass the test on it.

_____   10. I am attending college because my parents want me to.

Previewing Before You Read

You would not cross a city street without checking for traffic first. You would not pay to see a movie you had never heard of and knew nothing about. You would not buy a car without test-driving it or checking its mechanical condition.

Neither should you read an article or a textbook chapter without knowing what it is about or how it is organized. **Previewing** is a way of quickly familiarizing yourself with the organization and content of written material *before* beginning to read it. It is an easy method to use and will make a dramatic difference in how effectively you read.

How to Preview

When you preview, try to (1) find only the most important ideas in the material, and (2) note how they are organized. To do this, look only at the parts that state these important ideas and skip the rest. Previewing is a fairly rapid technique; it should take only a minute or two to preview any reading selection in this book. In fact, previewing is so fast that you should *not* take time to highlight or make notes. To preview an article or textbook chapter, look at the following parts:

- **Title and subtitle:** The title is a label that explains what the chapter is about. The subtitle, if there is one, suggests additional perspectives on the subject. For example, an article titled "Brazil" might be subtitled "The World's Next Superpower." In this instance, the subtitle tells which aspects of Brazil the article discusses.
- **First paragraph:** The first paragraph or introduction of a reading may provide an overview and offer clues about how a chapter or article is organized.
- **Section headings:** Section headings, like titles, identify and separate important topics and ideas.
- **First sentence under each heading:** The first sentence following a heading often further explains the heading. It may also state the central thought of the section it introduces.
- **Typographical aids:** Typographical aids are those features of a page that help to highlight and organize information. These include *italics,* **bold-faced type,** marginal notes, colored ink, underlining, and numbering.
- **Final paragraph or summary:** The final paragraph may review the main points of the reading or bring it to a close.

Demonstration of Previewing

The following excerpt, from a chapter of a communications textbook on nonverbal messages (messages that do not use words), discusses four major functions of eye communication. It has been included to help you understand previewing. Everything that you should look at or read has been highlighted. Preview this selection now, reading *only* the highlighted portions.

FUNCTIONS OF EYE COMMUNICATION

From Ben Jonson's poetic observation "Drink to me only with thine eyes, and I will pledge with mine" to the scientific observations of contemporary researchers, the eyes are regarded as the most important nonverbal message system. Researchers note four major functions of eye communication.

To Seek Feedback

You frequently use your eyes to seek feedback from others. In talking with someone, you look at her or him intently, as if to say, "Well, what do you think?" As you might predict, listeners gaze at speakers more than speakers gaze at listeners. Research shows that the percentage of interaction time spent gazing while listening was between 62 and 75 percent. However, the percentage of time spent gazing while talking was between 38 and 41 percent.

Women make eye contact more and maintain it longer (both in speaking and in listening) than do men. This holds true whether the woman is interacting with other women or with men. This difference in eye behavior may result from women's tendency to display their emotions more than men; eye contact is one of the most effective ways of communicating emotions. Another possible explanation is that women have been conditioned more than men to seek positive feedback from others. Women may thus use eye contact in seeking this visual feedback.

To Regulate the Conversation

A second function of eye contact is to regulate the conversation and particularly to pass the speaking turn from one person to another. You use eye contact, for example, to tell the listener that you are finished with your thought and that you would now like to assume the role of listener and hear what the other person has to say. Or, by maintaining a steady eye contact while you plan your next sentence, you tell the other person that although you are now silent, you don't want to give up your speaking turn. You also see this in the college classroom when the instructor asks a question and then locks eyes with a student—without saying anything, the instructor clearly communicates the desire for that student to say something.

To Signal the Nature of the Relationship

Eye contact is also used to signal the nature of the relationship between two people—for example, a focused attentive glance indicates a positive relationship, but avoiding eye contact shows one of negative regard. You may also signal status relationships with your eyes. This is particularly interesting because the same movements of the eyes may signal either subordination or superiority. The superior individual, for example, may stare at the subordinate or may glance away. Similarly, the subordinate may look directly at the superior or perhaps at the floor.

Eye movements may also signal whether the relationship between two people is amorous, hostile, or indifferent. Because some of the eye movements expressing these different relationships are so similar, you often use information from other areas, particularly the rest of the face, to decode the message before making any final judgments.

To Make Up for Increased Physical Distance

Last, eye movements may make up for increased physical distance. By making eye contact you overcome psychologically the physical distance between you and the other individual. When you catch someone's eye at a party, for example, you become psychologically close even though separated by a large physical distance. Not surprisingly, eye contact and other expressions of psychological closeness, such as self-disclosure, are positively related; as one increases, so does the other.

—DeVito, *Messages,* 4th Ed., p. 146

Although you may not realize it, you have gained a substantial amount of information from the minute or so that you just spent previewing. You have become familiar with the key ideas in this selection.

**Exercise
1–2**

Directions: Read the following statements and mark each one true (T) or false (F) based on what you learned by previewing the selection above.

_____ 1. The most important nonverbal message system involves the eyes.

_____ 2. We can obtain feedback from others by using just our eyes.

_____ 3. Eye movements cannot make up for physical distances.

_____ 4. The relationship between two people can be signaled through eye contact.

_____ 5. Eye contact regulates conversations.

This exercise tested your recall of some of the more important ideas in the article. Check your answers by referring back to the article. Did you get most or all of the above items correct? You can see, then, that previewing helps you learn the major ideas in a section before you read it.

Exercise 1–3

Directions: Carlos is taking a course in psychology and has been assigned to read an article from Psychology Today, *titled "Laughter: A Cure for What Ails You." He plans to preview the article before reading it. Choose the letter of the choice that best completes each of the following statements about this situation.*

_____ 1. The main reason that Carlos should preview his assignment is to
   a. memorize facts and details.
   b. evaluate the author's qualifications.
   c. identify the most important ideas in the material.
   d. decide how he feels about the topic.

_____ 2. Carlos can expect the subtitle, "A Cure for What Ails You," to
   a. indicate what aspect of laughter the article will discuss.
   b. reveal a personal story about the author.
   c. suggest that the author is going to list her reasons for liking or disliking laughter.
   d. explain how the author will organize her ideas.

_____ 3. The article contains five headings. Carlos can expect each heading to
   a. introduce a story or example.
   b. separate different kinds of research.
   c. continue with the same idea.
   d. introduce a new idea.

_____   4. Several sentences in the article appear in boldfaced print. When previewing, Carlos should
   a. skip them.
   b. read them.
   c. copy them.
   d. read them aloud to a classmate.

_____   5. Carlos should expect the last paragraph of the article to
   a. ask questions the reading leaves unanswered.
   b. suggest other uses of laughter.
   c. bring the article to a close.
   d. reveal the author's opinions on the topic.

Exercise 1–4

Directions: *Match the previewing step listed in column A with the type of information it provides in column B. Use each item only once. Write the letter of your choice in the space provided.*

Column A	Column B
_____ 1. title	a. provides an overview
_____ 2. first paragraph	b. summarizes the article
_____ 3. section headings	c. identify and separate main topics
_____ 4. typographical aids	d. indicate important information
_____ 5. last paragraph	e. identifies the subject

Guide Questions

Did you ever read an entire page or more and not remember anything you read? Have you found yourself going from paragraph to paragraph without really thinking about what the writer is saying? Guide questions can help you overcome these problems. **Guide questions** are questions you expect to be able to answer while or after you read. Most students form them mentally, but you can jot them in the margin if you prefer.

The following tips can help you form questions to guide your reading. It is best to develop guide questions *after* you preview but *before* you read.

- **Turn each major heading into a series of questions.** The questions should ask something that you feel is important to know.

- **As you read a section, look for the answers to your questions.** Highlight the answers as you find them.
- **When you finish reading a section, stop and check to see whether you can recall the answers.** Place check marks by those you cannot recall. Then reread.
- **Avoid asking questions that have one-word answers, like** *yes* **or** *no*. Questions that begin with *what, why,* or *how* are more useful.

Here are a few textbook headings and some examples of questions you might ask:

Heading	Questions
Reducing Prejudice	How can prejudice be reduced? What type of prejudice is discussed?
The Deepening Recession	What is a recession? Why is it deepening?
Newton's First Law of Motion	Who was Newton? What is his First Law of Motion?

Exercise 1–5

Directions: Choose the letter of the guide question that would be most helpful in improving your understanding of the textbook chapter sections that begin with the following headings:

_____ 1. Defining Loneliness
   a. Is loneliness unusual?
   b. What does loneliness mean?
   c. Are adults lonelier than children?
   d. Can loneliness ever be positive?

_____ 2. The Four Basic Functions of Management
   a. How important is management?
   b. Are there other functions of management?
   c. What are management's four basic functions?
   d. Do poor managers cause serious problems?

_____ 3. Surface Versus Depth Listening
   a. Is surface listening difficult?
   b. What is listening?
   c. How do surface and depth listening differ?
   d. Is depth listening important?

_____   4. The Origins of the Cold War
              a. How did the Cold War start?
              b. Is the Cold War still going on?
              c. How did the United States deal with the Cold War?
              d. Did the Cold War end through compromise?

_____   5. Some People Are More Powerful Than Others
              a. Does power affect relationships?
              b. Why are some people more powerful than others?
              c. What is power?
              d. Can people learn to become more powerful?

Putting Your Positive Attitude to Work

Throughout this chapter you have picked up many tips for being an active reader. You know that a positive attitude is important as are a workable environment for studying and the ability to pay attention. You've also learned how to preview material before you read and how to ask guide questions from major headings. Now you can put your positive attitude and active reading skills to work throughout the remainder of the book.

The Textbook Challenge

Part A: Student Resource Guide A

Preview Textbook Excerpt 2, "Food Safety: A Growing Concern," (p. 403) and then write five guide questions that will help you focus on chapter content. Read the excerpt and write answers to your guide questions.

Part B: A College Textbook

Choose a chapter from one of your textbooks for another course. Preview the chapter and then write a list of guide questions that will help you focus on chapter content as you read. Read the chapter and write answers to your guide questions.

What Have You Learned?

Directions: To check your understanding of the chapter and to review its major points, indicate whether each of the following statements is true (T) or false (F).

_____ 1. Worrying about failing a test can help you develop a positive attitude toward college.

_____ 2. Reading is not something you should rush through.

_____ 3. Where you study does not usually affect your concentration.

_____ 4. Setting goals and time limits for each assignment helps to keep you motivated.

_____ 5. Previewing is a quick way to become familiar with a chapter or article before you read it.

_____ 6. The best guide questions have one-word answers.

What Vocabulary Have You Learned?

Directions: The words in column A appear in exercises or examples in this chapter. Test your mastery of these words by matching the words in column A with their meanings in column B.

Column A

_____ 1. contemporary

_____ 2. conditioned

_____ 3. regulate

_____ 4. subordination

_____ 5. amorous

Column B

a. romantic

b. inferiority; lower status

c. trained or prepared

d. control

e. modern

Test-Taking Tip #1: Active Test-Taking

The attitude with which you approach a test is very important and can dramatically affect your performance. It is essential to think positively and approach the test actively. Use the following suggestions:

■ Remind yourself that you have worked hard and deserve to pass.

■ Think of the test as a chance to show what you have learned.

■ Don't panic if you cannot answer a question. Make a guess and move on to items you can answer.

■ If you do not immediately know an answer, *Think!* You may be able to reason it out. The tip boxes in other chapters will offer suggestions.

NAME _____   SECTION _____

DATE _____   SCORE _____

ACTIVE READING SKILLS

Directions: In the space provided, write the letter of the choice that best completes each of the following statements.

_____   1. Which of the following tips will *not* help you build a positive attitude toward college and reading?

    a. Look for key ideas as you read.

    b. Visualize the major problems you might encounter.

    c. Establish long-term goals for yourself.

    d. Send yourself positive messages.

_____   2. While studying and reading, you should

    a. speed up your reading whenever possible.

    b. stick with an assignment even if it is difficult.

    c. work on only one subject per week.

    d. set no time limits for yourself.

_____   3. To build your concentration, you should

    a. reward yourself after each hour of study.

    b. study in your bedroom.

    c. control the noise in your study environment.

    d. eliminate all time pressures.

_____   4. Previewing written material is a way to

    a. familiarize yourself with the material's important ideas.

    b. test your knowledge of the subject.

    c. draw conclusions from the material.

    d. determine the author's prejudices.

_____   5. When previewing a textbook chapter or article, you should read all of the following *except*

    a. the last paragraph.

    b. the section headings.

    c. the introductory paragraph.

    d. the references and footnotes.

_____ 6. Developing guide questions is primarily intended to
   a. give you practice answering test questions.
   b. help you remember what you have read.
   c. force you to read out loud.
   d. eliminate distractions.

_____ 7. The easiest way to form guide questions is to use the
   a. introduction.   c. summary.
   b. review questions.   d. headings.

_____ 8. One way to pay attention as you read and study is to
   a. save your most difficult subject for last.
   b. call your classmates for advice.
   c. take notes to keep your mind on the material.
   d. study at different times during the day.

_____ 9. The first paragraph of a chapter or reading usually provides
   a. review questions.
   b. an overview.
   c. the author's conclusion.
   d. a list of difficult vocabulary words.

_____ 10. Section headings are important because they usually
   a. identify the general subject.
   b. identify important topics and ideas.
   c. present summaries of the material.
   d. reveal the author's biases.

NAME _____ SECTION _____

DATE _____ SCORE _____

ACTIVE READING SKILLS

Directions: In the space provided, write the letter of the choice that best completes each of the following statements.

_____ 1. Guide questions should be asked

  a. before previewing.

  b. after previewing but before reading.

  c. after reading.

  d. during review.

_____ 2. Typographical aids include all of the following *except*

  a. introductions.   c. boldfaced type.

  b. colored ink.   d. underlining.

_____ 3. Which of the following guide questions would be the best to ask for a section in your history text on the Revolutionary War?

  a. When did it start?   c. Why did it start?

  b. Where did it start?   d. Did it last very long?

_____ 4. The main purpose of a distractions list is to

  a. keep your study area neat.

  b. organize your time after a study session.

  c. maintain your interest in a reading assignment.

  d. reduce the random thoughts that come to mind as you study.

_____ 5. The first sentence under a section heading usually

  a. gives the author's qualifications.

  b. further explains the heading.

  c. provides personal examples.

  d. announces the author's purpose for writing.

_____ 6. A useful type of guide question would probably begin with the word

  a. *Who*   c. *Where*

  b. *When*   d. *Why*

_____ 7. Building your concentration includes all of the following *except*

    a. eliminating distractions.

    b. increasing your reading speed.

    c. paying attention.

    d. rewarding yourself.

_____ 8. Maria has several reading assignments to complete in one evening. Before she begins, it is important for her to

    a. make a distractions list.

    b. reward herself.

    c. take some notes on the material.

    d. organize her study area.

_____ 9. Andrew has begun to preview an article called "Civil Rights and Issues of Race." He can tell that this article will probably discuss

    a. feminism.   c. sexual harassment.

    b. racial discrimination.   d. religious persecution.

_____ 10. The best guide question for an article titled "U.S. Voter Turnout: Among the Lowest in the World" would be

    a. What country has the highest turnout rate?

    b. What country has the lowest turnout rate?

    c. How many Americans voted in the last presidential election?

    d. Why is voter turnout so low in the United States?

PREVIEWING

Directions: The following excerpt is from a business marketing textbook. Preview by reading **only** the highlighted sections of the reading, and then, in the space provided, write the letter of the choice that best completes the statements that follow. Do **not** read the section completely.

THE PHYSICAL ENVIRONMENT IN STORES AND RESTAURANTS

It's no secret that people's moods and behaviors are strongly influenced by their physical surroundings. Despite all their efforts to presell consumers through advertising, marketers know that the store environment influences many purchases. For example, consumers decide on about two out of every three supermarket product purchases in the aisles. Therefore, the messages they receive at the time and their feelings about being in the store are important influences on their decisions.

Factors That Influence Shoppers

Two dimensions, *arousal* and *pleasure*, determine if a shopper will react positively or negatively to a store environment. In other words, the person's surroundings can be either dull or exciting (arousing), and either pleasant or not. Just because the environment is arousing doesn't necessarily mean it will be pleasant—we've all been in crowded, hot stores that are anything but! Maintaining an upbeat feeling in a pleasant context is one factor behind the success of theme parks such as Disney World, which try to provide consistent doses of carefully calculated stimulation to patrons.

The Appeal of Themed Environments

The importance of these surroundings explains why many retailers are combining two favorite consumer activities, shopping and eating, into elaborate *themed environments*. According to a recent Roper Starch survey, eating out is the top form of out-of-home entertainment, and innovative firms are scrambling to offer customers a chance to eat, buy, and be entertained all at once. Planet Hollywood, for example, is crammed full of costumes and props, and the chain now grosses over $200 million a year around the world.

Visual and Audio Elements in Restaurants

A lot of the appeal of these themed environments is that there are plenty of interesting things to look at while wolfing down your burger. In addition to visual stimuli, though, other sensory cues can also influence consumers—that's why the Harley-Davidson Café features the roar of a "hog" engine as part of its décor. Sounds and music can affect eating behavior—one study found that diners who listened to loud, fast music ate more and faster than those who listened to classical. The researchers concluded that diners who choose soothing music at mealtimes can increase weight loss by at least five pounds a month!

Indeed, a growing recognition of the important role played by a store or restaurant's audio environment has created a new market niche, as some companies now are selling musical collections tailored to different activities. These include RCA Victor's "Classical Music for Home Improvements" and Sony Classics' "Cyber Classics" that are billed as music specifically for computer hackers to listen to while programming! Sony's "Extreme Classics," packaged just for bungee jumpers, is claimed to be the "loudest and most dangerous music ever written."

—Solomon and Stuart, *Marketing*, pp. 161–162

1. The title suggests that the reading's general topic will be
   a. access for handicapped individuals.
   b. the physical surroundings within stores and restaurants.
   c. that personnel can influence business surroundings.
   d. how a store's surroundings can increase sales.

2. All of the following previewing aids are found in the selection *except*
   a. an introductory paragraph.
   b. a subtitle.
   c. typographical aids.
   d. section headings.

3. By reading the introductory paragraph as part of your preview, you would expect the reading to focus on
   a. the effects of advertising on shoppers.
   b. how supermarket products are sold.
   c. people's moods when they're not shopping.
   d. messages and feelings shoppers experience while in a store.

_____ 4. The most helpful guide question to ask for the heading "Factors That Influence Shoppers" is

    a. What factors influence shoppers?

    b. Why do stores want to influence shoppers?

    c. Are shoppers easily influenced?

    d. What is influence?

_____ 5. The two factors that are most likely to determine a shopper's response to a store's environment are

    a. convenience and location.

    b. arousal and pleasure.

    c. price and themes.

    d. crowds and arrangement of goods.

_____ 6. The most helpful guide question to ask for the heading "The Appeal of Themed Environments" is

    a. Where are themed stores located?

    b. Why are themed stores popular?

    c. When did theme restaurants first open?

    d. What kinds of shoppers like themed stores?

_____ 7. The two favorite consumer activities that themed stores combine are

    a. shopping and exercising.

    b. shopping and relaxing.

    c. shopping and socializing.

    d. shopping and eating.

_____ 8. The third heading, "Visual and Audio Elements in Restaurants," tells you that

    a. store elements must be visual.

    b. restaurant personnel should be seen but not heard.

    c. what consumers see and hear is important.

    d. audio and visual equipment sells quickly.

_____ 9. The sentence that follows the third heading, "Visual and Audio Elements in Restaurants," mentions only visual items. What other restaurant features would you expect to read about in this section?

a. hours of operation

b. sound and music

c. heating and cooling

d. service and friendliness

_____ 10. The typographical aid that the writer uses to emphasize important terms is

a. underlining.

b. numbering.

c. italics.

d. marginal notes.

PREVIEWING AND ASKING GUIDE QUESTIONS

A. Directions: Preview the following selection, which is from a study skills text. So that your instructor can see the parts you read, highlight each part you looked at. (Normally, it is too time-consuming to highlight while previewing.)

CHANGING YOUR HABITS TO REDUCE STRESS

This section describes four strategies for reducing stress by changing your habits. Experiment to discover which strategies will work for you.

1 **Control Your Own Time**

Take charge of your time; do not permit friends, roommates, or neighbors to consume it. Make clear when study times are planned, and don't allow interruptions. If people call or visit during those times, be brief and firm; insist that you must get back to work. If friends call to invite you to a movie, explain that this is a study hour and suggest a time that is convenient for you. Stay in control of your time. Apply the same firmness to family members who want you to drive them somewhere or to parents who want you to run errands. Suggest an alternate time when you can fulfill their requests.

2 **Give Yourself a Break**

Constantly pushing yourself increases stress. Take a break; give yourself some down time or personal space in which you can just be you. During your break, you are not a student, not an employee, not a parent, not the one who cooks dinner. Just be yourself. Think of something you enjoy—a special song, a favorite place, a friend whom you miss. Your break can be brief: Between one and five minutes is often enough to slow you down, provide relief from your routine, and reduce stress.

3 **Help Someone Out**

If you spend all your time thinking about yourself and the amount of work you have, your problems will grow out of proportion. Spend time helping someone else when you can afford the time. You might shop for an elderly relative, tutor a classmate, or volunteer at a soup kitchen or animal shelter. Once your mind is off yourself and you see others with problems, your problems will seem more manageable.

■ Here is one form of stress-reducing exercise.

4 **Get Some Exercise**

Build an exercise routine into your weekly schedule. Exercise can reduce stress by helping your body release hormones like endorphins that will improve your awareness and give you a sense of well-being. Fresh air is also helpful in reducing stress. It stimulates your mind and body and makes it easier for you to relax. Take a brisk walk outdoors when you feel stress mounting.

B. Directions: Write true (T) or false (F) before each of the following statements.

_____ 1. The title gives you a good idea of what the selection is about.

_____ 2. The last paragraph is a summary.

_____ 3. A useful guide question for the first heading is "How can I control my time?"

_____ 4. A useful guide question for the third heading is "Why should I help someone out?"

_____ 5. A useful guide question for the fourth heading is "Who should exercise?"

NAME _____   SECTION _____

DATE _____   SCORE _____

PREVIEWING AND ASKING GUIDE QUESTIONS

A. Directions: Preview the following selection, which is from a communications text. Highlight each part that you have looked at so that your instructor can see what you have read. (Normally, it is too time-consuming to highlight while previewing.)

TRY ACTIVE LISTENING

Active listening, an approach to listening developed by Thomas Gordon, is especially important in communicating with people. It's a method for encouraging the other person to explore his or her thoughts and talk about them.

Functions of Active Listening

Active listening serves several important functions. First of all, it helps you to check your understanding of what speakers mean. When you ask speakers about what they said, they can then confirm or deny your perceptions. Future messages will have a better chance of being meaningful.

Second, active listening enables you to say that you accept a speaker's feelings. Remember that a person's feelings—whether you see these as logical or illogical, reasonable or unreasonable—are extremely important to that person. A speaker needs to know that these feelings are accepted before he or she will talk about them.

Finally, and perhaps most important, active listening encourages the speaker to explore and express thoughts and feelings. For example, when you use active listening you provide Angela, who has expressed worry about getting fired, with the opportunity to explore these feelings in greater detail. You give Charlie, who hasn't had a date in four months, the opportunity to reflect openly on his feelings about dating and about his own loneliness. Active listening sets the stage for a dialogue of mutual understanding rather than one of attack and defense. In providing the speaker with the opportunity to talk through feelings, the active listener helps the speaker deal with them.

Techniques for Active Listening

Here are three techniques for effective active listening:

- **Paraphrase the speaker's thoughts.** When you paraphrase, you state in your own words what you think the speaker meant. This will help ensure understanding, since the speaker will be able to correct your restatement. It will show the speaker that you're interested in what is being said. The paraphrase also gives the speaker a chance to elaborate on or extend what was originally said. When you echo the speaker's thought, the speaker may then say more about his or her feelings. In your paraphrase, be especially careful that you do not lead the speaker in the direction you think he or she should go. Make your paraphrases as close to objective descriptions as you can.

- **Express understanding of the speaker's feelings.** In addition to paraphrasing the content, echo (repeat) the feelings you think the speaker expressed or implied. ("I can imagine how you must have felt. You must have felt really horrible.") Just as the paraphrase enables you to check on your ideas about the content, your expression of feelings enables you to check on your ideas about the speaker's feelings. This expression of feelings will also help the speaker to see his or her feelings more objectively. It's especially helpful when the speaker feels angry, hurt, or depressed. We all need that objectivity; we need to see our feelings from a somewhat less impassioned perspective if we are to deal with them effectively.

- **Ask questions.** Ask questions to make sure that you understand the speaker's thoughts and feelings and to obtain additional information ("How did you feel when you saw that grade?"). The questions should be designed to provide just enough stimulation and support for the speaker to express the thoughts and feelings he or she wants to convey. Questions should not pry into unrelated areas or challenge the speaker in any way. These questions will further confirm your interest and concern for the speaker.

If you follow these techniques, active listening will help you become a better communicator. Your relationships with friends, family members, and coworkers should improve.

—DeVito, *Messages*, p. 100

B. Directions: The following guide questions are based on the headings in the selection. Read the entire selection and then, in the space provided, write the letter of the choice that best answers each of the following questions.

_____ 1. What is the most important function of listening?

    a. It promotes acceptance of the speaker.

    b. It encourages understanding.

    c. It helps the listener clarify his or her thinking.

    d. It encourages the speaker to explore his or her feelings and ideas.

2. What is active listening?
    a. a method of encouraging people to communicate
    b. a process of understanding difficult messages
    c. a means of prying into hidden emotions
    d. a procedure for requesting information

3. What is paraphrasing?
    a. encouraging a speaker to explain an idea
    b. stating an idea in your own words
    c. correcting misinformation
    d. relying on visual cues

4. How does a listener express understanding of a speaker's feelings?
    a. by paraphrasing the content
    b. by repeating (echoing) the speaker's feelings
    c. by being considerate
    d. by admitting that feelings are important

5. Why is it useful to ask questions?
    a. to make sure you understand the speaker's thoughts and feelings
    b. to break up long explanations
    c. to help avoid arguments among friends
    d. to provide a format for a conversation

NAME *Miranda Garcia*   SECTION _____

DATE *9-20-10*   SCORE _____

TO LOVE AND TO CHERISH
Michelle Kearns

From a four-part series published in *The Buffalo News* on religious ceremonies, this reading explores wedding ceremonies. Preview and then read this selection to discover the traditions that various cultures include in marriage ceremonies.

Vocabulary Preview

These are some of the difficult words and phrases in this essay. The definitions here will help you if you can't figure out the meanings from the sentence context or words parts.

fortify (para. 2) strengthen

convened (para. 2) called together

articulate (para. 2) put into words

conviction (para. 2) belief

inevitable (para. 2) unavoidable; certain to happen

refracted (para. 2) turned or bent

covenant (para. 3) a solemn promise

nurture (para. 10) give nourishment; sustain

bliss (para. 10) pure joy

---

1   By government standards Beatrice Pardeep Singh-Arnone was married on a Tuesday by a judge in the town hall. "It still wasn't real for me," she said. Days later in the rose garden at Delaware Park, it was. She wore a dress in red, the color of happiness. For her **Sikh** ceremony, parents exchanged carnation garlands to symbolize the new bond between the bride and groom's families. And Singh-Arnone and her husband made four trips around the holy book that is the foundation of the religion, which began in India. Each time, the couple walked to a different prayer reading about the physical, mental, soul-uniting and godly aspects of their marriage. When they were done, friends and family showered them with flower petals, a kind of blessing.

2   Wedding rituals vary from religion to religion—from circling a holy book, as Sikhs do, to marrying under a canopy or chupah to show the beginning

Sikh: A follower of Sikhism—a branch of Hinduism marked by monotheism (having one god) founded in India in the 16th century.

■ A Sikh wedding.

Second Vatican Council: A meeting held by the Pope to address questions and issues in the Catholic Church. Many new policies and practices resulted from "Vatican II."

of a home together, as Jews do. Still, there is usually something universal among them: Religious rituals try to fortify couples in their lives together by showing support from God and the family, said Trevor Watt, a Protestant theologian at the **Second Vatican Council** convened by Pope John XXIII in the 1960s. "The most meaningful wedding ceremonies are the ones that name and articulate the values held by the couple getting married and hopefully by the family and their social community," said Watt. And, he said, the best rituals express an inner conviction. In some ceremonies love and its various forms—such as, romantic, friendship, physical and emotional—are described because they give the marriage strength "to get beyond the hurts and the anger that are inevitable," he said. "The reason that we seek a wedding ceremony is it's an acknowledgement of something that's ultimate," continued Watt, who is a religion professor at Canisius College and an ordained United Church of Christ minister at the Westminster Presbyterian Church in Buffalo. "In the Christian tradition it's called God's love," he said, "like light, it can be refracted into many different forms."

Christianity

sacrament: A formal Christian rite believed to be established by Jesus as a way to be with God.

3   For Catholics, the ceremony for the marriage **sacrament** gets part of its meaning from the bride and groom's work as ministers of their wedding service, said Father Matthew Zirnheld, a priest at Our Lady of Victory in Lackawanna. To prepare for their day, the couple has already planned for marriage by taking church classes that include children and keeping religion in

their lives. The modern service has changed some to reflect that a bride is no longer considered a possession of the family, as she once was, Zirnheld said. She can decide to have her father escort her to the altar to begin the service, or not. Instead, he said, Catholics now emphasize the importance of couples entering a marriage freely—so there is nothing to hold them back from keeping the union together. "It's not a contract. A contract can be broken. It's a covenant," he said. The couple demonstrates this by leading the wedding, which is their public commitment to each other. They choose the prayers, readings, music, said Zirnheld, who leads the exchange of vows. As modern evidence of the couple's leading role, it has become popular, within the last decade or so, to illustrate the new union with a "unity candle" that is lit with separate candles held by the bride and groom, Zirnheld said.

4   These candles are also popular at the African Methodist Episcopal Church in Buffalo, where couples include African traditions along with more traditional protestant steps, said Reverend Richard Stenhouse. After going to the altar for blessings and to exchange rings and vows, they may jump over a broom. This practice comes from times of slavery. Slaves were not allowed to marry, so couples used this tradition to "cross over from being separate to joined," said Stenhouse. A bride and groom may use another African ritual of pouring some water, the essence of life, on the ground. "It gives honor and recognition to those who've gone before," he said.

5   At the Hellenic Orthodox Church of the Annunciation in Buffalo—part of the Eastern Orthodox church led by **patriarchs** rather than the pope—the traditional Greek service is designed as preparation for heaven. Father James Doukas, the priest, places crowns of beaded circles on the bride and groom's heads to indicate that they're queen and king of their household and ready to begin a heaven-worthy life. Then the couple walks around the altar table three times in tribute to Jesus, the martyrs and the saints. The couple sips from a cup of wine to indicate they will drink the happiness of life together, as well as the sorrow.

patriarchs: Church leaders or bishops in the Orthodox faith.

Judaism

6   Jewish weddings can vary between temples and movements, such as reform, which is more liberal, and orthodox, which is more conservative. Yet

there are rituals common among them. One is the signing of the ktuba, a marriage contract describing the obligations to behave in an ethical and moral way. During the wedding ceremony, as the couple stands beneath a chupah, a rabbi reads the ktuba and offers seven blessings to encourage the couple to live in unity and love. When the service is over, the couple breaks a wine glass as reminder of the destruction of the temple in Jerusalem.

7   This is a signal for some that there is lots of work ahead, explained Rabbi Benjamin Arnold, of Temple Sinai in Amherst. "The wedding is a symbol of redemption and fulfillment," he said. "This wedding can be our inspiration." The couple sometimes retreats to a room with food, such as chocolate covered strawberries, so they can sit alone and break a pre-marriage fast. "It's a form of prayer, of asking God that he should be with this couple," said Rabbi Yirmiya Milevsky, of the Young Israel orthodox synagogue in Amherst.

Islam

8   Islam considers marriage a sacred duty, said Dawoud Adeyola, a leader of the Islamic Cultural Association of Western New York. "It's actually considered an act of worship," he said. Yet the ceremony itself is simple. First the couple must meet certain pre-conditions—they can't be closely related, the husband has to be able to support his wife—and have two Muslim witnesses. Adeyola will read a verse from the **Koran** about all of humankind being created from a single soul. The groom promises or gives a dowry chosen by the bride—a house, a car or a piece of jewelry. And the bride or the groom proposes marriage, the other accepts and the ceremony is complete after a prayer, said Adeyola.

Koran: The holy book of Islam, containing what followers believe to be revelations of Allah as told to Muhammad.

9   He has conducted spare ceremonies in a room and more elaborate ones in the rose garden at Delaware Park. It is important to dress up so that the couple stands out in recognition of the importance of the occasion. African Americans sometimes incorporate African traditions, such as African-style robes or food, said Adeyola remembering the yams served at his own Muslim wedding in 1969.

Lasting Power

10   In the nearly five years since Singh-Arnone was married, she has had two children and life struggles. Her 2-year-old son, who is now fine, was born pre-

maturely, which provoked a worrying few weeks. In such times she thinks back to her wedding and the memories of it nurture her still. "That was one of the most moving days of my life besides the birth of my children," she said. "I did feel surrounded by the presence of God." It was, she said, beyond happiness. It was bliss.

— ∙ —

Directions: In the space provided, write the letter of the choice that best completes each of the following statements.

CHECKING YOUR COMPREHENSION

 1. The purpose of this selection is to
    a. present research on the strength of religion-based marriages.
    b. criticize couples who do not have a religious wedding ceremony.
    c. encourage couples to put religion into their weddings.
    (d.) describe various religious marriage traditions.

 2. The topic of paragraph 3 is
    a. the unity candle.
    (b.) the Catholic ceremony.
    c. Father Matthew Zirnheld.
    d. marriage as a covenant.

_____ 3. The main idea of paragraph 4 is that
    a. candles are an important part of many ceremonies.
    (b.) couples may mix traditions from several cultures.
    c. an African tradition involves brooms.
    d. most rituals include recognition of people who have died.

_____ 4. All of the following reasons are given for the rituals of wedding ceremonies *except*
    (a.) to honor one's ancestors.
    b. to worship.
    c. to prepare for a large family.
    d. to seek redemption and fulfillment.

5. During the Sikh wedding ceremony, the parents of the bride and groom symbolize the new bond between the families by

   a. walking around the altar three times.

   b. lighting a unity candle.

   (c.) exchanging carnation garlands.

   d. jumping over a broom.

6. The religion that features crowns placed on the bride and groom's heads as part of the wedding ceremony is

   (a.) Greek Orthodox.

   b. African Methodist Episcopal.

   c. Judaism.

   d. Islam.

7. In the Jewish tradition, the *ktuba* is a

   a. pre-marriage fast.

   b. wedding gift from the groom to the bride.

   c. pre-wedding class.

   (d.) marriage contract.

8. Jewish wedding ceremonies

   a. vary, yet have some common rituals.

   b. use flowers to emphasize closeness to nature.

   (c.) are conservative, by Jewish law.

   d. all follow exactly the same rituals and format.

9. The last paragraph emphasizes

   a. that adversity strikes us all.

   b. the differences between Sikh and Christian views of marriage.

   (c.) the importance that ceremonies play in people's lives.

   d. that weddings do not change people's lives.

10. This selection includes quotes from all of the following people *except*

    a. a Sikh bride.   c. an orthodox rabbi.

    b. a Christian groom.   (d.) an Islamic leader.

_____ 11. The first paragraph of the reading

    a. provides an example of dual wedding ceremonies.

    b. explains why Sikh ceremonies are so long.

    c. emphasizes the importance of family participation.

    d. explains the differences between legal and religious ceremonies.

USING WHAT YOU KNOW ABOUT ACTIVE READING

_____ 12. The most useful guide question for the entire selection would be

    a. Where do most weddings take place?

    b. How do wedding rituals vary among different religions?

    c. How many weddings are performed each year?

    d. When do most couples get married?

_____ 13. The only previewing aids found in this selection are

    a. boldfaced headings.

    b. italics.

    c. marginal notes.

    d. underlining.

_____ 14. The best guide question for the heading "Judaism" is

    a. Who founded Judaism?

    b. What wedding rituals do Jews follow?

    c. How is Judaism different from Christianity?

    d. Why was Judaism founded?

_____ 15. The title of the reading

    a. provides little information about the reading.

    b. emphasizes that Christian ceremonies are least bound by tradition.

    c. focuses your attention on religious ceremonies throughout life.

    d. clearly identifies the topic and suggests the author's main point.

REVIEWING DIFFICULT VOCABULARY

Directions: Complete each of the following sentences by inserting a word from the Vocabulary Preview on page 25 in the space provided. A word should be used only once.

16. A special board meeting was ___convened___ to announce the sale of the company.

17. Mei had a strong ___conviction___ that her soccer team would be unbeatable this season.

18. Many people ___fortify___ their diets with vitamin supplements.

19. The cut-glass ornament ___refracted___ the sunlight into a beautiful design on the wall.

20. Sally was determined to ___nurture___ the injured bird until it could survive on its own.

QUESTIONS FOR DISCUSSION

1. A wedding is just the official beginning of a marriage. Discuss what couples really need to know about being husband and wife.

2. Discuss the wedding industry in America. Has it gotten out of control in terms of cost and importance in the lives of the bride and groom?

3. Discuss the rituals that you consider most important in a wedding. Is their significance based on religious tradition or something else?

WRITING ACTIVITIES

1. Write about a time that you witnessed or participated in a religious ceremony. What rituals were involved? Did the guests seem to recognize their significance?

2. Look at some sample nonreligious wedding ceremonies at the Web site http://www.nonreligiousweddings.com/samples.html. Write a paragraph comparing these ceremonies with what you know about religious weddings from this reading and your life.

3. Write an essay in which you take the position that religious rituals are or are not an important part of a marriage.

Chapter 1:   Reading Actively

Test	Number Right	Score
Practice Test 1-1	_____ × 10 =	_____%
Practice Test 1-2	_____ × 10 =	_____%
Practice Test 1-3	_____ × 10 =	_____%
Mastery Test 1-1	Part A (50 points)	_____*
Part B	_____ × 10 =	_____
Total (A + B)	=	_____%
Mastery Test 1-2	Part A (75 points)	_____*
Part B	_____ × 5 =	_____
Total (A + B)	=	_____%
Mastery Test 1-3	_____ × 4 =	_____%

EVALUATING YOUR PROGRESS

Based on your test performance, rate how well you have mastered the skills taught in this chapter by checking one of the boxes below or by writing your own evaluation.

☐ **Need More Improvement**
Tip: Try using the "Active Reading" Module on the Reading Road Trip Web site at **http://www.ablongman.com/readingroadtrip** to fine-tune the skills that you have learned in this chapter.

☐ **Need More Practice**
Tip: Try using the "Active Reading" Module on the Reading Road Trip Web site at **http://www.ablongman.com/readingroadtrip** to brush up on the skills you have learned in this chapter, or visit this textbook's companion Web site at **http://www.ablongman.com/mcwhorter** for extra practice.

☐ **Good**
Tip: To maintain your skills, quickly review this chapter by using this textbook's companion Web site by logging on to **http://ablongman.com/mcwhorter**.

☐ **Excellent**

YOUR EVALUATION: _____

_____

*Consult your instructor for scoring.

READ ME FIRST!

Study the cartoon below. What point does it make? Can you answer the question? If not, how could you find the answer? No doubt you would check a dictionary. A dictionary is an essential tool for college students. You will need one in a variety of situations. You will need one in a writing course to help you choose the precise words to use and spell them correctly. In other courses, you will come to rely on a dictionary to help you build and strengthen your vocabulary and figure out the meaning of unfamiliar words.

In this chapter, you will learn to use a dictionary and discover the wide variety of information it includes. You will also learn some basic rules of spelling and word pronunciation.

"Explain something to me. Are 'boned' and 'deboned' the same thing?"

CHAPTER **2**

Using Your Dictionary

Buying a Dictionary

Every writer needs a dictionary, not only to check spellings, but also to check meanings and the appropriate usage of words. You should have a desk or collegiate dictionary plus a pocket dictionary that you can carry with you to classes. Widely used dictionaries include:

The American Heritage Dictionary of the English Language

Merriam-Webster's Collegiate Dictionary

Webster's New World Dictionary of the American Language

Several dictionaries are available online. Two of the most widely used are *Merriam-Webster Online* (http://www.m-w.com) and *The American Heritage Dictionary* (http://yourdictionary.com/index.shtml). Both of these sites feature an audio component that allows you to hear how a word is pronounced.

If you have difficulty with spelling, a misspeller's dictionary is another valuable reference tool. It can help you locate correct spellings easily. Two commonly used online versions are *Webster's New World Misspeller's Dictionary* and *How to Spell It: A Handbook of Commonly Misspelled Words*.

Using a Dictionary

The first step in using your dictionary is to become familiar with the kinds of information it provides. In the sample entry on page 36, each kind of information is marked:

Pronunciation

Parts of speech

Meanings

Spelling of other forms of the entry word

Restrictive meanings

Etymology (word history)

curve (kurv) **n. 1a.** A line that deviates from straightness in a smooth continuous fashion. **b.** A surface that deviates from planarity in a smooth, continuous fashion. **c.** Something characterized by such a line or surface, especially a rounded line or contour of the human body. **2.** A relatively smooth bend in a road or other course. **3a.** A line representing data on a graph. **b.** A trend derived from or as if from such a graph: *"Once again, the politicians are behind the curve"* (Ted Kennedy). **4.** A graphic representation showing the relative performance of individuals as measured against each other, used especially as a method of grading students in which the assignment of grades is based on predetermined proportions of students. **5.** *Mathematics* **a.** The graph of a function on a coordinate plane. **b.** The intersection of two surfaces in three dimensions. **c.** The graph of the solutions to any equation of two variables. **6.** *Baseball* A curve ball. **7.** *Slang* Something that is unexpected or designed to trick or deceive. ◆ **v.** curved, curv • ing, curves – *intr.* To move in or take the shape of a curve: *The path curves around the lake* –*tr.* **1.** To cause to curve. See synonyms at bend. **2.** Baseball To pitch a curve ball to. **3.** To grade (students for example) on a curve. [From Middle English, curved, from Latin curvus, see **skar** in Appendix I. N., sense 6, short for CURVE BALL] –**curv'ed ness** n. –**curv'y** adj.

—American Heritage Dictionary of the English Language, 4th Ed., 2000

You can see that a dictionary entry provides much more than the definition of a word. Information about the word's pronunciation, part of speech, history, and special uses can also be found.

Exercise 2–1

Directions: Use the sample dictionary entry to complete the following exercises. Write your answer in the space provided.

1. Find three meanings for *curve* and write a sentence using each.

   _____

   _____

   _____

   _____

2. Explain what *curve* means when used in baseball.

   _____

3. Explain how the meaning of *curve* differs from the meaning of the word *bend*.

   _____

Exercise 2-2	*Directions: Find the following words in your dictionary. In the space provided, list all the different parts of speech each word can be used as.*

1. that _____

2. except _____

3. clear _____

4. fancy _____

5. record _____

The dictionary provides a great deal of information about each word. The following sections provide a brief review of the parts of a dictionary entry most often found confusing.

Abbreviations

All dictionaries provide a key to abbreviations used in the entry itself as well as some commonly used in other printed material. Most often this key appears on the inside front cover or in the first few pages of the dictionary.

Exercise 2-3	*Directions: Find the meaning of each of the following symbols and abbreviations in your dictionary. You may need to consult a list of abbreviations at the front or back of your dictionary. Write your answer in the space provided.*

1. v.t. _____

2. < _____

3. c. _____

4. Obs. _____

5. Fr. _____

6. pl. _____

Word Pronunciation

After each word entry, the pronunciation of the word is given in parentheses.

EXAMPLES

helmet (hĕl′mĭt)   connection (kə-nek′shən)

apologize (ə-pŏl′ə-jīz)   orchestra (or′kĭ-strə)

This part of the entry shows how to pronounce a word by spelling it the way it sounds. Different symbols are used to indicate certain sounds. Until you become familiar with this symbol system, you will need to refer to the pronunciation key. Most dictionaries include a pronunciation key at the bottom of every or every other page. Here is a sample key from the *American Heritage Dictionary:*

ă pat/ā pay/â care/ä father/b bib/ch church/d deed/ĕ pet/ē be/f fife/g gag/h hat/hw which/ĭ pit/i pie/îr pier/j judge/k kick/l lid, needle/m mum/n no, sudden/ng thing/ŏ not/ō toe/ô paw, for/oi noise/ou out/o͞o took/o͞o boot/p pop/r roar/s sauce/sh ship, dish/t tight/th thin, path/*th* this, bathe/ŭ cut/ûr urge/v valve/w with/y yes/z zebra, size/zh vision/ə about, item, edible, gallop, circus/

The key shows the sound the symbol stands for in a word you already know how to pronounce. For example, suppose you are trying to pronounce the word *helix* (hē′lĭks). The key shows that the letter *e* in the first part of the word sounds the same as the *e* in the word *be*. The *i* in *helix* is pronounced the same way as the *i* in *pit*. To pronounce a word correctly, you must also accent (put stress on) the appropriate part of the word. In a dictionary respelling, an accent mark (′) usually follows the syllable, or part of the word, that is stressed most heavily.

EXAMPLES

audience	ó′de- əns
football	fo͞ot′bôl
literacy	lĭt′ər-ə-sē
juror	jo͞or′ər
immediate	ĭ-mē′dē-ĭt

Some words have two accents—a primary stress and a secondary stress. The primary one is stressed more heavily and is printed in darker type than the secondary accent.

EXAMPLES   interstate   in'ter-sta-t'
            homicide   hôm'i-sīd'

Try to pronounce each of the following dictionary respellings, using the pronunciation key:

dĭ-vûr's-fī'   bŏosh'əl
chăl'ənj   bär'bĭ-kyo͞o'

Exercise 2-4

Directions: *Use the pronunciation key on the preceding page to sound out each of the following words. Write the word, spelled correctly, in the space provided.*

1. kə-mĭt' _____

2. kăp'chər _____

3. bə-röm'ĭ-tər _____

4. skĕj'o͞ol _____

5. i-den'te-fĭ-kā'shən _____

6. ĭn-dĭf'ər-əns _____

7. lûr'nĭd _____

8. lĭk'wĭd _____

9. no͞o'səns _____

10. fär'mə-sē _____

Etymology

Many dictionaries include information on each word's **etymology**—its origin and development. A word's etymology is its history, traced back as far as possible to its earliest use, often in another language. The sample dictionary entry on page 36 shows that the word *curve* was derived from the Latin word *curvus*.

Exercise 2-5

Directions: Find the origin of each of the following words in a dictionary. Write your answer in the space provided.

1. ginger _____

_____

_____

2. tint _____

3. calculate _____

4. fantastic _____

_____

5. authentic _____

_____

Source: American Heritage Dictionary

Restrictive Meanings

Many dictionaries include restrictive meanings of words. These are definitions that apply only when the word is being used with respect to a specific topic or field of study. The sample entry on page 36 gives two restrictive meanings for the word *curve*—one for baseball and another for math.

Exercise 2-6

Directions: Locate the following words in a dictionary and find the meaning that applies to the field of study given in parentheses after each word. Write the definitions in the space provided.

1. trust (law) _____

2. induction (logic) _____

3. compound (chemistry) _____

_____

4. primary (government) _____

_____

5. journal (accounting) _____

_____

Multiple Meanings

Because most words have more than one meaning, you must choose the meaning that fits the way the word is used in the sentence context. The following sample entry for the word *green* contains many meanings for the word.

Meanings
Grouped by
Parts of
Speech

7 Nouns

12 Adjectives

green (gren) **n. 1.** The hue of that portion of the visible spectrum lying between yellow and blue, evoked in the human observer by radiating energy with wavelengths of approximately 490 to 570 nanometers; any of a group of colors that may vary in lightness and saturation and whose hues is that of the emerald or somewhat less yellow than that of that of growing grass; one of the additive or light primaries; one of the psychological primary hues. **2.** Something green in color. **3. greens** Green growth or foliage, especially: **a.** The branches and leaves of plants used for decoration. **b.** leafy plants or plant part eaten as vegetables. **4.** A grassy lawn plot, especially: **a.** a grassy area located usually located at the center of a city or town and set aside for common use: a common. **b.** *Sports* A putting green. **5. greens** A green uniform: *"a young… sergeant in dress greens."* (**Nelson DeMille**). **6.** *Slang* Money. **7. Green** A supporter of a social and political movement that espouses global environmental protection, bioregionalism, social responsibility, and non-violence. ◆ *adj.* green er, green est **1.** Of the color green. **2.** Abounding in or covered with green growth or foliage; the green woods. **3.** Made with green or leafy vegetables: *a green salad.* **4.** Characterized by mild or temperate weather: a green climate. **5.** Youthful; vigorous: *at the green age of 18.* **6.** Not mature or ripe; young: *green tomatoes.* **7.** Brand-new; fresh. **8.** Not yet fully processed, especially: **a.** not aged: green wood. **b.** not cured or tanned: *green pelts.* **9.** Lacking training or experience. See synonyms at young. **10a.** Lacking sophistication or worldly experience; naive. **b.** easily duped or deceived; gullible. **11.** Having a sickly or unhealthy pallor indicative of nausea or jealousy, for example. **12a.** Beneficial to the environment: *green recycling policies.* **b.** Favoring or supporting environmentalism: *green legislators who strengthen pollution controls. tr.& intr.* **v. greened, green ing, greens** To make or become green. –idiom: **green around (or about) the gills.** Pale or sickly in appearance. [Middle English *grene,* from Old English *grene*; see ghr_- in Appendix I. N. sense 7, translation of German (*die*) *Grunen.* (the) Greens, from *grun,* green] **–green ly** adv. **– green ness** *n.*

Foliage

Grass area

Part of Golf
Course

Unripe Fruit

Inexperienced
Person

Sickly Pallor

—American Heritage Dictionary of the English Language, 4th Ed., 2000

The meanings are grouped by part of speech and are numbered consecutively in each group. Generally, the most common meanings of the word are listed first, with more specialized, less common meanings appearing toward the end of the entry. Now find the meaning that fits the use of the word *green* in the following sentence.

EXAMPLE

The local veterans' organization held its annual fund-raising picnic on the village green.

In this sentence, *green* refers to "an area of grass used for special purposes." Since this is a specialized meaning of the word, it appears toward the end of the entry.

Here are a few suggestions for choosing the correct meaning from among those listed in an entry:

1. **If you are familiar with the parts of speech, try to use these to locate the correct meaning.** For instance, if you are looking up the meaning of a word that names a person, place, or thing you can save time by reading only those entries given after *n.* (noun).

2. **For most types of college reading, you can skip definitions that give slang and colloquial (abbreviated *colloq.*) meanings.** Colloquial meanings refer to informal or spoken language.

3. **If you are not sure of the part of speech, read each meaning until you find a definition that seems correct.** Skip over restrictive meanings that are inappropriate.

4. **Test your choice by substituting the meaning in the sentence with which you are working.** Substitute the definition for the word and see whether it makes sense in context (see Chapter 3).

Suppose you are looking up the word *oblique* to find its meaning in the following sentence:

My sister's **oblique** answers to my questions made me suspicious.

Oblique is used in the preceding sentence as an adjective. Looking at the entries listed after *adj.* (adjective), you can skip over the definition under the heading *Mathematics,* as it wouldn't apply here: Definition 2 (*indirect, evasive*) best fits the way *oblique* is used in the sentence.

> **oblique** (ō-blēk′, ō-blīk′) *adj.* **1a.** Having a slanting or slopping direction, course, or position; inclined. **b.** *Mathematics* Designating geometric lines or planes that are neither parallel nor perpendicular. **2.** *Botany* Having sides of unequal length or form: *an oblique leaf.* **3.** *Anatomy* Situated in a slanting position; not transverse or longitudinal: *oblique muscles or ligaments.* **4a.** Indirect or evasive: *oblique political maneuvers.* **b.** Devious, misleading, or dishonest: *gave oblique answers to the questions.* **5.** Not direct in descent; collateral. **6.** *Grammar* Designating any noun case except the nominative or the vocative. N. **1.** An oblique thing, such as a line, direction, or muscle. **2.** *Nautical* The act of changing course by less than 90. *adv.* (ō-blēk′, ō-blīk′) At an angle of 45. [Middle English, from Old French, from Latin *obliquis*] —o·blique′-ly *adv.* o·blique′ness *n.*

**Exercise
2–7**

Directions: The following words have two or more meanings. Look them up in your dictionary and write two sentences with different meanings for each word.

1. culture _____

_____

2. perch _____

_____

3. surge _____

_____

4. apron _____

_____

5. irregular _____

_____

| Exercise 2–8 | ***Directions:*** *Use a dictionary to help you find an appropriate meaning for the boldfaced word in each of the following sentences. Insert your answer in the space provided.* |

1. The last contestant did not have a **ghost** of a chance.

_____

2. The race car driver won the first **heat.**

_____

3. The police took all possible **measures** to protect the witness.

_____

4. The orchestra played the first **movement** of the symphony.

_____

5. The plane stalled on the **apron.**

_____

Spelling

Every dictionary entry gives the correct spelling of a word. It also shows how the spelling changes when a word is made plural or endings (suffixes—see Chapter 4) are added, as in the following examples.

EXAMPLES	**Word**	**Word + Ending**
	budget	budgetary
		budgeter
	exhibit	exhibitor
		exhibition
	fancy	fancily
		fanciness
		fancier

Entries may also include alternative spellings of words when there are two acceptable ways to spell the word. If you see the word *also* or *or* following the entry word, you will know that either is acceptable. Usually, the first spelling is the preferred one.

EXAMPLES   medieval *also* mediaeval

archaeology *or* archeology

Each entry shows how the word is divided into syllables, so you know how to hyphenate a word when it appears at the end of a line of print (hyphens are placed only between syllables).

EXAMPLE   liv-a-ble   mil-li-me-ter   ob-li-ga-tion

For verbs, each entry contains the verb's principal parts: past tense, past participle, present participle (if different from the past), and third person singular present tense.

EXAMPLES   **go**   went, gone, going, goes

feed   fed, feeding, feeds

Exercise 2-9

Directions: Use a dictionary to answer the following questions. Write your answers in the space provided.

1. What is the plural form of *crisis?* _____

2. What is the alternative spelling of *judgment?* _____

3. If you had to hyphenate *surprise* at the end of a line, where would you divide it? _____

4. What is the past form of *burst?* _____

5. What is the adverb form of *criminal?* _____

Usage Notes

Some collegiate dictionaries contain a usage note or synonym section of the entry for words that are close in meaning to others. For example, a usage note for the word *indifferent* may explain how it differs in meaning from *unconcerned, detached,* and *uninterested.*

| Exercise 2-10 | *Directions:* Use a dictionary to explain the differences in meaning between the words in each of the following pairs. If your dictionary does not list usage notes, then look up each word separately. Write your explanations in the space provided. |

1. petite, diminutive _____

_____

2. careless, thoughtless _____

_____

3. odor, aroma _____

_____

4. grin, smirk _____

_____

5. hurt, damage _____

_____

_____

Idioms

An idiom is a phrase that has a meaning other than what the common definitions of the words in the phrase indicate. For example, the phrase "wipe the slate clean" is not about slates. It means "to start over." Most idiomatic expressions are not used in academic writing because they are considered trite or overused.

Exercise 2–11	*Directions:* Use a dictionary to help you explain the meanings of the following underlined idiomatic expressions. Write your explanation in the space provided.

1. One thousand dollars is nothing to <u>sneeze at</u>.

   _____

2. The home team <u>kicked off</u> the season with an easy win.

   _____

3. I intend to <u>turn over a new leaf</u> and work harder next semester.

   _____

4. The lake is two miles from here <u>as the crow flies</u>. (Hint: look under the entry for "crow.")

   _____

5. The owner's incompetent nephew was <u>kicked upstairs</u> rather than fired.

   _____

   _____

Other Aids

Many dictionaries (especially hardback editions) also contain numerous useful lists and tables. These are usually printed at the end of the dictionary. They frequently include tables of weights and measures and of periodic elements in chemistry, biographical listings for famous people, a pronouncing gazetteer (a geographical dictionary), and lists of standard abbreviations, colleges, and signs and symbols.

Pronouncing Unfamiliar Words

At one time or another, each of us comes across words that we are unable to pronounce. To pronounce an unfamiliar word, sound it out syllable by syllable. Here are a few simple rules for dividing words into syllables:

1. **Divide compound words between the individual words that form the compound word.**

EXAMPLES

house/broken   house/hold   space/craft

green/house   news/paper   sword/fish

2. **Divide words between prefixes (word beginnings) and roots (base words) and/or between roots and suffixes (word endings).**

EXAMPLES

Prefix + Root

pre/read   post/pone   anti/war

Root + Suffix

sex/ist agree/ment   list/ing

For a more complete discussion of prefixes, roots, and suffixes, see Chapter 4.

3. **Each syllable is a separate, distinct speech sound.** Pronounce the following words and try to hear the number of syllables in each:

EXAMPLES

expensive   ex/pen/sive = 3 syllables

recognize   rec/og/nize = 3 syllables

punctuate   punc/tu/ate = 3 syllables

complicated   com/pli/cat/ed = 4 syllables

4. **Each syllable has at least one vowel and usually one or more consonants.** The letters a, e, i, o, u, and sometimes y are vowels. All other letters are consonants.

EXAMPLES

as/sign   re/act   cou/pon   gen/er/al

5. **Divide words before a single consonant, unless the consonant is the letter r.**

EXAMPLES   hu/mid   pa/tron   re/tail   fa/vor   mor/on

6. **Divide words between two consonants appearing together.**

EXAMPLES   pen/cil   lit/ter   lum/ber   sur/vive

7. **Divide words between two vowel sounds that appear together.**

EXAMPLES   te/di/ous   ex/tra/ne/ous

These rules will prove helpful but, as you no doubt already know, there will always be exceptions.

Exercise 2–12

Directions: Use slash marks (/) to divide each of the following words into syllables.

1. pol/ka	6. in/no/va/tive	11. tan/ge/lo	16. te/nac/i/ty
2. pol/lute	7. ob/tuse	12. sym/me/try	17. mes/mer/ize
3. or/di/nal	8. ger/mi/cide	13. te/lep/a/thy	18. in/tru/sive
4. hal/low	9. fu/tile	14. or/gan/ic	19. in/fal/li/ble
5. ju/di/ca/ture	10. ex/toll	15. hid/e/ous	20. fa/nat/i/cism

Using Word Mapping to Expand Your Vocabulary

Word mapping is a visual method of expanding your vocabulary. It involves examining a word in detail by considering its meanings, synonyms (words similar in meaning), antonyms (words opposite in meaning), part(s) of speech, word parts, and usages. A word map is a form of word study. By the time you have completed the map, you will find that you have learned the word and are ready to use it in your speech and writing.

Here is a sample map for the word *intercept:*

Word Map

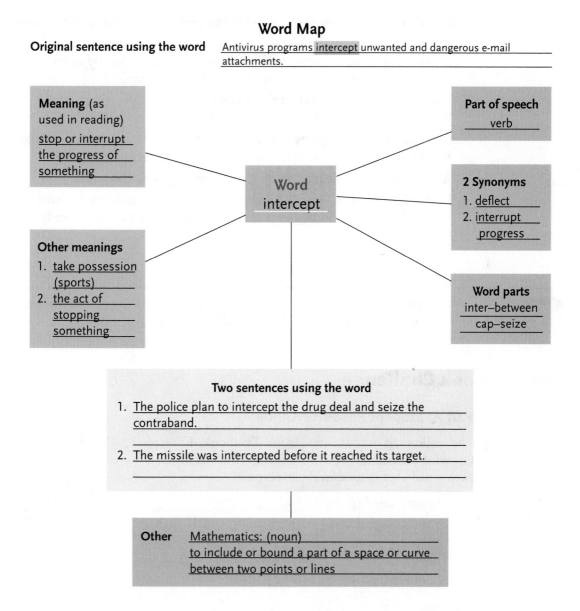

Original sentence using the word Antivirus programs intercept unwanted and dangerous e-mail attachments.

Meaning (as used in reading)
stop or interrupt the progress of something

Part of speech
verb

Word
intercept

2 Synonyms
1. deflect
2. interrupt progress

Other meanings
1. take possession (sports)
2. the act of stopping something

Word parts
inter–between
cap–seize

Two sentences using the word
1. The police plan to intercept the drug deal and seize the contraband.

2. The missile was intercepted before it reached its target.

Other Mathematics: (noun) to include or bound a part of a space or curve between two points or lines

Use the following steps in completing a word map:

1. **Write the sentence containing the word at the top of the map.**
2. **Look the word up in your dictionary.** Figure out which meaning fits the context of the sentence and write it in the box labeled "Meaning (as used in context)."

3. **In the "Part of speech" box, write in the word's part(s) of speech as used in context.**

4. **Study the dictionary entry to discover other meanings of the word.** Write them on the map in the box labeled "Other meanings."

5. **Find or think of two synonyms (words similar in meaning), and write them in the "Synonyms" box.** You might need a thesaurus for this.

6. **Analyze the word's parts and identify any prefixes, roots, or suffixes.** Write each word part and its meaning in the space provided.

7. **At the bottom of the map write two sentences using the word.**

8. **In the box labeled "Other," include any other interesting information about the word.** You might include antonyms, restrictive meanings, or word history.

Directions: Using a dictionary, complete a word map for one of the new words you are learning in one of your other courses.

The Textbook Challenge

Part A: Student Resource Guide A

The following words appear in Textbook Excerpt 2, "Food Safety: A Growing Concern." (p. 403) Using your dictionary, write a definition of each word as it is used in the excerpt.

1. contaminated (para. 1) _____

2. pathogens (para. 2) _____

3. virulence (para. 3) _____

4. opaque (para. 4) _____

5. toxic (para. 6) _____

6. anemia (para. 8) _____

7. microbes (para. 10) _____

8. antioxidants (para. 10) _____

9. dioxins (para. 11) _____

10. hormones (para. 11) _____

Part B: A College Textbook

Choose a chapter from one of your textbooks for another course. Identify ten difficult words and use a dictionary to write the definition of each.

What Have You Learned?

To check your understanding of the chapter and to review its major points, select the word or phrase from the box below that best completes each of the following sentences. Not all of the words will be used.

parentheses	root	suffix
usage notes	aids	one
part of speech	accent	abbreviation

1. Most words have more than___ meaning.

2. _____ explain similarities to and differences from other words.

3. To pronounce a word, divide it between its prefix and its___ .

4. To find the meaning of a word as it is used in a particular sentence, it is helpful to determine its_____ .

5. The pronunciation of a word is given in _____ following the word.

What Vocabulary Have You Learned?

Directions: Match the word in column A with its meaning in column B.

	Column A		Column B
_____	1. restrictive meanings	a.	information about a word's history
_____	2. idiom	b.	the part of a word that is most heavily stressed
_____	3. etymology	c.	meanings that apply to a specific field of study
_____	4. primary accent	d.	an expression that has a meaning other than what the common definitions of the words in the phrase mean.
_____	5. pronunciation key	e.	a listing of symbols that are used to explain how a word sounds

Test-Taking Tip #2: Taking Vocabulary Tests

Many vocabulary test items consist of a word and four or five choices for its definition. Often, the meaning of the word you are being asked to define does not appear in the context of a sentence. Use the following suggestions for approaching this type of vocabulary test:

■   **Try pronouncing the word to yourself.** "Hearing" the word may just make it more familiar.

■   **Read all the choices before you select and mark an answer.** Usually the directions tell you to choose the *best* answer. So while choice b may be somewhat close to the meaning or seem right at first, choice d may be a more exact and precise answer, as in the following example:

Example: 1. seniority

        a. degrees held

        b. age

        c. importance

        d. length of service

While you may see the word "senior" in the word "seniority" and think of age (choice b) as in senior citizen, and think that those who have seniority are usually older, the correct answer is choice d.

■   **Many vocabulary tests are timed and your score is based on the number of correct answers you get in a specific period of time.** Be sure to work at a steady, efficient pace. If you work too slowly, you will not have answered enough items to get a high score.

■   **Find out if there is a penalty for guessing (some tests subtract a percentage of a point for wrong answers but do not do so for those left blank).** If there is no penalty for guessing, be sure to guess at items you are not sure of. For an item containing four choices, you have a 25 percent chance of guessing correctly. For every four items you guess, you are likely to get one correct.

DICTIONARY SKILLS

Directions: Select the choice that indicates the correct pronunciation for each of the words listed below.

_____   1. documentary
   a. DOK you men ta rey
   b. dok youm EN trey
   c. do kum ENTRY
   d. DOK u men try

_____   2. glamour
   a. GL am or
   b. GLAM you r
   c. GLA moor
   d. GLAM err

_____   3. feasible
   a. FEE siz bull
   b. FEE za bull
   c. fe SA bell
   d. phe sa bell

_____   4. infinite
   a. IN fe nit
   b. INF i nite
   c. inf I nite
   d. infi NITE

_____   5. obligation
   a. OB lig shun
   b. ob lig E shun
   c. ob lee SHUN
   d. ob le GAY shun

NAME _____ SECTION _____

DATE _____ SCORE _____

DICTIONARY SKILLS

Directions: Use your dictionary to answer the following questions.

_____ 1. A restrictive meaning for the word **level** is
   a. a bit, element, or channel of information.
   b. a table or other flat surface.
   c. a computer input area.
   d. an unusual law that is difficult to enforce.

_____ 2. The restrictive meaning for the word **house** in a theater is
   a. floor.
   b. stage.
   c. pit.
   d. audience.

_____ 3. The restrictive meaning of the word **force** in physics is
   a. the distance from one point to another.
   b. an analytical measurement of speed.
   c. a vector quantity that tends to produce acceleration.
   d. the outcome of a vector analysis.

_____ 4. The abbreviation **FCC** stands for
   a. Federal Commission on Currency.
   b. Federal Communications Commission.
   c. Federal College Consultancy.
   d. Federal Carolina Commission.

_____ 5. The abbreviation **NRA** stands for
   a. National Rifle Association.
   b. National Regional Activists.
   c. North Regional Association.
   d. North Referral Association.

_____ 6. The abbreviation **MA** stands for
   a. Merchants Association.
   b. Michigan Arts.
   c. Mississippi Alumni.
   d. Master of Arts.

_____ 7. How is the word **inflammable** correctly divided into syllables?

    a. in/flam/ma/ble

    b. inf/lam/able

    c. infl/am/able

    d. inflam/able

_____ 8. How is the word **erratic** correctly divided into syllables?

    a. err/atic

    b. e/rr/atic

    c. err/a/tic

    d. er/rat/ic

_____ 9. How is the word **inflorescence** correctly divided into syllables?

    a. inf/lor/e/sc/ence

    b. in/flor/es/cence

    c. in/flo/res/cence

    d. inflor/es/cence

_____ 10. How is the word **compressible** correctly divided into syllables?

    a. com/pres/sible

    b. com/press/i/ble

    c. co/mpress/ib/le

    d. com/press/ible

NAME _____   SECTION _____

DATE _____   SCORE _____

DICTIONARY SKILLS

Directions: Select the choice that correctly defines each of the following idioms.

_____   1. turn over a new leaf
     a. start fresh in a new way
     b. criticize frequently
     c. complain angrily
     d. render useless

_____   2. to make no bones about
     a. to reveal information
     b. to ask for assistance
     c. to accept one's fate
     d. to speak openly and frankly

_____   3. in the dark
     a. unhappy
     b. unfriendly
     c. unaware
     d. uncooperative

_____   4. at the eleventh hour
     a. at the last minute
     b. just in time
     c. too late
     d. just before noon

_____   5. feeling blue
     a. feeling ambitious
     b. feeling sad
     c. feeling confused
     d. feeling angry

_____   6. to bad-mouth
     a. to have bad breath
     b. to frown or snarl

c. to say unpleasant things

d. to explain carefully

_____ 7. bull-headed

a. friendly

b. cow-like

c. aggressive

d. stubborn

_____ 8. to catch one's eye

a. to see poorly

b. to inspect closely

c. to capture someone's attention

d. to change one's mind frequently

_____ 9. to keep tabs on

a. to keep track of

b. to hinder progress

c. to offer help

d. to ask questions

_____ 10. to bite the bullet

a. to deal with a difficult situation

b. to arm oneself

c. to travel unsafely

d. to use time unwisely

NAME _____ SECTION _____

DATE _____ SCORE _____

DICTIONARY SKILLS

Directions: Each numbered sentence below is followed by a dictionary entry for the boldfaced word. Use this entry to select the choice that best fits the meaning of the word as it is used in the sentence.

_____ 1. At the entrance to the international exhibition hall, visitors are greeted by a **panoply** of flags representing every nation in the world.

> **pan•o•ply** (păn′ə-plē) *n., pl.* **-plies 1.** A splendid or striking array: *a panoply of colorful flags.* See synonyms at **display. 2.** Ceremonial attire with all accessories: *a portrait of the general in full panoply.* **3.** Something that covers and protects: *a porcupine's panoply of quills.* **4.** The complete arms and armor of a warrior. [Greek *panopliā* : *pan-*, pan- + *hopla*, arms, armor, pl. of *hoplon*, weapon.]
> **pan•op•tic** (păn-ŏp′tĭk) also **pan•op•ti•cal** (-tĭ-kəl) *adj.* Including everything visible in one view. [From Greek *panoptos*, fully visible : *pan-*, with respect to everything, fully; see PAN– + *optos*, visible; see **ok^w**- in Appendix I.]

    a. the complete arms and armor of a warrior

    b. ceremonial attire with all accessories

    c. something that covers and protects

    d. a splendid and striking array

_____ 2. At the town meeting, several citizens **ventilated** their concerns about the proposed increase in property taxes.

> **ven•ti•late** (věn′tl-āt′) *tr.v.* **-lat•ed, -lat•ing, -lates 1.** To admit fresh air into (a mine, for example) to replace stale or noxious air. **2.** To circulate through and freshen: *A sea breeze ventilated the rooms.* **3.** To provide with a vent, as for airing. **4.** To expose (a substance) to the circulation of fresh air, as to retard spoilage. **5.** To expose to public discussion or examination: *The students ventilated their grievances.* **6.** To aerate or oxygenate (blood). [Middle English *ventilaten*, to blow away, from Latin *ventilāre*, *ventilāt-*, to fan, from *ventulus*, diminutive of *ventus*, wind. See **wē-** in Appendix I.]

a. to admit fresh air in order to replace stale or noxious air

b. to circulate through and freshen

c. to expose to the circulation of fresh air, as to retard spoilage

d. to expose to public discussion or examination

_____ 3. Many people with coronary artery disease do not **manifest** symptoms until they have their first heart attack.

man•i•fest (măn′ə-fĕst′) *adj.* Clearly apparent to the sight or understanding; obvious. See synonyms at **apparent.** ❖ *tr.v.* **-fest•ed, -fest•ing, -fests 1.** To show or demonstrate plainly; reveal: "*Mercedes . . . manifested the chaotic abandonment of hysteria*" (Jack London). **2.** To be evidence of; prove. **3a.** To record in a ship's manifest. **b.** To display or present a manifest of (cargo). ❖ *n.* **1.** A list of cargo or passengers carried on a ship or plane. **2.** An invoice of goods carried on a truck or train. **3.** A list of railroad cars according to owner and location. [Middle English *manifeste,* from Old French, from Latin *manufestus, manifestus,* caught in the act, blatant, obvious. See **gʷhedh-** in Appendix I.] **—man′i•fest′ly** *adv.*

a. clearly apparent to the sight or understanding; obvious

b. to show or demonstrate plainly; reveal

c. to be evidence of; prove

d. to record in a ship's manifest

_____ 4. After receiving the Noble Prize, the winner is often **besieged** with requests for speaking engagements and public appearances.

be•siege (bĭ-sēj′) *tr.v.* **-sieged, -sieg•ing, -sieg•es 1.** To surround with hostile forces. **2.** To crowd around; hem in. **3.** To harass or importune, as with requests: *Reporters besieged the winner for interviews.* **4.** To cause to feel distressed or worried: *She was besieged by problems.* [Middle English *besegen,* probably alteration of *assegen,* from Old French *assegier,* from Vulgar Latin **assedicāre* : Latin *ad-,* ad- + Vulgar Latin **sedicāre,* to sit; see SIEGE.] **—be•siege′ment** *n.* **—be•sieg′er** *n.*

a. to cause to feel distressed or worried

b. to crowd around; hem in

c. to harass or importune, as with requests

d. to surround with hostile forces

_____ 5. The student task force obviously did not spend much time considering the problem of the limited number of parking spaces on campus; its **facile** solution to the problem disappointed all of us.

fac•ile (făs/əl) *adj.* **1.** Done or achieved with little effort or difficulty; easy. See synonyms at **easy. 2.** Working, acting, or speaking with effortless ease and fluency. **3.** Arrived at without due care, effort, or examination; superficial: *proposed a facile solution to a complex problem.* **4.** Readily manifested, together with an aura of insincerity and lack of depth: *a facile slogan devised by politicians.* **5.** *Archaic* Pleasingly mild, as in disposition or manner. [Middle English, from Old French, from Latin *facilis.* See **dhē-** in Appendix I.] —**fac/ile•ly** *adv.* —**fac/ile•ness** *n.*

a. done or achieved with little effort or difficulty; easy

b. working, acting, or speaking with effortless ease and fluency

c. arrived at without due care, effort, or examination; superficial

d. pleasingly mild, as in disposition or manner

DICTIONARY SKILLS

Directions: Use a dictionary to answer the following questions. Select the best answer.

_____ 1. The definition of the word **ligature** is
   a. legal suit.
   b. relief.
   c. coal.
   d. bond.

_____ 2. The most accurate phonetic spelling for the word **neuropathy** is
   a. nyu ro path e.
   b. nyur o path e.
   c. nyu ROP a the.
   d. nyu rop a te.

_____ 3. What part of speech is the word **tole?**
   a. noun
   b. verb
   c. adjective
   d. adverb

_____ 4. What is the origin of the word **hirsute?**
   a. French
   b. German
   c. Latin
   d. Middle English

_____ 5. The noun form of the word **infallible** is
   a. infallibility.
   b. infallibly.
   c. infallibleness.
   d. infallible.

_____ 6. The correct syllabication of the word **marsupial** is
  a. mar sup i al.
  b. mar su pi al.
  c. mars up ial.
  d. mar su pial.

_____ 7. What syllable or part of the word **developer** is stressed?
  a. de
  b. vel
  c. op
  d. er

_____ 8. Which of the following is a synonym for **gross?**
  a. net
  b. chaste
  c. total
  d. fumble

_____ 9. Which of the following is a synonym for **droll?**
  a. boring
  b. amusing
  c. elf
  d. confused

_____ 10. Which of the following is a synonym for **grip?**
  a. suitcase
  b. lost
  c. repel
  d. protest

NAME _____ SECTION _____

DATE _____ SCORE _____

WE DON'T HAVE AIDS, BUT WE SUFFER, TOO
Kerrel McKay

The author of this article, which first appeared in *Newsweek* magazine, works as an HIV/AIDS outreach officer for the Jamaican Ministry of Health. Read it to find out what Kerrel McKay learned from her own father's illness about the effects of AIDS on children and families.

Vocabulary Preview

These are some of the difficult words in this essay. The definitions here will help you if you can't figure out the meanings from the sentence context or word parts.

despondent (para. 7) without hope; despairing

hospice (para. 7) a program providing medical care and emotional support for terminally ill patients

anomaly (para. 9) an unusual or abnormal case

peers (para. 10) people of equal standing with others in a group

pandemic (para. 11) a disease that is spread over a wide geographic area, affecting an exceptionally high proportion of the population

Often it's the children of the dying who must care for them and keep it hidden from the rest of the world.

1   I was 9 years old when I found out my father was ill. It was 1994, but I can remember my mother's words as if it were yesterday: "Kerrel, I don't want you to take food from your father, because him have the AIDS. Be very careful when you are around him."

2   AIDS wasn't something we talked about in Jamaica when I was growing up. What I knew about AIDS could be summed up like this: If you were HIV-positive, you were going to die. You were going to suffer before you died. And you didn't expect anyone to treat you well, either.

3   From then on, I knew that this would be a family secret. My parents were not together anymore, and my dad lived alone. For a while he could take care of himself. But when I was 12, his condition worsened. My father's other children lived far away, so it fell to me to look after him.

■ NOWHERE TO TURN: The nurses would leave Dad's food on the table even though he was too weak to feed himself.

4   I tended to his every need. After school, I would cook, clean, shop for groceries and take my dad to the doctor. We couldn't afford all the necessary medication for him, and because Dad was unable to work, I had no money for school supplies and often couldn't even buy food for dinner. I would sit in class feeling completely lost, the teacher's words muffled as I tried to figure out how I was going to manage.

5   I did not share my burden with anyone. I had seen how people reacted to AIDS. Kids taunted and teased classmates who had parents with the disease. And even adults could be cruel. When my father was moved to the hospital, the nurses, who were not well educated about the virus and believed they could become infected easily, neglected to bathe him and would leave his food on the bedside table even though he was too weak to feed himself.

6   I had known from day one that he was going to die, but after so many years of keeping his condition a secret, I was completely unprepared when he reached his final days. All the questions I never asked, all the pain I felt, were bottled up inside. I couldn't bear the thought of watching him die or even hearing about his death. So I decided to kill myself first.

7   Despondent, I called a woman at the nonprofit Jamaica AIDS Support who had helped get my father to a caring hospice. That bleak day, she kept me on the phone for hours, and she left me with a sense of hope.

8   I was so lucky to find someone who cared. She saved my life. The most important thing I learned from her was this: I am not alone. In Jamaica, in the Caribbean, throughout the world, there are millions like me who first lose their childhood to a parent's illness and then lose their parent to AIDS.

9   Worldwide, there are 15 million children who have lost at least one parent to AIDS. Eighty percent of them are in sub-Saharan Africa; the rest are scattered all over the world, including my native Jamaica. Millions more children are living in the shadow of AIDS, forced to skip school to tend to sick parents, left to scrounge for food and medicine and grow up without parental protection, guidance and love. Most of these children are cared for by already overburdened relatives. Rarely do they get any outside help. I was fortunate enough to get counseling, but in this I was an anomaly. According to UNICEF, less than 10 percent of children affected by AIDS receive any public support or services.

10   My father's illness taught me all too well that young people must learn how to protect themselves from HIV. To do my part, I created a youth branch of my local Portland Parish AIDS Committee. The members of the group use drama, song and dance to educate their peers and adults about AIDS. We've even hosted a workshop with some of the nurses at the hospital where my father was treated. And every third Saturday, we choose a particular community to visit, walking to houses, parks and bars to talk honestly about HIV/AIDS and other sexually transmitted diseases. Young people are often too embarrassed to go looking for information, so we bring it to them.

11   When adults decide how to tackle the world's AIDS crisis, the way it affects children must become part of their thinking. The needs of young people must be addressed in national plans and budgets aimed at the AIDS pandemic. Children need medicine, health care and psychological support. They need help caring for their sick parents so they can continue to go to school. They need the care and stability of a strong family. And they need the education and services that will enable them to protect themselves from HIV.

12   I was 15 when my father died on Feb. 27, 2000. He took his secret to the grave, having never spoken about AIDS to anyone, even me. He didn't want to call attention to AIDS. I do.

—■ · ■—

Directions: In the space provided, write the letter of the choice that best completes each of the following statements.

CHECKING YOUR COMPREHENSION

 1. The author's main purpose in this selection is to
   a. describe the programs available to Jamaican families affected by AIDS.
   b. provide information about HIV/AIDS and other sexually transmitted diseases.
   c. report the most recent statistics about the spread of AIDS.
   (d.) draw attention to the needs of children everywhere affected by AIDS.

 2. When McKay found out that her father was ill, she knew that
   a. she would not have the support of her community.
   b. her father's illness would be a family secret.
   c. her father would die from his illness.
   (d.) all of the above.

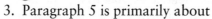 3. Paragraph 5 is primarily about
   a. why the author had no money for school supplies.
   b. how other children reacted to people with AIDS.
   c. why the author did not tell anyone about her father's illness.
   (d.) how the nurses at the hospital treated people with AIDS.

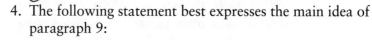 4. The following statement best expresses the main idea of paragraph 9:
   a. The majority of children who have lost at least one parent to AIDS live in sub-Saharan Africa.
   b. Millions of children affected by the AIDS crisis do not receive any kind of support or services.
   c. The children of adults with AIDS often skip school so they can tend to their parents.
   (d.) The author felt fortunate that she was able to get counseling in dealing with her father's illness.

 5. The author created a youth branch of her local Portland Parish AIDS Committee in order to
   (a.) educate young people and adults about AIDS.
   b. use drama, song, and dance to entertain children.
   c. provide food and medication to people with AIDS.
   d. offer an alternative to hospital care for AIDS patients.

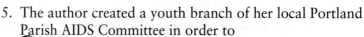

REVIEWING DIFFICULT VOCABULARY

Directions: Match each word in column A with its meaning in column B.

	Column A		Column B
d	6. despondent	a.	a geographically widespread disease affecting a high proportion of the population
e	7. hospice	b.	people of equal standing with others in a group
a	8. pandemic	c.	an unusual or abnormal case
c	9. anomaly	d.	hopeless
b	10. peers	e.	a program which provides medical and emotional care for terminally ill patients

STUDYING WORDS

a 11. The etymology of the word **burden** (para. 5) is
    a. Middle English.
    b. French.
    c. Latin.
    d. German.

a 12. The Latin form of the word **virus** (para. 5) means
    a. disease.
    b. health.
    c. germs.
    d. poison.

b 13. As a part of speech, the word **bathe** (para. 5) is
    a. a noun.
    b. a verb.
    c. an adjective.
    d. a pronoun.

b 14. Which one of the following correctly indicates how **anomaly** (para. 9) is pronounced?
    a. AN uh moll ee
    b. a NOM uh lee
    c. a NO moll ee
    d. an um ALL ee

Directions: Select the word or phrase from the box that best completes each of the following sentences. Not all the words in the box will be used.

irregularity	trapped	persuade	merciless	determined	state of health
overloaded	evaluation	spread	distant	discouraged	distressed

15. As used in paragraph 5, the word cruel means ___discourage___.

16. As used in paragraph 6, the word condition means ___state of health___

17. As used in paragraph 6, the phrase bottled up means ___trapped___.

18. As used in paragraph 9, the word scattered means ___spread___.

19. As used in paragraph 9, the word overburdened means ___overloaded___

20. As used in paragraph 9, the word anomaly means ___irregularity___.

QUESTIONS FOR DISCUSSION

1. What does the author say was the most important thing she learned from the woman at Jamaica AIDS Support? Why do you think that was so important?

2. Why was the author's photograph included with this selection? How do you think it affected your reading of her story?

3. What does this selection tell you about the status of children in the world? How is the author working to change it?

4. Why are people with AIDS treated differently from those with other terminal illnesses?

WRITING ACTIVITIES

1. The author learned about the cruelty of others as a result of her father's illness. Write a paragraph describing an experience in which you encountered either the best or worst aspects of your fellow humans. Explain how it left you feeling toward others.

2. The author is hoping to bring about change primarily by educating young people and raising the world's awareness about the AIDS crisis. Choose an issue that you believe could be improved through education and increased awareness and write a paragraph explaining how you would go about it.

3. How did this article change what you know about the effects of AIDS on families and children? Write a paragraph explaining your answer.

Chapter 2: Using Your Dictionary

RECORDING YOUR PROGRESS

Test	Number Right			Score
Practice Test 2-1	_____	× 10	=	_____%
Practice Test 2-2	_____	× 10	=	_____%
Practice Test 2-3	_____	× 10	=	_____%
Mastery Test 2-1	_____	× 10	=	_____%
Mastery Test 2-2	_____	× 10	=	_____%
Mastery Test 2-3	_____	× 5	=	_____%

EVALUATING YOUR PROGRESS

Based on your test performance, rate how well you have mastered the skills taught in this chapter by checking one of the boxes below or by writing your own evaluation.

☐ **Need More Improvement**
Tip: Try using the "Vocabulary" Module on the Reading Road Trip Web site at **http://www .ablongman.com/readingroadtrip** to fine-tune the skills that you have learned in this chapter.

☐ **Need More Practice**
Tip: Try using the "Vocabulary" Module on the Reading Road Trip Web site at **http://www .ablongman.com/readingroadtrip** to brush up on the skills you have learned in this chapter, or visit this textbook's companion Web site at **http://www.ablongman.com/mcwhorter** for extra practice.

☐ **Good**
Tip: To maintain your skills, quickly review this chapter by using the companion Web site that accompanies this textbook by logging on to **http://www.ablongman.com/mcwhorter**.

☐ **Excellent**

YOUR EVALUATION: _____

_____

_____

_____

READ ME FIRST!

The photograph below is striking and humorous because you do not see what you expect. It is obvious that the man's head and body are missing. You can tell what is missing by looking at the rest of the photograph; the image of a man's hands clutching the coat suggests that a person is present. When reading a sentence or paragraph, if you find a word is missing from your vocabulary, you can often figure out its meaning by studying the sentence or paragraph in which it appears. The words surrounding an unknown word provide clues to its meaning, just as the details in the photograph provide clues about what is missing.

CHAPTER 3

Building Vocabulary: Using Context Clues

What Is Context?

Studying the details of the photograph on the opposite page helped you understand its meaning. Likewise, by studying closely the words in a sentence you can figure out the meaning of a particular word within the sentence. Read the following brief paragraph. Several words are missing. Try to figure out the missing words and write them in the blanks.

Sally has never been to Mexico, but she loves _____ food. Her favorite dish is _____, those delicious tortilla chips covered with cheese, beef, and beans. Just thinking about them makes Sally _____.

Did you insert the word *Mexican* in the first blank, *nachos* in the second blank, and *hungry* in the third blank? You were probably able to correctly identify all three missing words. You could tell from each sentence which word to put in. The words around each word—the sentence **context**—gave you clues as to which word would fit and make sense. Such clues are called **context clues.**

Even though you won't find missing words on a printed page, you will often find words that you do not know. Context clues can help you figure out the meanings of unfamiliar words.

EXAMPLE

Tony noticed that the **wallabies** at the zoo looked like kangaroos.

From the sentence, you can tell that *wallabies* are "animals that look like kangaroos."

EXAMPLE

Many people have **phobias,** such as a fear of heights, a fear of water, or a fear of confined spaces.

You can figure out that *phobia* means "a fear of specific objects or situations."

Types of Context Clues

When you have trouble with a word, look for five types of context clues: (1) definition, (2) synonym, (3) example, (4) contrast, and (5) inference.

Definition Clues

Writers often define a word right after they use it. They may use words and phrases such as *means, is, refers to,* and *are called* to signal that a definition is to follow.

EXAMPLES

Broad, flat noodles that are served covered with sauce or butter are called **fettuccine.**

Corona refers to *the outermost part of the sun's atmosphere.*

At other times, rather than formally define a word, a writer may provide a clue to its meaning.

EXAMPLE

During the Christmas season, many people use decorative lights to **illuminate** their homes.

Here the word *lights* is a clue to the meaning of *illuminate*, which means to "light up."

Sometimes a definition is only part of a sentence. In this kind of sentence, a writer may use three kinds of punctuation (commas, dashes, or parentheses) to separate the definition from the rest of the sentence.

EXAMPLES

My Aunt Martha often serves **glog,** *a Swedish hot punch,* at her holiday parties.

The judge's **candor**—*his sharp, open frankness*—shocked the jury.

A leading cause of heart disease is a diet with too much **cholesterol** (*a fatty substance made of carbon, hydrogen, and oxygen*).

Textbook writers often use definition clues. As you read your texts, look for important words in **boldface type** or *italics*. These terms are usually right before or after a definition. Based on what you have just learned, what is the definition of **context** on page 71?

Directions: *Using the definition clues in each sentence, choose the letter of the choice that best defines each boldfaced word.*

_____   1. After taking a course in **genealogy,** Don was able to create a record of his family's history dating back to the eighteenth century.

a. the study of ancestry

b. creative writing

c. the study of plants

d. personal finance

_D_   2. Participants in a **triathlon** compete in long-distance swimming, bicycling, and running.

a. hiking trail   c. large group

b. three-part race   d. written test

_____   3. Louie's **dossier** is a record of his credentials, including college transcripts and letters of recommendation.

a. briefcase or valise

b. checking account statement

c. diploma

d. collection of materials

_____   4. **Audition,** the process of hearing, begins when a sound wave reaches the outer ear.

a. loud sound   c. deafness

b. sense of hearing   d. the inner ear

_____   5. A person who becomes an **entrepreneur** must be willing to take on both the risks and opportunities of his or her new business.

a. business owner   c. employee

b. stockbroker   d. designer

_____   6. After sketching out a design, a sculptor may create an **armature,** or rigid framework, to serve as a support for the sculpture.

    a. detailed design   c. small model

    b. supportive frame   d. alternative design

_____   7. Even though the patient was **asymptomatic**—not showing any symptoms—after his accident, the doctor decided to keep him in the hospital overnight for observation.

    a. not cooperative   c. in pain

    b. without symptoms   d. unable to talk

_____   8. In the business world, the funds that flow into a company from the sale of goods or services are called **revenues.**

    a. income   c. products

    b. benefits   d. expenses

_____   9. Across the front of the house was a **colonnade** (a row of columns connected by beams) where the children were playing hide-and-seek.

    a. playhouse   c. porch

    b. colonial structure   d. row of columns

_____ 10. When Anna became disabled, her husband was able to make legal and financial decisions on her behalf by obtaining a **proxy**—a document authorizing one person to act for another.

    a. consultation   c. promise

    b. legal authority   d. financial advice

Synonym Clues

At other times, rather than formally define a word, a writer may provide a synonym—a word or brief phrase that is close in meaning. The synonym may appear in the same sentence as the unknown word.

The main character in the novel was an **amalgam,** or *combination,* of several people the author met during the war.

Other times, it may appear anywhere in the passage, in an earlier or later sentence.

Betsy took a *break* from teaching in order to serve in the Peace Corps. Despite the **hiatus,** Betsy's school was delighted to rehire her when she returned.

**Exercise
3-2**

Directions: Using the synonym clues in each sentence, choose the letter of the choice that best defines each boldfaced word.

_____ 1. The noise in the nursery school was **incessant;** the crying, yelling, and laughing never stopped.

   a. careless   c. bold

   b. harmful   d. continuous

_____ 2. There was a **consensus**—or unified opinion—among the students that the exam was difficult.

   a. requirement   c. disagreement

   b. consequence   d. agreement

_____ 3. The family's decision to donate their land to the park system was **altruistic;** they were unselfish in their desire to do what was best for the community.

   a. shrewd   c. selfless

   b. thoughtless   d. greedy

_____ 4. After each course heading there was a **synopsis,** or summary, of the content and requirements for the course.

   a. correction   c. illustration

   b. brief description   d. continuation

_____ 5. When preparing job application letters, Serena develops one standard letter or **prototype.** Then she changes that letter to fit the specific jobs she is applying for.

   a. variation   c. detail

   b. model   d. introduction

_____ 6. The mayor worried that the town council was trying to **usurp** her power, but how could she prevent the council members from taking over?

   a. support   c. improve

   b. take away   d. allow

_____ 7. Joe was **hesitant** about asking Katy for a date because he was unsure if she liked him.

    a. definite   c. casual

    b. uncertain   d. heroic

_____ 8. The old man avoided his family; in fact, he **eschewed** the company of anyone who knew about his past.

    a. sought out   c. shunned

    b. enjoyed   d. welcomed

_____ 9. Rico approves of the new drunk driving laws, but he does not **endorse** taking away drunk drivers' cars.

    a. stop   c. start

    b. regret   d. support

_____ 10. The teenager died from drinking a **lethal** amount of alcohol during a party.

    a. harmless   c. deadly

    b. moderate   d. excessive

Example Clues

Writers, especially textbook writers, often include examples to help explain or clarify a word. Suppose you do not know the meaning of the word *toxic,* and you find it used in a science text:

> **Toxic** materials, such as arsenic, asbestos, pesticides, and lead, can cause bodily damage.

This sentence gives four examples of toxic materials, all of which are poisonous substances. You could conclude, then, that *toxic* means "poisonous." When writers put examples in a sentence, they often introduce them with the words *like, such as, for example,* or *including.*

EXAMPLES

In the past month, we have had almost every type of **precipitation,** including rain, snow, sleet, and hail.

Newsmagazines, like *Time* or *Newsweek,* are more detailed than newspapers.

Lena doesn't mind planting her favorite **annuals**—marigolds and zinnias—even though she has to do it every year.

By using the example clues, can you figure out that *precipitation* means "the forms in which water returns to earth" and that *newsmagazines* are "magazines that give in-depth coverage of news events"? Can you also tell that *annuals* are "plants that can't survive the winter"?

Copyright © 2007 by Kathleen T. McWhorter

Exercise 3–3

Directions: Using the example clues in each sentence, choose the letter of the choice that best defines each boldfaced word.

_____ 1. Many **pharmaceuticals,** including morphine and penicillin, are not readily available in some countries.

   a. aspirin tablets
   b. pharmacists
   c. drugs
   d. substances

_____ 2. Jerry's child was **reticent** in every respect; she would not speak, refused to answer questions, and avoided looking at anyone.

   a. reserved
   b. noisy
   c. undisciplined
   d. rigorous

_____ 3. Most **condiments,** such as pepper, mustard, and catsup, are used to improve the flavor of foods.

   a. ingredients
   b. seasonings for food
   c. sauces
   d. appetizers

_____ 4. Dogs, cats, parakeets, and other **sociable** pets can provide senior citizens with companionship.

   a. weak
   b. friendly
   c. dangerous
   d. unattractive

_____ 5. Paul's grandmother is a **sagacious** businesswoman; once she turned a small ice cream shop into a popular restaurant and sold it for a huge profit.

   a. old fashioned
   b. shrewd
   c. dishonest
   d. foolish

_____ 6. Rosie's dog was **submissive**—crouching, flattening its ears, and avoiding eye contact.

   a. friendly and excitable
   b. yielding to the control of another
   c. aggressive
   d. active

_____ 7. Many things about the library make it **conducive** to study, including good lighting and many reference books.

    a. unattractive   c. helpful

    b. uncomfortable   d. sociable

_____ 8. Clothing is available in a variety of **fabrics**, including cotton, wool, polyester, and linen.

    a. types of leather   c. materials

    b. styles   d. fashions

_____ 9. The raccoons were a **menace** to our backyard. They ate all of our tomato plants and dug holes in the grass.

    a. help   c. threat

    b. barrier   d. force

_____ 10. Murder, rape, and armed robbery are **reprehensible** crimes.

    a. reasonable   c. very bad

    b. unusual   d. rural

Contrast Clues

Sometimes you can determine the meaning of an unknown word from an **antonym**—a word or phrase that has an opposite meaning. Notice how the antonym *resisted* in the following sentence provides a clue to the meaning of the boldfaced term:

> One of the dinner guests **succumbed** to the temptation to have a second piece of cake, but the others resisted.

Since the others resisted a second dessert, you can tell that one guest gave in and had a piece. Thus, *succumbed* means the opposite of *resist*; that is, "to give in to." When writers use contrasting words or phrases, they often introduce them with words such as *but, though,* and *whereas.*

EXAMPLES   The professor **advocates** testing on animals, but many of her students are opposed to it.

Though Liz felt sad and depressed, most of the graduates were **elated.**

My Uncle Saul is quite **portly,** whereas his wife is very thin.

Can you tell from the contrast clues that *advocates* means "favors," *elated* means "happy," and *portly* means "heavy"?

Exercise 3-4

Directions: Using the contrast clues or antonyms in each sentence, choose the letter of the choice that best defines each boldfaced word or phrase.

_____ 1. Freshmen are often **naive** about college at first, but by their second semester they are usually quite sophisticated in the ways of their new school.

a. innocent   c. annoyed
b. sociable   d. elated

_____ 2. Although most members of the class agreed with the instructor's evaluation of the film, several strongly **objected.**

a. agreed   c. obliterated
b. debated   d. disagreed

_____ 3. Little Jill hid shyly behind her mother when she met new people, yet her brother Matthew was very **gregarious.**

a. insulting   c. concerned
b. sociable   d. embarrassed

_____ 4. The child remained **demure** while the teacher scolded but became violently angry afterward.

a. quiet and reserved   c. cowardly
b. boisterous   d. upset and distraught

_____ 5. Some city dwellers are **affluent;** others live in or near poverty.

a. poor   c. wealthy
b. arrogant   d. agreeable

_____ 6. I am certain that the hotel will hold our reservation; however, if you are **dubious,** call to make sure.

a. confused   c. sure
b. doubtful   d. energetic

_____ 7. The speaker **denounced** certain legal changes while praising other reforms.

a. laughed at   c. spoke out against
b. cherished   d. denied

_____ 8. The woman's parents **thwarted** her marriage plans though they liked her fiancé.

a. prevented   c. idolized
b. encouraged   d. organized

_____ 9. Extroverted people tend to be outgoing and talkative, while introverted people are more **reticent.**

   a. reserved   c. overbearing

   b. showy   d. helpless

_____ 10. Unlike other male-dominated species, Indian elephants live in a **matriarchal** society.

   a. aggressive   c. led by females

   b. nonthreatening   d. passive

Inference Clues

When you read, you often figure out the meaning of an unknown word through **inference**—a process that uses logic and reasoning skills. For instance, look at the following sentence:

> Bob is quite versatile: he is a good student, a top athlete, an excellent car mechanic, and a gourmet cook.

Since Bob is successful at many different types of activities, you could infer that *versatile* means "capable of doing many things well."

EXAMPLES   When my friend tried to pay with Mexican **pesos,** the clerk explained that the store accepted only U.S. dollars.

On hot, humid summer afternoons, I often feel **languid.**

The vase must have been **jostled** in shipment because it arrived with several chips in it.

By using logic and your reasoning skills, can you figure out that *pesos* are a kind of "Mexican money"? Can you also tell that *languid* means "lacking energy" and *jostled* means "bumped"?

Exercise 3–5   *Directions: Using logic and your own reasoning skills, choose the letter of the choice that best defines each boldfaced word.*

________ 1. To **compel** Clare to hand over her wallet, the mugger said he had a gun.

   a. discourage   c. force

   b. entice   d. imagine

_D_   2. Student journalists are taught how to be **concise** when writing in a limited space.

    a. peaceful   c. proper

    (b.) clear and brief   d. wordy

_C_   3. There should be more **drastic** penalties to stop people from littering.

    a. dirty   (c.) extreme

    b. suitable   d. dangerous

_B_   4. To **fortify** his diet while weightlifting, Monty took 12 vitamins a day.

    a. suggest   c. avoid

    (b.) strengthen   d. approve of

_B_   5. On our wedding anniversary, my husband and I **reminisced** about how we first met.

    a. sang   c. argued

    (b.) remembered   d. forgot

_d_   6. For their own safety, household pets should be **confined** to their own yards.

    a. led   (c.) shown

    b. restricted   (d.) used

_B_   7. The quarterback **sustained** numerous injuries: a fractured wrist, two broken ribs, and a hip injury.

    a. caused   c. displayed

    (b.) experienced   d. noticed

_a_   8. Sam's brother advised him to be **wary** of strangers he meets on the street.

    (a.) suspicious   c. congenial with

    b. trusting   d. generous toward

_C_   9. The lawyer tried to confuse the jury by bringing in many facts that weren't **pertinent** to the case.

    a. obvious   (c.) relevant

    b. continuous   d. harmful

10. We keep candles in the house to **avert** being left in the dark during power failures.

    (a.) prevent   c. accommodate

    b. ensure   d. begin

**Exercise
3–6**

Directions: *Choose the answer that best defines each boldfaced word from the passage below.*

Worms and *viruses* are rather unpleasant terms that have entered the **jargon** of the computer industry to describe some of the ways that computer systems can be invaded.

A worm can be defined as a program that transfers itself from computer to computer over a network and plants itself as a separate file on the target computer's disks. One worm was **injected** into an electronic mail network where it multiplied uncontrollably and clogged the memories of thousands of computers until they could no longer function.

A virus is a set of illicit instructions that passes itself on to other programs or documents with which it comes in contact. It can change or delete files, display words or obscene messages, or produce bizarre screen effects. In its most **vindictive** form, a virus can slowly **sabotage** a computer system and remain undetected for months, contaminating data or wiping out an entire hard drive. A virus can be dealt with using a vaccine, or antivirus, which is a computer program that stops the virus from spreading and often **eradicates** it.

—adapted from Capron, *Computers: Tools for an Information Age,* 5th Ed., p. 233.

_____ 1. jargon

    a. language   c. confusion

    b. system   d. security

_____ 2. injected

    a. avoided   c. removed

    b. introduced   d. discussed

_____ 3. vindictive

    a. creative   c. harmful

    b. simple   d. typical

_____ 4. sabotage

    a. prevent   c. transfer

    b. destroy   d. produce

_____   5. eradicates

        a. eliminates   c. repeats

        b. allows   d. produces

Using All of the Context Clues

When you read a chapter in a textbook or a story, you probably use all four types of context clues. You may find a definition here, an example there, and a contrasting word someplace else. You also put on your thinking cap and use your common sense and reasoning to figure out other words you don't know. Sometimes, though, there are no context clues, or they don't go far enough in explaining what a difficult word really means. For this reason, you need to develop other kinds of vocabulary skills, which are covered in the next chapter.

The Textbook Challenge

Part A: Student Resource Guide A

The following words appear in Textbook Excerpt 2, "Food Safety: A Growing Concern" (p. 403). For each word, use context to write a definition of the word as it is used in the excerpt.

1. tinge (para. 2) _____

2. food irradiation (para. 5) _____

3. dispenses (para. 6) _____

4. enhance (para. 8) _____

5. fortification (para. 8) _____

6. supplements (para. 8) _____

Part B: A College Textbook

Choose a chapter from one of your textbooks for another course. Identify ten words that you are able to determine the meaning of from context. Write the words and their meanings.

What Have You Learned?

Directions: To check your understanding of the chapter, select the word or phrase from the box below that best completes each of the following sentences. Keep in mind that not all of the words will be used.

examples	inference	definitions
context clues	parts	word group
antonym	synonym	context

1. The words around an unfamiliar word in a sentence are known as its
   _____.

2. _____ are hints or tips that help you figure out
   a word you don't know.

3. A _____ has the same meaning as another
   word, whereas an antonym has an opposite meaning.

4. The two types of context clues that textbook authors often use are
   _____ and examples.

5. When you figure out the meaning of a word by using logic and your
   reasoning skills, you are using _____.

Test-Taking Tip #3: Answering Vocabulary Questions

When answering questions on a reading test about the meaning of a word in a sentence or paragraph, use the following suggestions:

■   Test writers do not ask questions that students are unable to answer. So, if you are being asked the meaning of a particular word, there is probably a way to figure it out.

■   Read beyond the word in question. Look beyond the word to find a clue to its meaning. Sometimes the context clue appears after the unknown word, either in the same sentence or in a later sentence.

Example: The economy was in a constant state of *flux.* One month inflation increased; the next month it decreased.

In this example, the clue to the meaning of *flux* appears in the sentence following the one in which the word is used.

■   When you are unsure of your answer to a multiple choice question about the meaning of a word in a sentence or paragraph, first try to eliminate one or more choices. Then substitute the choice(s) you are considering for the unknown word in the sentence in which it appears. Choose the choice that makes the most sense and seems to fit.

Example: After the shopper *succumbed* to the temptation of buying an expensive new dress, she was filled with regret.

a. gave in

b. resisted

c. alerted

d. ridiculed

Choice a is correct. Choice b, *resisted,* does not fit because the shopper would not be filled with regret if she had resisted. Choice c, *alerted to temptation* does not make sense—temptation usually does not alert us. Choice d does not make sense because temptation is usually not ridiculed.

USING CONTEXT CLUES

Directions: Using context clues, in the space provided write the letter of the choice that best defines each boldfaced word.

_____ 1. The cat and her newborn kittens had to be **isolated** from the family dog after he tried to attack them.

    a. combined   c. separated

    b. heated up   d. rejected

_____ 2. All of the movies I wanted to rent were taken, so as an **alternative** I went home and watched television.

    a. command   c. assignment

    b. design   d. another option

_____ 3. The baby birds needed a place of **refuge** from the summer storm.

    a. shelter   c. building

    b. rejection   d. separation

_____ 4. Mike's efforts to buy a car were **futile,** so he continued to ride his bike to work.

    a. helpful   c. necessary

    b. useless   d. careless

_____ 5. Janice **persistently** asked her mother to buy a new car, so her mother finally gave in and bought one.

    a. constantly   c. brief

    b. lazy   d. unenthusiastic

_____ 6. The meal was prepared perfectly, but the young woman found it **repugnant.**

    a. overpriced   c. distasteful

    b. lovely   d. delicious

_____ 7. Getting our car fixed after the accident was an **ordeal.**

    a. good time   c. unexpected event

    b. relaxing opportunity   d. painful experience

_____ 8. Candace wore a red, low-cut dress to the party, but her sister was dressed more **decorously.**

    a. fashionably   c. fancy

    b. warmly   d. modestly

_____ 9. Monica let a few weeks **elapse** before returning her ex-boyfriend's phone call.

    a. separate   c. slow down

    b. pass   d. speed up

_____ 10. Gorillas can **convey** messages to humans through gestures and sounds.

    a. invent   c. communicate

    b. allow   d. approve of

USING CONTEXT CLUES

Directions: Using context clues, in the space provided write the letter of the choice that best defines each boldfaced word.

_____ 1. When several members of the president's staff were charged with various crimes, the public's confidence in the government **eroded.**

a. grew   c. healed

b. deteriorated d. repeated

_____ 2. People who suffer from migraine headaches are frequently advised to avoid foods that can **precipitate** an attack, such as chocolate and some cheeses.

a. prevent   c. follow

b. trigger   d. delay

_____ 3. When solving a complex math problem, it is better to be **punctilious** and get it right than to be careless and risk getting it wrong.

a. timely   c. mistaken

b. careful   d. risky

_____ 4. Being extremely thin has become a **compulsion** for many teenage girls.

a. behavior   c. punishment

b. obsession   d. separation

_____ 5. The veterinarian gave the puppies vitamins to **stimulate** their appetites.

a. arouse   c. stop

b. confuse   d. delay

_____ 6. The children looked angelic, but after their parents left they became more and more **obstreperous.**

a. agreeable   c. sad

b. unruly or rowdy d. intellectual

7. After visiting the dark cave, it was difficult to make the **transition** into the sunlight.
   a. purchase
   c. change
   b. invention
   d. repetition

8. My **conservative** grandparents were disappointed when I served a vegetarian meal for Thanksgiving.
   a. resistant to change
   c. not definite
   b. opinionated
   d. understanding

9. The fact that Tim was ten years older than Sandy was enough to **deter** her from dating him.
   a. damage
   c. prevent
   b. refuse
   d. dislike

10. Our senator **advocates** stricter gun control laws; she favors lengthening the waiting period for the purchase of guns.
    a. eliminates
    c. supports
    b. opposes
    d. indulges

NAME _____ SECTION _____
DATE _____ SCORE _____

USING CONTEXT CLUES

Directions: Select the word from the box below that best defines the bold-faced word in each of the following sentences. Keep in mind that not all of the words will be used.

generous	exceed	travel plan	not intended
gruesome	silent	weaknesses	trusting relationship
lively	helpful	useless	
change	limit	burned	

1. The economy was in a state of continual **flux;** inflation increased one month and decreased the next. _____

2. Art is always talkative, but Ed is usually **taciturn.**

   _____

3. Many **debilities** of old age, including poor eyesight and loss of hearing, can be treated medically. _____

4. The soap opera contained numerous **morbid** events: the death of a young child, the suicide of her father, and the murder of his older brother. _____

5. After long hours of practice, Peter finally learned to type; Sam's efforts, however, were **futile.** _____

6. The newspaper's error was **inadvertent;** the editor did not intend to include the victim's name. _____

7. To save money, we have decided to **curtail** the number of CDs we buy each month. _____

8. Steam from the hot radiator **scalded** the mechanic's hand.

   _____

9. Sonia's **itinerary** outlined her trip and listed Cleveland as her next stop.

   _____

10. Steven had very good **rapport** with his father, but he was unable to get along with his mother. _____

NAME _____ SECTION _____

DATE _____ SCORE _____

USING CONTEXT CLUES

Directions: Using context clues, select the word from the box below that best defines each of the boldfaced words in the following paragraph. Keep in mind that not all of the words will be used.

Can looking at a color affect your behavior or **alter** your mood? Some researchers are **skeptical,** but others believe color can **influence** how you act and feel. A number of experiments have been conducted that **demonstrate** the effects of color. In 1979 a psychologist named Schauss **evaluated** the effect of the color pink. He found out that the color relaxed the subjects so much that they could not perform simple strength tests as well as they did when looking at other **hues.** The officer in charge of a U.S. Navy **brig** in Washington noticed Schauss's findings and allowed Schauss to test his calm-color **hypothesis** on inmates. Today, many **institutions,** such as jails, juvenile correction facilities, and holding centers, put individuals in pink rooms when their tempers **flare.**

—Geiwitz, *Psychology*, p. 189

colors	change	erupt	calm down
equaled	places of confinement	doubtful	show
theory	studied	prison	
demoralize	asylums	affect	

1. alter _____

2. skeptical _____

3. influence _____

4. demonstrate _____

5. evaluated _____

6. hues _____

7. brig _____

8. hypothesis _____

9. institutions _____

10. flare _____

USING CONTEXT CLUES

Directions: Using context clues, select the word from the box below that best defines each of the boldfaced words in the following paragraph. Keep in mind that not all of the words will be used.

The homeless are among the extremely poor. They are by definition people who sleep in streets, parks, shelters, and places not intended as **dwellings,** such as bus stations, lobbies, or **abandoned** buildings. Homelessness is not new. There have always been homeless people in the United States. But the homeless today differ in some ways from their **counterparts** of the 1950s and 1960s. More than 30 years ago, most of the homeless were old men, only a **handful** were women, and **virtually** no families were homeless. Today the homeless are younger, and include more women and families with young children. Today's homeless also are more **visible** to the general public because they are much more likely to sleep on the streets or in other public places in great numbers. They also suffer greater **deprivation.** Although in the past homeless men on Skid Row were **undoubtedly** poor, their average income from casual and **intermittent** work was three to four times more than what the current homeless receive. In addition, many of the older homeless had small but **stable** pensions, which today's homeless do not have.

—Thio, *Sociology*, p. 235

large group	dependable	almost	those who are similar
noticeable	blind	houses	given up completely
few	hardship	never	
definitely	integrated	not continuous	

1. dwellings _____   6. visible _____

2. abandoned _____   7. deprivation _____

3. counterparts _____   8. undoubtedly _____

4. handful _____   9. intermittent _____

5. virtually _____   10. stable _____

NAME _____ SECTION _____

DATE _____ SCORE _____

ONLINE DATING SITES AREN'T HOLDING PEOPLE'S HEARTS
Randy Dotinga

The multi-million dollar business of online dating is described in this article, which first appeared in the *Christian Science Monitor* in January 2005. Read it to find out what new options are being offered by sites trying to gain and keep customers.

Vocabulary Preview

These are some of the difficult words in this essay. The definitions here will help you if you can't figure out the meanings from the sentence context or word parts.

bane (para. 1) source of annoyance

cutthroat (para. 2) ruthless; without mercy

stagnation (para. 2) lack of activity or growth

compatibility (para. 3) ability to get along with another person or to form a harmonious relationship

profiling (para. 5) analyzing a person's characteristics in order to make predictions about the person

zaftig (para. 10) having a full, shapely figure

felon (para. 10) a person who has committed a serious crime

As their growth slows, dating Web sites offer plenty of new options—from background checks to more detailed questionnaires.

1   Kristin, a 20-something property manager from Tempe, Ariz., isn't sold on online dating just yet. Recently, she posted an ad on Match.com, a leading personal-ad website. "I was just looking for an alternative to the regular singles scene," Kristin says. "In my first 24 hours, I received 150 e-mails and 'winks.' That's a little intimidating." She's annoyed that some of the responders live outside the US, and worried about encountering the bane of online daters—the "weirdo." But her ad is still up, boasting in the headline that she's "exceptional—looking for same."

2   As they face cutthroat competition and the threat of stagnation, online dating sites are working furiously to convince millions of singles such as Kristin to stick around despite their misgivings. Within the past few months, several top sites have overhauled the online dating experience, and up-and-coming companies are wooing people like the marriage-minded, the security-conscious, and the religious.

3   All in all, the changes may be turning online dating into a more friendly world. Video and audio links, which have yet to become wildly popular, offer singles the opportunity to see and hear one another before the traditional coffee date. It's easier to reject someone who contacts you through an e-mail or the quick hello known as a wink—sites now helpfully provide canned responses for unimpressed members to send. And complex compatibility surveys aim to match people who have similar outlooks on life and love, not just a shared fascination with Woody Allen or "Desperate Housewives."

4   At stake is a share of the huge online dating business, whose growth is leveling out. From the beginning of 2001 to the end of 2003, customer spending on the sites rocketed from $8 million to $117 million, according to the Online Publishers Association and comScore Networks. But in the second quarter of 2004, the spending was stagnant at $114 million.

5   The sites were less complicated back in the go-go days of online dating. The process of matching on dating sites—alerting a customer to other users who might be right for him or her—used to be based simply on factors like who has blue eyes and blond hair, says Rochelle Adams, spokeswoman for Yahoo Personals. "Now, you're talking about temperament and personality through deep relationship 'profiling.' These are all things working to help people get matches that are really going to work for them."

6   One dating site, eHarmony.com, is pushing the compatibility testing idea to its limit. Users answer a whopping 463 questions about everything from energy level and ambition to sense of humor and spirituality.

For Relationships That Last

7   "Our whole focus is on putting people together, making compatible matches that have the possibility of the long term," says senior vice presi-

dent Marylyn Warren. "If you want a date for Saturday night, we probably are just not the place to come." Perhaps following eHarmony's lead, Yahoo Personals has developed a premium service—it will cost an extra $15 a month beyond the usual $19.95 fee—for people interested in more than casual dating. Ms. Warren is impressed to hear that companies such as Yahoo are following eHarmony's approach. "We've gotta go deeper," she says.

8   The most difficult challenge, however, is the same as always: Just as a man in a singles bar might tell a woman he's an astronaut when he's really an accountant, online daters often fudge the truth. "Both sexes complain that the other side is lying," says Michael Kantor, owner of eDateReview.com, which offers advice about online dating.

Is He Already Married?

9   Enter True.com, a new site that runs background checks on customers. About 5 percent of potential users are banished because they may have criminal records, and about 4 percent get the boot because public records suggest they're married, says spokeswoman Taylor Cole. If they're actually single, they can try again to join the service. "We're very gratified that we've saved a lot of people from potential physical and emotional hazards," says founder and CEO Herb Vest. The checking "doesn't totally eliminate that hazard, but it does lower the incidence of it."

Little White Lies

10   True.com doesn't launch other kinds of investigations, however. Does "Fun-Loving Romeo" really like long walks on the beach, or does he spend weekends in front of the television? And what about the claim by "Ready for Adventure" that she's a petite athlete? Maybe she's zaftig and hasn't put on a pair of sneakers since high school. "Most lying isn't about whether someone is a felon, but exaggeration lying, which I don't think [sites] will be able to spot," says Mr. Kantor of eDateReview.com. "When someone lists their weight, unless someone actually comes to their apartment and weighs them, that's going to slip by."

11   Other problems may be unsolvable, too. "Men mostly complain about having to send out too many e-mails, and nobody responds," Kantor says.

"Women complain they get too many e-mails, and they're all from losers."
Perhaps the course of online dating—like true love—will never run smooth.

━ ▪ ━

Directions: In the space provided, write the letter of the choice that best completes each of the following statements.

CHECKING YOUR COMPREHENSION

_____ 1. The main point of the reading is that

   a. most singles today rely on online dating sites to find a compatible match.

   b. customer spending on online dating sites has leveled out.

   c. online dating sites are offering a variety of new options to attract customers.

   d. most people are dishonest about themselves on online dating sites.

_____ 2. According to the article, a "wink" refers to a

   a. traditional coffee date.

   b. quick hello online.

   c. perfect match.

   d. little white lie.

_____ 3. Paragraph 3 is primarily about

   a. changes in online dating.

   b. video and audio links.

   c. profiling.

   d. compatibility surveys.

_____ 4. The Web site that offers advice about online dating is called

   a. True.com.   c. Match.com.

   b. eHarmony.com.   d. eDateReview.com.

_____ 5. "Exaggeration lying" on a dating Web site can be defined as

   a. presenting irrelevant information.

   b. withholding essential information.

   c. misrepresenting one's self in order to present a more positive image.

   d. bragging about one's accomplishments.

USING YOUR CONTEXT CLUES

_____ 6. In paragraph 1, the word **encountering** means

    a. fighting.   c. meeting.

    b. becoming.   d. liking.

_____ 7. In paragraph 2, the word **misgivings** means

    a. goals.   c. disagreements.

    b. lies.   d. doubts.

_____ 8. In paragraph 2, the word **overhauled** means

    a. made changes and improvements.

    b. brought to an end.

    c. settled legal problems.

    d. took control

_____ 9. In paragraph 3, the meaning of the word **wink** is suggested by which type of context clue?

    a. synonym   c. example

    b. contrast   d. inference

_____ 10. In paragraph 3, the word **canned** means

    a. fired.

    b. expanded.

    c. prepared in a standard format.

    d. preserved or sealed.

_____ 11. In paragraph 3, the word **complex** means

    a. grouped together.

    b. complicated.

    c. uncertain.

    d. confused.

_____ 12. In paragraph 6, the word **ambition** means

    a. sense of humor.

    b. desire for success or power.

    c. job or career.

    d. education.

_____ 13. In paragraph 9, the word **banished** means
      a. thrown out.   c. allowed.
      b. scolded.   d. tested.

_____ 14. In paragraph 9, the word **gratified** means
      a. paid back.   c. pleased.
      b. criticized.   d. sorry.

_____ 15. In paragraph 9, the word **incidence** means
      a. the number of times something occurs.
      b. accidents or mistakes.
      c. hazards.
      d. investigation.

REVIEWING DIFFICULT VOCABULARY

Directions: Complete each of the following sentences by inserting a word from the Vocabulary Preview on page 93 in the space provided. A word should be used only once.

16. The company's new advertising campaign featured ____ women instead of the usual ultra-thin models.

17. Although the bike route was generally flat, there was one steep hill that was the ____ of every rider.

18. Most dating services rely on some form of _____ to help them find a good match for their customers.

19. In order to prevent _____, key employees and managers were invited on several company retreats each year.

20. _____ is the key to the success of most relationships.

STUDYING WORDS

Directions: Use a dictionary to answer the following questions.

_____ 21. Which one of the following correctly indicates how **intimidating** (para. 1) is pronounced?

     a. in time eh DAY ting

     b. in TIM eh day ting

     c. IN tim eh day ting

     d. in tim eh day TING

_____ 22. As a part of speech, the word **furiously** (para. 2) is

     a. a noun.

     b. a verb.

     c. an adjective.

     d. an adverb.

_____ 23. The etymology of the word **petite** (para. 10) is

     a. German.

     b. English.

     c. French.

     d. Latin.

_____ 24. The correct meaning of the word **premium** (para. 7) as it is used in this reading is

     a. of superior quality or value.

     b. a prize or an award.

     c. the amount paid for an insurance policy.

     d. payment for professional training.

_____ 25. The etymology of the word **zaftig** (para. 10) is

     a. French.

     b. English.

     c. Yiddish.

     d. Latin.

QUESTIONS FOR DISCUSSION

1. Discuss whether you would want to use an online dating site. Which of the options described in the article are appealing to you, if any? If you have used a dating site, describe your experience and compare it with the information in the article.

2. Discuss compatibility surveys. Are they useful? Explain why or why not.

3. Why do you think people are dishonest about themselves online? What would be your reaction to the kind of "exaggeration lying" described in the article?

4. According to the article, customer spending on online dating sites has leveled out after dramatic growth. Discuss possible reasons for the current status of the online dating business after the initial burst of customer spending from 2001 to 2003.

WRITING ACTIVITIES

1. Matchmaking has been around in various forms for centuries. Write a paragraph comparing modern matchmaking methods such as those offered by dating Web sites to more old-fashioned methods (for example, blind dates). Which do you prefer?

2. In the past few years, online dating has become a multi-million dollar industry. What do you think this says about human nature and modern life? Write an essay explaining your answer.

3. Create your own compatibility survey. Write at least ten questions (or list at least ten qualities) that would help you determine whether a person would be a good match for you.

Chapter 3: Building Vocabulary: Using Context Clues

RECORDING YOUR PROGRESS

Test	Number Right		Score
Practice Test 3-1	_____ × 10	=	_____ %
Practice Test 3-2	_____ × 10	=	_____ %
Practice Test 3-3	_____ × 10	=	_____ %
Mastery Test 3-1	_____ × 10	=	_____ %
Mastery Test 3-2	_____ × 10	=	_____ %
Mastery Test 3-3	_____ × 4	=	_____ %

EVALUATING YOUR PROGRESS

Based on your test performance, rate how well you have mastered the skills taught in this chapter by checking one of the boxes below or by writing your own evaluation.

☐ **Need More Improvement**
Tip: Try using the "Vocabulary" Module on the Reading Road Trip Web site at **http://www .ablongman.com/readingroadtrip** to fine-tune the skills that you have learned in this chapter.

☐ **Need More Practice**
Tip: Try using the "Vocabulary" Module on the Reading Road Trip Web site at **http://www .ablongman.com/readingroadtrip** to brush up on the skills you have learned in this chapter, or visit this textbook's companion Web site at **http://www.ablongman.com/mcwhorter** for extra practice.

☐ **Good**
Tip: To maintain your skills, quickly review this chapter by using the companion Web site that accompanies this textbook by logging on to **http://www.ablongman.com/mcwhorter**.

☐ **Excellent**

YOUR EVALUATION: _____

_____

_____

_____

_____

READ ME FIRST!

Look at the photograph showing Maria baking delicious chocolate chip cookies. Even though she hasn't made this dessert before, she can figure out how to do it. She reads the recipe, gathers all the ingredients together, and combines everything in the correct sequence.

When you see a word you don't know, you may also be able to figure out its meaning by looking at its "ingredients" or parts.

CHAPTER 4

Building Vocabulary: Using Word Parts

What Are Word Parts?

Just as Maria baked the cookies she hadn't made before by working with the ingredients presented in a recipe, you can learn many new words by studying their "ingredients" or parts.

Although many people build their vocabulary word by word, studying word parts is a better and faster way to do it. For example, if you learn that *pre-* means *before,* then you can begin to figure out hundreds of words that begin with *pre* (premarital, premix, prepay).

Suppose you came across the following sentence in a child psychology text:

The parents thought their child was **unteachable.**

If you did not know the meaning of *unteachable,* how could you figure it out? Since there are no clues in the sentence context, you might decide to look up the word in a dictionary. An easier way, though, is to break the word into parts. Many words in the English language are made up of word parts called *prefixes*, *roots*, and *suffixes*. A **prefix** comes at the beginning of a word, and a **suffix** comes at the end of a word. The **root**, which contains a word's basic meaning, forms the middle.

Let's look at the word *unteachable* again and divide it into three parts: its prefix, root, and suffix.

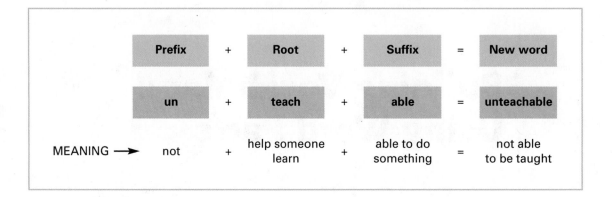

By using word parts, you can see that *unteachable* means "not able to be taught."

My friend Josh is **nonconformist.**

non- = not
conform = go along with others
-ist = one who does something
nonconformist = someone who does not go along with others

To use word parts effectively, you should learn some of the most common ones. The prefixes and roots listed in Tables 4-1 and 4-2 on pages 105 and 108 are a good place to start. By knowing just *some* of these prefixes and roots, you can figure out the meanings of thousands of words without looking them up in the dictionary. For instance, more than 10,000 words can begin with the prefix *non-*. Another common prefix, *pseudo-* (which means "false") is used in more than 400 words. As you can see, by learning only a few word parts, you can add many new words to your vocabulary.

Prefixes

Though some English words do not have a prefix, many of them do. Prefixes appear at the *beginnings* of words and change the meaning of the root to which they are connected. For example, if you add the prefix *re-* to

TABLE 4-1 Common Prefixes

Prefix	Meaning	Sample Word
Prefixes Referring to Amount or Number		
mono/uni	one	monocle/unicycle
bi/di/du	two	bimonthly/divorce/duet
tri	three	triangle
quad	four	quadrant
quint/pent	five	quintet/pentagon
deci	ten	decimal
centi	hundred	centigrade
milli	thousand	milligram
micro	small	microscope
multi/poly	many	multipurpose/polygon
semi	half	semicircle
equi	equal	equidistant
Prefixes Meaning "Not" (Negative)		
a	not	asymmetrical
anti	against	antiwar
contra	against, opposite	contradict
dis	apart, away, not	disagree
in/il/ir/im	not	incorrect/illogical/irreversible/impossible
mis	wrongly	misunderstand
non	not	nonfiction
un	not	unpopular
pseudo	false	pseudoscientific
Prefixes Giving Direction, Location, or Placement		
ab	away	absent
ad	toward	adhesive
ante/pre	before	antecedent/premarital
circum/peri	around	circumference/perimeter
com/col/con	with, together	compile/collide/convene
de	away, from	depart
dia	through	diameter
en/em	into, within	encase/embargo
ex/extra	from, out of, former	ex-wife/extramarital
hyper	over, excessive	hyperactive
inter	between	interpersonal
intro/intra	within, into, in	introduction
post	after	posttest
re	back, again	review
retro	backward	retrospect
sub	under, below	submarine
super	above, extra	supercharge
tele	far	telescope
thermo	heat	thermometer
trans	across, over	transcontinental

the word *read,* the word *reread* is formed, meaning "to read again." If *dis-* is added to the word *respect,* the word *disrespect* is formed, meaning "lack of respect."

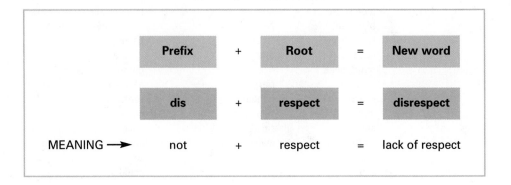

Prefix	+	Root	=	New word
dis	+	respect	=	disrespect

MEANING ⟶   not   +   respect   =   lack of respect

**Exercise
4–1**

Directions: Using the list of common prefixes in Table 4-1, match each word in column A with its meaning in column B. Write the letter of your choice in the space provided.

	Column A		Column B
_____	1. misplaced	a.	half a circle
_____	2. interoffice	b.	build again
_____	3. exhale	c.	unusual
_____	4. semicircle	d.	between offices
_____	5. nonprofit	e.	not fully developed
_____	6. reconstruct	f.	put in the wrong position
_____	7. triathlete	g.	build up electrical power again
_____	8. atypical	h.	not for making money
_____	9. recharge	i.	breathe out
_____	10. immature	j.	one who participates in three-part sporting events

Exercise 4–2

Directions: *Select a prefix from the box below that will complete the word indicated in each of the following sentences. One of the prefixes is used more than once.*

bi	inter	re
dis	ir	retro
im	mis	sub

1. A person who speaks two languages is _____ lingual.

2. My new sweater had a snag; I returned it to the store because it was _____ perfect.

3. The flood damage in Carl's hometown was permanent and _____ reversible.

4. Sheila was not given the correct date and time; she was _____ informed.

5. The magazine didn't interest me, so I _____ continued my subscription.

6. Clothing that does not pass factory inspection is considered _____ standard and is often sold at a discount.

7. The raise I got on April 1 will apply to last month's salary as well; it will be _____ active to March 1.

8. The attorneys acted as _____ mediaries between the angry, divorcing couple.

9. Because the results of the research study were unexpected, the research team decided to _____ plicate the experiment.

10. The draperies in Juan's apartment are _____ colored because they were exposed to the sun for too long.

Roots

Think of roots as being at the core of a word's meaning. You already know many roots—like *bio* in *biology* and *sen* in *insensitive*—because they are used in everyday speech. Thirty-one of the most common and useful roots are listed in Table 4-2. Learning the meanings of these roots will help

TABLE 4-2   Common Roots

Root	Meaning	Sample Word
aud/audit	hear	audible/auditory
aster/astro	star	asteroid/astronaut
bene	good, well	benefit
bio	life	biology
cap	take, seize	captive
chron(o)	time	chronology
corp	body	corpse
cred	believe	incredible
dict/dic	tell, say	dictate/predict
duc/duct	lead	introduce/conduct
fact/fac	make, do	factory/factor
graph	write	telegraph
geo	earth	geophysics
log/logo/logy	study, thought	logic/psychology
mit/miss	send	permit/dismiss
mort/mor	die, death	immortal/mortician
path	feeling	sympathy
phono	sound, voice	telephone
photo	light	photosensitive
port	carry	transport
scop	seeing	microscope
scrib/script	write	scribe/inscription
sen/sent	feel	sensitive/sentiment
spec/spic/spect	look, see	retrospect/spectacle
tend/tent/tens	stretch or strain	tendon/tension
terr/terre	land, earth	terrain/territory
theo	god	theology
ven/vent	come	convention/venture
vert/vers	turn	invert/inverse
vis/vid	see	invisible/video
voc	call	vocation

you unlock the meanings of many words. For example, if you knew that the root *dic/dict* means "tell or say," then you would have a clue to the meanings of such words as *dictate* (to speak for someone to write down) or *dictionary* (a book that "tells" what words "say," or mean).

When you see a word you don't know, and you can't figure it out from the sentence context, follow these tips:

1. **Look for the root first.**
2. **Keep in mind that the spelling of a root may change a bit if it is combined with a suffix.**

(Table 4-2 has some examples of spelling changes.)

Exercise 4–3

Directions: Using the list of common roots in Table 4-2, match each word in column A with its meaning in column B. Write the letter of your choice in the space provided. To help you, the roots in each word in column A are in italics.

Column A	Column B
_____ 1. *aud*ible	a. undertaker
_____ 2. *miss*ive	b. went back
_____ 3. *sent*iment	c. able to respond to light
_____ 4. *mort*ician	d. come between two things
_____ 5. inter*vene*	e. channel or pipe that brings water from a distance
_____ 6. re*vert*ed	f. use the voice
_____ 7. aque*duct*	g. blessing; expression of good wishes
_____ 8. *photo*active	h. letter or message
_____ 9. *voc*alize	i. able to be heard
_____ 10. *bene*diction	j. expression of a feeling

Exercise 4–4

Directions: *Select the word from the box below that best completes each of the following sentences. Refer to the list of roots in Table 4-2 if you need help.*

apathetic	extraterrestrial	prescribed	spectators	verdict
deduce	graphic	scriptures	synchronized	visualize

1. After hearing the testimony, the jury brought in its _____ quickly.

2. Religious or holy writings are called _____.

3. Tina closed her eyes and tried to _____ the license plate number.

4. As they watched the football game, the _____ became tense.

5. Henry's doctor _____ two types of medication for his rash.

6. The murderer seemed _____ when the judge pronounced her sentence.

7. Just before the race, the runners _____ their watches.

8. My history text contains many _____ aids, including maps, charts, and diagrams.

9. Emily's favorite movie is about a(n) _____, a creature not from earth.

10. By putting together many clues, the detective was finally able to _____ who committed the crime.

Suffixes

Suffixes are word *endings*. Think of them as add-ons that make a word fit grammatically into a sentence. For example, adding the suffix *y* to the noun *cloud* forms the adjective *cloudy*. The words *cloud* and *cloudy* are used in different ways:

EXAMPLE

The rain **cloud** above me looked threatening.

It was a **cloudy**, rainy weekend.

You can often form several different words from a single root by adding different suffixes.

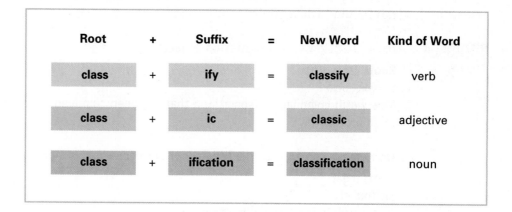

Root	+	Suffix	=	New Word	Kind of Word
class	+	ify	=	classify	verb
class	+	ic	=	classic	adjective
class	+	ification	=	classification	noun

As you know, when you find a word that you do not recognize, you should look for the root first. Then try to figure out what the word means with the suffix added. A list of common suffixes and their meanings appears in Table 4-3.

TABLE 4-3   Common Suffixes

Suffix	Sample Word	Suffix	Sample Word
Suffixes Referring to a State, Condition, or Quality			
able	touchable	ive	permissive
ance	assistance	like	childlike
ation	confrontation	ment	amazement
ence	reference	ness	kindness
ful	playful	ous	jealous
ible	tangible	ty	loyalty
ion	discussion	y	creamy
ity	superiority		
Suffixes Meaning "One Who"			
an	Italian	ent	resident
ant	participant	er	teacher
ee	referee	ist	activist
eer	engineer	or	advisor
Suffixes Meaning "Pertaining to or Referring to"			
al	autumnal	hood	brotherhood
ship	friendship	ward	homeward

Sometimes you may find that the spelling of the root word changes because of the suffix. For instance, a final *e* may be dropped, a final consonant may be doubled, or a final *y* may be changed to *i*. Keep these possibilities in mind when you're trying to identify a root word.

EXAMPLES

David's article was a **compilation** of facts.

Root: compil(e)
Suffix: -ation
New word: compilation (something that has been compiled, or put together, in an orderly way)

We were concerned with the **legality** of our decision about our taxes.

Root: legal
Suffix: -ity
New word: legality (legal matters)

Our college is one of the most **prestigious** in the state.

Root: prestig(e)
Suffix: -ious
New word: prestigious (having prestige or distinction)

In the examples above, which root word did not have a spelling change when the suffix was added? Did you notice that *compile* and *prestige* both lost an *e?*

Exercise 4–5

Directions: For each list of four words, select the choice that best completes the following sentence. Write your answer in the space provided.

1. *conversely, converse, conversation, conversing*

   Our phone _____ lasted ten minutes.

2. *assist, assistant, assisted, assists*

   My doctor's _____ labels each patient's blood samples.

3. *qualifications, qualify, qualifies, qualifying*

   As Bill spoke to the interviewer, he outlined his

   _____ for the job.

4. *intern, interned, internship, interning*

   Dr. Bernard completed her _____ at Memorial Medical Center.

5. *eating, eat, eater, eaten*

   We did not realize that the blossoms of the plant could be

   _____.

6. *audition, audio, audible, audioed*

   Theresa spoke so softly that her voice was not

   _____.

7. *sincerer, sincere, sincerity, sincerest*

   When my best friend lied to me, I began to question her

   _____.

8. *permitted, permit, permissive, permission*

   Beverly's professor granted her _____ to miss class.

9. *instructor, instructive, instructs, instructed*

   The lecture on Freud was very _____.

10. *remembrance, remember, remembering, remembered*

    A wealthy businessman donated the building in

    _____ of his deceased father.

11. *mortal, mortally, mortals, mortality*

    The _____ rate in Ethiopia is very high.

12. *presidency, president, presidential, presidentship*

    The _____ race was full of surprises.

13. *femininely, feminine, feminism, feminist*

    She called herself a _____ , but she never actively supported equal rights for women.

14. *hazarding, hazardous, hazard, hazardousness*

    When there is toxic waste in a lake, it is _____
    to health.

15. *destiny, destined, destinies, destine*

    Robert felt it was his _____ to become a priest.

16. *different, differences, differ, differing*

    The physical _____ among the three brothers
    were striking.

17. *friend, friendly, friendlier, friendship*

    A true _____ with another person sometimes
    lasts a lifetime.

18. *comforted, comfortable, comforting, comfort*

    I felt _____ in my role as counselor.

19. *popularize, popular, popularity, popularly*

    The rock group's _____ rose after their first
    hit song.

20. *apologetic, apology, apologizing, apologize*

    Kelly seemed _____ about the temper tantrum
    she had last night.

Using Word Parts

When you're reading your favorite magazine or one of your textbooks,
you'll often be able to figure out new words from context, as you did in
Chapter 3. Now, though, you have even stronger vocabulary skills because
you know how to work with word parts. As you work with prefixes, roots,
and suffixes, remember these tips:

1. **Look for the *root* first and try to figure out its meaning, even if a few of
   its letters are missing.**

2. **Look for a *prefix* and see how it changes the meaning of the root word.**

3. **Find a *suffix* and see how it further changes or adds to the meaning.**

When you use word parts every day, you will find that your vocabulary grows by leaps and bounds.

The Textbook Challenge

Part A: Student Resource Guide A

The following words appear in Textbook Excerpt 2, "Food Safety: A Growing Concern" (p. 403). For each word, use word parts and a dictionary, if necessary, to write a definition of the word as it is used in the excerpt.

1. perishables (para. 4) _____

2. radioactive (para. 5) _____

3. replicating (para 5) _____

4. microorganisms (para. 6) _____

5. environmentalists (para. 7) _____

6. inadvertently (para. 11) _____

7. interactions (para. 12) _____

Part B: A College Textbook

Choose a chapter from one of your textbooks for another course. Identify ten words that you are able to determine the meaning of from word parts. Write the words and their meanings.

What Have You Learned?

Directions: Mark each of the following statements true (T) or false (F).

_____ 1. A word part that comes at the beginning of a word is known as a suffix.

_____ 2. Prefixes change the meaning of a word.

_____ 3. All English words have prefixes.

_____ 4. A suffix helps a word fit grammatically into a sentence.

_____ 5. The part of a word that carries its core meaning is known as a root.

_____ 6. When a suffix is added to a root, the spelling of the root always changes.

Test-Taking Tip #4: Using Word Parts

Use your knowledge of word parts to help you figure out the meaning of vocabulary test items. Here are some specific suggestions:

▪ Pronounce the word in question to yourself. By saying the word, you may hear a part (prefix, root, or suffix) that is familiar.

Example: *Configuration* means

a. detail.

b. distance.

c. shape.

d. reason.

If you hear the word *figure* in the word *configuration,* then you may be able to reason that *configuration* means shape (choice c) or form.

▪ If you do not recognize the root of a word, concentrate on the prefix, if there is one. Often, knowing the meaning of the prefix can help you figure out the right answer, or at least help you identify one or more choices as wrong.

Example: A *monologue* is

a. a debate among politicians.

b. secrets shared by friends.

c. an intimate conversation.

d. a long, uninterrupted speech.

If you know that *mono-* means "one," then you can figure out that the right answer is choice d, because choices a, b, and c each involve two or more people.

▪ Pay attention to suffixes. Like prefixes, they can help you figure out a word, even if you do not know the root.

Example: Someone who believes in positive outcomes is a(an)

a. isogonic.

b. micelle.

c. feticide.

d. optimist.

If you know that the suffix *-ist* means "someone who," then choice d is a reasonable choice.

NAME _____ SECTION _____

DATE _____ SCORE _____

USING WORD PARTS

Directions: In each of the following sentences, the boldfaced word contains a root and a prefix and/or suffix. Using your knowledge of word parts, in the space provided write the letter of the choice that best defines each word.

_____ 1. Enoch was a lawyer before he turned to **theology.**

    a. writing   c. study of religion

    b. teaching   d. study of life

_____ 2. The **antiwar** movement of the 1960s helped bring about U.S. withdrawal from Vietnam.

    a. before war   c. in favor of war

    b. against war   d. during war

_____ 3. If you use spaces instead of tabs in your computer document, your columns will **misalign.**

    a. be against one line   c. form a small line

    b. skip a line   d. line up wrong

_____ 4. The juggler's performance **captivated** the audience.

    a. bored   c. misjudged

    b. seized the attention of   d. quieted

_____ 5. Peter's English instructor told him he had written a **creditable** paper.

    a. very poor   c. deserving credit

    b. detailed   d. lacking credit

_____ 6. The coroner prepared a **postmortem** report on the drowning victim.

    a. before life   c. written again

    b. after death   d. confused

_____ 7. The Supreme Court's decisions are **irreversible.**

    a. capable of great injury

    b. not able to be turned around

    c. unacceptable

    d. flawless

_____ 8. As we watched the movie, the music seemed to **foretell** the murder of the heroine.

a. predict   c. delay

b. repeat   d. cover up

_____ 9. My congressman pledged to put an end to **substandard** wages in our district.

a. illegal   c. below normal

b. under investigation   d. dishonest

_____ 10. A famous **economist** predicted that unemployment would increase.

a. person who studies economics

b. theories of economics

c. former studies of the economy

d. the quality of the economy

NAME _____ SECTION _____

DATE _____ SCORE _____

USING WORD PARTS

Directions: Using your knowledge of word parts, in the space provided write the letter of the choice that best defines each word.

_____ 1. multistage rocket
   a. rocket with two stages   c. rocket with several stages
   b. rocket with three stages   d. multipurpose rocket

_____ 2. noncommittal
   a. unwilling to reveal attitude or feeling
   b. unable to perform a task
   c. unwilling to make an effort
   d. unwilling to change

_____ 3. equidistant
   a. of specific distances   c. of unlike distances
   b. of uneven distances   d. of equal distances

_____ 4. triennial
   a. occurring once a year
   b. occurring every two years
   c. occurring every three years
   d. occurring every four years

_____ 5. transcultural
   a. differences in cultures   c. among cultures
   b. within cultures   d. extending across cultures

_____ 6. chronometer
   a. machine to control velocity
   b. device to control friction
   c. instrument for measuring time
   d. instrument for measuring speed

_____ 7. disaffiliated
   a. not associated   c. weakly associated
   b. partially associated   d. strongly associated

_____ 8. territory
   a. area of land   c. upper surface area
   b. related to fear   d. resulting from terror

_____ 9. astrology
   a. study of positions of stars   c. form of heat
   b. study of types of sound   d. type of lens

_____ 10. photosensitive cell
   a. cell sensitive to heat   c. cell sensitive to color
   b. cell sensitive to light   d. cell sensitive to friction

NAME _____ SECTION _____
DATE _____ SCORE _____

USING WORD PARTS

Directions: Select a word part from the box below that will complete the word indicated in each of the following sentences. Each word part should be used only once.

dict	thermo	un	ver	vis
terr	trans	uni	vert	voc

1. The instant replay provided _____ ification that our team had won the football game.

2. The _____ ain was too rocky for planting vegetables.

3. Even though Karen dropped her expensive vase, it remained _____ broken.

4. During the job interview, Joe was asked what he en _____ ioned doing in five years.

5. My cousin con _____ ed his Canadian currency to American dollars.

6. The minister's in _____ ation began the morning services.

7. All of the children in the marching band were required to wear _____ forms.

8. Many students were able to pre _____ their exam grades.

9. When I _____ planted the tree to a different location, it grew much bigger.

10. _____ dynamics deals with the connection between heat and mechanical energy.

USING WORD PARTS

Directions: Read the paragraph below. Using your knowledge of word parts, write the correct meaning for each word listed.

When Dimitri and his wife Carol began to renovate their old house, they underestimated the amount of time and effort it would take. They were careless in their planning, and they miscalculated the amount of money they would need. Since the bank was hesitant to provide more money for their project, the young couple was fearful that they would have to forgo the house of their dreams. Eventually, though, Dimitri and Carol overcame their financial problems, and their friends and families pitched in on a multitude of tasks—rewiring, painting, and even putting on a new roof. In less than a year, their old rundown house was transformed into a lovely Victorian.

1. renovate _____

2. underestimated _____

3. careless _____

4. miscalculated _____

5. hesitant _____

6. fearful _____

7. forgo _____

8. overcame _____

9. multitude _____

10. transformed _____

NAME _____ SECTION _____
DATE _____ SCORE _____

USING WORD PARTS

Directions: Using your knowledge of word parts, select the word from the box below that best completes each of the following sentences. Each word should be used only once.

flexible	benefits	endanger	snakelike	location
dramatic	tension	erroneously	strenuous	peaceful

Lu-chin loves to exercise. She knows, though, that too much exercise or exercise done _____ could _____ her health. To get ready for a _____ workout, she stretches and bends to make her body _____.

Once Lu-chin is warmed up, she likes to jog around the quiet, _____ park near her home. Its winding, _____ trails and _____ views make it a perfect _____ for her early morning run. When she has finished, she walks and stretches again to relieve the _____ in her body. Because Lu-chin knows how to exercise correctly, her running truly _____ her health.

NAME _____ SECTION _____
DATE _____ SCORE _____

MASTERY TEST 4-3

SAVED BY THE KINDNESS OF A VIRTUAL STRANGER
Mark Zelermyer

This essay first appeared in *Newsweek* magazine in August 2004. Read it to find out how the author and his wife benefited from an entirely generous and unexpected gift.

Vocabulary Preview

These are some of the difficult words in this essay. The definitions here will help you if you can't figure out the meanings from the sentence context or word parts.

phenomenon (para. 1) a remarkable or unusual development

macrobiotic (para. 1) the practice of promoting health, primarily through a diet of whole beans and grains

cadaveric (para. 2) from a dead body

regimen (para. 2) a systematic course of treatment

dialysis (para. 2) a medical procedure which treats kidney failure by cleaning the blood

---

My wife needed a kidney, but we didn't know how to ask friends for help. Turns out we didn't have to.

1   I grew up thinking that if miracles existed at all, they were larger than life, spectacular acts that suspended the laws of nature (think Cecil B. DeMille's "The Ten Commandments"). Even as an adult, whenever I read about some medical phenomenon that doctors were hard pressed to explain, like a late-stage tumor that disappeared long after a patient's treatment was discontinued, I chalked it up to the sort of inexplicable divine intervention that trumps macrobiotic diets and crystals. It was something to hope for in your darkest hour, perhaps, but not to expect. So when I learned that my wife would need a kidney transplant within two years, I focused on what modern medicine had to offer.

2   Her polycystic kidney disease had been controlled with medication for some 20 years, but in the spring of 2001 it began to worsen. The nephrologist explained that her best shot at regaining her health was to receive a living kidney, which would function better and longer than a cadaveric kidney. The challenge was to find a healthy person with the same type O blood who was

willing to undergo a regimen of tests and ultimately donate a kidney. Otherwise, she would have to start the time-consuming, punishing process of dialysis in order to get on the five-year waiting list for a cadaveric transplant.

3   I was quickly ruled out as a donor because my blood type didn't match my wife's. Her family produced no candidates either. In fact, her mother had died from complications of the same genetic disease, and her brother had received a cadaveric transplant the year before.

4   We desperately needed help, and yet we felt uncomfortable asking for it. After all, how do you ask another person to give up a kidney? We finally turned to our friends, and one of them, our rabbi, gave an impassioned appeal during Yom Kippur services. A number of congregants agreed to be tested, but all of them were eliminated after the first stage of screening. It looked as if we had hit a wall.

5   Then one evening I rode home on the train with Carolyn Hodges, a friend of mine from work. I was feeling particularly low that day, and I told her about our situation. The next day she stopped by my office and told me that she and her husband were type O's and longtime blood and platelet donors who were listed with the bone-marrow registry. They had talked it over and decided they were willing to be tested as potential matches. Carolyn was eliminated shortly thereafter, but John, whom we barely knew, emerged as the surgeon's donor of choice.

6   John is a scientist by training, and once he got the news he began diligently researching kidney disease and transplant surgery. By the time he met with the surgeon, he had compiled a list of incredibly detailed questions, the likes of which the doctor had never seen before. Most donors are blood relations who are more likely to beg the surgeon to take their kidney than grill him on the latest studies.

7   Despite his thorough research, John encountered a fair amount of resistance from his family members and close friends. They'd ask, "Why should someone in good health put himself on the line for a person he hardly knows?" But John strongly believed that this was a way for him to actively make the world a better place. He would simply tell them he had considered every potential danger and determined that the rewards—for my wife, her family and himself—outweighed the risks. He was even more reassured after talking with his daughter's teacher, who had donated a kidney to her brother years before, and his good friend who was a transplant counselor.

8   By the beginning of this past May, my wife's condition had deteriorated to the point that she was in danger of being too sick for the transplant operation. To make matters worse, the procedure required two operating rooms and a 20-person surgical team—and both were booked solid for nearly two months. We were scared.

9   Thankfully, one week later there was a last-minute cancellation, and we received word one afternoon to go to the hospital at once for pre-op work—the surgery would begin the following morning at 6:30. Without hesitation, John dropped everything and drove over.

10   I am happy to report that the operation was a success. "Little Johnny," as my wife calls her new kidney, is working exceptionally well. After John spent a few weeks recovering at home, he was able to ease back to work and resume his normal routine.

11   Except that life will never really be the way it was before the surgery for either of our families. A tremendous bond now joins us. We will forever be connected by John's generous, selfless gift of life.

12   I've learned that miracles come in myriad forms, including human. John and Carolyn Hodges are living proof.

■ ▪ ■

Directions: In the space provided, write the letter of the choice that best completes each of the following statements.

CHECKING YOUR COMPREHENSION

_____   1. The author's main purpose in this selection is to
   a. explain the various aspects of kidney disease.
   b. describe the events surrounding his wife's kidney transplant.
   c. convince readers to register as organ donors.
   d. describe medical miracles and unexplained cures.

_____   2. The phrase that best describes the author's belief about his wife's successful transplant is
   a. "divine intervention."
   b. "medical phenomenon."
   c. "a generous, selfless gift of life."
   d. "macrobiotic diets and crystals."

_____ 3. John Hodges, the kidney donor, was
    a. a lifelong friend of the Zelermyers.
    b. a distant relative of the Zelermyers.
    c. a member of the Zelermyers' congregation.
    d. married to a work friend of Mr. Zelermyer.

_____ 4. Mr. Zelermyer was ruled out as a donor because
    a. he was not healthy enough.
    b. he had already donated a kidney to his brother-in-law.
    c. his blood type did not match his wife's.
    d. spouses are not allowed to donate organs.

_____ 5. When the author says in paragraph 4 that "It looked as if we had hit a wall," the phrase **hit a wall** means that they
    a. got very angry.
    b. were unable to make progress.
    c. asked someone for a favor.
    d. succeeded at something difficult.

_____ 6. The main point of paragraph 5 is that
    a. the author was discouraged about his wife's health.
    b. Carolyn and John Hodges were listed with the bone-marrow registry.
    c. the author and his wife barely knew John Hodges.
    d. the Hodges were willing to be considered as potential donors.

_____ 7. According to the selection, most donors are
    a. blood relatives.
    b. close friends.
    c. acquaintances.
    d. total strangers.

_____ 8. The statement that best describes the reaction to Mr. Hodges' decision to be a donor is
    a. His family and friends wholeheartedly supported his decision.
    b. His family and friends did not understand why he would risk his health for a stranger.

c. Members of his family refused to give permission for him to be a donor.

d. His family and friends researched the latest studies in order to convince him not to be a donor.

_____ 9. Mr. Hodges agreed to be a donor primarily because

a. he determined that the rewards outweighed the risks.

b. his mother had died from complications of kidney disease.

c. he had a scientific interest in the donation process.

d. his good friend was a transplant counselor.

_____ 10. In paragraphs 10–12, the author reports that the

a. transplant operation was a success.

b. donor has been able to resume his normal routine.

c. families consider themselves joined by a special bond.

d. all of the above.

USING CONTEXT AND WORD PARTS

_____ 11. In paragraph 1, the word **inexplicable** means

a. difficult or impossible to explain.

b. not true.

c. obvious.

d. mistaken.

_____ 12. In paragraph 1, the word **trumps** means

a. announces.

b. pretends.

c. gets the better of.

d. collects.

_____ 13. In paragraph 2, the word **nephrologist** means

a. referring to the condition of kidneys.

b. referring to specific medical treatment.

c. pertaining to the study of kidneys.

d. one who specializes in the study of kidney function and disease.

_____ 14. In paragraph 4, the word **congregants** means

a. the condition of a church or synagogue.

b. those who gather as a group for religious worship.

c. moving in an opposite direction.

d. the quality of friendship.

_____ 15. In paragraph 6, the word **diligently** means

a. without confidence.

b. in a hurry.

c. carefully and steadily.

d. fearfully.

REVIEWING DIFFICULT VOCABULARY

Directions: Match each word in column A with its meaning in column B.

Column A	Column B
_____ 16. phenomenon	a. from a dead body
_____ 17. macrobiotic	b. a remarkable or unusual development
_____ 18. cadaveric	c. a systematic course of treatment
_____ 19. regimen	d. a medical procedure for treating kidney failure
_____ 20. dialysis	e. a diet based on whole grains, beans, and vegetables

STUDYING WORDS

Directions: Use a dictionary to answer the following questions.

_____ 21. The correct meaning of the word **divine** (para. 1) as it is used in this reading is

a. relating to God.

b. extremely pleasant.

c. clergyman or minister.

d. to guess.

_____ 22. Which one of the following correctly indicates how **cadaveric** (para. 2) is pronounced?

a. kuh DAV er ik

b. kad uh VAIR ik

c. KAD uh ver ik

d. KAY duh ver ik

_____ 23. Which one of the following correctly indicates how **dialysis** (para. 2) is pronounced?

    a. die uh LIE sis

    b. die AL uh sis

    c. die uh LIS is

    d. DIE all sis

_____ 24. In parts of speech, the word **impassioned** (para. 4) is

    a. an adjective.   c. a verb.

    b. a noun.   d. an adverb.

_____ 25. The etymology of the word **myriad** (para. 12) is

    a. German.   c. Greek.

    b. English.   d. French.

QUESTIONS FOR DISCUSSION

1. Discuss John Hodges' motivation for, and his family's reaction to, his kidney donation. Should family members have the right to prevent a relative from donating an organ?

2. Discuss organ donation. Who should and who should not be allowed to donate? Should restrictions be placed on who can receive donated organs? Should donors be paid?

3. Brainstorm a list of things people could do to make the world a better place. (You may include organ donation on your list!)

WRITING ACTIVITIES

1. Consider how the author's attitude toward miracles changed as a result of the events described in this reading. Write a paragraph describing your own beliefs and attitudes about miracles.

2. Would you consider donating an organ to a non-family member? Write a paragraph giving at least three reasons why you would or would not make such a donation.

3. Write a paragraph describing a situation in which you either helped a stranger or a stranger helped you. Describe how the act made you feel.

Chapter 4: Building Vocabulary: Using Word Parts

Test	Number Right			Score
Practice Test 4-1	_____	× 10	=	_____ %
Practice Test 4-2	_____	× 10	=	_____ %
Practice Test 4-3	_____	× 10	=	_____ %
Mastery Test 4-1	_____	× 10	=	_____ %
Mastery Test 4-2	_____	× 10	=	_____ %
Mastery Test 4-3	_____	× 4	=	_____ %

EVALUATING YOUR PROGRESS

Based on your test performance, rate how well you have mastered the skills taught in this chapter by checking one of the boxes below or by writing your own evaluation.

☐ **Need More Improvement**
Tip: Try using the "Vocabulary" Module on the Reading Road Trip Web site at **http://www.ablongman.com/readingroadtrip** to fine-tune the skills that you have learned in this chapter.

☐ **Need More Practice**
Tip: Try using the "Vocabulary" Module on the Reading Road Trip Web site at **http://www.ablongman.com/readingroadtrip** to brush up on the skills you have learned in this chapter, or visit this textbook's companion Web site at **http://www.ablongman.com/mcwhorter** for extra practice.

☐ **Good**
Tip: To maintain your skills, quickly review this chapter by using this textbook's companion Web site by logging on to **http://www.ablongman.com/mcwhorter**.

☐ **Excellent**

YOUR EVALUATION: _____

_____

_____

_____

_____

READ ME FIRST!

Look at the photograph below—a movie still from the classic film *King Kong*. Just by looking at the photo, you can get a *general idea* of what this movie is about—a giant gorilla is terrorizing a large city and the woman in his clutches. Until you see the whole movie, though, you won't know the movie's *main idea*—the most important point the film is making.

When you study a paragraph, you also start with its general idea and then try to figure out its main idea.

CHAPTER 5

Locating Main Ideas

What Is a Main Idea?

When a friend asks you to go to a movie you haven't heard of, you probably ask "What's it about?" As you watch the movie, you come to understand the characters and the story. Eventually, you grasp the point the film is making—you realize what all the conversations and action, taken together, mean.

Understanding a paragraph involves a similar process. You first need to know what the paragraph is about, then you have to understand each of the sentences and how they relate to one another. Finally, to understand the paragraph's main point, you need to grasp what all the sentences, taken together, mean.

The one general subject a whole paragraph is about is called the **topic.** The most important point a whole paragraph makes is called the **main idea.** For example, read the following paragraph:

> Despite its increase in popularity, hypnotism has serious limitations that restrict its widespread use. First of all, not everyone is capable of being hypnotized. Second, a person who does not cooperate with the hypnotist is unlikely to fall into a hypnotic trance. Finally, there are limits to the commands a subject will obey when hypnotized. In many cases, subjects will not do anything that violates their moral code.

In this paragraph, the topic is "hypnotism," and the main idea is that "hypnotism has serious limitations that restrict its widespread use."

Here the main point of the paragraph is stated in the first sentence. The rest of the sentences then support or back up the main idea. As you will see later, however, the main idea doesn't always come first.

Understanding General Versus Specific Ideas

To identify topics and main ideas in paragraphs, it helps to understand the difference between general and specific. A *general* idea applies to a large number of individual items. The term *clothing* is general because it refers to a large collection of individual items—pants, suits, blouses, shirts, and so on. A *specific* idea or term is more detailed or particular. It refers to an individual item. The word *scarf,* for example, is more specific than the word *clothing.* The phrase *plain red scarf* is even more specific.

EXAMPLES				
General:	Pies		*General:*	Fruit
Specific:	chocolate cream		*Specific:*	grapes
	apple			lemons
	cherry			pineapple
General:	Countries		*General:*	Word Parts
Specific:	Britain		*Specific:*	prefix
	Finland			root
	Brazil			suffix

Exercise 5–1

Directions: Choose the letter that represents the most general term in each group of words.

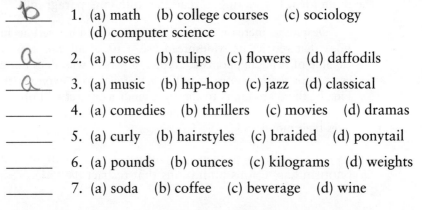

___b___   1. (a) math   (b) college courses   (c) sociology
      (d) computer science

___a___   2. (a) roses   (b) tulips   (c) flowers   (d) daffodils

___a___   3. (a) music   (b) hip-hop   (c) jazz   (d) classical

_____   4. (a) comedies   (b) thrillers   (c) movies   (d) dramas

_____   5. (a) curly   (b) hairstyles   (c) braided   (d) ponytail

_____   6. (a) pounds   (b) ounces   (c) kilograms   (d) weights

_____   7. (a) soda   (b) coffee   (c) beverage   (d) wine

_____ 8. (a) soap operas   (b) news   (c) TV programs
(d) sports special

_____ 9. (a) home furnishings   (b) carpeting   (c) drapes
(d) wall hangings

_____ 10. (a) sociology   (b) social sciences   (c) anthropology
(d) psychology

Exercise 5-2

Directions: *For each list of items, choose the letter of the choice that best applies to that grouping.*

_____ 1. dogs, canaries, tigers, elephants, panda bears

    a. household pets   c. endangered animals

    b. animals   d. zoo animals

_____ 2. alcohol, tobacco, heroin

    a. liquids   c. addictive substances

    b. illegal substances   d. legal substances

_____ 3. for better health, to fit into old clothes, for vanity

    a. reasons to visit your doctor

    b. reasons to go on a diet

    c. reasons to take vitamins

    d. reasons to buy new clothes

_____ 4. mosquito, wasp, gnat, butterfly

    a. living creatures   c. insects

    b. pests   d. harmful insects

_____ 5. Martha Washington, Hillary Clinton, Jacqueline Kennedy

    a. famous twentieth-century women

    b. famous American parents

    c. wives of American presidents

    d. famous wives

Now that you are familiar with the difference between general and specific, you will be able to use these ideas in the rest of the chapter.

Identifying the Topic

You already know that the topic is the general subject of an entire paragraph. Every sentence in a paragraph in some way discusses or explains this topic. To find the topic of a paragraph, ask yourself: What is the one idea the author is discussing throughout the paragraph? Read the following paragraph with that question in mind:

> Nutrition is the process of taking in and using food for growth, repair, and maintenance of the body. The science of nutrition is the study of foods and how the body uses them. Many North Americans define nutrition as eating a healthful diet. But what is healthful? Our food choices may be influenced by fads, advertising, or convenience. We may reflect on the meaning of nutrition while pushing a cart down a supermarket aisle, or while making a selection from a restaurant menu.
>
> —Byer and Shainberg, *Living Well: Health in Your Hands*, p. 256

In this example, the author is discussing one topic—nutrition—throughout the paragraph. Notice that the word *nutrition* is used several times.

Look again at the paragraph about hypnotism on page 133. How many times does the author use the word *hypnotism* or a version of that word? As you can see, the repeated use of a word often serves as a clue to the topic.

Exercise 5–3

Directions: After reading each of the following paragraphs, choose the letter of the choice that best represents the topic of the paragraph.

B 1. Some plants require more light than others as a result of the colors of their leaves. Plants with shades of white, yellow, or pink in their leaves need more light than plants with completely green foliage. For example, a Swedish ivy plant with completely green leaves requires less light per day than a variegated Swedish ivy that contains shades of white, yellow, and green in its leaves.

   a. how plants grow   c. light
   (b.) plants and light   d. green foliage

C 2. Mental illness is usually diagnosed from abnormal behavior. A woman is asked the time of day, and she begins to rub her arms and recite the Apostles' Creed. A man is so convinced that someone is "out to get him" that he refuses to leave his apartment. Unusual behaviors like these are taken as evidence that the mental apparatus is not working quite right, and mental illness is the resulting diagnosis.

—Schaie and Geiwitz, *Adult Development and Aging*, pp. 371–372

a. psychology
b. mental health
c. mental illness
d. evidence

A ∅ ∉
3. Discrimination doesn't go away: it just aims at whatever group appears to be out of fashion at any given moment. One expert feels that *age* is the major factor in employment discrimination today, although studies have shown older workers may be more reliable than young workers and just as productive. The Age Discrimination in Employment Act gives protection to the worker between forty and sixty-five. If you're in this age range, your employer must prove that you have performed unsatisfactorily before he can legally fire you. This act also prohibits age discrimination in hiring, wages, and benefits.

—George, *The New Consumer Survival Kit*, p. 212

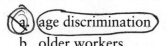

a. age discrimination
b. older workers
c. employment
d. protection of workers

d
4. Magazines are a means of communication halfway between newspapers and books. Until the 1940s most consumer (general) magazines offered both fiction and nonfiction articles as well as poetry and short humor selections. With television providing so much entertainment for the American home, many magazines discovered a strong demand for nonfiction articles, their almost exclusive content today.

—Agee, Ault, and Emery, *Introduction to Mass Communication*, p. 153

a. communication
b. nonfiction articles
c. newspapers and books
d. magazines

C ∅
5. Slavery has taken a number of different forms. War captives and their descendants formed a class of slaves in some societies; in others, slaves were owned and could be bought and sold. The rights granted to a slave varied, too. In ancient Greece, a slave could marry a free person, but in the southern United States before the Civil War, slaves were not allowed even to

marry each other because they were not permitted to engage in legal contracts. Still, slaves in the South often lived together as husband and wife throughout their adult lives, forming families that remained tightly knit until they were separated at the auction block.

—Hicks and Gwynne, *Cultural Anthropology,* p. 270

a. rights of slaves

b. slavery in Greece

c. forms of slavery

d. slavery in the southern United States

Directions: *After reading the following passage, select the topic of each paragraph from the box below. Note that not all of the words in the box will be used.*

A.   The basic chemical compounds that make up food are generally referred to as nutrients. Nutrients that are essential to health include proteins, carbohydrates, fiber, fats, vitamins, minerals, and water. (Although water contains no nutritious value, it is essential for life; therefore it is considered an essential nutrient.)

B.   Proteins are the building blocks of the body. They provide the structural framework for the skin, hair, nails, cartilage, tendons, and muscles. They provide an important structural part of the bones and are essential for the body's growth as well as maintenance, the regulation of body processes, and the replacement of body cells. In fact, proteins are a vital part of every cell.

C.   Proteins are made up of over twenty amino acids. Most of these amino acids can be made, or synthesized, by the body. Nine amino acids cannot be synthesized by the body yet are considered essential for health, so they must be consumed every day to ensure an adequate protein supply.

D.   A complete protein in food is one that contains all nine of the essential amino acids in amounts that correspond to human needs or amounts needed to make body protein. Complete proteins are found in animal products such as eggs, meat, milk, poultry, fish, and cheese. Unfortunately, many of these sources of complete protein are also high in fat and cholesterol. Soy protein is a low-fat alternative.

E.   An incomplete protein is one in which one or more of the essential amino acids are missing or in short supply relative to the need for protein synthesis. Plants contain incomplete proteins and are divided into three groups: grains, legumes (starchy peas, beans, and lentils), and vegetables. An incomplete protein, such as a grain, must be combined with other foods to form a complete protein.

—adapted from Pruitt and Stein, *Decisions for Healthy Living*, pp. 49–51

amino acids proteins	protein synthesis food	complete proteins incomplete proteins	cholesterol nutrients

1. The topic of paragraph A is ___nutrients___.
2. The topic of paragraph B is ___Proteins___.
3. The topic of paragraph C is ___Protein Synthesis___.
4. The topic of paragraph D is _____.
5. The topic of paragraph E is _____.

Finding the Main Idea

You learned earlier that the **main idea** of a paragraph is its most important point. The main idea is also the most *general* statement the writer makes about the topic. Pick out the most general statement among the following sentences:

1. People differ according to height.
2. Hair color distinguishes some people from others.
3. People differ in a number of ways.
4. Each person has his or her own personality.

Did you choose item 3 as the most general statement? Now we will change this list into a paragraph by rearranging the sentences and adding a few facts.

People differ in numerous ways. They differ according to physical characteristics, such as height, weight, and hair color. They also differ in personality. Some people are friendly and easygoing. Others are more reserved and formal.

In this brief paragraph, the main idea is expressed in the first sentence. This sentence, known as the **topic sentence,** is the most general statement in the paragraph. All the other sentences are specific details that explain this main idea.

Tips for Finding the Main Idea

Here are some tips that will help you find the main idea:

1. **Identify the topic.** As you did earlier, figure out the general subject of the entire paragraph. In the previous sample paragraph, "how people differ" is the topic.

2. **Locate the most general sentence (the topic sentence).** This sentence must be broad enough to include all of the other ideas in the paragraph. The topic sentence in the sample paragraph ("People differ in numerous ways.") covers all of the other details in that paragraph. The tips in the next section will help you locate topic sentences.

3. **Study the rest of the paragraph.** The main idea must make the rest of the paragraph meaningful. It is the one idea that ties all of the other details together. In the sample paragraph, sentences 2, 3, 4, and 5 all give specific details about how people differ.

Tips for Locating the Topic Sentence

Although a topic sentence can be located anywhere in a paragraph, it is usually *first* or *last*.

Topic Sentence First   In most paragraphs, the topic sentence comes first. The author states his or her main point and then explains it.

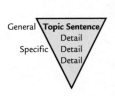

    Good listeners follow specific steps in order to achieve accurate understanding. First, whenever possible, good listeners prepare in advance for the speech or lecture they are going to attend. They study the topic to be discussed and find out about the speaker and his or her beliefs. Second, when they arrive at the place where the speech is to be given, they choose a seat where it is easy to see, hear, and remain alert. Finally, when the speech is over, effective listeners review what was said and evaluate the ideas that were expressed.

In the first sentence, the writer states that good listeners follow specific steps. The rest of the paragraph lists those steps.

Topic Sentence Last   The second most likely place for a topic sentence to appear is last in a paragraph. When using this arrangement, a writer leads up to the main point and then states it at the end. Here is a paragraph almost identical to the preceding one, but with the topic sentence last:

Whenever possible, good listeners prepare in advance for the speech or lecture they plan to attend. They study the topic to be discussed and find out about the speaker and his or her beliefs. When they arrive at the place where the speech is to be given, they choose a seat where it is easy to see, hear, and remain alert. And when the speech is over, they review what was said and evaluate the ideas that were expressed. <u>Thus, effective listeners follow specific steps in order to achieve accurate understanding</u>.

This paragraph lists all the steps that good listeners follow. Then, at the end, the writer states the main idea.

Topic Sentence in the Middle   If a topic sentence is placed neither first nor last, then it may appear somewhere in the middle of a paragraph. In this arrangement, the sentences before the topic sentence lead up to or introduce the main idea. Those that follow the main idea explain or describe it.

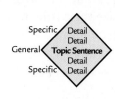

Whenever possible, good listeners prepare in advance for the speech or lecture they plan to attend. They study the topic to be discussed and find out about the speaker and his or her beliefs. <u>Effective listeners, then, take specific steps to achieve accurate understanding of the lecture</u>. Furthermore, when they arrive at the place where the speech is to be given, they choose a seat where it is easy to see, hear, and remain alert. Finally, when the speech is over, effective listeners review what was said and evaluate the ideas that were expressed.

This paragraph begins with two examples of what good listeners do. Then the writer states the main idea and continues with more examples.

Topic Sentence First and Last   Occasionally writers put the main idea at the beginning of a paragraph and again at the end. Writers may do this to emphasize the main point or to clarify it.

General | Topic Sentence
Specific | Detail / Detail / Detail
General | Topic Sentence

<u>Good listeners follow specific steps in order to achieve accurate understanding</u>. First, whenever possible, good listeners prepare in advance for the speech or lecture they are going to attend. They study the topic to be discussed and find out about the speaker and his or her beliefs. Second, when they arrive at the place where the speech is to be given, they choose a seat where it is easy to see, hear, and remain alert. Finally, when the speech is over, they review what was said and evaluate the ideas that were expressed. <u>Effective listening, then, is an active process in which listeners deliberately take certain actions to ensure that accurate communication has occurred</u>.

The first and last sentences both state, in slightly different ways, the main idea of the paragraph—that good listeners follow certain steps.

Exercise 5-5

Directions: Underline the topic sentence in each of the following paragraphs. Keep in mind that topic sentences can appear at the beginning, middle, or end of a paragraph.

1. Fast foods tend to be short on fresh fruits and vegetables, and are low in calcium, although calcium can be obtained in shakes and milk. Pizza is a fast-food exception. It contains grains, meat, vegetables, and cheese, which represent four of the food groups. Pizza is often only about 25 percent fat, most of which comes from the crust. Overall, studies have shown pizza to be highly nutritious.

   —Byer and Shainberg, *Living Well: Health in Your Hands,* p. 289

2. Earlier we examined the concept of irreversibility, the idea that once something is said, it cannot be unsaid. Perhaps the most common method for defending or justifying something that has been said and may be perceived negatively is "the excuse." Excuses pervade all forms of communication and behavior. Although we emphasize their role in conversation, recognize that the excuse is applicable to all human behaviors, not just the conversational ones.

   —adapted from DeVito, *Human Communication,* p. 170

3. You could be the greatest genius since Thomas Edison, but if no one knows about your talent or is in a position to judge it, you're wasting your time. Being in the right field is important. But within that field, it's also a good idea to maintain a high degree of visibility. If you've got the potential to be a brilliant corporate planner, you may be wasting your time working for a small company. You'd be better off working for a large corporation where you have the opportunity to take off in many directions, learn how the different departments work together, and thus have a larger arena to test your skills.

   —Weinstein, *Jobs for the 21st Century,* p. 118

4. Dirty words are often used by teenagers in telling off-color stories and this can be considered part of their sex education. As their bodies grow and change, both boys and girls wonder and worry. To keep from being overwhelmed by these fears, they turn them into jokes or dirty-word stories. By telling and retelling off-color stories, they learn that they aren't the only ones in the group disturbed about their future roles in courtship and marriage. Using dirty words and stories to laugh at sexual doubts and fears may make them less frightening.

   —Brothers, "What Dirty Words Really Mean" from *Good Housekeeping*

5. When consumers are in a store to buy an expensive product, they may feel pressured to purchase immediately. The sales staff may exert pressure, or they may create their own pressure. After all, the trip has cost time and effort, and the buyers don't want to appear indecisive. For important purchases, it is often advisable to invest a bit more time before making a final decision. In fact, consumers should go home and evaluate and weigh the purchase decision. At home consumers are free of external pressures exerted by the sales environment and the sales staff. Consumers can also ask themselves important questions such as "Can I really afford this?" and "Is this the best product I can find for the price?"

6. The 1950s were to most Americans a time of great security. After World War II, the people prospered in ways they had never known before. Our involvement in the Korean war was thought to be successful from the point of view of national image. We saw ourselves as *the* world power, who had led the fight for democracy. When Dwight D. Eisenhower was elected president, we entered a period in American history where everything was all right, everyone was getting richer, and tomorrow would always be better than today.

—Weirich, *Personal Financial Management,* p. 155

7. Suppose you are preparing to give a speech to a group of people. Assume you are in a position where you can observe the group. What are they wearing? Are they dressed casually, formally, informally, trendy, classy, or wildly? Do they seem well-to-do or frugal? What are their hobbies? What sports are they involved with? To what age range do most of the group members belong? What are their occupations? Are they professional or blue-collar workers? Assessing the characteristics of your audience will allow you to make inferences about its values and interests and enable you to tailor your speech to those interests.

8. The words "effortless exercise" are a contradiction in terms. Muscles grow in strength only when subjected to overload. Flexibility is developed only by extending the normal range of body motion. Endurance is developed only through exercise that raises the pulse rate enough to achieve a training effect on the heart, lungs, and circulatory system. In all cases, the benefits from exercise come from extending the body beyond its normal activity range. What this requires is, precisely, effort.

—Dorfman, *Well Being: An Introduction of Health,* p. 263

9. Burger King Corporation offers both a service and a product to its customers. Its service is the convenience it offers the consumer—the location of its restaurants and its fast food service. Its product is *the total*

Burger King experience, which starts from the time you drive into the restaurant's parking lot and ends when you drive out. It includes the speed of service, the food you order, the price you pay, the friendliness and courtesy you are shown, the feeling of satisfaction—in short, an experience. Burger King, then, is marketing a positive experience, as promised by its advertising and promotional efforts and delivered by its product.

—Fox and Wheatley, *Modern Marketing,* p. 142

10. In the United States, Australia, and Western Europe people are encouraged to be independent. Members of these cultures are taught to get ahead, to compete, to win, to achieve their goals, to realize their unique potential, to stand out from the crowd. In many Asian and African countries, people are taught to value an interdependent self. Members of these cultures are taught to get along, to help others, and to not disagree or stand out. Thus, there are significant cultural differences in the way people are taught to view themselves.

—adapted from DeVito, *Human Communication,* p. 78

Learning More About Paragraphs

When you read a paragraph now, you should be pretty good at figuring out its topic and finding its topic sentence. Obviously, though, there is more to a paragraph than these two items. What about all of the other sentences? These are the **details**—the sentences that explain the main idea. To connect sentences, writers use **transitions,** words like *first, however,* and *finally.* You will learn more about details and transitions in the next chapter.

The Textbook Challenge

Part A: Student Resource Guide A

Using Textbook Excerpt 1, "Civil Liberties and the Right to Privacy," (p. 400) highlight the topic sentence of each paragraph.

Part B: A College Textbook

Choose a chapter that you have been assigned to read in a textbook for one of your other courses. For the first five pages, underline the topic sentence of each paragraph.

What Have You Learned?

Directions: Circle the letter of the choice that best completes each statement.

_____ b 1. The topic of a paragraph is the
      a. subject of the paragraph.
      b. main idea of the paragraph.
      c. noun that is the subject of a sentence.
      d. object of the predicate.

_____ a 2. The best clue to use in identifying the topic of a paragraph is
      a. the arrangement of the sentences.
      b. the use of directional words.
      c. a frequently repeated key word.
      d. the order of details.

_____ c 3. The sentence that expresses the main idea of a paragraph is known as the
      a. opening sentence.   c. topic sentence.
      b. general sentence.   d. main sentence.

_____ a 4. In what position are you most likely to find the topic sentence in a paragraph?
      a. first   c. last
      b. second   d. in the middle

_____ b 5. Occasionally, writers who want to clarify or emphasize a main idea might put a topic sentence
      a. first.   c. last.
      b. first and last.   d. in the middle.

What Vocabulary Have You Learned?

Directions: The words in column A appear in exercises in this chapter. Test your mastery of these words by matching each word in column A with its meaning in column B.

	Column A		Column B
_____	1. prohibits	a.	produced or made
_____	2. vital	b.	spread throughout
_____	3. synthesized	c.	does not allow
_____	4. pervade	d.	succeeded financially
_____	5. prospered	e.	necessary

Test-Taking Tip #5: Questions on the Topic and Main Idea

Reading comprehension tests often include questions that ask you to identify the topic and main idea of a paragraph. Test writers do not always use the terms "topic" and "main idea." Once you understand what a test item is asking you to identify, you'll probably be able to answer it.

■ **Topic**—Here are a few ways reading tests may ask you to identify the topic of a paragraph:

- This paragraph is primarily about . . .
- This paragraph concerns . . .
- This paragraph focuses on . . .
- The best title for the paragraph would be . . .

■ **Main Idea**—Here are a few words reading tests may use to mean the main idea of a paragraph:

- Thesis
- Central point
- Central idea
- Controlling idea
- Most important idea
- Primary idea

So a question that asks, "Which of the following statements expresses the central point of the paragraph?" is really asking you to identify the main idea.

RECOGNIZING GENERAL AND SPECIFIC

Directions: In the space provided, write the letter of the choice that best describes each grouping.

_____ 1. touchdown, home run, 3-pointer, 5 under par
  a. types of errors in sports   c. types of scoring in sports
  b. types of activities   d. types of sports

_____ 2. Oprah Winfrey, David Letterman, Jay Leno, Dr. Laura Schlesinger
  a. rock stars   c. comedians
  b. talk-show hosts   d. movie stars

_____ 3. for companionship, to play with, because you love animals
  a. reasons to visit the zoo
  b. reasons to feed your cat
  c. reasons to get a pet
  d. reasons to become a veterinarian

_____ 4. taking a hot bath, going for a walk, watching a video, listening to music
  a. ways to relax   c. ways to listen
  b. ways to help others   d. ways to solve problems

_____ 5. Road Runner, Donald Duck, Mickey Mouse, Tweety Bird
  a. movie characters   c. historical figures
  b. live animals   d. cartoon characters

_____ 6. lamp, toaster, radio, computer
  a. machinery   c. electrical devices
  b. luxuries   d. good birthday gifts

_____ 7. listen, be helpful, be generous, be forgiving
  a. ways to get a job
  b. ways to keep a friend
  c. ways to learn
  d. ways to appreciate a movie

_____ 8. Lake Huron, Mississippi River, Atlantic Ocean, Gulf of Mexico

    a. bodies of water   c. areas of conflict

    b. vacation spots   d. U.S. landmarks

_____ 9. take your blood pressure, record your weight, ask how you're feeling

    a. tasks doctors usually perform

    b. tasks mothers usually perform

    c. tasks friends usually perform

    d. tasks nurses usually perform

_____ 10. soccer, baseball, basketball, football

    a. sports that use similar scoring systems

    b. sports that are popular all over the world

    c. team sports that use a ball

    d. the safest sports

NAME _____ SECTION _____

DATE _____ SCORE _____

RECOGNIZING GENERAL AND SPECIFIC

Directions: For each general idea, write four specific ideas that "fit" within it. An example is provided for each entry.

1. <u>General idea</u>: types of exercise   <u>sit-ups</u>

   _____ _____ _____ _____

2. <u>General idea</u>: fast-food restaurants   <u>McDonald's</u>

   _____ _____ _____ _____

3. <u>General idea</u>: musical instruments   <u>saxophone</u>

   _____ _____ _____ _____

4. <u>General idea</u>: types of personalities   <u>outgoing</u>

   _____ _____ _____ _____

5. <u>General idea</u>: models of cars   <u>Ford Mustang</u>

   _____ _____ _____ _____

6. <u>General idea</u>: breakfast drinks   <u>coffee</u>

   _____ _____ _____ _____

7. <u>General idea</u>: food categories   <u>meat</u>

   _____ _____ _____ _____

8. <u>General idea</u>: summer sports   <u>swimming</u>

   _____ _____ _____ _____

9. <u>General idea</u>: popular singers   <u>Whitney Houston</u>

   _____ _____ _____ _____

10. <u>General idea</u>: tools   <u>hammer</u>

   _____ _____ _____ _____

NAME _____ SECTION _____
DATE _____ SCORE _____

PRACTICE TEST 5-3

IDENTIFYING TOPICS AND TOPIC SENTENCES

Directions: For each of the following paragraphs, (1) in the space provided, write the letter of the choice that best represents the topic of the paragraph, and (2) underline the topic sentence.

_____ 1. There are a number of reasons why there has been an increase in the demand for nurses, not the least of which is the aging of the U.S. population. Older people use hospitals more and have chronic ailments that require more nursing. Moreover, as hospitals reduce the length of stay of patients, people who are discharged earlier than in previous years need more home care, usually provided by nurses. While demand has been rising, the supply of nurses has decreased somewhat—there are now fewer women between the ages of 18 and 24. Because this is the group from which nurses traditionally come, there have been fewer potential nurses. In addition, women have more alternatives in the labor market than they did years ago.

—Miller, *Economics Today,* p. 84

    a. aging population

    b. demand for nurses

    c. age distribution of women

    d. other job choices for nurses

_____ 2. When good writers use the word revision, they don't mean the sort of minor changes implied in the old elementary school phrase "Copy it over in ink." Revision doesn't even mean writing your paper over again. Instead, it means reading your draft carefully in order to make effective changes in the existing text. It means stepping outside the draft you've created; looking at its strengths and weaknesses as if you were a reader seeing it for the first time; and deciding what parts of the draft need to be expanded, clarified, elaborated, illustrated, reworded, restructured, modified—or just plain cut.

—Anson and Schwegler, *The Longman Handbook for Writers and Readers,* p. 78

    a. writing   c. what revision means

    b. what drafting means   d. rewording a paper

_____ 3. Young women who suffer from *anorexia nervosa,* an eating disorder, severely limit their food intake to the point of significant weight loss and near starvation. Many young women also have *bulimia nervosa,* another serious eating disorder, which involves frequent binges (overeating) followed by purges (self-induced vomiting or the use of laxatives). In the United States approximately 10 million women experience one of these disorders. Both of these life-threatening eating disorders involve an obsessive relationship with food, and women who have these disorders must be treated professionally before they permanently damage their bodies.

a. young women   c. bulimia nervosa

b. eating disorders   d. anorexia

_____ 4. Narratives are stories, and they are often useful as supporting materials in a speech. Narratives give the audience what it wants: a good story. Listeners seem to perk up automatically when a story is told. If the narrative is a personal one, it will make you more believable and show you as a real person. Listeners like to know about speakers, and the personal narrative meets this desire. Notice how you remember the little stories noted personalities tell in television interviews.

—DeVito, *The Elements of Public Speaking,* p. 164

a. supporting materials   c. listeners

b. speeches   d. narratives in speeches

_____ 5. We might like to think of ourselves as so sophisticated that physical attractiveness does not move us. We might like to claim that sensitivity, warmth, and intelligence are more important to us. However, we might never learn about other people's personalities if they do not meet our minimal standards for physical attractiveness.

—Rathus, *Human Sexuality,* p. 189

a. learning about personalities

b. importance of physical attractiveness

c. factors in dating

d. factors in relationships

IDENTIFYING MAIN IDEAS

Directions: After reading the following passage, in the space provided, write the letter of the choice that best completes each of the statements below.

The most common form of Internet abuse is spam. *Spam* is unsolicited impersonal e-mail from a party who is unknown to you or with whom you have no consenting relationship. Anyone who sends out an announcement to millions of e-mail addresses is a spammer. Most e-mail spam is commercial in nature. But spam can also contain political calls for action, religious sermons, or the incoherent ravings of someone with a mental problem.

If you're worried about avoiding spam, you'll need to learn more about the various ways that spammers obtain e-mail addresses. Whenever you are asked to provide personal information over the Web or via e-mail, you should know what, if any, privacy policies will be applied to protect your privacy online. No laws in the United States protect the privacy rights of consumers, so users must be savvy about what goes on behind the scenes. If a company offers you a "free" e-mail account, how much information do you have to give up in order to participate? Data resellers generate a lot of revenue by selling Internet user profiles to advertisers, marketing organizations, and scam artists. Whenever anyone on the Internet offers you a free service in exchange for information, understand that you are probably being bought and sold. If the service is worth it to you, fine. But most people don't realize that they are really trading personal privacy for a free e-mail account or free space on a Web page server.

—Lehnert, *Light on the Internet*, pp. 53, 55

_____ 1. The topic of the first paragraph is
   a. e-mail.   c. political calls for action.
   b. spam.   d. privacy issues.

_____ 2. In the first paragraph, the topic sentence begins with the words
   a. "The most common."   c. "Most e-mail."
   b. "Anyone who."   d. "But spam."

_____ 3. In paragraph 1, the word **unsolicited** means
   a. unusual.   c. not requested.
   b. dangerous.   d. not proven.

_____ 4. In paragraph 1, the word **consenting** means

    a. convenient.   c. close.

    b. caring.   d. agreed upon.

_____ 5. In paragraph 1, the word **incoherent** means

    a. not pleasant.   c. not quiet.

    b. not understandable.   d. not teachable.

_____ 6. The topic of the second paragraph is

    a. how to generate spam.

    b. the privacy rights of consumers.

    c. free e-mail accounts.

    d. how spammers obtain e-mail addresses.

_____ 7. In the second paragraph, the topic sentence begins with the words

    a. "If you're worried."   c. "Data resellers."

    b. "No laws."   d. "But most people."

_____ 8. According to the selection, which of the following is _not_ correct?

    a. A religious sermon might be spam.

    b. Data resellers sell personal information to advertisers and others.

    c. You may lose personal privacy to get a free e-mail account.

    d. U.S. laws protect the privacy of personal e-mail.

_____ 9. According to the selection, one way that spammers obtain e-mail addresses is by

    a. buying them from data resellers.

    b. violating laws that protect the privacy rights of consumers.

    c. responding to requests for information.

    d. sending out requests for names.

_____ 10. The two paragraphs in this reading support the idea that a topic sentence usually comes

    a. in the middle.   c. last.

    b. first.   d. first and last

IDENTIFYING MAIN IDEAS

Directions: After reading the following passage, in the space provided, write the letter of the choice that best completes each of the statements below.

Many people start relationships because of loneliness. Loneliness and being alone are not synonymous. Loneliness is a state of painful isolation, of feeling cut off from others. Being alone, a state of solitude, can be quite desirable, since it allows us to work, study, or reflect on the world around us. Solitude is usually a matter of choice; loneliness is not.

Lonely people tend to spend a lot of time by themselves, eat dinner alone, spend weekends alone, and participate in few social activities. They are unlikely to date. Some lonely people report having many friends, but a closer look suggests that these "friendships" are shallow. Lonely people are unlikely to share confidences. Loneliness tends to peak during adolescence. This is when most young people begin to supplant family ties with peer relationships. Loneliness is often connected with feelings of depression and with a feeling of being "sick at heart."

Loneliness is even reported among some married people. In one study, lonely wives tended to feel less liking and love for their partners and expressed less marital satisfaction. Lonely husbands reported less liking for their wives and less intimacy in their relationships.

—Rathus, *Human Sexuality,* p. 221

_____ 1. The topic of the first paragraph is
  a. how to begin relationships.
  b. solitude and loneliness.
  c. solitude.
  d. isolation and pain.

_____ 2. The topic sentence of the first paragraph begins with the words
  a. "Many people start."   c. "Being alone."
  b. "Loneliness and being." d. "Solitude is."

_____ 3. In paragraph 1, the word **synonymous** means
  a. different.   c. serious.
  b. the same.   d. relevant.

4. In the first paragraph, what is the easiest way to figure out the meaning of the word **isolation?**

   a. by using word parts

   b. by using a dictionary

   c. by using sentence context

   d. by rereading the paragraph

5. The topic of the second paragraph is

   a. how lonely people behave.

   b. what lonely people want.

   c. the difference between loneliness and solitude.

   d. why lonely people are depressed.

6. In the second paragraph, the topic sentence begins with the words

   a. "Lonely people tend."   c. "Lonely people are."

   b. "Some lonely people."   d. "Loneliness is often."

7. In paragraph 2, the word **confidences** means

   a. factual information.   c. family histories.

   b. knowledge of others.   d. personal stories.

8. In paragraph 2, the word **supplant** means

   a. reject.   c. lessen.

   b. replace.   d. encourage.

9. The topic of the third paragraph is

   a. marriage.

   b. lonely wives.

   c. lonely husbands.

   d. loneliness among married people.

10. According to the selection,

    a. loneliness is desirable.

    b. lonely people date quite a bit.

    c. solitude can be desirable.

    d. married people are usually lonely.

DON'T ASK
Deborah Tannen

Men and women differ in many ways, including how they communicate. You'll probably recognize some of the differences Deborah Tannen describes in this excerpt from her book, *You Just Don't Understand*. Read this selection to find out why many men do not like to ask for directions.

Vocabulary Preview

These are some of the difficult words in this essay. The definitions here will help you if you can't figure out the meanings from the sentence context or word parts.

paradox (para. 4) contradiction

metamessages (para. 4) meanings that appear beneath the surface; hidden meanings

hierarchical (para. 5) arranged in a specified order

framed (para. 5) placed within a context

implicit (para. 6) not directly stated

asymmetrical (para. 8) having a lack of harmony or balance

status (para. 8) position or rank; one's standing in relation to others

1 Talking about troubles is just one of the many conversational tasks that women and men view differently, and that consequently causes trouble in talk between them. Another is asking for information.

2 A man and a woman were standing beside the information booth at the Washington Folk Life Festival, a sprawling complex of booths and displays. "You ask," the man was saying to the woman. "I don't ask."

3 Sitting in the front seat of the car beside Harold, Sybil is fuming. They have been driving around for half an hour looking for a street he is sure is close by. Sybil is angry not because Harold does not know the way, but because he insists on trying to find it himself rather than stopping and asking someone. Her anger stems from viewing his behavior through the lens of her own: If she were driving, she would have asked directions as soon as she realized she didn't know which way to go, and they'd now be comfortably

ensconced in their friends' living room instead of driving in circles, as the hour gets later and later. Since asking directions does not make Sybil uncomfortable, refusing to ask makes no sense to her. But in Harold's world, driving around until he finds his way is the reasonable thing to do, since asking for help makes him uncomfortable. He's avoiding that discomfort and trying to maintain his sense of himself as a self-sufficient person.

4   Why do many men resist asking for directions and other kinds of information? And, it is just as reasonable to ask, why is it that many women don't? By the paradox of independence and intimacy, there are two simultaneous and different metamessages implied in asking for and giving information. Many men tend to focus on one, many women on the other.

5   When you offer information, the information itself is the message. But the fact that you have the information, and the person you are speaking to doesn't, also sends a metamessage of superiority. If relations are inherently hierarchical, then the one who has more information is framed as higher up on the ladder, by virtue of being more knowledgeable and competent. From

CLOSE TO HOME   JOHN McPHERSON

"Ha! I TOLD you I could find my way back to the interstate without stopping to ask directions!"

this perspective, finding one's own way is an essential part of the independence that men perceive to be a prerequisite for self-respect. If self-respect is bought at the cost of a few extra minutes of travel time, it is well worth the price.

6   Because they are implicit, metamessages are hard to talk about. When Sybil begs to know why Harold won't just ask someone for directions, he answers in terms of the message, the information: He says there's no point in asking, because anyone he asks may not know and may give him wrong directions. This is theoretically reasonable. There are many countries, such as, for example, Mexico, where it is standard procedure for people to make up directions rather than refuse to give requested information. But this explanation frustrates Sybil, because it doesn't make sense to her. Although she realizes that someone might give faulty directions, she believes this is relatively unlikely, and surely it cannot happen every time. Even if it did happen, they would be in no worse shape than they are in now anyway.

7   Part of the reason for their different approaches is that Sybil believes that a person who doesn't know the answer will say so, because it is easy to say, "I don't know." But Harold believes that saying "I don't know" is humiliating, so people might well take a wild guess. Because of their different assumptions, and the invisibility of framing, Harold and Sybil can never get to the bottom of this difference; they can only get more frustrated with each other. Keeping talk on the message level is common, because it is the level we are most clearly aware of. But it is unlikely to resolve confusion since our true motivations lie elsewhere.

8   To the extent that giving information, directions, or help is of use to another, it reinforces bonds between people. But to the extent that it is asymmetrical, it creates hierarchy: Insofar as giving information frames one as the expert, superior in knowledge, and the other as uninformed, inferior in knowledge, it is a move in the negotiation of status.

9   It is easy to see that there are many situations where those who give information are higher in status. For example, parents explain things to children and answer their questions, just as teachers give information to stu-

dents. An awareness of this dynamic underlies one requirement for proper behavior at Japanese dinner entertainment, according to anthropologist Harumi Befu. In order to help the highest-status member of the party to dominate the conversation, others at the dinner are expected to ask him questions that they know he can answer with authority.

10 Because of this potential for asymmetry, some men resist receiving information from others, especially women, and some women are cautious about stating information that they know, especially to men. For example, a man with whom I discussed these dynamics later told me that my perspective clarified a comment made by his wife. They had gotten into their car and were about to go to a destination that she knew well but he did not know at all. Consciously resisting an impulse to just drive off and find his own way, he began by asking his wife if she had any advice about the best way to get there. She told him the way, then added, "But I don't know. That's how I would go, but there might be a better way." Her comment was a move to redress the imbalance of power created by her knowing something he didn't know. She was also saving face in advance, in case he decided not to take her advice. Furthermore, she was reframing her directions as "just a suggestion" rather than "giving instructions."

— · —

Directions: In the space provided, write the letter of the choice that best completes each of the following statements.

CHECKING YOUR COMPREHENSION

_____ 1. The main point of the passage is
  a. men and women differ on asking for information because of how they think about relationships.
  b. men and women ask for directions in different ways.
  c. women are willing to ask for help because they are bad at remembering directions.
  d. you shouldn't give information to others because you will embarrass them.

_____ 2. In paragraph 3, the main reason Sybil is angry is because

    a. they are late arriving at their friend's home.

    b. they are lost.

    c. Harold will not ask for directions.

    d. Harold doesn't know the way.

_____ 3. According to paragraph 7,

    a. information is more important than what motivates Harold and Sybil.

    b. Harold and Sybil have unspoken assumptions about what motivates people.

    c. Harold and Sybil know they have similar approaches to asking for information.

    d. Harold and Sybil can never understand each other.

_____ 4. According to Harold's reasoning, when asked for directions, most people will

    a. try to embarrass him for having asked for help.

    b. be uncomfortable and avoid his question.

    c. lead him to his destination.

    d. give wrong directions rather than say "I don't know."

_____ 5. In the last example in the passage, the wife said she wasn't sure her directions were the best because

    a. she had forgotten how to reach their destination.

    b. she was being considerate of her husband's feelings.

    c. she would prefer to ask for directions along the way.

    d. she wanted to confuse her husband with unclear advice.

_____ 6. The topic of paragraph 3 is

    a. driving.   c. Sybil's anger.

    b. asking for directions.   d. Harold's discomfort.

_____ 7. The topic sentence of paragraph 6 begins with the words

    a. "Because they are."   c. "Although she realizes."

    b. "This is theoretically."   d. "Even if it did."

8. The topic of paragraph 8 is
   a. creating bonds.   c. giving information.
   b. communication.   d. being an expert.

9. The topic sentence of paragraph 9 begins with the words
   a. "It is easy."   c. "An awareness."
   b. "For example."   d. "In order."

10. The topic sentence of paragraph 10 begins with the words
    a. "They had gotten."   c. "Furthermore, she."
    b. "Consciously resisting." d. "Because of this."

USING CONTEXT CLUES AND WORD PARTS

11. In paragraph 3, the word **ensconced** means
    a. settled.   c. expected.
    b. waiting.   d. enlisted.

12. In paragraph 3, the word **self-sufficient** means
    a. able to take care of oneself.
    b. able to rely on others for care.
    c. able to trust others.
    d. able to present one's own problems.

13. In paragraph 5, the word **superiority** means
    a. being worse than someone else.
    b. being different from someone else.
    c. being better than someone else.
    d. being the same as someone else.

14. In paragraph 5, the word **prerequisite** means
    a. something that is necessary.
    b. something that is important.
    c. something that is confusing.
    d. something that is distracting.

15. In paragraph 7, the word **humiliating** means
    a. courageous.   c. harmful to one's self-respect.
    b. helpful to one's purpose. d. cowardly.

REVIEWING DIFFICULT VOCABULARY

Directions: Complete each of the following sentences by inserting a word from the Vocabulary Preview on page 156 in the space provided. A word should be used only once.

16. Because José had not _____ the question correctly, I didn't understand what he meant.

17. In terms of income, the poor, the middle-class, and the wealthy can be arranged in a _____ order.

18. If two sisters love each other but also get so angry that they hate each other, this situation might be called a _____.

19. Since Wanda is well educated, has a good-paying job, and has famous parents, her _____ is higher than mine.

20. One leg of Amy's old jeans is three inches shorter than the other. The legs of her jeans are _____.

STUDYING WORDS

Directions: Use a dictionary to answer the following questions.

_____ 21. What part of speech is the word **simultaneous** (para. 4)?
   a. adjective
   b. verb
   c. noun
   d. adverb

_____ 22. What is the correct pronunciation of the word **implicit** (para. 6)?
   a. IMP lis it
   b. im PL sit
   c. im PLISS it
   d. imp liss SIT

_____ 23. Another meaning for the word **fuming** (para. 3) that is not used in the reading is to have
   a. extinguishing a fire.
   b. giving off smoke or gas.
   c. releasing fumaric acid.
   d. issuing an attack.

_____ 24. The word **paradox** (para. 4) originated from which of the following languages?
   a. Spanish
   b. French
   c. Latin
   d. English

_____ 25. The restrictive meaning of the word **frame** (para. 5) in baseball is
   a. pitch.
   b. home run.
   c. outfield.
   d. inning.

QUESTIONS FOR DISCUSSION

1. Does this selection match or not match your own experiences about asking for directions?
2. Discuss whether your own generation has a different perspective toward hierarchical relationships than your grandparents' or parents' generation.
3. Observe the communication styles of men and women within your college classroom. What differences did you observe?

WRITING ACTIVITIES

1. Choose an event, such as a ball game, a party, or a concert. Make a list of the differences you have observed between the ways that men and women communicate during the event.

2. Brainstorm a list of situations, other than asking directions, in which one person assumes a higher status than the other. Note how the behavior and speech of the person of higher status differs from that of the person of lower status.

3. Consider your own relationships. Write one paragraph about your relationship with someone whose knowledge in a particular area is superior to your own and another paragraph about a relationship in which your knowledge is superior. Be sure to include a description of how you communicate with each person.

Chapter 5: Locating Main Ideas

Test	Number Right	Score
Practice Test 5-1	_____ × 10 =	_____ %
Practice Test 5-2	_____ × 10 =	_____ %
Practice Test 5-3	_____ × 10 =	_____ %
Mastery Test 5-1	_____ × 10 =	_____ %
Mastery Test 5-2	_____ × 10 =	_____ %
Mastery Test 5-3	_____ × 4 =	_____ %

EVALUATING YOUR PROGRESS

Based on your test performance, rate how well you have mastered the skills taught in this chapter by checking one of the boxes below or by writing your own evaluation.

☐ **Need More Improvement**
Tip: Try using the "Main Idea" Module on the Reading Road Trip Web site at **http://www.ablongman.com/readingroadtrip** to fine-tune the skills that you have learned in this chapter.

☐ **Need More Practice**
Tip: Try using the "Main Idea" Module on the Reading Road Trip Web site at **http://www.ablongman.com/readingroadtrip** to brush up on the skills you have learned in this chapter, or visit this textbook's companion Web site at **http://www.ablongman.com/mcwhorter** for extra practice.

☐ **Good**
Tip: To maintain your skills, quickly review this chapter by using this textbook's companion Web site by logging on to **http://www.ablongman.com/mcwhorter**.

☐ **Excellent**

YOUR EVALUATION: _____

_____

_____

_____

READ ME FIRST!

Look at the photograph below, which shows everyone having a good time at a party. Did this party just "happen," or did someone have an idea and then follow it up with work and planning? Suppose you decide to have a birthday party for your best friend. Your *main idea* is that it will be a surprise party and that you will serve pizza, your friend's favorite food. In order for the party to be successful, though, you also need to pay attention to the *details*—inviting people, doing the grocery shopping, getting a birthday cake, and so forth.

Studying a paragraph can be a little bit like planning a party. First you find the paragraph's main idea and then you look for the details that support it.

CHAPTER 6

Identifying Supporting Details and Transitions

What Are Supporting Details?

Just as grocery shopping and inviting friends are details that help you throw a party, the details writers use in a paragraph help them back up the point they want to make. **Supporting details** are those facts and ideas that prove or explain the main idea of a paragraph. As you read, you will notice that some details are more important than others. Pay particular attention to the **major details**—the most important details that directly explain the main idea. You should also note **minor details**—details that may provide additional information, offer an example, or further explain one of the major details.

Figure 6-1 on page 168 shows how details relate to the main idea. As you recall from Chapter 5, the main idea is usually stated in a topic sentence.

Read the following paragraph and then study the diagram in Figure 6-2 on page 168.

The skin of the human body has several functions. First, it serves as a protective covering. In doing so, it accounts for 17 percent of the body's weight. Skin also protects the organs within the body from damage or harm. The skin serves as a regulator of body functions. It controls body temperature and water loss. Finally, the skin serves as a receiver. It is sensitive to touch and temperature.

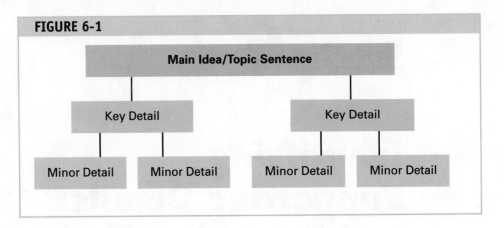

FIGURE 6-1

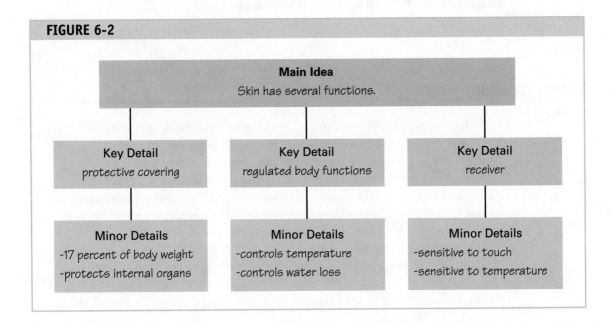

FIGURE 6-2

From Figure 6-2 you can see the major details that state the three main functions of the skin. The minor details, such as "controls temperature," provide further information and are less important than the major details.

Look at the paragraph again, and notice how the author has used **transitions**—words that lead you from one major detail to the next. The words *first, also,* and *finally* are a few of the transitions that can help you find the major details in a paragraph. Be on the lookout for transitions as you read; they will be discussed more fully later in this chapter.

Exercise 6-1

A. Directions: *Read the following paragraph and then complete the diagram that follows. Some of the items have been filled in for you.*

Communication occurs with words and gestures, but did you know it also occurs through the sense of smell? Odor can communicate at least four types of messages. First, odor can signal attraction. Animals give off scents to attract members of the opposite sex. Humans use fragrances to make themselves more appealing or attractive. Smell also communicates information about tastes. The smell of popcorn popping stimulates the appetite. If you smell a chicken roasting, you can anticipate its taste. A third type of smell communication is through memory. A smell can help you recall an event that occurred months or even years ago, especially if the event was an emotional one. Finally, smell can communicate by creating an identity or image for a person or product. For example, a woman may wear only one brand of perfume. Or a brand of shaving cream may have a distinct fragrance, which allows users to recognize it.

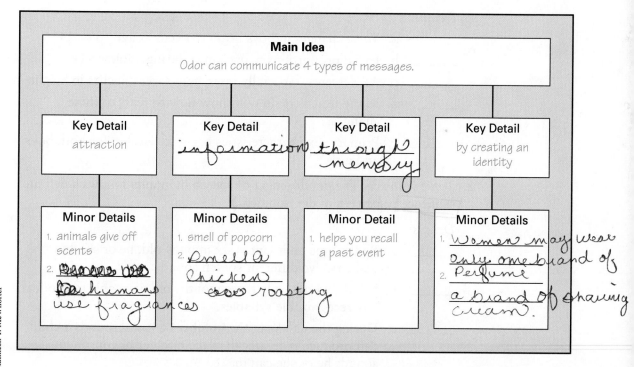

Main Idea

Odor can communicate 4 types of messages.

Key Detail	Key Detail	Key Detail	Key Detail
attraction	*information through memory*	*memory*	by creating an identity

Minor Details	Minor Details	Minor Detail	Minor Details
1. animals give off scents 2. *for humans use fragrances*	1. smell of popcorn 2. *Smell a Chicken roasting*	1. helps you recall a past event	1. *Women may wear only one brand of Perfume* 2. *a brand of shaving cream.*

B. Directions: *Read the paragraph again and list the four transitions the writer uses to help you find the four major details.*

1. *first* 2. *also* 3. *third* 4. *finally*

The diagram you completed in Exercise 6–1 is a **map**—a visual way of organizing information. By filling in—or drawing—maps you can "see" how ideas in a paragraph or essay are related. Chapter 8 gives you more information about mapping (see p. 242) and about other ways of organizing information.

Exercise 6–2	***Directions:*** *Each of the following topic sentences states the main idea of a paragraph. After each topic sentence are sentences containing details that may or may not support the topic sentence. Read each sentence and put a check mark beside those that contain major details that support the topic sentence.*

1. *Topic sentence:* Many dramatic physical changes occur during adolescence, between the ages of 13 and 15.

   Details:

   _____ a. Voice changes in boys begin to occur at age 13 or 14.

   _____ b. Facial proportions may change during adolescence.

   _____ c. Adolescents, especially boys, gain several inches in height.

   ___✓___ d. Many teenagers do not know how to react to these changes.

   _____ e. Primary sex characteristics begin to develop for both boys and girls.

2. *Topic sentence:* The development of speech in infants follows a definite sequence or (pattern of development.)

   Details:

   _____ a. By the time an infant is six months old, he or she can make twelve different speech sounds.

   _____ b. Mindy, who is only three months old, is unable to produce any recognizable syllables.

   _____ c. During the first year, the number of vowel sounds a child can produce is greater than the number of consonant sounds he or she can make.

   _____ d. Between six and twelve months, the number of consonant sounds a child can produce continues to increase.

   _____ e. Parents often reward the first recognizable word a child produces by smiling or speaking to the child.

3. *Topic sentence:* The main motives for attending a play are the desire for recreation, the need for relaxation, and the desire for intellectual stimulation.

   Details:

   _____ a. By becoming involved with the actors and their problems, members of the audience temporarily forget about their personal cares and concerns and are able to relax.

   _____ b. In America today, the success of a play is judged by its ability to attract a large audience.

   _____ c. Almost everyone who attends a play expects to be entertained.

   _____ d. Even theater critics are often able to relax and enjoy a good play.

   _____ e. There is a smaller audience that looks to theater for intellectual stimulation.

4. *Topic sentence:* Licorice is used in tobacco products because it has specific characteristics that cannot be found in any other single ingredient.

   Details:

   _____ a. McAdams & Co. is the largest importer and processor of licorice root.

   _____ b. Licorice blends with tobacco and provides added mildness.

   _____ c. Licorice provides a unique flavor and sweetens many types of tobacco.

   _____ d. The extract of licorice is present in relatively small amounts in most types of pipe tobacco.

   _____ e. Licorice helps tobacco retain the correct amount of moisture during storage.

5. *Topic sentence:* An *oligopoly* is a market structure in which only a few companies sell a certain product.

   Details:

   _____ a. The automobile industry is a good example of an oligopoly, even though it gives the appearance of being highly competitive.

   _____ b. The breakfast cereal, soap, and cigarette industries, although basic to our economy, operate as oligopolies.

_____ c. Monopolies refer to market structures in which only one industry produces a particular product.

_____ d. Monopolies are able to exert more control and price fixing than oligopolies.

_____ e. In the oil industry there are only a few producers, so each producer has a fairly large share of the sales.

Exercise 6–3

Directions: *Read the following paragraph and answer the questions that follow.*

The larger-scale and more technologically sophisticated a society, the weaker its ties of marriage, for several reasons. First, in large-scale societies, especially mobile ones like Western society, individuals continually meet new people of the opposite sex. Second, people are likely to live longer in technologically advanced societies, and longevity sometimes leads to marital discontent. Third, many of the functions of marriage in large-scale, technologically sophisticated societies are fulfilled by other institutions. A married person's economic support, for example, does not depend on cooperation with a spouse when both spouses earn paychecks outside their joint household and can continue to do so even if they part.

—Hicks and Gwynne, *Cultural Anthropology*, p. 258

1. Does the topic sentence occur first, last, or in the middle of the paragraph? _____

2. List the paragraph's three major details:

   _____

   _____

   _____

3. What transition words does the writer use to take the reader from one major detail to the next? *enumeration*

4. In the third sentence, what does the word **longevity** mean?

   _____

5. Is the last sentence the main idea of the paragraph, a major detail, or a minor detail? _____

What Are Transitions?

Transitions are linking words or phrases that lead the reader from one idea to another. If you get into the habit of recognizing transitions, you will see that they often help you read a paragraph more easily.

In the following paragraph, notice how the underlined transitions lead you from one detail to the next.

> When Su-ling gets ready to study at home, she follows a certain proce-dure. <u>First of all</u>, she tries to find a quiet place, far away from her kid sisters and brothers. This place might be her bedroom, <u>for example</u>, or it might be the porch or the basement, depending on how much noise the younger chil-dren are making. <u>Next</u>, she finds a snack to eat while she is studying, <u>such as</u> chips, an apple, or a candy bar. Sometimes, <u>however</u>, she skips the snack, especially if she is on a diet. <u>Finally</u>, Su-ling takes her books and notes to the quiet spot she has found. She usually does her most difficult homework first <u>because</u> she is more alert at the beginning.

Not all paragraphs contain such obvious transitions, and not all transi-tions serve as such clear markers of details. As you can see, transitions may be used for a variety of reasons. They may alert you to what will come next in the paragraph, they may tell you that an example will follow, or they may predict that a different, opposing idea is coming. Table 6-1 lists some of the most common transitions and indicates what they tell you.

TABLE 6-1   Common Transitions

Type of Transition	Example	What They Tell the Reader
Time sequence	first, later, next, finally	The author is arranging ideas in the order in which they happened.
Example	for example, for instance, to illustrate, such as	An example will follow.
Enumeration	first, second, third, last, another, next	The author is marking or identifying each major point. (Sometimes these may be used to suggest order of importance.)
Continuation	also, in addition, and, further, another	The author is continuing with the same idea and is going to provide additional information.
Contrast	on the other hand, in contrast, however	The author is switching to a different, opposite, or contrasting idea than previously discussed.
Comparison	like, likewise, similarly	The writer will show how the previous idea is similar to what follows.
Cause/effect	because, thus, therefore, since, consequently	The writer will show a connection between two or more things, how one thing caused another, or how something happened as a result of something else.

Directions: *Select the transitional word or phrase from the box below that best completes each of the following sentences. Two of the transitions in the box will be used more than once.*

on the other hand	for example	because	in addition
similarly	later	next	however

1. As a young poet, e. e. cummings was traditional in his use of punctuation and capitalization. _____, he began to create his own grammatical rules.

2. Many fruits are high in calories; vegetables, _____, are usually low in calories.

3. In order to sight-read music, you should begin by scanning it. _____, you should identify the tempo and whether the piece is written in a major or minor key.

4. Many rock stars have met with tragic ends. _____, John Lennon was gunned down, Buddy Holly and Ritchie Valens were killed in a plane crash, and Janis Joplin died of a drug overdose.

5. Hernando's sister made a delicious birthday cake for him. _____, she surprised him with a big party.

6. Using your birthdate as your computer password is not advisable _____ hackers may be able to guess your password and access your files.

7. Some scientists believe that intelligence is determined equally by heredity and environment. Other scientists, _____, believe that heredity accounts for about 60 percent of intelligence and environment for the other 40 percent.

8. Tigers tend to grow listless and unhappy in captivity. _____, pandas grow listless and have a difficult time reproducing in captivity.

9. American voters tend to vote according to the state of the economy. _____, if the economy is good, they tend to vote for the party in power and if the economy is poor, they tend to vote for the party not in power.

10. Liz refused to go to her friend's wedding _____ she knew her ex-husband would be there.

Exercise 6-5

Directions: Many transitions have similar meanings and can sometimes be used interchangeably. Match each transition in column A with a similar transition in column B. Write the letter of your choice in the space provided.

	Column A		Column B
_____	1. because	a.	therefore
_____	2. in contrast	b.	also
_____	3. for instance	c.	likewise
_____	4. thus	d.	after that
_____	5. first	e.	since
_____	6. one way	f.	finally
_____	7. similarly	g.	on the other hand
_____	8. next	h.	one approach
_____	9. in addition	i.	in the beginning
_____	10. to sum up	j.	for example

Exercise 6-6

Directions: Read each paragraph below and then complete the items that follow.

A. You can help prevent heat stress by following certain precautions. First, proper acclimatization to hot and/or humid climates is essential. Heat acclimatization increases your body's cooling efficiency; in this process, you increase activity gradually over 10 to 14 days in the hot environment. Second, avoid dehydration by replacing the fluids you lose during and after exercise. Third, wear clothing appropriate for your activity and the environment. And finally, use common sense—for example, on a day when the temperature is 85 degrees and the humidity is 80 per-cent, postpone your usual lunchtime run until the cool of evening.

—Donatelle, *Health: The Basics*, 5th Ed., pp. 290–291

List the transitional words or phrases in this paragraph that suggest enu-meration.

1. _____   2. _____   3. _____   4. _____

B. One indicator of good advertising is, of course, the impression it makes on consumers. But how can this impact be defined and measured? Two basic measures of impact are *recognition* and *recall*. In the typical recog-nition test, subjects are shown ads one at a time and asked if they have seen them before. In contrast, free recall tests ask consumers to think of what they have seen without being prompted for this information first. Under some conditions, these two memory measures tend to yield the same results; however, recognition scores tend to be more reliable and do not decay over time the way recall scores do. Recall tends to be more important in situations in which consumers do not have product data at their disposal, so they must rely on memory to generate this information. On the other hand, recognition is more likely to be an important factor in a store, where consumers are confronted with thousands of product options and the task may simply be to recognize a familiar package.

—adapted from Solomon, *Consumer Behavior: Buying, Having, and Being*, 5th Ed., pp. 92–93

List the transitional words or phrases in this paragraph that suggest contrast.

1. _____   2. _____   3. _____

C. Tuition vouchers are a set amount of money given by the government to parents that can only be used to pay for public or private school tuition. Supporters of tuition vouchers argue that by giving parents a choice in where they send their children to school, schools will have to pay more attention to the needs of students and their parents or risk losing stu-dents to competitive schools with better services. They also argue that schools that are guaranteed students solely because of their location have no incentive to improve. Further, voucher advocates argue that it is unfair that rich families have the ability to choose which school their children attend, but poor families do not.

—adapted from Edwards et al., *Government in America*, 10th Ed., pp. 654–655

List the transitional words or phrases in this paragraph that suggest con-tinuation.

1. _____   2. _____

D. The process of making an etching begins with the preparation of a metal plate with a *ground*—a protective coating of acid-resistant material that covers the copper or zinc. The printmaker then draws easily through the ground with a pointed tool, exposing the metal. Finally, the plate is immersed in acid. Acid "bites" into the plate where the drawing has exposed the metal, making a groove that varies in depth according to the strength of the acid and the length of time the plate is in the bath.

—Preble and Preble, *Artforms,* 7th Ed., p. 144

List the transitional words or phrases in this paragraph that suggest time sequence.

1. _____   2. _____   3. _____

E. Dangerous and dramatic mass movements, such as rock slides and mud-flows, can occur on steep slopes, especially during wet conditions. Steep slopes are prone to rock slides because the force of gravity pushing down on the rocks is likely to exceed the strength of the rocks. Landslides on steep slopes can follow intense rains, because material with a high water content is heavier, weaker, and less able to resist the force of gravity. The sliding material may break down into fluid mud, which flows downhill. Houses built on very steep slopes—along the west coast of North America, for example—risk damage from landslides and mudflows.

—adapted from Bergman and Renwick, *Introduction to Geography,* 2nd Ed., p. 106

List the transitional words or phrases in this paragraph that suggest the illustration and example pattern.

1. _____   2. _____

Putting It All Together

In Chapters 5 and 6 you have learned the four essential ingredients of a paragraph and how to find them. You know how to locate the general *topic* of a paragraph and its *main idea* in a topic sentence. You also know how to identify *details* and how to use *transitions* to help you. In short, you can recognize and put together all of the important parts of a paragraph. Sometimes, though, as you have probably noticed in your reading, the main idea of a paragraph is not always stated directly. Instead of being in a topic sentence—like the paragraphs you've been working with—a main idea may be **implied.** Paragraphs with implied main ideas will be covered in Chapter 7.

The Textbook Challenge

Part A: Student Resource Guide A

Using Textbook Excerpt 1, "Civil Liberties and the Right to Privacy" (p. 400), highlight the major supporting details of each paragraph. Circle the transitions.

Part B: A College Textbook

Choose a chapter that you have been assigned to read in a textbook for one of your other courses. For the first five pages, underline the major supporting details of each paragraph. Circle the transitions.

What Have You Learned?

Directions: To check your understanding of the chapter, select the word or phrase from the box below that best completes each of the following sentences. Keep in mind that five of the choices will not be used.

finally	next	minor details	on the other hand
first	transitions	main idea	major details
because	for example		

1. The details in a paragraph are intended to prove or explain the

   _____.

2. The most important details in a paragraph are its

   _____.

3. _____ are words or phrases that lead the

   reader from one idea to another.

4. Words such as *first*, *next*, and _____ tell you

   that the writer is putting ideas in the order in which they happened.

5. The phrase _____ tells you that the writer is

   switching to a different idea.

What Vocabulary Have You Lea

Directions: The words in colum
your mastery of these words b
meaning in column B.

Column A

_____ 1. anticipate

_____ 2. distinct

_____ 3. sophisticated

_____ 4. longevity

_____ 5. acclimatization   e. ad

Test-Taking Tip #6: Answering Detail Questions

Comprehension tests often include questions about supporting details in the paragraph or passage. Test writers do not usually use the term *supporting details*. Instead, they just ask questions that test your ability to understand the supporting details in a paragraph or passage. Use the following suggestions to answer questions about supporting details:

■ Don't try to memorize factual information as you read the passage the first time. You are usually allowed to look back to the passage in order to answer questions based on it.

■ As you read, pay attention to how the writer supports the main idea. You may discover the writer is giving a definition, making a comparison, or offering an example.

■ Don't trust your memory. If a question asks you a factual question, look back to the passage and find the answer. For example, if a question asks you to identify the date on which something happened or to identify the name of a person who performed an action, look back to the passage to find the date or name.

■ It may be necessary to consider several details together in order to answer a question. For example, a passage may give the date of one event and state that a second event occurred ten years later. (BuildingBlocks, Inc. was founded in 1991. . . . Ten years later the company began its first national advertising campaign.) The question may ask you to identify the date on which the second event occurred. (On what date did BuildingBlocks, Inc. begin its national advertising campaign?)

...ING SUPPORTING DETAILS

...ions: Read the following paragraph and then complete the diagram ...ow. Some of the items have been filled in for you.

There are four main types of sunglasses. The traditional *absorptive* glasses soak up all the harmful sun rays. *Polarizing* sunglasses account for half the market. They're the best buy for knocking out glare and reflections from snow and water, but they may admit more light rays than other sunglasses. *Coated* sunglasses usually have a metallic covering that itself reflects light. They are often quite absorptive, but a cheap pair of coated glasses may have an uneven or nondurable coating that could rub off after a short period of time. New on the market are the somewhat more expensive *photochromatic* sunglasses. Their chemical composition causes them to change color according to the brightness of the light: in the sun, they darken; in the shade, they lighten. This type of sunglasses responds to ultraviolet light only, and will not screen out infrared rays, so they're not the best bet for continual exposure to bright sun.

—George, *The New Consumer Survival Kit*, p. 114

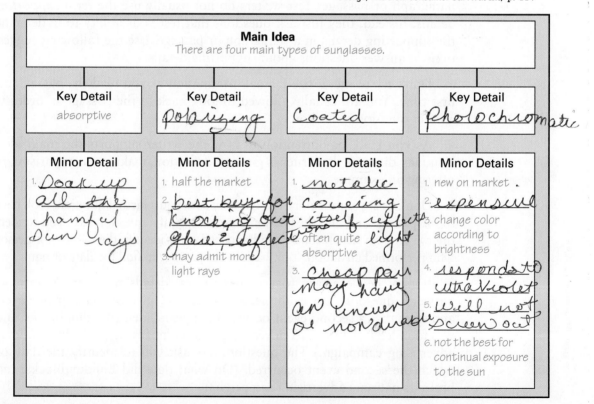

Main Idea
There are four main types of sunglasses.

Key Detail	Key Detail	Key Detail	Key Detail
absorptive	Polarizing	Coated	Photochromatic

Minor Detail	Minor Details	Minor Details	Minor Details
1. Soak up all the harmful sun rays	1. half the market 2. best buy for knocking out glare & reflections 3. may admit more light rays	1. metalic covering itself reflects 2. often quite absorptive 3. cheap pair may have an uneven or non'durable	1. new on market 2. expensive 3. change color according to brightness 4. responds to ultraviolet 5. Will not screen out 6. not the best for continual exposure to the sun

NAME _____ SECTION _____
DATE _____ SCORE _____

IDENTIFYING SUPPORTING DETAILS

Directions: Select the transitional word or phrase from the box below that best completes each of the following sentences. Use each transition only once.

also	because
~~second~~	finally
on the other hand	~~first~~
another	to illustrate
likewise	such as

When you begin to put together a new computer, you should *first* read the directions. *Second*, make sure that you have all of the various components, _____ the monitor, keyboard, and mouse. If you have everything, you can proceed with the assembly. _____, if you are missing an item, you might have to contact the store where you bought the computer. You might _____ have to wait for the missing component.

Once you actually begin to put the computer together, _____ point to remember is to work carefully, following the directions step by step. _____ you are working with electronic equipment, it is important to connect all of the components correctly. _____, if the printer is not plugged in properly, you will not be able to print out an e-mail message or an assignment for one of your classes. _____, the monitor must be connected at the right place or you won't have a screen on which to work. _____, when you have attached all of the components, you are ready to turn on your new computer and enjoy it.

IDENTIFYING SUPPORTING DETAILS

Directions: After reading the paragraph below, in the space provided, write the letter of the choice that best completes each of the statements that follow.

      The role of affirmative action in our multicultural society lies at the center of a national debate about how to steer a course in race and ethnic relations. In affirmative action, quotas based on race (and gender) are used in hiring and college admissions. Liberals, both white and minority, defend affirmative action, saying that it is the most direct way to level the playing field of economic opportunity. If whites are passed over, this is an unfortunate cost we must pay if we are to make up for past discrimination. Conservatives, in contrast, both white and minority, agree that opportunity should be open to all, but say that putting race (or sex) ahead of people's ability to perform a job is reverse discrimination. Because of their race (or sex), qualified people who had nothing to do with past discrimination are being discriminated against. They add that affirmative action stigmatizes the people who benefit from it because it suggests that they hold their jobs because of race (or sex), rather than merit.

—Henslin, *Essentials of Sociology*, p. 239

_____ 1. The topic of the paragraph is
    a. race relations.   c. affirmative action.
    b. discrimination.   d. economic opportunity.

_____ 2. The topic sentence occurs
    a. first.   c. last.
    b. second.   d. first and last.

_____ 3. The third sentence, which begins with the word "Liberals," is
    a. a transition.   c. the paragraph's main idea.
    b. a major detail.   d. a minor detail.

_____ 4. When the author moves to his second major detail, the transition he uses to provide a signal for the reader is
    a. *because.*   c. *in contrast.*
    b. *however.*   d. *but.*

_____ 5. The last sentence of the paragraph is
    a. its main idea.   c. a transitional statement.
    b. a major detail.   d. a minor detail.

NAME _____ SECTION _____

DATE _____ SCORE _____

IDENTIFYING SUPPORTING DETAILS

Directions: After reading the paragraph below, in the space provided, write the letter of the choice that best completes each of the statements that follow.

Several types of experiences influence how people feel about being touched. Our experiences as a child are one thing that affects our attitudes toward touching. Little girls, for example, are generally kissed and hugged more than little boys. As a result, women often like touching more than men. Our feelings about being touched also depend on our cultural background. Latin Americans and southern Europeans, for example, casually touch each other more than northern Europeans and most Americans. Social context as well influences our willingness to touch and be touched. Even men who are usually uneasy about touching may hug one another at an exciting sporting event.

_____ 1. The general topic of the paragraph is
   a. types of childhood experiences.
   b. how men and women feel about each other.
   c. how the fear of touching influences our lives.
   d. what affects our feelings about touching.

_____ 2. The topic sentence of the paragraph begins with the words
   a. "Several types."   c. "Social context."
   b. "As a result."   d. "Even men."

_____ 3. The major supporting details of the paragraph are
   a. Latin Americans, southern Europeans, and men at sporting events.
   b. childhood experiences, cultural background, and social context.
   c. willingness to be touched, and discomfort at being touched.
   d. little girls, little boys, and differences in being touched.

_____ 4. The first major supporting detail is signaled by the transitional word or phrase
   a. *one thing.*   c. *also.*
   b. *for example.*   d. *as well.*

_____ 5. Sentence 3, which begins with the words "Little girls," is

      a. a minor detail.   c. a transition.

      b. a major detail.   d. the paragraph's main idea.

_____ 6. The transition "as a result" in sentence 4 indicates

      a. the writer is putting ideas in order.

      b. an example will follow.

      c. the writer is continuing with the same idea.

      d. the writer will show how one thing caused another.

_____ 7. You know the author is moving to his second major supporting detail because he uses the transitional word or words

      a. _one._   c. _for example._

      b. _also._   d. _as well._

_____ 8. Sentence 6, which begins with the words "Latin Americans," provides

      a. minor details.

      b. the paragraph's main idea.

      c. major details.

      d. additional transitions.

_____ 9. The last major detail is about

      a. why northern Europeans dislike touching.

      b. why women like touching.

      c. how social context affects touching.

      d. how cultural background affects touching.

_____ 10. According to the paragraph,

      a. men never like to hug each other.

      b. Latin Americans casually touch each other more than southern Europeans.

      c. women who were never hugged as children will still like to be touched.

      d. two men might hug one another at an exciting baseball game.

IDENTIFYING SUPPORTING DETAILS

Directions: After reading the selection below, in the space provided, write the letter of the choice that best completes each of the statements that follow.

Corporations may be either public or private. The stock of a public corporation is widely held and available for sale to the general public. For example, anyone who has the money can buy shares of Caterpillar, Digital Equipment, or Time Warner. The stock of a private corporation, on the other hand, is held by only a few people and is not available for sale to the general public. The controlling group of stockholders may be a family, a management group, or even the firm's employees. Gallo Wine, Levi Strauss, and United Parcel Service are all private corporations. Because few investors will buy unknown stocks, most new corporations start out as private corporations. As the corporation grows and investors see evidence of success, it may issue shares to the public as a way to raise additional money. For example, Netscape Communications publicly issued stock for the first time in 1995. The firm quickly sold 81 million shares and raised over a billion dollars for new product development and expansion.

Corporations have several advantages. The biggest advantage is limited liability: The liability of investors is limited to their personal investments in the corporation. In the event of failure, the courts may seize and sell a corporation's assets but cannot touch the personal possessions of investors. For example, if you invest $1,000 in a corporation that goes bankrupt, you may lose your $1,000, but no more. In other words, $1,000 is the extent of your liability. Another corporate advantage is continuity. Because it has a legal life independent of its founders and owners, a corporation can, at least in theory, go on forever. Shares of stock, for example, may be sold or passed on from generation to generation. Moreover, most corporations also benefit from the continuity provided by professional management. Finally, corporations have advantages in raising money. By selling more stock, for instance, they can expand the number of investors and the amount of available funds. Continuity and the legal protections afforded to corporations also tend to make lenders more willing to grant loans.

—Griffin and Ebert, *Business,* p. 43

_____ 1. The topic sentence of the first paragraph begins with the words

    a. "The firm."   c. "Corporations may."

    b. "The controlling group."   d. "Because few."

_____ 2. The second sentence in paragraph 1, which begins with the words "The stock of a public corporation," is

   a. the paragraph's main idea.

   b. a major detail.

   c. a minor detail.

   d. an additional transition.

_____ 3. When the writer moves the discussion in paragraph 1 to private corporations, he uses the transition

   a. *for example.*   c. *in contrast.*

   b. *because.*   d. *on the other hand.*

_____ 4. The last sentence of paragraph 1 is

   a. a minor detail.

   b. a transition.

   c. a major detail.

   d. the paragraph's main idea.

_____ 5. The major supporting details of paragraph 2 are

   a. corporate advantages and disadvantages.

   b. limited liability, continuity, and raising money.

   c. investing and selling stock.

   d. corporations, founders, and owners.

_____ 6. In paragraph 2, the word **liability** means

   a. accuracy.   c. responsibility.

   b. honesty.   d. awareness.

_____ 7. In paragraph 2, the word **continuity** means

   a. having the ability to change.

   b. going on without interruption.

   c. knowing something is true.

   d. having the experience to succeed.

_____ 8. The last major detail in paragraph 2 begins with the transition

   a. *finally.*   c. *for example.*

   b. *also.*   d. *moreover.*

_____ 9. According to the selection,

    a. people should not invest in corporations.

    b. new corporations usually begin as private corporations.

    c. corporations often have difficulty raising money.

    d. Levi Strauss is a public corporation.

_____ 10. When the writer wants to add some specific information, he often uses the transition

    a. *another.*   c. *in other words.*

    b. *on the other hand.*   d. *for example.*

WHY GO VEG?
Barbara Tunick

Why become a vegetarian? This author describes some of the personal, social, and environmental reasons why people adopt a vegetarian lifestyle.

Vocabulary Preview

These are some of the difficult words in this essay. The definitions here will help you if you can't figure out the meanings from the sentence context or word parts.

chronic (para. 6) marked by long duration or frequent recurrence

degenerative (para. 6) tending to cause progressive deterioration of tissue or organs

mortality (para. 7) the state of being subject to death

arresting (para. 7) stopping

eschew (para. 12) to avoid habitually on moral or practical grounds

intolerant (para. 12) unable or unwilling to endure

sentient (para. 14) finely sensitive in perception or feeling

wreak havoc (para. 15) to cause confusion or destruction

vogue (para. 16) in fashion at a particular time

pacifist (para. 17) strongly and actively opposed to conflict

1   It's hip to be vegetarian today and we don't mean hip as in hippie. Sure, some of us might have love beads still hanging in the closet, but for the estimated 5 million Americans who have chosen a meat-free diet, reasons for going veg are as varied as our favorite '60s rock stars.

2   Some of us want to live longer, healthier lives or do our part to reduce pollution. Others of us have made the switch to preserve the earth's natural resources or because we've always loved animals and are ethically opposed to eating them.

3   Thanks to an abundance of scientific research that demonstrates the health and environmental benefits of a plant-based diet, even the federal government is recommending that Americans consume the majority of their calories from grain products, vegetables and fruits.

4   Why go veg? Here are six great reasons.

Get Healthy

5   The No. 1 reason most of us switch to a plant-based diet is because we're concerned about our health, says the Baltimore-based Vegetarian Resource Group. And there's good reason: An estimated 70 percent of all diseases—including one-third of all cancers—are related to diet.

6   A vegetarian diet reduces the risk for several chronic degenerative diseases, such as obesity, coronary artery disease, high blood pressure, diabetes and certain types of cancer—including colon, breast, prostate, stomach, lung and esophageal cancer. The China-Cornell-Oxford Project, a study of the diet and health of 6,500 people from 65 countries, found in the 1980s that rural Chinese people who consumed the least amount of fat and animal products had the lowest risks of cancer, heart attack and other chronic degenerative diseases, compared to those who consumed more animal products.

7   As for cardiovascular disease—the leading cause of death in the United States—not only is mortality lower in vegetarians than in nonvegetarians, but vegetarian diets have also been successful in arresting and reversing coronary artery disease, says Joel Fuhrman, MD, spokesperson for Physicians Committee for Responsible Medicine and author of *Eat to Live: The Revolutionary Plan for Fast and Sustained Weight Loss*.

Feel Younger; Live Longer

8   "If you switch from a normal American diet to a vegetarian diet, you can add about 13 healthy years to your life," says Michael F. Roizen, MD, dean of the School of Medicine, SUNY Upstate, Syracuse, New York, and author of *The Real Age Diet*. "People who consume saturated, four-legged fat have a shorter life span and more disability at the end of their lives. Animal products dog your arteries, zap your energy and slow down your immune system. Meat-eaters also experience accelerated cognitive and sexual dysfunction at a younger age."

9   In a 1976–1988 study of 34,000 Seventh-Day Adventists, researchers at Loma Linda University in California found that vegetarians live about seven

years longer than meat-eaters, and vegans—people who consume no animal products—live about eight years longer.

Lose Weight

10   Meat consumption is linked to obesity. According to the National Center for Health Statistics and the American Society for Clinical Nutrition, 61 percent of adults and 20 percent of U.S. children are overweight. A study from 1986–1992 by Dean Ornish, MD, a *Vegetarian Times* board member, found that overweight people who followed a low-fat, vegetarian diet lost an average of 24 pounds in the first year and had kept off that weight five years later.

11   Overweight people who adopted a low-fat, vegetarian diet lost weight without counting calories, measuring portions or, most importantly, feeling hungry. "It makes sense that you'll lose weight if you follow a low-fat, plant-based diet since you're eating less fat, no cholesterol and higher fiber," says Fuhrman. "Eliminating dairy from your diet is the first step to losing weight."

Resolve Digestive Difficulties

12   A number of people who become vegetarians eschew all milk and dairy products because they cause digestive complaints. According to the American Gastroenterological Association, close to 50 million Americans are lactose-intolerant or have trouble digesting the sugar, or lactose, found in milk and dairy products. As a result, they may experience abdominal bloating, flatulence, nausea or diarrhea after consuming milk or dairy products.

13   "Many people are also sensitive to milk protein," says John McDougall, MD, author of The McDougall Program for Women, which advocates a low-fat, vegetarian diet for optimum wellness. "Your immune system recognizes cow protein as foreign and makes antibodies against it. Unfortunately, these same antibodies attack our own tissues and cause problems like severe arthritis and even Type-1 diabetes."

Spare Animals

14   Many vegetarians give up meat because of their concern for animals. Eight billion animals are slaughtered for human consumption each year. And,

unlike farms of yesteryear where animals roamed freely, today most animals are "factory farmed"—crammed into cages where they can barely move and fed a diet tainted with pesticides. "If you believe that animals are sentient beings, how can you simply disregard their needs and comfort?" asks Polly Walker, MD, MPH, associate director for programs at Johns Hopkins University's Center for a Livable Future.

Reduce Pollution

15   Some people become vegetarian after realizing the devastation the meat industry is having on the environment. According to the U.S. Environmental Protection Agency, chemical and animal waste runoff from factory farms is responsible for more than 173,000 miles of polluted rivers and streams. "By concentrating thousands of animals into a small area, industrial animal production creates threats to both the environment and human health," says Walker. "Factory farms have the potential to wreak havoc on the environment, as was experienced in North Carolina during Hurricane Floyd in 1999."

Summing It Up

16   Health reasons, environmental concerns, ethics—whatever your motivation for choosing vegetarianism, you're in good company. Even though your love beads probably won't come back into style, good health will always be in vogue.

17   Beverly Cappel, DVM, always knew she wanted to be a veterinarian. "Even as a little girl I collected sick or injured animals," says Cappel, who runs a holistic veterinary care center in Chestnut Ridge, New York. "Our basement was filled with boxes and cages and crates of hurt birds, squirrels, chipmunks, cats and dogs." Cappel became a vegetarian in 1969, during her pre-veterinary training. "I've always loved animals, and I've always been a pacifist, so it makes perfect sense that I would be a vegetarian," she says. "I have to say, though, that while I became a vegetarian solely for ethical reasons, I would now have to include the health benefits as well."

━ · ━

Directions: In the space provided, write the letter of the choice that best completes each of the following statements.

CHECKING YOUR COMPREHENSION

_____   1. The main point of the selection is that
   a. vegetarians tend to be healthier than people who eat meat.
   b. the desire to improve body image is the main reason for becoming a vegetarian.
   c. people become vegetarians for emotional rather than physical reasons.
   d. there are a variety of reasons why people become vegetarians.

_____   2. The meat industry harms the environment by
   a. raising unhealthy animals.
   b. polluting the air.
   c. creating chemical and animal-waste run-off.
   d. producing meat that contains harmful chemicals.

_____   3. The primary (no. 1) reason for choosing a vegetarian diet is concern for
   a. one's health.
   b. digestive problems.
   c. animal rights.
   d. pollution.

_____   4. People who are lactose intolerant and consume dairy products may experience
   a. weight gain.
   b. nausea.
   c. guilt.
   d. asthmatic conditions.

_____   5. According to paragraph 10, people who follow a low-fat vegetarian diet
   a. learn to hate the taste of meat.
   b. lose and keep weight off.

c. usually feel hungry.

d. do not live longer than those on a high-fat diet.

USING WHAT YOU KNOW ABOUT SUPPORTING DETAILS

_____ 6. In paragraph 6, the phrase "such as" tells the reader that

a. an example will follow.

b. the author will show how one thing caused another.

c. the author will switch to a contrasting idea.

d. the author will identify each major point.

_____ 7. In paragraph 6, the topic sentence is expressed

a. in the first sentence.

b. in the second sentence.

c. in the middle.

d. in the last sentence.

_____ 8. In paragraph 17, the sentence that begins with the words "Our basement was filled" is a

a. transition.   c. major detail.

b. topic sentence.   d. minor detail.

_____ 9. In paragraph 15, the sentence that begins with the words "Some people become" is

a. a transition.

b. a major detail.

c. a minor detail.

d. the paragraph's main idea.

_____ 10. What percentage of diseases, including cancer, are related to diet?

a. 20 percent

b. 35 percent

c. 50 percent

d. 70 percent

USING CONTEXT CLUES AND WORD PARTS

_____ 11. In paragraph 1, the word **hip** means
- a. convenient.
- b. logical and reasonable.
- c. difficult and trying.
- d. aware of what is current.

_____ 12. In paragraph 3, the word **abundance** means
- a. defective quality.
- b. amply quantity.
- c. important ingredient.
- d. insignificant amount.

_____ 13. In paragraph 8, the word **consume** means
- a. eat.
- b. enjoy.
- c. eliminate.
- d. cook.

_____ 14. In paragraph 13, the word **sensitive** means
- a. care about.
- b. reject.
- c. dislike.
- d. affected by.

_____ 15. In paragraph 14, the word **tainted** means
- a. deposited.
- b. energized.
- c. contaminated.
- d. injected.

REVIEWING DIFFICULT VOCABULARY

Directions: Complete each of the following sentences by inserting a word from the Vocabulary Preview on page 188 in the space provided. Use each word only once.

16. Maria decided to _____ cigarette smoking.

17. Tattoos and other forms of body decoration are currently in _____ among some teenage groups.

18. My psychology instructor is _____ toward students who try to talk among themselves during a class lecture.

19. My father's _____ illness left him weak and discouraged.

20. Researchers hope to identify drugs that will be successful in _____ the spread of lung cancer.

STUDYING WORDS

_____ 21. The expression **"saturated, four-legged fat"** (para. 8) refers to
  a. low-fat meat.
  b. cholesterol-producing fat.
  c. processed fat.
  d. animal fat.

_____ 22. The word **coronary** (para. 6) is derived from which of the following languages?
  a. Latin
  b. Greek
  c. Spanish
  d. Arabic

_____ 23. What part of speech is the word **dairy** as used in paragraph 11?
  a. adjective
  b. noun
  c. adverb
  d. verb

_____ 24. The specialized meaning of the word **fiber** (para. 11) in the field of health is
  a. coarse substance that aids digestion.
  b. a thin, narrow root.
  c. a thread.
  d. a fundamental characteristic.

_____ 25. The word **obesity** (para. 10) is correctly pronounced
  a. AH beez i ty
  b. AHB eez ity
  c. OOH bees ity
  d. OHB ess ety

QUESTIONS FOR DISCUSSION

1. If a vegetarian lifestyle is healthier than a traditional American diet, why are more Americans not vegetarians?

2. Which of the six reasons offered in this reading for becoming a vegetarian do you find most reasonable and convincing? Which is least convincing?

3. Discuss what efforts are made in your campus's dining facilities to accommodate vegetarians.

WRITING ACTIVITIES

1. Try a vegetarian meal and write a paragraph describing your experience.

2. As mentioned in the article, obesity is becoming a serious problem in America. Write a paragraph discussing other ways to combat obesity.

3. Dr. Cappel describes how she loved animals as a child, which led her to become a veterinarian. Describe a hobby or interest you had as a child that might lead you to a particular profession, decision, or position on an issue.

Chapter 6: Identifying Supporting Details

RECORDING YOUR PROGRESS

Test	Number Right			Score	
Practice Test 6-1	_____	× 10	=	_____	%
Practice Test 6-2	_____	× 10	=	_____	%
Practice Test 6-3	_____	× 10	=	_____	%
Mastery Test 6-1	_____	× 10	=	_____	%
Mastery Test 6-2	_____	× 10	=	_____	%
Mastery Test 6-3	_____	× 4	=	_____	%

EVALUATING YOUR PROGRESS

Based on your test performance, rate how well you have mastered the skills taught in this chapter by checking one of the boxes below or by writing your own evaluation.

☐ **Need More Improvement**
Tip: Try using the "Supporting Details" Module on the Reading Road Trip Web site at **http://www. ablongman.com/readingroadtrip** to fine-tune the skills that you have learned in this chapter.

☐ **Need More Practice**
Tip: Try using the "Supporting Details" Module on the Reading Road Trip Web site at **http://www. ablongman.com/readingroadtrip** to brush up on the skills you have learned in this chapter, or visit this textbook's companion Web site at **http://www.ablongman.com/mcwhorter** for extra practice.

☐ **Good**
Tip: To maintain your skills, quickly review this chapter by using this textbook's companion Web site by logging on to **http://www.ablongman.com/mcwhorter**.

☐ **Excellent**

YOUR EVALUATION: _____

_____

_____

_____

_____

READ ME FIRST!

Study the cartoon below. The point the cartoonist is making is clear—"The dog ate my homework" is a common excuse given by students. Notice, however, that this point is not stated directly; instead, it is implied. To get the cartoonist's point, you have to study the details and dialogue in the cartoon and then figure out what the cartoonist is trying to say.

When you read a paragraph that lacks a topic sentence, you need to use the same reasoning process. You have to study all of the details and figure out the writer's main point. This chapter will show you how to figure out implied main ideas.

"Oh no, not homework again."

CHAPTER 7

Understanding Implied Main Ideas

What Does Implied Mean?

Just as you figured out the cartoonist's main point, you often have to figure out the implied main ideas of speakers and writers. When an idea is **implied,** it is suggested but not stated outright. Suppose your favorite shirt is missing from your closet and you know that your roommate often borrows your clothes. Thus, you say to your roommate, "If my blue plaid shirt is back in my closet by noon, I'll forget it was missing." This statement does not directly accuse your roommate of borrowing the shirt, but your message is clear—Return my shirt! Your statement implies or suggests to your roommate that he has borrowed the shirt and should return it.

Speakers and writers often imply ideas rather than state them directly.

Here is another statement. What is the writer implying?

EXAMPLE   I wouldn't feed that dessert to a dog.

You can figure out that the writer dislikes the dessert and considers it inedible even though this is not stated directly.

Exercise 7–1

Directions: For each of the following statements, choose the letter of the choice that best explains what the writer is implying or suggesting.

_____ 1. Jane's hair looked as if she just came out of a wind tunnel.

    a. Jane needs a haircut.   c. Jane needs a hat.

    (b.) Jane's hair is messed up.   d. Jane's hair needs coloring.

_____ 2. Dino would not recommend Professor Wright's class to his worst enemy.

    a. Dino likes Professor Wright's class.

    (b.) Dino dislikes Professor Wright's class.

    c. Professor Wright's class is popular.

    d. Professor Wright's class is unpopular.

_____ 3. The steak was overcooked and tough, the mashed potatoes were cold, the green beans were withered, and the chocolate pie was mushy.

    a. The dinner was tasty.

    b. The dinner was nutritious.

    (c.) The dinner was prepared poorly.

    d. The dinner was served carelessly.

_____ 4. Professor Rodriguez assigns three 5-page papers, gives pop quizzes, and requires both a midterm and final exam. In addition to reading chapters in the text every week, Leah must read three or four other articles. It is difficult to keep up.

    (a.) Professor Rodriguez's course is demanding.

    b. Professor Rodriguez is not a good teacher.

    c. Professor Rodriguez likes to give homework.

    d. Professor Rodriguez's course is unpopular.

_____ 5. The floor of the theater was scattered with popcorn; my feet stuck to the floor where soda had been spilled; the aisles were cluttered with candy wrappers.

    a. The theater's management is not well trained.

    b. The theater is well attended.

    (c.) The theater has not been cleaned.

    d. The theater was crowded.

Remembering the Difference Between General and Specific Ideas

When trying to figure out the implied main idea in a paragraph, it is important to remember the distinction between general and specific. From Chapter 5 you know that a *general* idea applies to many items or ideas, whereas a *specific* idea refers to a particular item. The word *color,* for instance, is general because it refers to many other specific colors—purple, yellow, red, and so forth. The word *shoe* is general because it can apply to many types, such as running shoes, high heels, loafers, and bedroom slippers. (For more information on general and specific ideas, see Chapter 5, page 134.)

Exercise 7–2	***Directions:*** *For each set of specific items or ideas, choose the letter of the choice that best applies to them. When choosing a general idea, be careful that it is not too general or too narrow.*

_____ 1. sledding, skiing, ice hockey, snowmobiling

      a. men's activities   c. winter sports

      b. Olympic events   d. recreational activities

_____ 2. cleaning the house, having a yard party, planting flowers, having a garage sale

      a. homeowner activities   c. general responsibilities

      b. daily chores   d. weekend jobs

_____ 3. answering the phone politely, taking accurate messages, being outgoing and positive

      a. how to be successful

      b. how to keep a job

      c. how to be a good receptionist

      d. how to assert yourself

_____ 4. cutting calories, jogging, eliminating desserts, working out at a gym

      a. ways to exercise

      b. ways to lose weight

      c. ways to make friends

      d. ways to improve your well-being

_____   5. to lower heating costs, to reduce drafts, to keep your house warmer

      a. reasons to insulate your house

      b. reasons to stay inside

      c. reasons to turn up the heat

      d. reasons to move south in the winter

You also know from Chapter 5 that the main idea of a paragraph is not only its most important point but also its most *general* idea. *Specific* details back up or support the main idea. In the paragraphs you studied in Chapters 5 and 6, the main idea was always stated in a topic sentence. In this chapter, however, because main ideas are implied, you have to look at the specific details to figure out the main idea. Like main ideas that are stated directly, implied main ideas are usually larger, more important, and more general than the details.

What larger, more general idea do the following specific details and the accompanying photograph point to?

Snow
wind

The wind was blowing at 35 mph.

The windchill was 5 degrees below zero.

Snow was falling at the rate of 3 inches per hour.

Together, these three details and the photograph suggest that a snowstorm or blizzard was occurring.

What general idea do the following specific sentences suggest?

The child refused to speak.

The child crossed his arms and turned his back.

The child then threw himself facedown on the floor.

You probably determined that the child was angry or having a temper tantrum.

Exercise 7-3

Directions: Read the specific details in each exercise, and then select the word or phrase from the box below that best completes the general idea in the sentence that follows. Make sure that each general idea fits all of its specific details. Not all words or phrases in the box will be used.

in an accident	a power outage	going too fast	dying
tonsillitis	the flu	a burglary	closed

1. The child has a headache.

   The child has a queasy stomach.

   The child has a mild fever.

   General idea: The child has ___the flu___.

2. The plant's leaves were withered.

   Its blossoms had dropped.

   Its stem was drooping.

   General idea: The plant was ___dying___.

3. The windshield of the car was shattered.

   The door panel was dented.

   The bumper was crumpled.

   General idea: The car had been ___in an accident___

4. The lights went out.

   The clock radio flashed.

   The refrigerator stopped running.

   General idea: There was ___a power outage___

5. The supermarket door was locked.

The parking lot was nearly empty.

A few remaining customers were checking out.

General idea: The supermarket was _____.

Directions: Study the photo shown here and then answer each of the following questions.

1. What do you think is happening in the photograph?

   _____

2. What general idea is the photographer trying to express through the photograph?

   _____

   _____

   _____

How to Find Implied Main Ideas in Paragraphs

As you know, when a writer leaves his or her main idea unstated, it is up to you, the reader, to look at the details in the paragraph and figure out the writer's main point.

The details, when taken together, will all point to a general and more important idea. You might want to think of such a paragraph as the pieces of a puzzle. You must put together the pieces or details to determine the meaning of the paragraph as a whole. Use the following steps as a guide to find implied main ideas:

1. **Find the topic.** As you know from earlier chapters, the *topic* is the general subject of the entire paragraph. Ask yourself: "What is the one thing the author is discussing throughout the paragraph?"

2. **Figure out what is the most important idea the writer wants you to know about that topic.** Look at each detail and decide what larger idea is being explained.

3. **Express this main idea in your own words.** Make sure that the main idea is a reasonable one. Ask yourself: "Does it apply to all of the details in the paragraph?"

EXAMPLE

Some advertisers rely on star power. Commercials may use celebrities, for example, to encourage consumers to purchase a product. Other commercials may use an "everyone's buying it" approach, arguing that thousands of consumers could not possibly be wrong in their choice, so the product must be worthwhile. Still other commercials may use visual appeal to catch the consumers' interest and persuade them to make purchases.

—Solomon, *Consumer Behavior: Buying, Having, and Being,* 4th Ed., pp. 49–50

The general topic of this paragraph is commercials. More specifically, the paragraph is about the various persuasive devices used in commercials. Three details are given: (1) star power, (2) the everyone's-buying-it approach, and (3) visual appeal. Each of the three details is a different persuasive device. The main point the writer is trying to make, then, is that commercials use a variety of persuasive devices to appeal to consumers. You can figure out this writer's main idea even though no single sentence states this directly. The diagram on page 206 can help you visualize the paragraph.

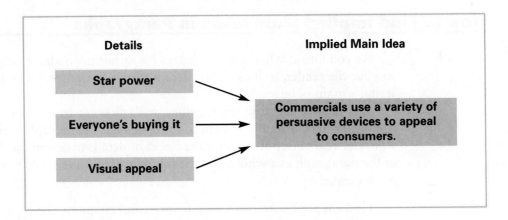

Here is another paragraph. Read it and then fill in the diagram that follows:

EXAMPLE

Yellow is a bright, cheery color; it is often associated with spring and hope-fulness. Green, since it is a color that appears frequently in nature (trees, grass, plants), has come to suggest growth and rebirth. Blue, the color of the sky, may suggest eternity or endless beauty. Red, the color of both blood and fire, is often connected with strong feelings such as courage, lust, and rage.

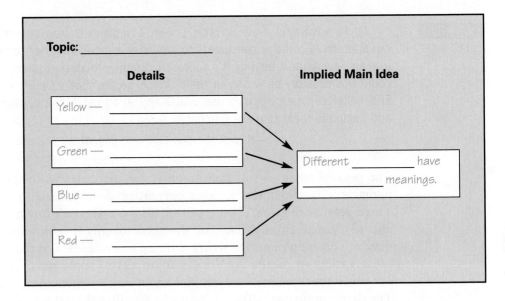

After you come up with a main idea, make sure it is broad enough. Every sentence in the paragraph should support the idea you have chosen. Work through the paragraph sentence by sentence. Check to see if each sentence explains or gives more information about the main idea. If some sentences do not explain your chosen idea, it probably is not broad enough. You may need to expand your idea and make it more general.

Exercise 7–5

Directions: After reading each of the following paragraphs, complete the diagram that follows.

1. In 1920 there was one divorce for every seven marriages in the United States. Fifty years later the rate had climbed to one divorce for every three marriages, and today there is almost one divorce for every two marriages. The divorce rate in the United States is now the highest of any major industrialized nation, while Canada is in a rather distant second place.

   —Coleman and Cressey, *Social Problems*, p. 130

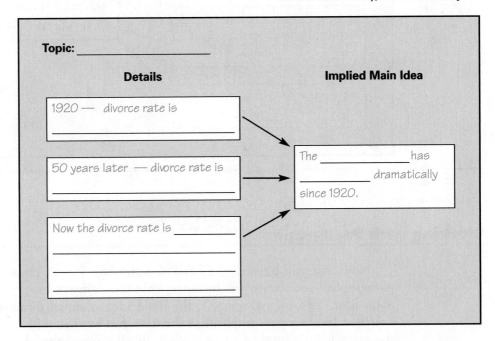

2. Immigration has contributed to the dramatic population growth of the United States over the past 150 years. It has also contributed to the country's shift from a rural to an urban economy. Immigrants provided inexpensive labor, which allowed industries to flourish. Native-born children of immigrants, benefiting from education, moved into professional

and white collar jobs, creating a new middle class. Immigration also increased the U.S. mortality rate. Due to crowded housing and unhealthy living conditions, disease and fatal illness were common.

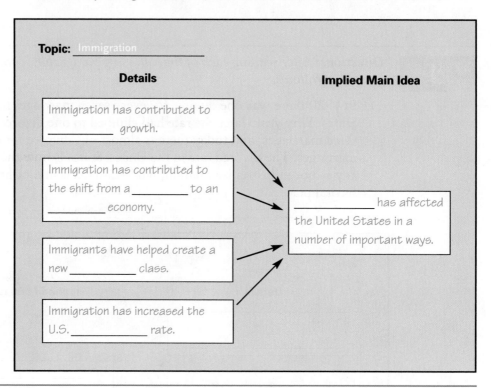

Topic: Immigration

Details

Immigration has contributed to _____ growth.

Immigration has contributed to the shift from a _____ to an _____ economy.

Immigrants have helped create a new _____ class.

Immigration has increased the U.S. _____ rate.

Implied Main Idea

_____ has affected the United States in a number of important ways.

Working with Paragraphs

Now that you have read Chapters 5 through 7, you know a lot about paragraphs. You know, for instance, that they always have a *topic* and a *main idea*. In some paragraphs, the main idea is stated directly in a *topic sentence*. In other paragraphs, like the ones you worked with in this chapter, the main idea is *implied* or suggested. In all paragraphs, the main idea is backed up by *details*. As you move on to Chapter 8, you will learn some ways to keep track of the kinds of information you've been learning. The methods in that chapter will help you with all kinds of reading—for this course, for other college courses, and for reading you do on the job or just for fun.

The Textbook Challenge

Part A: Student Resource Guide A

Using Textbook Excerpt 2 in Student Resource Guide A, page 403, write a topic sentence for each of the following paragraphs that have an unstated main idea.

1. Paragraph 10:_____

   _____

   _____

2. Paragraph 11:_____

   _____

   _____

Part B: A College Textbook

As you read chapters in your textbooks for other courses, mark any paragraphs that do not have a stated main idea. When you have finished reading your assignment, write topic sentences below for three of those paragraphs.

1. _____

   _____

2. _____

   _____

3. _____

   _____

What Have You Learned?

Directions: To check your understanding of the chapter, select the word or phrase from the box below that best completes each of the following sentences. Not all of the words or phrases in the box will be used.

important	in the writer's words	general
missing	specific	details
in your own words	implied	identity

1. When an idea is _____, it is suggested but not stated directly.

2. To figure out the main idea of a paragraph, it is important to understand the distinction between _____ and _____.

3. Main ideas are larger, more general, and more _____ than details.

4. When a writer does not state the main idea directly, you have to look at a paragraph's specific _____ in order to figure out the main idea.

5. Once you figure out the main idea in a paragraph, you should be able to express this idea _____.

What Vocabulary Have You Learned?

Directions: The words in column A appear in exercises in this chapter. Test your mastery of these words by matching each word in column A with its meaning in column B.

Column A	Column B
_____ 1. industrialized	a. in a city
_____ 2. distant	b. deadly
_____ 3. urban	c. become successful; thrive
_____ 4. flourish	d. having production or manufacturing companies
_____ 5. fatal	e. far away

Test-Taking Tip #7: Answering Questions about Implied Main Ideas

On reading comprehension tests you may encounter questions that ask you to understand and answer questions about implied main ideas. That is, you may find that the answer to a question is not directly stated in the paragraph or passage. Use the following suggestions to answer implied main idea questions:

▪ Concentrate on the details. Ask yourself: "What do all these details mean when taken together?"

■. Main ideas, whether implied or directly stated, are broad ideas. If you are unsure of an answer, choose a broad idea rather than a specific one. Here is a sample question based on a paragraph on the topic of body language:

Example: The main idea of the paragraph is that

a. women use body language to flirt.

b. a raised eyebrow signals interest.

c. a smile can be seductive.

d. the neck is considered important in flirting.

In this question, choice A is the broadest statement, while the others are more specific. Choice A is more likely to be an implied main idea than the remaining choices. The remaining choices are facts that offer specific information.

■   Once you have chosen a statement as the implied main idea of a paragraph, apply the following test. Reread each sentence of the paragraph. Check to be sure that each sentence supports or explains the statement you have chosen as the implied main idea. If you encounter one or more sentences that do not support the statement you have chosen, then reconsider your choice. Here is an example:

Paragraph: Some best sellers become best sellers because buyers recognize the author's name. John Grisham and Stephen King are good examples. The timing of a book's release also influences its sales. A book released in time for holiday sales or the beach reading season is more likely to succeed than books released midseason. Publicity also sells a book. If the book or author is featured on television talk shows, people are inspired to buy and read the book.

Question: The implied main idea of the paragraph is that

a. John Grisham is a best-selling author; people recognize his name.

b. Releasing books for the holiday season can help their sales.

c. Publicity can help make a book successful.

d. Numerous factors contribute to making a book a best seller.

Analysis:

Choice A: Not all sentences in the paragraph are about John Grisham, so it is not the implied main idea.

Choice B: Not all sentences in the paragraph are about the timing of a book's release, so it is not the implied main idea.

Choice C: Not all sentences are about publicity, so it is not the main idea.

Choice D: This is the correct answer. Each sentence in the paragraph is concerned with a factor that contributes to a book's sales.

UNDERSTANDING IMPLIED MAIN IDEAS

Directions: Read the specific details in each exercise and then select the word or phrase from the box below that best completes the general idea in the sentence that follows. Not all of the words in the box will be used.

cancelled	validated	impatient
spoiled	St. Patrick's Day	speeding ticket
dining	Super Bowl	overexposure
eating disorder	late	allergy
camping	vandalized	party

1. The window was shattered.

   Dresser drawers were emptied; clothing was thrown about.

   Furniture was overturned.

   General idea: The apartment had been _____.

2. The broccoli soup was left sitting unrefrigerated all afternoon.

   The soup was served to everyone at the banquet.

   Everyone who ate the soup got sick.

   General idea: The soup was _____.

3. The child was in the hot sun for four hours.

   She began to feel queasy.

   Her skin reddened.

   General idea: She was suffering from _____ to the sun.

4. The family unpacked tents.

   Everyone wore boots and warm clothing.

   Their food was hung from a rope in a tree.

   General idea: The family was _____.

5. Players on both teams were introduced.

   The national anthem was sung.

   The stadium was filled with cheering fans.

   General idea: The _____ was about to begin.

6. Janine, a teenager, was dangerously thin.

   She thought she needed to lose more weight.

   She often forced herself to vomit.

   General idea: Janine suffered from an _____.

7. The lecture hall in which the class was scheduled to meet was locked.

   There was a message posted on the door.

   Several classmates read the message and walked away.

   General idea: The class was _____.

8. It was a rainy day in March in Buffalo.

   Many people wore green.

   There were parades, and restaurants served corned beef and cabbage.

   General idea: It was _____.

9. A woman was seated alone at a table in a restaurant.

   She tapped her foot impatiently.

   She kept glancing at her watch.

   General idea: She was meeting someone who was _____.

10. Jeremy was driving 55 miles per hour.

    The speed limit in the residential area was 35 mph.

    In his rearview mirror he saw a police car with its lights flashing.

    General idea: Jeremy was going to get a _____.

UNDERSTANDING IMPLIED MAIN IDEAS

Directions: After reading each of the following paragraphs, complete the diagram that follows by filling in each blank line.

1. Severe punishment may generate such anxiety in children that they do not learn the lesson the punishment was designed to teach. Moreover, as a reaction to punishment that they regard as unfair, children may avoid punitive parents, who therefore will have fewer opportunities to teach and guide the child. In addition, parents who use physical punishment provide aggressive models. A child who is regularly slapped, spanked, shaken, or shouted at may learn to use these forms of aggression in interactions with peers.

—Newcombe, *Child Development,* p. 354

Topic: _____Severe Punishment_____

Details

Punishment may prevent _____ .

Punishment may cause children to _____ their parents, who will then have fewer _____ to teach and guide their children.

Parents who use physical punishment may provide _____ models for their children, who may then learn to use aggression with their _____ .

Implied Main Idea

Physical punishment has four negative _____ .

2. Traffic is directed by color. Pilot instrument panels, landing strips, and road and water crossings are regulated by many colored lights and signs. Factories use colors to distinguish between thoroughfares and work areas. Danger zones are painted in special colors. Lubrication points and removable parts are accentuated by color. Pipes for transporting water, steam, oil, chemicals, and compressed air are designated by different colors. Electrical wires and resistances are color coded.

—Gerritsen, *Theory and Practice of Color,* p. 9

Topic: _____

Details	**Implied Main Idea**

Color is used to direct _____.

Color is used in factories to _____
_____.

Color is used to identify danger _____.

Color is used to label _____.

Color is used to designate _____.

Color is used to label _____.

Color is used to _____
_____.

3. Jack Schultz and Ian Baldwin found last summer that trees under attack by insects or animals will release an unidentified chemical into the air as a distress signal. Upon receiving the signal, nearby trees step up their production of tannin—a poison in the leaves that gives insects indigestion. The team learned, too, that production of the poison is in proportion to the duration and intensity of the attack.

—"Trees Talk to One Another," *Science Digest*, p. 47

Topic: _____

Details	**Implied Main Idea**

Trees release _____ as a distress signal.

Nearby trees increase production of _____.

Production is in proportion to the _____ and _____ of the attack.

Trees have a process to protect themselves when they are _____.

NAME _____ SECTION _____

DATE _____ SCORE _____

UNDERSTANDING IMPLIED MAIN IDEAS

Directions: After reading each of the following paragraphs, select the letter of the choice that best answers each of the questions below.

Paragraph A

When President Lincoln was shot, the word was communicated by telegraph to most parts of the United States, but because we had no links to England, it was five days before London heard of the event. When President Reagan was shot, journalist Henry Fairlie, working at his typewriter within a block of the shooting, got word of it by telephone from his editor at the *Spectator* in London, who had seen a rerun of the assassination attempt on television shortly after it occurred.

—Naisbitt, *Megatrends*, p. 23

  1. What is the topic?

    a. communication of information

    b. President Lincoln

    c. assassinations

    d. President Reagan

_C_ 2. What main idea is the writer implying?

    a. U.S. presidents are in danger.

    b. The telegraph is outdated.

    c. The speed of communication has increased dramatically.

    d. Communication links between countries need to be built.

Paragraph B

The perceived richness or quality of the material in clothing, bedding, or upholstery is linked to its "feel," whether rough or smooth, flexible or inflexible. A smooth fabric such as silk is equated with luxury, although denim is considered practical and durable. Fabrics that are composed of scarce materials or that require a high degree of processing to achieve their smoothness or fineness tend to be more expensive and thus are seen as being higher class. Similarly, lighter, more delicate textures are assumed to be feminine. Roughness is often positively valued for men, and smoothness is sought by women.

—Solomon, *Consumer Behavior: Buying, Having, and Being*, 4th Ed., pp. 49–50

_____A_____ 3. What is the topic?

    (a.) the feel of fabrics

    b. expense in producing fabrics

    c. luxury clothing

    d. roughness in clothing

d 4. What is the writer saying about the topic?

    a. Denim is a practical and durable fabric.

    (b.) Men and women differ in their perception of quality.

    c. Fabrics made of scarce materials are expensive.

    (d.) The feel of a fabric influences how consumers regard its quality.

Paragraph C

A study by the market research department of the *New York Times* found that when choosing between two similar food or beverage products, 81 percent of consumers would choose one they could both smell and see over one they could only see. Samuel Adams beer was one of the first non-perfume products to be advertised with a scent strip that smelled of hops, and Rolls Royce distributed ads scented with the smell of leather. However, a note of caution: This technique adds at least 10 percent to the cost of producing an ad, so marketers will need to watch their dollars and scents.

—Solomon, *Consumer Behavior: Buying, Having, and Being,* 4th Ed., p. 48

_____ 5. What is the topic?

    a. market research study

    b. beer advertisements

    c. cost of advertisements

    d. the use of smells in advertising

_____ 6. What main idea is the writer implying?

    a. People have difficulty choosing between similar products.

    b. Advertisers are beginning to use scent as part of their advertisements.

    c. Advertising is expensive.

    d. Advertisers should control their spending.

_____ 7. Which one of the following details does *not* support the paragraph's implied main idea?

   a. Samuel Adams beer used scent strips.

   b. Consumers must always choose between two similar products.

   c. Rolls Royce used scented ads.

   d. Consumers prefer to both see and smell products.

Paragraph D

Your e-mail address will eventually become available to a lot of people you don't know. Some of these people may contact you with unsolicited information or with queries that you are not qualified to answer. If you are in a work situation in which it is appropriate to forward a query to someone else, then you have a legitimate right to pass mail on without further comment. Exercise your good judgment in these situations. Perhaps you will choose to reply to a message that interests you even if it might have been misdirected. But if you find yourself pressed for time and you discover yourself talking to perfect strangers about things that you aren't being paid to discuss, you need to get serious and ignore more of your mail. At the very least, forward legitimate queries to other people if you aren't the appropriate respondent.

—Lehnert, *Internet 101: A Beginner's Guide to the Internet and World Wide Web*, p. 95

_____ 8. What is the topic?

   a. legitimate queries   c. inappropriate e-mail responses

   b. unsolicited information   d. responding to e-mail

_____ 9. What is the writer saying about the topic?

   a. All e-mail messages deserve acknowledgement or responses.

   b. It is not always necessary to respond to e-mail messages.

   c. Work situations require a different type of e-mail response than personal situations.

   d. You should protect your e-mail address and restrict its use.

_____ 10. Which one of the following details does *not* support the paragraph's implied main idea?

   a. The use of e-mail programs will get easier in future years.

   b. E-mail can be forwarded to the appropriate respondent.

   c. Some e-mail can be ignored.

   d. It may not be your job to answer some e-mail.

UNDERSTANDING IMPLIED MAIN IDEAS

Directions: After reading each of the following paragraphs, select the letter of the choice that best completes each of the statements below.

Paragraph A

When a homemaker is killed in an auto accident, that person's family can often sue for the value of the services that were lost. Attorneys (who rely on economists) are often asked to make an attempt to estimate this value to present to the court. They add up the cost of purchasing babysitting, cooking, housecleaning, and tutoring services. The number turns out to be quite large, often in excess of $30,000 a year. Of course one of the problems in measuring the value of unpaid housework in such a way is that we could often purchase the services of a full-time live-in housekeeper for less money than if we paid for the services of the various components of housekeeping. And what about quality? Some homemakers serve fabulous gourmet meals; others simply warm up canned and frozen foods. Should they be valued equally? Another problem lies in knowing when to stop counting. A person can hire a valet to help him or her get dressed in the morning. Should we therefore count the time spent in getting dressed as part of unpaid work? Both men and women perform services around the house virtually every day of the year. Should all of those unpaid services be included in a "new" measure of GDP (Gross Domestic Product)? If they were, measured GDP would be increased dramatically.

—Miller, *Economics Today,* 8th Ed., p. 185

_____ 1. The implied main idea of the paragraph is

  a. it is difficult to place a dollar value on a homemaker's services.

  b. homemakers are not all valued equally.

  c. full-time housekeepers are expensive.

  d. homemakers provide a variety of services.

_____ 2. The statement that can reasonably be inferred from the details given in the paragraph is that

  a. all homemakers are underpaid.

  b. not all homemakers provide the same services.

  c. homemakers cannot fairly represent themselves in legal disputes.

  d. most homemakers are not recognized fairly by the people in their households.

_____ 3. A valet is a
   a. tutor.   c. homemaker.
   b. cook.   d. personal assistant.

_____ 4. It is cheaper to hire a full-time live-in housekeeper than it is to hire
   a. a number of different workers to handle each part of housekeeping.
   b. a valet.
   c. inexperienced workers.
   d. two half-time employees.

_____ 5. When the author says one of the problems is "knowing when to stop counting," he means
   a. costs add up quickly if one doesn't keep track.
   b. it is impossible to count a housekeeper's hours of work.
   c. assigning number values to homemakers' work is insulting.
   d. it is difficult to know what services to include in determining value.

Paragraph B

   In 1970 the federal government passed the Comprehensive Drug Abuse, Prevention and Control Act (also known as the Controlled Substance Act). That act did not contain a rigid penalty system but rather established only upper bounds for the fines and prison terms to be imposed for offenses. In 1984 the act was amended in order to impose fixed penalties, particularly for dealers. For anyone caught with more than 1 kilogram of heroin, 50 grams of cocaine base, or 1,000 kilograms of marijuana, the applicable penalty was raised to imprisonment from 10 years to life plus a fine of $4 million. A variety of other prison penalties and fines were outlined in that amendment. Another amendment passed in 1988 included the death penalty for "drug kingpins."

—Miller, _Economics Today_, 8th Ed., p. 513

_____ 6. The implied main idea of this paragraph is that
   a. drug laws are focused on users, not dealers.
   b. drug laws are becoming less effective.
   c. drug laws have become increasingly more strict.
   d. drug laws are effective in reducing drug abuse.

_____ 7. Drug laws have more severe penalties for
  a. drug users.
  b. underage users.
  c. dealers.
  d. countries that supply drugs.

_____ 8. The author arranged his details in the paragraph
  a. from least to most important.
  b. in the order in which events happened.
  c. from most to least important.
  d. in no particular order.

_____ 9. The 1984 amendment was probably designed to penalize
  a. recreational users.   c. dealers.
  b. underage users.   d. repeat offenders.

_____ 10. As used in the paragraph, the term **rigid** means
  a. weak.   c. lenient.
  b. fair.   d. strict.

NAME _____ SECTION _____
DATE _____ SCORE _____

UNDERSTANDING IMPLIED MAIN IDEAS

Directions: Read the following excerpt from an essay titled "My Grand-mother, the Bag Lady" by Patsy Neal. Then read each statement and decide whether it is an implied idea that can reasonably be drawn from the information presented in the passage. If the statement is reasonable, write **R** in the space provided; if it is not reasonable, write **NR**.

Almost all of us have seen pictures of old, homeless ladies, moving about the streets of big cities with everything they own stuffed into a bag or a paper sack.

My grandmother is 89 years old, and a few weeks ago I realized with a jolt that she, too, had become one of them. Before I go any further, I had best explain that I did not see my grandmother's picture on TV. I discovered her plight during a face-to-face visit at my mother's house—in a beautiful, comfortable, safe, middle-class environment with good china on the table and turkey and chicken on the stove.

My grandmother's condition saddened me beyond words, for an 89-year-old should not have to carry around everything she owns in a bag. It's enough to be 89, without the added burden of packing the last fragments of your existence into a space big enough to accommodate only the minutest of treasures.

Becoming a bag lady was not something that happened to her over-night. My grandmother had been in a nursing home these last several years; at first going back to her own home for short visits, then less fre-quently as she became older and less mobile.

No matter how short these visits were, her greatest pleasure came from walking slowly around her home, touching every item lovingly and spending hours browsing through drawers and closets. Then, I did not understand her need to search out all her belongings.

As she spent longer days and months at the nursing home, I could not help noticing other things. She began to hide her possessions under the mattress, in her closet, under the cushion of her chair, in every conceiv-able, reachable space. And she began to think that people were "stealing" from her.

_____ 1. The behavior of the author's grandmother changed as a result of living in a nursing home.

_____ 2. The grandmother is homeless.

_____ 3. The grandmother's bag may contain items she valued, such as jewelry, photographs, or family mementos.

_____ 4. The grandmother felt as if she could not trust others in the nursing home.

_____ 5. The grandmother is fond of her granddaughter.

_____ 6. The author feels sorry for her grandmother.

_____ 7. The grandmother's physical condition has gradually worsened.

_____ 8. When returning to her own home from the nursing home, the grandmother enjoyed being surrounded by her own possessions.

_____ 9. The author is pleased with the lifestyle a nursing home offers.

_____ 10. The writer thinks that the elderly are not capable of owning and managing property.

PRIMARY COLORS
Kim McLarin

This essay, originally published in the *New York Times Magazine*, describes a mother's response to her interracial child. Read it to discover how a mother copes with racial stereotypes.

Vocabulary Preview

These are some of the difficult words in this essay. The definitions here will help you if you cannot figure out the meanings from the sentence context or word parts.

albino (para. 2) person lacking pigment, so skin and hair are white

retrospect (para. 5) reviewing the past

eccentricities (para. 6) oddities

mischievous (para. 8) playful in a naughty or teasing way

abduction (para. 9) kidnapping

disconcerting (para. 10) upsetting

condemnation (para. 13) strong criticism or disapproval

allegiances (para. 13) loyalties

denounce (para. 13) to criticize openly

align (para. 14) join with others

---

1   A few weeks after my daughter was born, I took her to a new pediatrician for an exam. The doctor took one look at Samantha and exclaimed: "Wow! She's so light!" I explained that my husband is white, but it didn't seem to help. The doctor commented on Sam's skin color so often that I finally asked what was on her mind.

2   "I'm thinking albino," she said.

3   The doctor, who is white, claimed she had seen the offspring of many interracial couples, but never a child this fair. "They're usually a darker, coffee-with-cream color. Some of them are this light at birth, but by 72 hours you can tell they have a black parent."

4   To prove her point, she held her arm next to Samantha's stomach. "I mean, this could be my child!"

5   It's funny now, in retrospect. But at the time, with my hormones still raging from childbirth, the incident sent me into a panic. Any fool could see that Samantha wasn't albino—she had black hair and dark blue eyes. It must be a trick. The doctor, who had left the room, probably suspected me of kidnapping this "white" child and was outside calling the police. By the time she returned I was ready to fight.

6   Fortunately, her partner dismissed the albino theory, and we escaped and found a new pediatrician, one who knows a little more about genetic eccentricities. But the incident stayed with me because, in the months since, other white people have assumed Samantha is not my child. This is curious to me, this inability to connect across skin tone, especially since Samantha has my full lips and broad nose. I'll admit that I myself didn't expect Sam to be quite so pale, so much closer to her father's Nordic coloring than my own umber tones. My husband is a blue-eyed strawberry blond; I figured that my genes would take his genes in the first round.

7   Wrong.

8   Needless to say, I love Sam just as she is. She is amazingly, heartbreakingly beautiful to me in the way that babies are to their parents. She sweeps me away with her mischievous grin and her belly laugh, with the coy way she tilts her head after flinging the cup from her highchair. When we are alone and I look at Samantha, I see Samantha, not the color of her skin.

9   And yet I admit that I wouldn't mind if she were darker, dark enough so that white people would know she was mine and black people wouldn't give her a hard time. I know a black guy who, while crossing into Canada, was suspected of having kidnapped his fair-skinned son. So far no one has accused me of child abduction, but I have been mistaken for Samantha's nanny. It has happened so often that I've considered going into business as a nanny spy. I could sit in the park and take notes on your child-care worker. Better than hiding a video camera in the living room.

10   In a way it's disconcerting, my being mistaken for a nanny. Because, to be blunt, I don't like seeing black women caring for white children. It may be because I grew up in the South where black women once had no choice but to leave their own children and suckle the offspring of others. The weight of that past, the whiff of a power imbalance, still stains such pairings for me. That's unfair, I know, to the professional, hard-working (mostly Caribbean) black nannies of New York. But there you are.

11   On the flip side, I think being darker wouldn't hurt Samantha with black people, either. A few weeks ago, in my beauty shop, I overheard a woman trashing a friend for "slathering" his light-skinned children with sunscreen during the summer.

12   "Maybe he doesn't want them getting skin cancer," suggested the listener. But my girl was having none of that.

13   "He doesn't want them getting black!" she said, as full of righteous condemnation as only a black woman in a beauty shop can be. Now, maybe the woman was right about her friend's motivation. Or maybe she was 100 percent wrong. Maybe because she herself is the color of butterscotch she felt she had to declare her allegiances loudly, had to place herself prominently

high on the unofficial black scale and denounce anyone caught not doing the same. Either way, I know it means grief for Sam.

14   I think that as time goes on my daughter will probably align with black people anyway, regardless of the relative fairness of her skin. My husband is fine with that, as long as it doesn't mean denying him or his family.

15   The bottom line is that society has a deep need to categorize people, to classify and, yes, to stereotype. Race is still the easiest, most convenient way of doing so. That race tells you, in the end, little or nothing about a person is beside the point. We still feel safer believing that we can sum up one another at a glance.

━━ ▪ ━━

Directions: Select the letter of the choice that best completes each of the following statements.

CHECKING YOUR COMPREHENSION

_____ 1. The main point of this selection is that

     a. people classify others on the basis of skin color because it is what they notice first.

     b. being the mother of an interracial child has more negative than positive moments.

     c. having an interracial child is easier in the North than in the South.

     d. although people are still aware of race, most people realize that race is not important.

_____ 2. The main idea of paragraph 10 is that

     a. the author has negative feelings about black women caring for white children.

     b. black women have always cared for white children.

     c. Caribbean nannies are hardworking professionals.

     d. the author is used to seeing nannies because she grew up in the South.

3. One reason the author wishes her daughter were darker is that she

   a. wants Sam to identify more with her father's family.

   b. doesn't want Sam to have to use sunscreen.

   c. wants to travel to Canada with Sam.

   d. doesn't want black people to criticize Sam.

4. The details in paragraphs 1 through 6 are presented

   a. in the order in which they occurred.

   b. in random order.

   c. from the child's perspective.

   d. from the pediatrician's perspective.

5. Which statement best describes Sam's physical appearance?

   a. Sam is an albino.

   b. Sam flings her cup from her highchair.

   c. Sam has fair skin, dark hair, and blue eyes.

   d. Sam has dark skin and dark hair.

USING WHAT YOU KNOW ABOUT IMPLIED MAIN IDEAS

6. The main idea of paragraph 9 is that

   a. having people think she is not Samantha's mother has several advantages.

   b. people usually think a dark-skinned adult is not the parent of a light-skinned child.

   c. white people have more difficulty than black people in accepting skin tone differences in a parent and child.

   d. having a light-skinned child is easier for the author than having a dark-skinned child.

7. The incident at the pediatrician's office upset the author because she was afraid that

   a. her daughter might have a genetic abnormality.

   b. the doctor thought Samantha was not her child.

   c. her child might have been switched at birth.

   d. the doctor would harm Samantha.

_____ 8. The main idea of paragraph 8 is that

    a. Sam is a beautiful, teasing child.

    b. the author is most aware of Sam's skin tone when she is with other people.

    c. skin color does not come between the author and her daughter.

    d. the author feels guilty for wishing Sam were darker.

_____ 9. The author found a new pediatrician because the first one

    a. called in her partner to help her.

    b. had never examined an interracial child.

    c. seemed to know very little about genetics and interracial children.

    d. accused the author of kidnapping her child.

_____ 10. Which statement most accurately summarizes the author's attitude toward the incident with the first pediatrician?

    a. She feared she would be arrested.

    b. She still does not understand the incident.

    c. She believes the pediatrician should lose her license to practice medicine.

    d. She was upset at the time, but now understands that others will make the same mistakes.

USING CONTEXT AND WORD PARTS

_____ 11. In paragraph 1, a **pediatrician** is a doctor who

    a. cares for feet.

    b. treats the elderly.

    c. deals with emotional problems.

    d. cares for children.

_____ 12. In paragraph 6, **umber** means

    a. having reddish tones.   c. without color.

    b. a shade of brown.   d. pale.

_____ 13. In paragraph 10, **imbalance** means
        a. knowing too little.   c. having too much power.
        b. unevenness.   d. not understood.

_____ 14. In paragraph 11, **slathering** means
        a. artificially coloring.   c. scrubbing thoroughly.
        b. covering thickly.   d. applying unevenly.

_____ 15. In paragraph 15, **categorize** means
        a. to put into groups.   c. to reverse.
        b. to join.   d. to explain.

REVIEWING DIFFICULT VOCABULARY

Directions: Complete each of the following sentences by inserting a word from the Vocabulary Preview on page 000 in the space provided.

16. In _____, I wish I had majored in biology instead of history.

17. The judge's _____ of the rapist was severe.

18. My grandmother's _____ make her even more lovable and charming.

19. The news of his father's illness was very _____ to Jamall.

20. The child's _____ was the feature story on the national news.

STUDYING WORDS

_____ 21. The idiom **"on the flip side"** (para. 11) means
        a. in special cases.
        b. under no circumstances.
        c. considering the opposite point of view.
        d. finding fault with something.

_____ 22. The word **eccentricities** (para. 16) is correctly pronounced
   a. EK sen tris it tees.
   b. ek SEN ti sit eez.
   c. ek sen trisit EEZ.
   d. EK sen treez it ezz.

_____ 23. The word **prominently** (para. 13) is derived from which of the following languages?
   a. Greek
   b. French
   c. Spanish
   d. Latin

_____ 24. The specialized meaning of the word **Nordic** (para. 6) in the field of anthropology is
   a. abnormal coloration or shading.
   b. unique characteristic of the Normans.
   c. striking and unusual.
   d. tall, fair, and blue-eyed.

_____ 25. What parts of speech can the word **stereotype** (para. 15) be?
   a. noun and verb
   b. verb and adjective
   c. adjective and adverb
   d. noun and adjective

QUESTIONS FOR DISCUSSION

1. Identify categories other than race that people use to classify and stereotype others.
2. What stereotypes, either positive or negative, are associated with college students? Discuss ways to overcome these stereotypes.
3. People often assumed that Samantha was not the author's child. Discuss ways the author could respond to such people.

WRITING ACTIVITIES

1. Write a brief summary of the issues this reading addresses.

2. This selection originally appeared in the *New York Times Magazine*. Imagine that you first read it there, and write a letter to the editor expressing your reaction to Ms. McLarin's story.

3. In paragraph 13, a black woman declares her allegiances loudly. Write a paragraph describing a situation in which you felt compelled to declare your own "allegiances" on a particular issue.

4. Choose a stereotype that you feel is particularly unfair. Write a paragraph explaining why it is unfair and suggesting steps that can be taken to combat the stereotype.

Chapter 7: Understanding Implied Main Ideas

RECORDING YOUR PROGRESS

Test	Number Right			Score	
Practice Test 7-1	_____	× 10	=	_____	%
Practice Test 7-2	_____	× 10	=	_____	%
Practice Test 7-3	_____	× 10	=	_____	%
Mastery Test 7-1	_____	× 10	=	_____	%
Mastery Test 7-2	_____	× 10	=	_____	%
Mastery Test 7-3	_____	× 4	=	_____	%

EVALUATING YOUR PROGRESS

Based on your test performance, rate how well you have mastered the skills taught in this chapter by checking one of the boxes below or by writing your own evaluation.

☐ **Need More Improvement**
Tip: Try using the "Main Idea" Module on the Reading Road Trip Web site at **http://www.ablongman.com/readingroadtrip** to fine-tune the skills that you have learned in this chapter.

☐ **Need More Practice**
Tip: Try using the "Main Idea" Module on the Reading Road Trip Web site at **http://www.ablongman.com/readingroadtrip** to brush up on the skills you have learned in this chapter, or visit this textbook's companion Web site at **http://www.ablongman.com/mcwhorter** for extra practice.

☐ **Good**
Tip: To maintain your skills, quickly review this chapter by using this textbook's companion Web site by logging on to **http://www.ablongman.com/mcwhorter**.

☐ **Excellent**

YOUR EVALUATION: _____

_____

_____

_____

READ ME FIRST!

Suppose you were planning a two-week vacation through the state of Texas next summer. You might use a basic map to figure out your driving time and to highlight the main places you wanted to see. You could also go to a website such as MapQuest.com to determine the best route to take, as shown below. In addition, you might jot down a list of major cities and the attractions you didn't want to miss. Under "San Antonio," for example, you would probably write "the Alamo."

Just as there are several ways to keep track of information when you plan a vacation, there are several ways to keep track of information when you read.

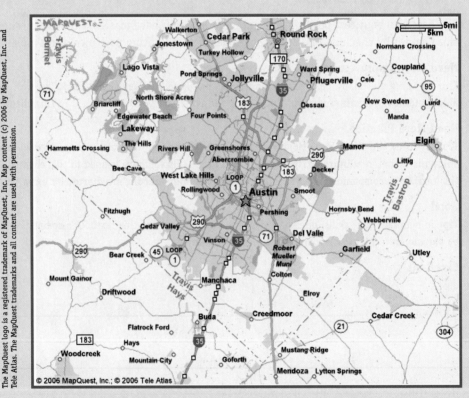

CHAPTER 8

Keeping Track of Information

Why Keep Track of Information?

As you plan a vacation, you often begin to collect all sorts of information—newspaper articles on various cities, brochures, restaurant suggestions from friends, and so forth. If you don't keep track of the various pieces of information, you soon discover that they are hard to find and thus are not very useful. For a trip to Texas, for instance, you might decide to sort what you've collected by city, putting everything for San Antonio in one large envelope, everything for Dallas in another envelope, and so forth.

When you read, the ideas and details you are learning about also become more useful if you can organize them in some way. In the preceding chapters, you discovered how to find main ideas and the details that support them. This chapter will show you five ways to keep track of this kind of information: (1) highlighting, (2) marking, (3) outlining, (4) mapping, and (5) summarizing. You may decide to use only a few of these methods, or you may decide to use different ones for different kinds of reading assignments. Whatever approach you take, keep in mind that all of these methods can help you remember what you have read—an important skill for studying and taking tests in college.

Highlighting and Marking

Highlighting and marking important facts and ideas as you read are effective ways to keep track of information. They are also big time-savers for college students. Suppose it took you four hours to read an assigned chapter in sociology. One month later you might need to review that chapter to prepare for an exam. If you did not highlight or mark the chapter the first time, then you might have to spend another four hours rereading it. However, if you had highlighted and marked as you read, you could review the chapter fairly quickly.

Highlighting Effectively   Here are a few basic suggestions for highlighting effectively:

1. **Read a paragraph or section first.** Then go back and highlight what is important.
2. **Highlight important portions of any topic sentence.** Also highlight any supporting details you want to remember (see Chapter 6).
3. **Be accurate.** Make sure your highlighting reflects the content of the passage.
4. **Highlight the right amount.** If you highlight too little, you may miss valuable information. On the other hand, if you highlight too much, you are not zeroing in on the most important ideas, and you will wind up rereading too much material when you study. As a general rule of thumb, highlight no more than 20 to 30 percent of the material.

Read the following paragraph. Notice that you can understand its meaning from the highlighted parts alone.

> Obviously, everybody spends part of his or her life as a single person. Traditionally, it was common that as adolescents entered adulthood, they felt compelled to find both jobs and marriage partners. Today, expectations and goals are changing. As an adolescent moves through high school, and perhaps college, he or she faces a number of decisions regarding the future. Marrying right after school is no longer a top priority for many, and the social stigma against remaining single is rapidly disappearing. In fact, single adults are now one of the fastest-growing factions in the United States; in the past two decades, the number of singles has more than doubled and now represents more than one-fourth of all households.

Exercise 8-1

Directions: Read the following paragraph, which has been highlighted two different ways. Look at each highlighted version, then write your answers to the questions that follow in the spaces provided.

Example 1

Money (or actually the lack of it) is a major source of stress for many people. In a sense, this is one of the most "valid" stressors because so many of our basic survival needs require money. Anyone struggling to survive on a small income is likely to feel plenty of stress. But money has significance beyond its obvious value as a medium of exchange. Even some of the wealthiest people become stressed over money-related issues. To some people, wealth is a measurement of human value and their self-esteem is based on their material assets. Stress management for such people requires taking an objective look at the role money plays for them.

—Byer and Shainberg, *Living Well: Health in Your Own Hands*, 2nd Ed., pp. 78–79

Example 2

Money (or actually the lack of it) is a major source of stress for many people. In a sense, this is one of the most "valid" stressors because so many of our basic survival needs require money. Anyone struggling to survive on a small income is likely to feel plenty of stress. But money has significance beyond its obvious value as a medium of exchange. Even some of the wealthiest people become stressed over money-related issues. To some people, wealth is a measurement of human value and their self-esteem is based on their material assets. Stress management for such people requires taking an objective look at the role money plays for them.

1. The topic sentence begins with the word _____.

2. Is example 1 or example 2 the better example of effective highlighting? _____

3. Why isn't the highlighting in the other example effective?

   _____

4. According to the writer, what two kinds of people may be stressed by money or the lack of it?

   a. _____   b. _____

Marking   Although highlighting can be very helpful, sometimes you may want to circle a word, ask a question, or write some other kind of note to yourself as you read. In these instances, try making notes in the margin in addition to highlighting.

Here are just a few ways to use marking:

1. **Circle words you do not know.**
2. **Mark definitions with "def."**
3. **Make notes to yourself**—such as "good example," "test question," "reread," or "ask instructor."
4. **Put question marks next to confusing words or passages.**

In the following passage, a student taking an introduction to business course has used marking as well as highlighting:

> U.S. companies have several (options) as to the products they sell outside the United States. They can sell the same product abroad that they sell at home, they can modify the product for foreign markets, or they can develop an entirely new product for foreign markets.
>
> *def*
>
> The simplest strategy is known as *product extension,* which involves offering the same product in all markets, domestic and foreign. This approach has worked successfully for companies including Pepsico, Coca-Cola, Kentucky Fried Chicken, and Levis. Pepsi and Coke are currently battling for market share in both Russia and Vietnam, countries with small but growing soft-drink markets. Both firms are producing and selling the same cola to the Russian and Vietnamese markets that they sell to other markets around the world. Not all companies that have attempted it, however, have found success with product extension. When Duncan Hines introduced its rich, moist American cakes to England, the British found them too messy to hold while sipping tea. Japanese consumers disliked the coleslaw produced by Kentucky Fried Chicken; it was too sweet for their tastes. KFC responded by cutting the sugar in half.
>
> *good examples of product extension not working*
>
> —Kinnear, Bernhardt, and Krentler, *Principles of Marketing,* 4th Ed., p. 132

Notice how the student has used marking to circle a word he's not sure of, to point out a definition, and to comment on some examples.

Exercise 8-2

Directions: Read the following paragraphs, which are a continuation of the preceding passage. Highlight and mark the paragraphs in a way that would help you remember the material and study it later.

When companies modify a product to meet local preferences or conditions, this strategy is known as *product adaptation.* Cosmetics companies produce different colors to meet the differing preferences of European consumers. French women like bold reds while British and German women prefer pearly pink shades of lipstick and nail color. Nestle's sells varieties of coffee to suit local tastes worldwide. Unilever produces frozen versions of local delicacies such as Bami Goreng and Madras Curry for markets in Indonesia and India.

Product invention consists of developing a new product to meet a market's needs and preferences. The opportunities that exist with this strategy are great since many unmet needs exist worldwide, particularly in developing and less-developed economies. Marketers have not been quick, however, to attempt product invention. For example, despite the fact that an estimated 600 million people worldwide still scrub clothes by hand, it was the early 1980s before a company (Colgate-Palmolive) developed an inexpensive, all plastic, manual washing machine with the tumbling action of an automatic washer for use in homes without electricity.

—Kinnear, Bernhardt, and Krentler, *Principles of Marketing,* 4th Ed., p. 132

Outlining

Making an outline is another good way to keep track of what you have read. **Outlining** involves listing major and minor ideas and showing how they are related. When you make an outline, follow the writer's organization. An outline usually follows a format like the one below:

I. First major topic
   A. First major idea
      1. First key supporting detail
      2. Second key supporting detail
   B. Second major idea
      1. First key supporting detail
         a. Minor detail or example
         b. Minor detail or example
      2. Second key supporting detail
II. Second major topic
   A. First major idea

Suppose you had just read a brief essay about your brother's vacation in Texas. An outline of the essay might begin like this:

I. Favorite cities
   A. San Antonio—beautiful, interesting history
      1. The Alamo
      2. Riverwalk
   B. Houston—friendly people
      1. Seeing Houston Astros play
         a. Excitement of game
         b. Getting lost after leaving Astrodome

Notice that the most important ideas are closer to the left margin. The rule of thumb to follow is this: The less important the idea, the more it should be indented.

Here are a few suggestions for using the outline format:

1. **Don't worry about following the outline format exactly.** As long as your outline shows an organization of ideas, it will work for you.
2. **Use words and phrases or complete sentences,** whichever is easier for you.
3. **Use your own words, and don't write too much.**
4. **Pay attention to headings.** Be sure that all the information you place underneath a heading explains or supports that heading. In the outline above, for instance, the entries "San Antonio" and "Houston" are correctly placed under the major topic "Cities." Likewise, "the Alamo" and "Riverwalk" are under "San Antonio."

Read the following paragraph on fashions, and then study its outline:

Why do fashions occur in the first place? One reason is that some cultures, like ours, *value change*: what is new is good, even better. Thus, in many modern societies clothing styles change yearly, while people in traditional societies may wear the same style for generations. A second reason is that many industries promote quick changes in fashion to increase sales. A third reason is that fashions usually trickle down from the top. A new style may occasionally originate from lower-status groups, as blue jeans did. But most fashions come from upper-class people who like to adopt some style or artifact as a badge of their status. But they cannot monopolize most status symbols for long. Their style is adopted by the middle class, maybe copied or modified for use by lower-status groups, offering many people the prestige of possessing a high-status symbol.

—Thio, *Sociology,* 5th Ed., p. 534

I. Why fashions occur
    A. Some societies like change.
        1. Modern societies—yearly changes
        2. Traditional societies—may be no change for many years
    B. Industries encourage changes to increase sales.
    C. Changes generally start at top.
        1. Blue jeans an exception—came from lower class
        2. Usually start as upper-class status symbol, then move to other classes

---

In this outline, the major topic of the paragraph, "Why fashions occur," is listed first. The writer's three main reasons are listed as A, B, and C. Supporting details are then listed under the reasons. When you look at this outline, you can easily see the writer's most important points.

Exercise 8–3

***Directions:** After reading the passage below and the incomplete outline that follows, fill in the missing information in the outline.*

CHANGING MAKEUP OF FAMILIES AND HOUSEHOLDS

The traditional definition of a typical U.S. household was one that contained a husband, a nonworking wife, and two or more children. That type of household accounts for only about 9 percent of households today. In its place we see many single-parent households, households without children, households of one person, and other nontraditional households.

A number of trends have combined to create these changes in families and households. Americans are staying single longer—more than one-half of the women and three-quarters of the men between 20 and 24 years old in the United States are still single. Divorce rates are at an all-time high. It is predicted that almost two-thirds of first marriages may end up in divorce. There is a widening gap between the life expectancy of males and females. Currently average life expectancy in the United States is 74 years for men and 78 years for women. Widows now make up more than one-third of one-person households in the United States. These trends have produced a declining average size of household.

The impact of all these changes is significant for marketers. Nontraditional households have different needs for goods and services than do traditional households. Smaller households often have more income per person than larger households, and require smaller houses, smaller cars, and smaller package sizes for food products. Households without children often spend more on personal entertainment and respond more to fads than do traditional households. More money may be spent on travel as well.

—Kinnear, Bernhardt, and Krentler, *Principles of Marketing*, 4th Ed., pp. 39–40

I. Typical U.S. household has changed
   A. Traditional household
      1. Husband
      2. Nonworking wife
      3. _____
   B. _____
      1. _____
      2. _____
      3. _____
II. Trends that created these changes
   A. _____

        1. One-half of women age 20–24

        2. Three-quarters of men age 20–24

    B. Divorce rates higher

        1. May be two-thirds of first marriages

    C. _____

        1. Women (78 years) live longer than men (74).

        2. Women are one-third of one-person households.

III. Impact of changes for marketers

    A. Different goods and services needed for traditional vs. nontraditional households

    B. Characteristics of smaller households

        1. _____

        2. _____

        3. _____

        4. _____

Mapping

In Chapter 6 you learned a little bit about **mapping** (p. 168), which is a visual method of organizing information. It involves drawing diagrams to show how ideas in a paragraph or chapter are related. Some students prefer mapping to outlining because they feel it is freer and less tightly structured.

Maps can take many forms. You can draw them in any way that shows the relationships between ideas. Figures 8-1 and 8-2 show two sample maps of the paragraph about fashions. Look at the maps and then look again at the outline of the fashions paragraph. Notice how the important information is included in each method—it's just presented differently.

As you draw a map, think of it as a picture or diagram that shows how ideas are connected. You can hand draw them or use a word processor. Use the following steps, which can be seen in Figures 8-1 and 8-2:

1. **Identify the overall topic or subject.** Write it in the center or at the top of the page.

2. **Identify major ideas that relate to the topic.** Using a line, connect each piece of information to the central topic.

3. **As you discover supporting details that further explain an idea already mapped, connect those details with new lines.**

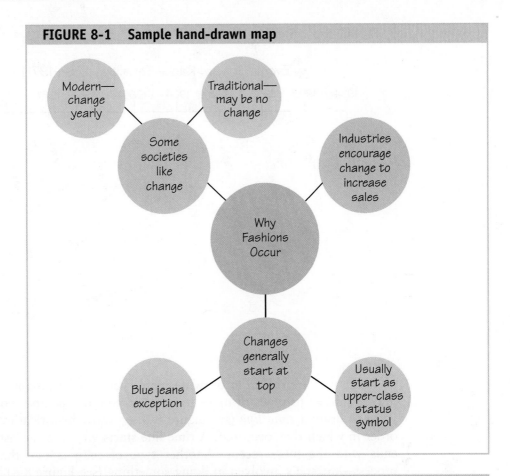

FIGURE 8-1   Sample hand-drawn map

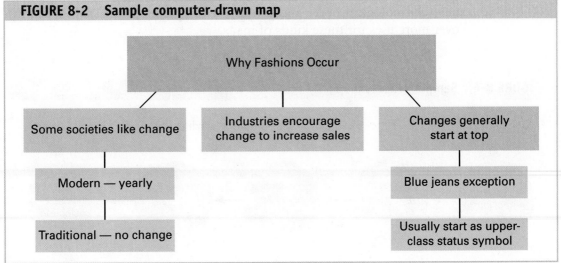

FIGURE 8-2   Sample computer-drawn map

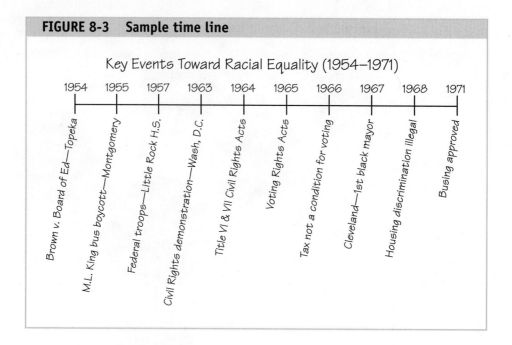

FIGURE 8-3   Sample time line

Key Events Toward Racial Equality (1954–1971)

1954 — Brown v. Board of Ed—Topeka
1955 — M.L. King bus boycott—Montgomery
1957 — Federal troops—Little Rock H.S.
1963 — Civil Rights demonstration—Wash, D.C.
1964 — Title VI & VII Civil Rights Acts
1965 — Voting Rights Acts
1966 — Tax not a condition for voting
1967 — Cleveland—1st black mayor
1968 — Housing discrimination illegal
1971 — Busing approved

Once you are skilled at drawing maps, you can become more creative, drawing different types of maps to fit what you are reading. For example, you can draw a *time line* (see Figure 8-3) to show historical events in the order in which they occurred. A time line starts with the earliest event and ends with the most recent. Another type of map is one that shows a process—the steps involved in doing something (see Figure 8-4). When you study chronological order and process in Chapter 9 (p. 281), you will discover more uses for these kinds of maps.

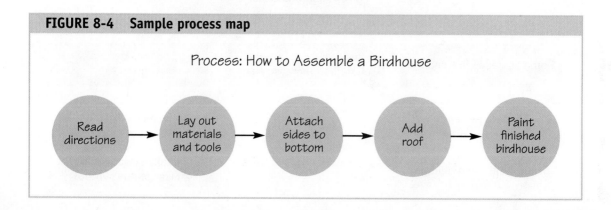

FIGURE 8-4   Sample process map

Process: How to Assemble a Birdhouse

Read directions → Lay out materials and tools → Attach sides to bottom → Add roof → Paint finished birdhouse

Exercise 8–4

Directions: Read the following paragraph and complete the map below, filling in the writer's main points in the spaces provided. Then answer the question that follows the map.

When your college work load increases, it is tempting to put things off. Here are some suggestions to help you overcome *procrastination,* which is the tendency to postpone tasks that need to be done. First, clear your desk. Move everything except the materials for the task at hand. Once you start working you will be less likely to be distracted. Second, give yourself five minutes to start. If you are having trouble beginning a task, working on it for just five minutes might spark your motivation. Next, divide the task into manageable parts. Working with just a part of a task is usually less overwhelming. Then, start somewhere, no matter where. It is better to do something rather than sit and stare. Finally, recognize when you need more information. Sometimes you may avoid a task because you're not sure how to do it. Discuss your questions with classmates or with your professor.

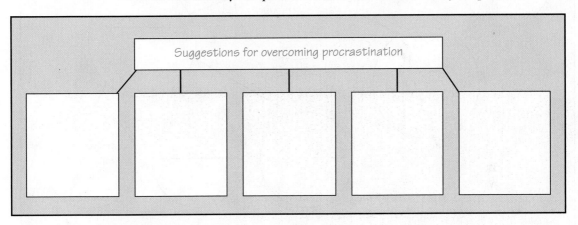

Suggestions for overcoming procrastination

1. What five transition words does the writer use to introduce the main points?

   a. _____   b. _____   c. _____   d. _____   e. _____

Exercise 8–5

Directions: After reading the following paragraphs, complete each section of the map in which a blank line appears. Fill in the writer's main points as well as some supporting details.

Animal diets vary *enormously,* and so do methods of feeding. Certain parasites—tapeworms, for instance—are absorptive feeders; lacking a mouth or digestive tract, they absorb nutrients through their body surface. In contrast, the majority of animals, including the great whales, are ingestive feeders; they eat (ingest) living or dead organisms, either plants or animals or both, through a mouth.

Animals that ingest both plants and animals are called omnivores. We humans are omnivores, as are crows, cockroaches, and raccoons. In contrast, plant-eaters, such as cattle, deer, gorillas, and a vast array of aquatic species that graze on algae are called herbivores. Carnivores, such as lions, sharks, hawks, spiders, and snakes, eat other animals.

—Campbell, Mitchell, and Reece, *Biology,* p. 430

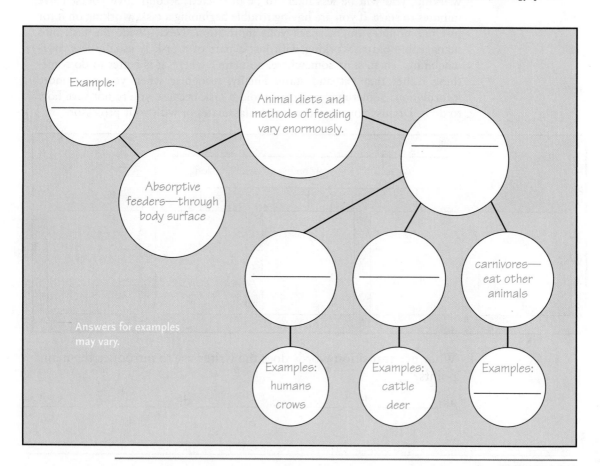

Summarizing

Summarizing is another good way to remember and keep track of information. A **summary** is a brief statement that pulls together the most important ideas in something you have read. It is much shorter than an outline and contains less detailed information. At times, you may want to summarize a paragraph, an essay, or even a chapter.

To write a good summary you need to understand the material and identify the writer's major points. Here are some tips to follow:

1. **Underline each major idea in the material.**

2. **Write one sentence that states the writer's most important idea.** This sentence will be the topic sentence of your summary.

3. **Be sure to use your own words rather than those of the author.**

4. **Focus on the author's major ideas,** not on supporting details.

5. **Keep the ideas in the summary in the same order as in the original material.**

Read the following summary of "Changing Makeup of Families and Households," which appeared in Exercise 8-3 on page 241.

> The typical U.S. household has changed from a husband, nonworking wife, and two or more children to a smaller sized unit that might contain a single parent, no children, or even only one person. Three trends have caused this change: people are staying single longer, divorce rates are higher, and women are outliving men by four years or more. Because of these changes, marketers have found that the current, smaller household needs different goods and services, has more income per person, tends to purchase smaller items, and spends more on entertainment, fads, and travel than the typical household of the past.

Notice that this summary contains only the most important ideas. Details are not included. The first sentence shows how the typical household has changed, the second sentence lists the three trends that are causing this change, and the last sentence lists the implication for marketers.

Exercise 8–6

A. Directions: *Read the following statements and mark each one true (T) or false (F).*

_____ 1. Summaries usually contain a lot of detailed information.

_____ 2. When writing a summary, it is important to use your own words.

_____ 3. The ideas in a summary should be in the same order as in the original material.

B. Directions: After reading the following paragraphs, choose the letter of the choice that best summarizes each one.

_____ 4. When a group is too large for an effective discussion or when its members are not well informed on the topic, a *panel* of individuals may be selected to discuss the topic for the benefit of others, who then become an audience. Members of a panel may be particularly well informed on the subject or may represent divergent views. For example, your group may be interested in UFOs (unidentified flying objects) and hold a discussion for your classmates. Or your group might tackle the problems of tenants and landlords. Whatever your topic, the audience should learn the basic issues from your discussion.

—Gronbeck et al., *Principles of Speech Communication*, p. 302.

a. Panel members are usually well informed on the subject, even though they may express different views. Members of a panel on UFOs, for example, may disagree about whether they exist.

b. Whatever topic a panel discusses, it is important that the audience learns basic information about the topic. For this reason, only well-informed people should participate in panels.

c. If a group is very large, or if its members are not familiar with a particular topic, a panel of people is sometimes chosen to talk about the topic. The rest of the group should get essential information from the panel's discussion.

d. Panels work effectively in large groups, such as in classrooms. Panels also work well when a group's members don't know very much about a topic. For example, a panel might talk about the problems of tenants and landlords to a group that was not familiar with such problems.

_____ 5. The process of becoming hypnotized begins when the people who will be hypnotized find a comfortable body position and become thoroughly relaxed. Without letting their minds wander to other matters, they focus their attention on a specific object or sound, such as a metronome or the hypnotist's voice. Then, based on both what the hypnotherapist [hypnotist] expects to occur and actually sees occurring, she or he tells the clients how they will feel as the hypnotic process continues. For instance, the hypnotist may say, "You are feeling completely relaxed" or "Your eyelids are becoming heavy." When people being hypnotized recognize that their feelings match the hypnotist's comments, they are likely to believe that some change is taking place. That belief seems to increase their openness to other statements made by the hypnotist.

—Uba and Huang, *Psychology*, p. 148

a. The first step in being hypnotized is for people to feel comfortable and at ease. Then, they pay close attention to a particular item or sound while the hypnotist tells them how they will feel. If they believe their feelings are the same as what the hypnotist is saying, they will be more likely to accept other comments the hypnotist makes.

b. If the hypnotist says, "Your eyelids are becoming heavy," then the person being hypnotized would believe such a statement. The person being hypnotized would also continue to believe other statements the hypnotist makes.

c. The most important part of being hypnotized is to feel comfortable and relaxed. If you are uncomfortable at the beginning, you might not be willing to accept what the hypnotist is saying. To feel relaxed try to focus on changes that are taking place.

d. If the hypnotist says that "You are feeling completely relaxed," people being hypnotized have to believe that this is true. If such belief does not occur, then it is unlikely that hypnosis will happen. Once the subject feels relaxed, his or her eyelids get heavy.

Good Reasons to Keep Track of Information

As you know, you will do a lot of reading in your college courses, and you will often be tested on what you have read. If you keep track of information as you go along, you will remember more of the material, and studying for tests or exams will be much easier. Instead of rereading everything, you can study from the notes, outlines, or maps you have already made. You now know five ways to keep track of information—highlighting, marking, outlining, mapping, and summarizing. Try out a few of these methods as you read the next chapters.

The Textbook Challenge

Part A: Student Resource Guide A

1. Using Textbook Excerpt 1 in Student Resource Guide A, page 400, read, highlight, and mark the selection.

2. Using Textbook Excerpt 1 in Student Resource Guide A, page 400, draw a time line showing historical documents or cases that address the right to privacy, either implicitly (indirectly) or directly.

3. Using Textbook Except 2 in Student Resource Guide A, page 403, write an outline of paragraphs 8–11.

4. Using Textbook Excerpt 3 in Student Resource Guide A, page 407, draw a map of paragraph 4.

Part B: A College Textbook

1. Choose a chapter you have been assigned. Read, highlight, and mark the chapter.

2. Choose a section of the chapter you used in #1, above. Write a summary of that section.

3. Choose another section of the chapter you used in #1 above. Write an outline of that section.

4. Choose another section of the chapter you used in #1 above. Draw a map of that section.

5. Evaluate each technique that you used above. Which worked best? Which helped you learn the information? Why?

What Have You Learned?

Directions: To test your understanding of the chapter and to review its major points, mark each of the following statements true (T) or false (F).

_____ 1. If people highlight too much material, they are probably not focusing on the most important ideas.

_____ 2. Highlighting is helpful if you want to circle a word, ask a question, or make a note to yourself as you read.

_____ 3. Outlining involves listing major and minor ideas and showing how they are related.

_____ 4. When you make an outline, the most important ideas are closer to the right margin.

_____ 5. Mapping is more structured than outlining.

_____ 6. A summary is a brief statement that pulls together the most important ideas in something you have read.

_____ 7. A time line is a kind of summary.

What Vocabulary Have You Learned?

Directions: The words in column A appear in exercises in this chapter. Test your mastery of these words by matching each word in column A with its meaning in column B.

Column A	Column B
_____ 1. significance	a. general tendencies
_____ 2. modify	b. eat
_____ 3. trends	c. different
_____ 4. ingest	d. meaning
_____ 5. divergent	e. change

Test-Taking Tip #8: Using Highlighting and Summarizing

Highlighting and summarizing can be helpful in certain test-taking situations. Use the following suggestions:

■ As you read a lengthy passage on a test, it may be helpful to quickly mark important ideas. For example, if a passage states that there are four key factors that contribute to building a successful Web site, as you find each of the factors, quickly mark or circle them. Then, as you answer detail questions, you can move back quickly to the appropriate section of the passage. (Be sure that you are allowed to write in your test booklet.)

■ If a question asks you to choose a statement that best summarizes the paragraph or passage, choose the statement that is the best restatement of the paragraph or passage's main idea.

■ If you are having trouble finding the main idea of a paragraph or passage, look away from it and try to summarize it in one sentence in your own words. Your summary statement will be the main idea. Try to find a choice that comes closest to your summary.

NAME _____ SECTION _____
DATE _____ SCORE _____

PRACTICE TEST 8-1

SUMMARIZING

Directions: After reading the following article, "Hispanic Americans," select the words and phrases from the box that follows the selection that best complete the summary. Use each word or phrase only once. Not all words and phrases in the box will be used.

HISPANIC AMERICANS

1   The umbrella term "Hispanic" describes people of many different backgrounds. According to the 2000 Census, nearly 60 percent of Hispanic Americans are of Mexican descent. The next largest group, Puerto Ricans, make up just fewer than 10 percent of Hispanics. Other groups counted in this category include Central Americans, Dominicans, South Americans, and Cubans.

2   The Hispanic subculture is a sleeping giant that until recently was largely ignored by many U.S. marketers. The growth and increasing affluence of this group has now made it impossible to overlook, and major corporations avidly court Hispanic consumers. Marketers especially like the fact that Hispanics tend to be brand loyal. In one study, about 45 percent reported that they always buy their usual brand, whereas only one in five said they frequently switch brands. Another study found that Hispanics who strongly identify with their ethnic origin are more likely to seek Hispanic vendors, to be loyal to brands used by family and friends, and to be influenced by Hispanic media. This segment is also highly concentrated geographically by country of origin, which makes them relatively easy to reach. More than 50 percent of all Hispanic Americans live in the Los Angeles, New York, Miami, San Antonio, San Francisco, and Chicago metropolitan areas.

3   Many initial efforts to market to Hispanic Americans were, to say the least, counterproductive. Companies bumbled in their efforts to translate advertising adequately or to compose copy that could capture desired nuances. These mistakes do not occur so much anymore as marketers are more sophisticated in dealing with this segment and tend to involve Hispanics in advertising production to ensure they are getting it right. The following are some translation mishaps that have slipped through in the past.

- The Perdue slogan, "It takes a tough man to make a tender chicken," was translated as "It takes a sexually excited man to make a chick affectionate."
- Budweiser was promoted as the "queen of beers."
- A burrito was called a *burrada,* which means "big mistake."
- Braniff, promoting the comfortable leather seats on its airplanes, used the headline, *Sentado en cuero,* which was interpreted as "Sit naked."
- Coors beer's slogan to "get loose with Coors" appeared in Spanish as "get the runs with Coors."

4   Nike made history in 1993 by running the first Spanish-language commercial ever broadcast in prime time on a major American network. The spot, which ran during the All-Star baseball game, featured boys in tattered clothes playing ball in the *Dominican Republic,* or *La Tierra de Mediocampistas* (the land of Shortstops). This title refers to the fact that more than 70 Dominicans have played for major league ball clubs, many of whom started at the shortstop position. This groundbreaking spot also laid bare some of the issues involved in marketing to Hispanics: Many found the commercial condescending (especially the ragged look of the actors), and felt that it promoted the idea that Hispanics don't really want to assimilate into mainstream Anglo culture.

5   If nothing else, though, this commercial by a large corporation was a wake-up call for many companies. Many are rushing to sign Hispanic celebrities, such as Daisy Fuentes and Rita Moreno, to endorse their products. Others are working hard to add more Hispanic consumers; CBS recently introduced Spanish-speaking characters on its soap opera *The Bold and the Beautiful*. Even the well-known movie star Raquel Welch is now 'repositioning" herself by reclaiming her Hispanic heritage. After starring in several movies and TV shows featuring Hispanic characters, Jo-Raquel Tejada (her real name) recently proclaimed, "Latinos are here to stay." The president of an ad agency specializing in the Latino market refers to this phenomenon as "Hispanization—or the Ricky Martin effect." She notes that firms are consciously using Hispanic references because these are cool and hip now. That's the thinking behind the new Dulce de Leche caramel variety of M&Ms, for example.

—Solomon, *Consumer Behavior: Buying, Having, and Being,* 6th Ed., pp. 480–481

Hispanization	Anglo life	celebrities
Daisy Fuentes	Nike	variety of people
made history	advertisers	Hispanic culture
geographic areas	assimilate	mistakes
Spanish-speaking	background	Budweiser
TV shows	cool	

SUMMARY

The term *Hispanic* is used to describe a wide _____ from different _____. Until recently, Hispanics have been ignored by advertisers. _____ are now interested in Hispanics because they are growing in wealth, they are brand loyal, and they live together in identifiable _____. Many efforts to reach Hispanics have not worked out and have resulted in embarrassing, and sometimes humorous, _____. _____ was the first company to run a Spanish-language commercial, and the commercial raised questions about how Hispanics should be portrayed and whether Hispanics want to be part of the _____. However, this commercial caught the attention of other companies, resulting in a rush to sign _____ and the increased presence of _____ characters in movies and _____.
As a result, references to Hispanics are now considered popular and hip.

KNOWING WHAT TO HIGHLIGHT

Directions: After reading the following passage, taken from a communications textbook, select the letter of the choice that best completes each of the statements that follow.

HUMOROUS APPEALS

1   The use of humor can be tricky, particularly since what is funny to one person may be offensive or incomprehensible to another. Specific cultures may have different senses of humor and use funny material in diverse ways. For example, commercials in the United Kingdom are more likely to use puns and satire than they are in the United States.

2   Does humor work? Overall, humorous advertisements do get attention. One study found that recognition scores for humorous liquor ads were better than average. However, the verdict is mixed as to whether humor affects recall or product attitudes in a significant way. One function it may play is to provide a source of *distraction*. A funny ad inhibits the consumer from counterarguing, thereby increasing the likelihood of message acceptance.

3   Humor is more likely to be effective when the brand is clearly identified and the funny material does not "swamp" the message. This danger is similar to that of beautiful models diverting attention from copy points. Subtle humor is usually better, as is humor that does not make fun of the potential consumer. Finally, humor should be appropriate to the product's image. An undertaker or a bank might want to avoid humor, but other products adapt to it quite well. Sales of Sunsweet pitted prunes improved dramatically based on the claim, "Today the pits, tomorrow the wrinkles."

4   An antismoking public campaign recently sponsored by the State of Arizona illustrates how humor can be used to transmit a serious message to an audience that may not be otherwise receptive to it. In a television commercial, a teenager sitting in a movie theater with his date spits gooey chewed tobacco in a cup. His date, who doesn't realize this, reaches over and takes a drink. The caption says, "Tobacco: a tumor-causing, teeth-staining, smelly, puking habit." The campaign is also selling merchandise with the slogan through its Smelly, Puking Habit Merchandise Center.

—Solomon, *Consumer Behavior: Buying, Having, and Being,* 4th Ed., pp. 252–253

1. In paragraph 1, which of the following word groups is *most* important to highlight?

   a. use of humor can be tricky

   b. in diverse ways

   c. particularly since what is funny

   d. commercials in the United Kingdom

2. In paragraph 1, which word or phrase serves as a transition?

   a. in the United States   c. for example

   b. specific cultures   d. more likely

3. In paragraph 2, which of the following word groups is *most* important to highlight?

   a. one study found

   b. in a significant way

   c. one function it may play

   d. humorous advertisements do get attention

4. Paragraph 2 begins with the question "Does humor work?" According to the passage, the best answer to that question is

   a. yes.

   b. no.

   c. only if humor serves as a distractor.

   d. the verdict is mixed.

5. The main idea of paragraph 3 is that

   a. there are several guidelines to follow in using humor in advertisements.

   b. undertakers and bankers might want to avoid humor.

   c. subtle humor is usually better.

   d. "Today the pits, tomorrow the wrinkles."

6. In paragraph 3, all of the following word groups are important to highlight *except*

   a. funny material does not "swamp" the message.

   b. subtle humor is usually better.

   c. humor should be appropriate to the product's image.

   d. sales of Sunsweet pitted prunes improved dramatically.

_____ 7. In paragraph 3, the Sunsweet pitted prune advertisement is
   a. the unstated main idea.   c. the main point.
   b. an example.   d. a transition.

_____ 8. In paragraph 4, the term **receptive** means
   a. open to.   c. angered by.
   b. opposed to.   d. object to.

_____ 9. The main idea of paragraph 4 is that humor can be used
   a. with audiences not willing to accept the advertiser's message.
   b. with teenagers.
   c. with controversial products.
   d. without offending the audience.

_____ 10. In paragraph 4, which of the following word groups is *most* important to highlight?
   a. reaches over and takes a drink
   b. humor can be used to transmit a serious message
   c. sponsored by the State of Arizona
   d. Smelly, Puking Habit Merchandise Center

OUTLINING

Directions: After reading the following passage, taken from a health text-book, fill in the missing information in the outline that follows.

CAFFEINE

Caffeine is the most popular and widely consumed drug in the United States. Almost half of all Americans drink coffee every day, and many others use caffeine in some other form, mainly for its well-known "wake-up" effect. Drinking coffee is legal, even socially encouraged. Many people believe caffeine is a nondrug item and not really addictive. Besides, it tastes good. Coffee and other caffeine-containing products seem harmless; with no cream or sugar added, they are calorie-free and therefore a good way to fill yourself up if you are dieting. If you share these attitudes, you should think again, because research in the last decade has linked caffeine to certain health problems.

Caffeine is a drug derived from the chemical family called *xanthines*. Two related chemicals, *theophylline* and *theobromine,* are found in tea and chocolate, respectively. The xanthines are mild central nervous system stimulants. They enhance mental alertness and reduce the feeling of fatigue. Other stimulant effects include increases in heart muscle contraction, oxygen consumption, metabolism, and urinary output. These effects are felt within 15 to 45 minutes of ingesting a caffeine-containing product.

Side effects of the xanthines include wakefulness, insomnia, irregular heartbeat, dizziness, nausea, indigestion, and sometimes mild delirium. Some people also experience heartburn. As with some other drugs, the user's psychological outlook and expectations will influence the stimulant effects of xanthine-containing products.

—Donatelle, *Health: The Basics,* 4th Ed., p. 213

    I. Caffeine—popular and widely consumed _____.

       A. Uses and benefits

          1. _____

          2. _____

          3. _____

       B. May create health problems

II. Physical effects of caffeine as a member of the drug family xanthine

   A. Mild stimulant

   B. _____

   C. Increases heart muscle contractions

   D. _____

   E. Increases metabolism

   F. _____

III. _____

   A. Wakefulness

   B. _____

   C. Dizziness

   D. Nausea

   E. Indigestion

   F. _____

   G. Heartburn

   H. User's state of mind may influence the effects of caffeine products

MAPPING

Directions: After reading the following passage, taken from a health text-book, fill in the missing information in the map that follows.

THIS THING CALLED LOVE

What is love? Finding a definition of love may be more difficult than listing characteristics of a loving relationship. The term *love* has more entries in *Bartlett's Familiar Quotations* than does any other word except *man*. This four-letter word has been written about and engraved on walls; it has been the theme of countless novels, movies, and plays. There is no one definition of *love*, and the word may mean different things to people depending on cultural values, age, gender, and situation.

Many social scientists maintain that love may be of two kinds: *companionate* and *passionate*. Companionate love is a secure, trusting attachment, similar to what we may feel for family members or close friends. In companionate love, two people are attracted, have much in common, care about each other's well-being, and express reciprocal liking and respect. Passionate love is, in contrast, a state of high arousal, filled with the ecstasy of being loved by the partner and the agony of being rejected. The person experiencing passionate love tends to be preoccupied with his or her partner and to perceive the love object as being perfect. According to Hatfield and Walster, passionate love will not occur unless three conditions are met. First, the person must live in a culture in which the concept of "falling in love" is idealized. Second, a "suitable" love object must be present. If the person has been taught by parents, movies, books, and peers to seek partners having certain levels of attractiveness or belonging to certain racial groups or having certain socioeconomic status and none is available, the person may find it difficult to allow him- or herself to become involved. Finally, for passionate love to occur, there must be some type of physiological arousal that occurs when a person is in the presence of the object of desire. Sexual excitement is often the way in which such arousal is expressed.

In his article "The Triangular Theory of Love," researcher Robert Sternberg attempts to clarify further what love is by isolating three key ingredients:

- *Intimacy:* The emotional component, which involves feelings of closeness.

- *Passion:* The motivational component, which reflects romantic, sexual attraction.

- *Decision/commitment:* The cognitive component, which includes the decision you make about being in love and the degree of commitment to your partner.

According to Sternberg's model, the higher the levels of intimacy, passion, and commitment, the more likely a person is to be involved in a healthy, positive love relationship.

—Donatelle, *Health: The Basics,* 4th Ed., p. 99

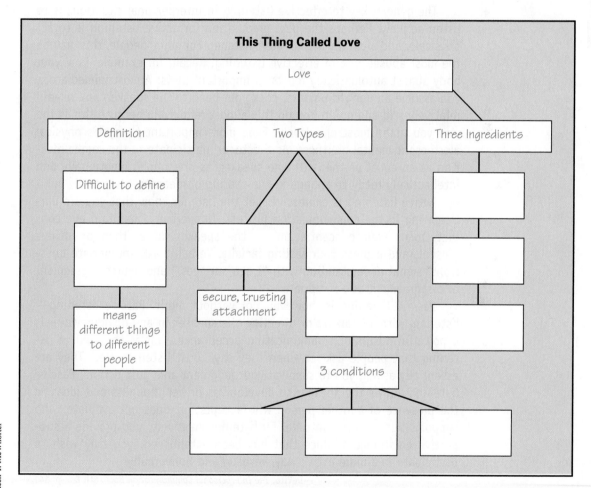

OUTLINING

Directions: After reading the following passage, fill in the missing information in the outline that follows.

ACTIVE AND PASSIVE LISTENING

The general key to effective listening in interpersonal situations is to listen actively. Perhaps the best preparation for active listening is to act physically and mentally like an alert listener. For many people, this may be the most abused rule of effective listening. Recall, for example, how your body almost automatically reacts to important news: Almost immediately, you assume an upright posture, cock your head to the speaker, and remain relatively still and quiet. You do this almost reflexively because this is the way you listen most effectively. Even more important than this physical alertness is mental alertness. As a listener, participate in the communication as an equal partner with the speaker, as one who is emotionally and intellectually ready to engage in the sharing of meaning.

Active listening is expressive. Let the listener know that you are participating in the communication process. Nonverbally, maintain eye contact, focus your concentration on the speaker rather than on others present, and express your feeling facially. Verbally, ask appropriate questions, signal understanding with "I see" or "yes," and express agreement or disagreement as appropriate.

Passive listening is, however, not without merit. Passive listening—listening without talking or directing the speaker in any obvious way—is a powerful means of communicating acceptance. This is the kind of listening that people ask for when they say, "Just listen to me." They are essentially asking you to suspend your judgment and "just listen." Passive listening allows the speaker to develop his or her thoughts and ideas in the presence of another person who accepts but does not evaluate, who supports but does not intrude. By listening passively, you provide a supportive environment. Once that has been established, you may wish to participate in a more active way, verbally and nonverbally.

—DeVito, *The Interpersonal Communication Book,* 8th Ed., p. 141

A. Active listening
1. Physical alertness
   a. Sit straight
   b. Tilt your _____
   c. Remain quiet
2. _____ alertness
   a. Be an equal partner
   b. Be ready to share _____
B. Letting the listener know you are participating
1. Nonverbal clues
   a. _____
   b. Pay attention to the speaker
   c. Express feeling with your _____
2. _____ clues
   a. Ask _____
   b. Signal understanding with words
   c. Express _____ or disagreement
C. Passive listening
1. Definition
   a. Listening without _____
   b. Listening without giving the speaker
      _____
2. Benefits
   a. Communicates acceptance
   b. Allows speakers to develop their own ideas
   c. Provides supportive environment

BODY PIERCING AND TATTOOING
Rebecca Donatelle

Tattoos and body piercings are increasingly popular. Read this selection, which first appeared in a college health textbook, to find out why "body art" is growing in popularity and to learn about the health risks associated with it.

> **Vocabulary Preview**
>
> These are some of the difficult words in this essay. The definitions here will help you if you cannot figure out the meanings from the sentence context or word parts.
>
> **enclaves** (para. 1) distinct groups or communities
>
> **medium** (para. 2) a means of conveying something
>
> **elitism** (para. 2) a perceived superiority
>
> **pathogens** (para. 6) disease-causing agents (germs)
>
> **adverse** (para. 6) unfavorable

1   One look around college campuses and other enclaves for young people reveals a trend that, while not necessarily new, has been growing in recent years. We're talking, of course, about body piercing and tattooing, also referred to as "body art." For decades, tattoos appeared to be worn only by motorcyclists, military guys, and general roughnecks; and in many people's eyes, they represented the rougher, seedier part of society. Body piercing, on the other hand, was virtually nonexistent in our culture except for pierced ears, which didn't really appear until the latter part of the twentieth century. Even then, pierced ears were limited, for the most part, to women.

2   Various forms of body art, however, can be traced throughout human history when people "dress themselves up" to attract attention or be viewed as acceptable by their peers. Examinations of cultures throughout the world, both historical and contemporary, provide evidence of the use of body art as a medium of self- and cultural expression. Ancient cultures often used body piercing as a mark of royalty or elitism. Egyptian pharaohs underwent rites of passage by piercing their navels. Roman soldiers demonstrated manhood by piercing their nipples.

The Popularity of Body Art

3   But why the surge in popularity of body art in current society, particularly among young people? Today, young and old alike are getting their ears and bodies pierced in record numbers, in such places as the eyebrows, tongues, lips, noses, navels, nipples, genitals, and just about any place possible. Many people view the trend as a fulfillment of a desire for self-expression, as this University of Wisconsin—Madison student points out:

> The nipple (ring) was one of those things that I did as a kind of empowerment, claiming my body as my own and refuting the stereotypes that people have about me . . . The tattoo was kind of a lark and came along the same lines and I like it, too . . . (T)hey both give me a secret smile.

4   Whatever the reason, tattoo artists are doing a booming business in both their traditional artistry of tattooing as well as in the "art" of body piercing. Amidst the "oohing" and "aahing" over the latest artistic additions, however, the concerns over health risks from these procedures have been largely ignored. Despite warnings from local health officials and federal agencies, the popularity of piercings and tattoos has grown.

Common Health Risks

5   The most common health-related problems associated with tattoos and body piercing include skin reactions, infections, and scarring. The average healing times for piercings depend on the size of the insert, location, and the person's overall health. Facial and tongue piercings tend to heal more quickly than piercings of areas not commonly exposed to open air and light and which are often teeming with bacteria, such as the genitals. Because the hands are great germ transmitters, "fingering" of pierced areas poses a significant risk for infection.

6   Of greater concern, however, is the potential transmission of dangerous pathogens that any puncture of the human body exacerbates. The use of unsterile needles—which can cause serious infections and can transmit HIV, hepatitis B and C, tetanus, and a host of other diseases—poses a very real risk. Body piercing and tattooing are performed by body artists, unlicensed "professionals" who generally have learned their trade from other body artists. Laws and policies regulating body piercing and tattooing vary greatly by state. While some states don't allow tattoo and body-piercing parlors, others may regulate them carefully, and still others provide few regulations and standards by which parlors have to abide.

Standards for safety usually include minimum age of use, standards of sanitation, use of aseptic techniques, sterilization of equipment, informed risks, instructions for skin care, record keeping, and recommendations for dealing with adverse reactions. Because of this varying degree of standards regulating the business and the potential for transmission of dangerous pathogens, anyone who receives a tattoo, body piercing, or permanent makeup tattoo cannot donate blood for one year.

Important Advice

7   Anyone who does opt for tattooing or body piercing should remember the following points:

- *Look for clean, well-lit work areas, and ask about sterilization procedures.*
- *Before having work done, watch the artist work. Tattoo removal is expensive and often undoable. Make sure the tattoo is one you can live with.*
- *Right before piercing or tattooing, the body area should be carefully sterilized and the artist should wear new latex gloves and touch nothing else while working.*
- *Packaged, sterilized needles should be used only once and then discarded. A piercing gun should not be used because it cannot be sterilized properly.*
- *Only jewelry made of noncorrosive metal, such as surgical stainless steel, niobium, or solid 14-karat gold, is safe for new piercing.*
- *Leftover tattoo ink should be discarded after each procedure.*
- *If any signs of pus, swelling, redness, or discoloration persist, remove the piercing object and contact a physician.*

Directions: Select the letter of the choice that best completes each of the following statements.

CHECKING YOUR COMPREHENSION

_____   1. The primary purpose of this selection is to
   a. discuss the use of body art throughout history.
   b. promote the use of body art as a form of self-expression.
   c. explain the cultural bases of body piercing.
   d. describe the health risks associated with body art.

_____   2. The selection focuses on the trend in body piercing and tattooing among
   a. women.
   b. ancient cultures.

    c. young people.

    d. people in the military.

_____ 3. According to the selection, anyone who has received a tattoo or body piercing must wait a year before

    a. donating blood.

    b. getting another tattoo.

    c. getting another piercing.

    d. having a tattoo removed.

_____ 4. One of the greatest health risks from body piercing and tattooing results from

    a. leftover ink.

    b. unsterile needles.

    c. allergic reactions.

    d. overexposure to air or light.

_____ 5. The laws and policies regulating body piercing and tattooing can best be described as

    a. strict in every state.

    b. moderate in every state.

    c. varying from state to state.

    d. completely nonexistent.

USING WHAT YOU KNOW ABOUT KEEPING TRACK OF INFORMATION

_____ 6. In paragraph 2, which sentence would be the most important to highlight?

    a. sentence 1   c. sentence 4

    b. sentence 2   d. sentence 5

_____ 7. Which of the following statements best summarizes paragraph 4?

    a. Local health officials and federal agencies are being ignored.

    b. Tattooing and body piercing have become more popular in spite of the health risks.

    c. The latest artistic additions in tattooing and body piercing have made body art more popular.

    d. Tattoo artists do a booming business.

The following map of paragraph 7 is referred to in questions 8, 9, and 10:

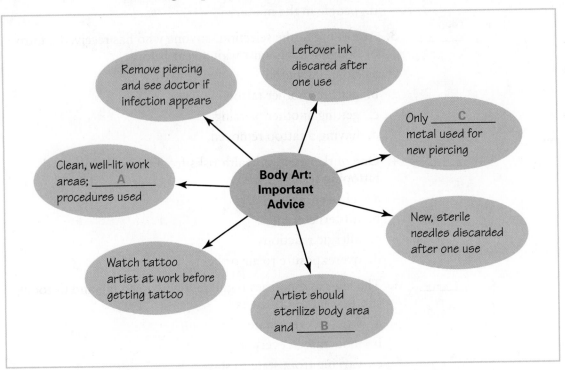

_____ 8. The word that belongs in the space marked A is

a. sterilization.   c. piercing.

b. medical.   d. regulation.

_____ 9. The words that belong in the space marked B are

a. demonstrate design.   c. guarantee work.

b. wear new gloves.   d. clean work area.

_____ 10. The word that belongs in the space marked C is

a. gold or silver.   c. jewelry.

b. brand new.   d. noncorrosive.

USING CONTEXT AND WORD PARTS

_____ 11. In paragraph 3, the word **surge** means

a. disapproval.   c. improvement.

b. increase.   d. decline.

_____ 12. In paragraph 5, the word **teeming** means
      a. lacking.   c. paired up.
      b. disappearing.   d. full of or overflowing with.

_____ 13. In paragraph 5, the word **transmitters** means
      a. carriers.   c. imitators.
      b. creators.   d. destroyers.

_____ 14. In paragraph 7, the word **discarded** means
      a. made clean.   c. untouched.
      b. thrown away.   d. used again.

_____ 15. In paragraph 7, the word **discoloration** means
      a. brightening.   c. fading or darkening.
      b. reduction in size.   d. infection.

REVIEWING DIFFICULT VOCABULARY

Directions: Match each word in column A with its meaning in column B.

Column A	Column B
_____ 16. enclave	a. a perceived superiority
_____ 17. medium	b. unfavorable
_____ 18. elitism	c. distinct group or community
_____ 19. pathogens	d. a means of conveying something
_____ 20. adverse	e. disease-causing agents

STUDYING WORDS

_____ 21. The meaning of the word **examinations** (para. 2) as it is used in the reading is
      a. interrogations in a court of law.
      b. close studies and analyses.
      c. test situations.
      d. studies of samples for medical diagnoses.

_____ 22. The word **pathogens** (para. 6) is correctly pronounced
      a. pat O gens.
      b. PA the o gens.

    c. PATH o gens.

    d. pa the OGENS.

_____ 23. The word **tetanus** (para. 6) is derived from which of the following languages?

    a. Latin

    b. French

    c. Spanish

    d. German

_____ 24. The restrictive meaning of the word **medium** (para. 2) in the field of biology is

    a. someone who communicates with the dead.

    b. neither large nor small.

    c. substance in which an organism grows.

    d. state between extremes.

_____ 25. What part of speech is the word **seedier** (para. 1)?

    a. adverb

    b. verb

    c. noun

    d. adjective

QUESTIONS FOR DISCUSSION

1. Do you have a tattoo or a piercing, or do you know someone who does? Discuss your reasons for (or against) getting a tattoo or a piercing.

2. Do you think the popularity of body art has increased its acceptability in society? How do you think older and younger generations perceive body art?

3. Discuss other means of self-expression that you have observed (or participate in yourself). How do they compare with body art?

WRITING ACTIVITIES

1. Write a letter to a friend in which you make a case for or against that person getting a tattoo. Try to present a convincing argument.

2. Write a summary of paragraphs 5 and 6.

3. Create an outline of the selection.

Chapter 8: Keeping Track of Information

Test	Number Right		Score
Practice Test 8-1	_____	× 10 =	_____%
Practice Test 8-2	_____	× 10 =	_____%
Practice Test 8-3	_____	× 10 =	_____%
Mastery Test 8-1	_____	× 10 =	_____%
Mastery Test 8-2	_____	× 10 =	_____%
Mastery Test 8-3	_____	× 4 =	_____%

EVALUATING YOUR PROGRESS

Based on your test performance, rate how well you have mastered the skills taught in this chapter by checking one of the boxes below or by writing your own evaluation.

☐ **Need More Improvement**
Tip: Try using the "Outlining, Summarizing, Mapping, & Paraphrasing" Module on the Reading Road Trip Web site at **http://www.ablongman.com/readingroadtrip** to fine-tune the skills that you have learned in this chapter.

☐ **Need More Practice**
Tip: Try using the "Outlining, Summarizing, Mapping, & Paraphrasing" Module on the Reading Road Trip Web site at **http://www.ablongman.com/readingroadtrip** to brush up on the skills you have learned in this chapter, or visit this textbook's companion Web site at **http://www.ablongman.com/ mcwhorter** for extra practice.

☐ **Good**
Tip: To maintain your skills, quickly review this chapter by using this textbook's companion Web site by logging on to **http://www.ablongman.com/mcwhorter**.

☐ **Excellent**

YOUR EVALUATION: _____

_____

_____

_____

READ ME FIRST!

Imagine that your bedroom looks like one of the pictures below. If you were looking for your favorite sweatshirt and a clean pair of socks, finding them would be a problem in the room on the left. The other room, however, is pretty neat and organized, so socks and sweatshirts are probably in a particular drawer or on a certain shelf. Being organized may not always be fun, but it makes it easier to find what you're looking for.

Organization is also important in paragraphs and in longer pieces of writing. Good writers try to follow a clear *pattern* when they write so that readers can easily find and understand the important points they are making.

CHAPTER 9

Recognizing the Basic Patterns of Organization

What Are Patterns of Organization?

Just as there is no one way to organize a room, there is no one way to organize a paragraph or essay. Writers use a variety of *patterns of organization,* depending on what they want to accomplish. These patterns, then, are the different ways that writers present their ideas.

To help you think about patterns a bit, complete each of the following steps:

1. Study each of the drawings below for a few seconds (count to ten as you look at each one).
2. Cover up the drawings and try to draw each from memory.
3. Check to see how many you had exactly correct.

You probably drew all but the fourth correctly. Why do you think you got that one wrong? How does it differ from the others?

Drawings 1, 2, 3, and 5 have patterns. Drawing 4, however, has no pattern; it is just a line that goes in random directions.

From this experiment you can see that it is easier to remember drawings that have a pattern—a clear form of organization. The same is true of written material. If you can see how a paragraph or essay is organized, it is easier to understand and remember. In this chapter you will learn about some of the common patterns writers use and how to recognize them: (1) example, (2) definition, (3) chronological order and process, and (4) listing.

Example

One of the clearest ways to explain something is to give an example. This is especially true when a subject is unfamiliar. Suppose, for instance, that your younger brother asks you to explain what anthropology is. You might give him examples of the topics you study, such as apes and early humans, and the development of modern humans. Through examples, your brother would get a fairly good idea of what anthropology is all about.

When organizing a paragraph, a writer often states the main idea first and then follows it with one or more examples. The preceding paragraph takes this approach. The main idea in the topic sentence is supported by the example about explaining anthropology to a younger brother. In some paragraphs, of course, a writer might use several examples. And in a longer piece of writing, a separate paragraph may be used for each example.

Here is one way that the example pattern in a paragraph can be visualized:

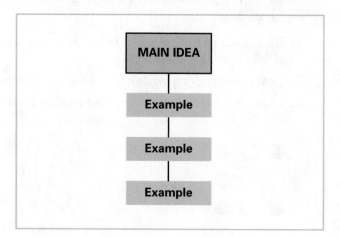

Notice how this example pattern is developed in the following paragraph:

Static electricity is all around us. We see it in lightning. We receive electric shocks when we walk on a nylon rug on a dry day and then touch something (or someone). We can see sparks fly from a cat's fur when we pet it in the dark. We can rub a balloon on a sweater and make the balloon stick to the wall or the ceiling. Our clothes cling together when we take them from the dryer.

—Newell, *Chemistry: An Introduction,* p. 11

In the preceding paragraph, the writer explains static electricity through the use of everyday examples. You could visualize the paragraph as follows:

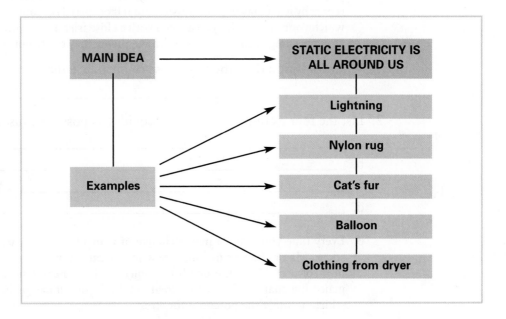

As you recall from Chapter 6, sometimes writers use transitional words—*for example, for instance,* or *such as*—to signal the reader that an example is to follow. The writer of the following paragraph uses transitions in this way:

Charlie agrees with the old saying that "a dog is a man's best friend." When he comes home from work, *for instance,* his dog Shadow is always happy to see him. He wags his tail, licks Charlie's hand, and leaps joyously around the room. Shadow is also good company for him. The dog is always there, *for example,* when Charlie is sick or lonely or just needs a pal to take for a walk. Many pets, *such as* cats and parakeets, provide companionship for their owners. But Charlie would put his dog Shadow at the top of any "best friend" list.

By using examples and transitions, the writer explains why Shadow is Charlie's best friend. Although writers don't always use transitions with examples, be on the lookout for them as you read.

Exercise 9-1

Directions: The following paragraphs, all of which are about stress, use the example pattern. Read each of them and answer the questions that follow in the space provided.

A. Any single event or situation by itself may not cause stress. But, if you experience several mildly disturbing situations at the same time, you may find yourself under stress. For instance, getting a low grade on a biology lab report by itself may not be stressful, but if it occurred the same week during which your car "died," you argued with a close friend, and you discovered your checking account was overdrawn, then it may contribute to stress.

1. What transition does the writer use to introduce the examples?

   _____

2. List the four examples the writer provides as possible causes of stress.
   a. _____
   b. _____
   c. _____
   d. _____

B. Every time you make a major change in your life you are susceptible to stress. Major changes include a new job or career, marriage, divorce, the birth of a child, or the death of someone close. Beginning college is a major life change. Try not to create multiple simultaneous life changes, which multiply the potential for stress.

3. Does the topic sentence occur first, second, or last?

   _____

4. The writer gives six examples of major changes. List them briefly.
   a. _____   d. _____
   b. _____   e. _____
   c. _____   f. _____

C. Because you probably depend on your job to pay part or all of your college expenses, your job is important to you and you feel pressure to perform well in order to keep it. Some jobs are more stressful than others. Those, for example, in which you work under constant time pressure tend to be stressful. Jobs that must be performed in loud, noisy, crowded, or unpleasant conditions—a hot kitchen, a noisy machine shop, with coworkers who don't do their share—can be stressful. Consider changing jobs if you are working in very stressful conditions.

5. Does the topic sentence occur first, second, or last? _____

6. What transition does the writer use to introduce the first type of jobs?

_____

7. To help you understand "jobs that must be performed in loud, noisy, crowded, or unpleasant conditions," the writer provides three examples. List these examples in the diagram below.

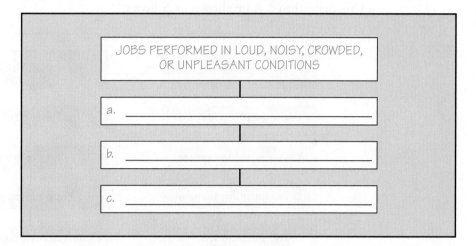

D. People who respond well to stress focus on doing the best they can, not on how they might fail. It's not that the potential problems have disappeared, it's that successful people believe in the possibility of success. Once success is seen as possible, you can focus on completing the task to the best of your ability. For example, instead of saying "I cannot do this on time," leave out the word _not_. Ask yourself: "How _can_ I finish this task on time?" and "How well _can_ I do this?"

8. Does the topic sentence occur first, second, or last?

_____

9. What transition does the author use to introduce the example?

_____

10. What does the example tell you to do?

_____

Definition

Another pattern writers follow is definition. Let's say that you see an opossum while driving in the country and you mention this to a friend. Since your friend does not know what an opossum is, you have to define it. Your definition should describe an opossum's characteristics or features, explaining how it is different from other animals. Thus, you might define an opossum as follows:

> An opossum is an animal with a ratlike tail that lives in trees. It carries its young in a pouch. It is active at night and pretends to be dead when trapped.

This definition can be shown as follows:

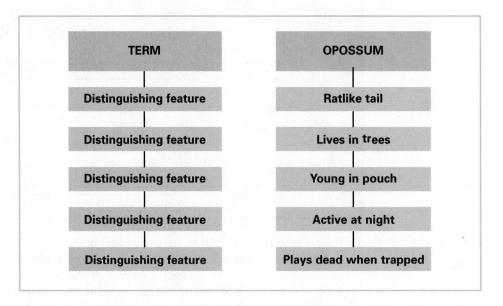

As you read passages that use the definition pattern, keep these questions in mind:

1. What is being defined?
2. What makes it different from other items or ideas?

Apply these questions to the following paragraph:

> Ragtime music is a piano style that developed at the turn of the twentieth century. Ragtime music usually has four themes. The themes are divided into four musical sections of equal length. In playing ragtime music, the left hand plays chords and the right hand plays the melody. There is an uneven accenting between the two hands.

When you ask yourself the preceding questions, you can see, first of all, that *ragtime music* is being defined. In addition, the definition lists four ways that ragtime is different from other piano styles: (1) there are four themes, (2) the left hand plays chords, (3) the right hand plays the melody, and (4) there is uneven accenting.

Combining Definition and Example

It is important to note that definitions are often combined with examples. For instance, if someone asks you to define the term *comedian,* you might begin by saying that a comedian is an entertainer who tells jokes and makes people laugh. You might also give some examples of well-known comedians, such as David Letterman or Eddie Murphy. When definition and example are used together in this way, you can visualize this pattern as follows:

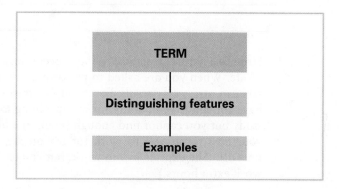

You will often encounter the definition and example pattern in your text-books. An author will define a term and then use examples to explain it further, as shown in this passage from a psychology text:

> Everyone has **central traits**—a few dominant traits that are thought to summarize an individual's personality. For example, Oprah Winfrey's central traits might include a desire to do good works, honesty, a sense of humor, and a strong work ethic.

> —Uba and Huang, *Psychology,* p. 483

First the author defines *central traits,* and then she uses the example of Oprah Winfrey to make the definition more understandable. You have probably already noticed that textbook authors often put an important term in **boldface** type just before they define it. This makes it easier for students to find definitions as they read or study for tests.

Exercise 9–2

Directions: Read each of the following paragraphs and answer the questions that follow.

A. A partnership is a form of ownership used primarily in small business firms. Two or more owners comprise a partnership. The partners establish the conditions of the partnership, contribution of each partner to the business, and division of profits. They also decide on the amount of authority, duties, and liability each will have.

—Pickle and Abrahamson, *Introduction to Business*, p. 40

1. What term is being defined? _____

2. The writer mentions several distinguishing features of this term. List three of them.

   _____

   _____

B. Stress is a natural response to the expectations, demands, and challenges of life. When you are asked to perform more (or better) than you think you can, stress may result. For example, stress can occur when you don't have enough time to study for an upcoming exam (you are expected to study but you cannot find enough time). In addition, stress occurs when your boss wants you to work for her on the weekend so she can take time off. (She expects you to work, but you cannot give up study time to work extra hours.)

3. What term is being defined? _____

4. Does this paragraph have a definition and example pattern? _____

5. What two transitional phrases does the writer use?

   _____

C. The Small Business Administration (SBA) is an independent agency of the federal government that was created by Congress when it passed the Small Business Act in 1953. The purposes of the SBA are to assist people in getting into business, to help them stay in business, to help small firms win federal contracts, and to act as a strong advocate for small business.

—Pickle and Abrahamson, *Introduction to Business*, p. 119

6. What term is being defined? Enter it in the diagram on the next page.

7. In defining this term, the writer mentions four distinguishing features. List them in the diagram on the next page.

8. Does this paragraph have a definition and example pattern? _____

D. **Assimilation** is what you do when you fit new information into your present system of knowledge and beliefs or into your mental categories of things and people. Suppose that little Harry learns the category for "dog" by playing with the family schnauzer. If he then sees the neighbor's collie and says "doggie!" he has assimilated the new information about

TERM:

Distinguishing features:

a. _____

b. _____

c. _____

d. _____

the neighbor's pet into his category for dogs. **Accommodation** is what you do when, as a result of undeniable new information, you must change or modify your existing categories. If Harry sees the neighbor's Siamese cat and still says "doggie!" his parents are likely to laugh and correct him. Harry will have to modify his category for *dogs* to exclude cats, and he will have to create a category for *cats*. In this way, he accommodates the new information that a Siamese cat is not a dog.

—Wade and Tavris, *Psychology*, 5th Ed., p. 499

9. What two terms are being defined?

_____

10. After defining each of these terms, how does the writer make them clearer?

_____

Chronological Order and Process

The terms *chronological order* and *process* both refer to the order in which something occurs or is done. When writers tell a story, they usually present events in chronological order. In other words, they start with the first event, continue with the second, and so on. For example, if you were telling a friend that a police officer stopped you for speeding, you would probably start with the fact of being "pulled over," continue with the conversation between you and the officer, and end with the result—did you get a ticket? You would put events in order according to the *time* they occurred, beginning with the first event.

Common Transitions in Chronological Order and Process		
first	before	following
second	after	last
later	then	during
next	in addition	when
another	also	until
as soon as	finally	meanwhile

When you read stories for an English class or material in a history of political science text, you will often encounter chronological order. When writers use this pattern, they often include time transitions, such as *first, next,* and *finally* (see box above). They may also use actual dates to help readers keep track of the sequence of events.

EXAMPLE

In the early 1930s, the newly established Federal Bureau of Narcotics took on a crucial role in the fight against marijuana. Under the directorship of Harry J. Anslinger, a rigorous campaign was waged against the drug and those using it. By 1937 many states had adopted a standard bill making marijuana illegal. In that same year, the federal government stepped in with the Marijuana Tax Act, a bill modeled after the Harrison "Narcotics" Act. Repressive legislation continued, and by the 1950s severe penalties were imposed on those convicted of possessing, buying, selling, or cultivating the drug.

—Barlow, *Criminal Justice in America*, p. 332

As you can see in this paragraph from a history text, the writer uses chronological order to discuss the actions taken to limit the use of marijuana. He uses three phrases with dates to show the reader the time sequence—*in the early 1930s, by 1937,* and *by the 1950s.* As you read, look for such phrases as well as for time transitions.

Writers also follow a time sequence when they use the **process pattern**— when they explain how something is done or made. When writers explain how to put together a bookcase, how to knit a sweater, or how bees make honey, they use steps to show the appropriate order.

EXAMPLE

To plant a tulip bulb, follow a few easy steps. First, dig a hole large enough for the bulb and about six inches deep. Next, place the bulb in the hole, making sure that the pointed end of the tulip is facing up. Then fill the hole firmly with dirt and sprinkle some bulb fertilizer on top. Finally, water the spot where you have planted the tulip.

This writer uses four time transitions—*first, next, then,* and *finally*—to make the order clear for the reader. Note that she also uses the word *steps* in the topic sentence. In the process pattern and in other patterns as well, the topic sentence often provides a clue to the kind of pattern that will be used.

You can visualize and draw the chronological order and process patterns as follows:

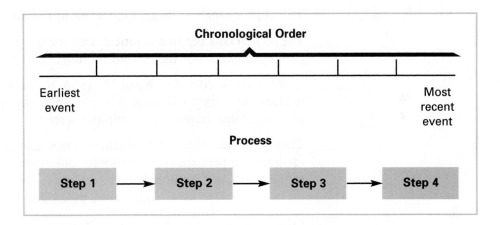

Sample maps showing chronological order and process appear in Chapter 8 (see Figures 8-3 and 8-4, p. 244).

**Exercise
9–3**

Directions: Using either chronological order or process, put each of the following groups of sentences in the correct order. Insert a number from 1 to 4 in the space provided for each sentence, beginning with the topic sentence.

1. _____ Vassar College opened its doors in 1865, followed by Smith in 1871, Wellesley in 1877, and Bryn Mawr in 1880.

_____ In spite of varied protests, the 1800s saw the admission of women into higher education.

_____ Today the great majority of the more than 2,000 institutions of higher learning in the United States are coeducational.

_____ Meanwhile, the University of Michigan had admitted women in 1870, and by the turn of the century coed colleges and universities were becoming commonplace.

—adapted from Kephart and Jedlicka, *The Family, Society, and the Individual*, p. 332

2. _____ Next, it involves evaluating why the reaction or response occurred as it did.

_____ First, it involves monitoring the impact or influence of our messages on the other person.

_____ Finally, it involves adjusting or changing our future messages.

_____ In communication, the process of *feedback* has three steps.

—adapted from Weaver, *Interpersonal Communication,* p. 123

3. _____ The blips meant one thing: high levels of radiation.

_____ The technicians began a frantic search for the problem at their own plant, but they found nothing.

_____ At 9:00 AM on Monday, April 28, 1986, technicians at a nuclear plant sixty miles north of Stockholm began to see alarming blips across their computer screens.

_____ They concluded that the problem was not with their own facilities but perhaps with the Soviet Union's nuclear plant to the south, at Chernobyl.

—adapted from Wallace, *Biology,* 7th Ed., p. 572

4. _____ He soon had one-third of all Americans over 65 enrolled in his Townsend clubs, demanding that the federal government provide $200 a month for every person over 65—the equivalent of about $2,000 a month today.

_____ The Great Depression made matters even worse, and in 1930 Francis Townsend, a social reformer, started a movement to rally older citizens.

_____ Because the Townsend Plan was so expensive, Congress embraced President Franklin Roosevelt's more modest Social Security plan in June 1934.

_____ In the 1920s, before Social Security provided an income for the aged, two-thirds of all citizens over 65 had no savings and could not support themselves.

—adapted from Henslin, *Essentials of Sociology,* 2nd Ed., p. 272

5. _____ When you revise, you step back to see whether you have expressed your thoughts adequately; you review your message and rewrite it.

_____ Writing a business message may be organized into three simple stages.

_____ In the writing stage, you decide on the organization and put your message on paper, including details and examples.

_____ During the planning stage, you think about your basic message, your audience, and the best way to convey your thoughts.

—adapted from Thill and Bovee, *Excellence in Business Communication*, 4th Ed., p. 79

Listing

Although writers often want to put events or items in a specific time sequence, sometimes they just want to list them. **Listing,** then, is used when a particular order isn't so important. If you were telling a friend about three movies or TV shows you liked, you might just list them. It wouldn't matter which movie or show was listed first.

EXAMPLE

Maria goes to the movies often, and she likes old movies as well as new ones. Three of them, however, are her favorites. She loves *Gone with the Wind* because she is a Civil War buff and a big fan of Clark Gable. *Titanic* is another favorite because of the dramatic love story, the tragedy that occurred, and the intense drama. Maria also likes *Grumpy Old Men;* it makes her laugh a lot, and she appreciates the comic acting of the late Jack Lemmon and Walter Matthau.

In the preceding paragraph, the writer might have put any of the movies first. The order simply depends on how the writer wants to present the material. Specific steps or time sequences are not important. Note, however, that the writer uses the transitions *another* and *also* to link the movies together.

You can visualize the listing pattern as follows:

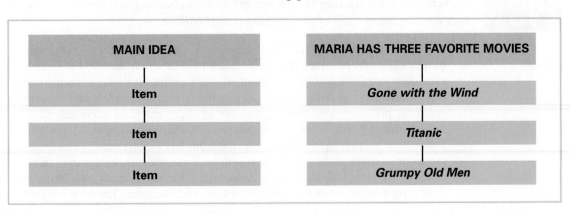

Textbook authors often use listing when they want to present information. The order is the way *they* want to present the material. It is not determined by time or steps.

EXAMPLE

Audiences favor speakers who communicate in a personal rather than an impersonal style, who speak *with* them rather than *at* them. There are several ways to develop a personal style. First, use personal pronouns, such as *I, me, he, she,* and *you,* which will create bridges to the audience. Using personal pronouns is better than using impersonal expressions such as "One is lead to believe . . . ." In addition, try to involve the audience by asking questions. When you direct questions to your listeners, they feel that they are part of the public speaking experience. You should also try to create immediacy—a sense of connectedness—with your audience. You can do this in numerous ways, such as by using personal examples, complimenting the audience, or referring to what you and the audience have in common.

—DeVito, *Elements of Public Speaking,* 7th Ed., p. 164

The author of this passage, Joseph DeVito, could have listed his advice in a different order. He might, for example, have discussed immediacy first and personal pronouns last. The decision was up to him because he was not talking about something related to time.

As in the paragraph about Maria's favorite movies, textbook writers also use transitions to link the items in a list. In the preceding example, the transitions *first, in addition,* and *also* tie together the three ways of developing a personal style. Other transitions—such as *one* and *finally*—are also used in the listing pattern.

Exercise 9-4

Directions: After reading the paragraph below, choose the letter of the choice that best answers each of the questions that follow.

Many companies—including Johnson & Johnson, McDonald's, and Burger King—have adopted written codes of ethics that formally acknowledge their intent to do business in an ethical manner. Indeed, the number of such companies has risen dramatically in the last three decades. In 1968, for example, polls revealed that 32 percent of the companies surveyed maintained ethical codes. A mere two years later, the number was 75 percent. Today, over 90 percent of all Fortune 500 firms have such codes. These codes serve one or more of the following functions. First, they increase public confidence in the firm. They also lessen the potential for government regulation by indicating a commitment to self-control. In addition, they improve internal operations by providing a consistent blueprint for acceptable conduct. Last but not least, they prescribe a response when unethical behavior does occur.

—Griffin and Ebert, *Business*, 5th Ed., p. 83

_____ 1. The topic of the paragraph is
   a. public confidence in business.
   b. written codes of ethics.
   c. Fortune 500 firms.
   d. unethical behavior.

_____ 2. In the third, fourth, and fifth sentences, the writer presents an example. What pattern of organization do these sentences follow?
   a. chronological order   c. definition
   b. process   d. listing

_____ 3. At the end of the paragraph, the writer mentions several functions of the codes. What pattern of organization do these functions follow?
   a. process   c. listing
   b. chronological order   d. example

4. What four transition words does the writer use to link the functions of the codes?

   _____ _____ _____ _____

5. Complete the following outline of the paragraph. Some items have been filled in for you.

   I. Main idea: Many companies now have written codes of ethics.
      A. _____.
         1. 32 percent had codes in 1968.
         2. _____.
         3. 90 percent have codes today.
      B. The codes serve several functions.
         1. _____.
         2. They lessen potential for government regulation.
         3. _____.
         4. _____.

Combining Patterns of Organization

As you saw in Exercise 9-4, some pieces of writing may have more than one pattern. In the beginning of this chapter, for instance, you learned how definition and example could be combined, with a writer defining a term and then giving examples to clarify the definition. As you read textbooks, novels, magazine articles, and newspapers, you will see that writers often combine other patterns as well. Within a story that is in chronological order, for instance, a writer might include a list of items. And writers almost always use examples, regardless of the overall pattern they are following. In the next chapter you will learn about two more patterns—comparison/contrast and cause/effect—and how these patterns, too, are often combined with lists, examples, and definitions.

The Textbook Challenge

Part A: Student Resource Guide A

Using Textbook Excerpt 2 in Student Resource Guide A, page 403, identify at least one paragraph for each of the following patterns of organization:

Pattern	Paragraph #
Example _____	_____
Listing _____	_____
Definition _____	_____
Process _____	_____

Part B: A College Textbook

Using a chapter from one of your textbooks, identify at least one paragraph for each of the following patterns of organization:

Pattern	Paragraph #
Example _____	_____
Listing _____	_____
Definition _____	_____
Chronological Order _____	_____
Process _____	_____

What Have You Learned?

Directions: To check your understanding of the chapter, select the word or phrase from the box below that best completes each of the following sentences. Not all of the words in the box will be used.

listing	next	definition
patterns of organization	distinguishing features	main ideas
for instance	chronological order	thus
process	example	

1. The different ways that writers present their ideas are called

   _____.

2. Textbook writers often use the _____

   and example patterns to help explain unfamiliar subjects.

3. When writers tell a story, they usually present events in

   _____.

4. A(n) _____ pattern is used when

   a particular order is not important.

5. A transition that signals an example is to follow is

   _____.

6. A definition always includes _____.

7. The _____ pattern is used to explain how

   something is done or made.

8. A transition that signals chronological order is

   _____.

What Vocabulary Have You Learned?

Directions: The words in column A appear in exercises in this chapter. Test your mastery of these words by matching each word in column A with its meaning in column B.

	Column A		Column B
_____	1. comprise	a.	provide as a guide
_____	2. advocate	b.	fitting new information into your present set of knowledge, beliefs, or mental categories
_____	3. assimilation	c.	changing your mental categories in order to include new information
_____	4. accommodation	d.	one who promotes or supports
_____	5. prescribe	e.	make up or form

Test-Taking Tip #9: Answering Questions About Patterns

Reading comprehension tests often contain questions about organizational patterns and their transitions. Use the following suggestions to answer these questions correctly:

▪   If you are uncertain about the pattern of a particular paragraph, study the transitions. These may suggest the pattern.

▪   If you are having trouble identifying a pattern, ask yourself the following question: "How does the author explain his or her main idea?" You will hear yourself saying things such as "by giving examples" (the example pattern), "by explaining how it is done" (the process pattern), or "by telling what it is" (the definition pattern).

▪   A question may not use the term "pattern of organization" but it may be asking you to identify the pattern.

Example: In the above paragraph, the writer supports her ideas by

a. giving examples.

b. listing information.

c. offering definitions.

d. making comparisons.

RECOGNIZING PATTERNS

Directions: Select the letter of the choice that best answers each of the following questions.

_____ 1. If you want to explain *defense mechanisms* to someone who is unfamiliar with the term, the best pattern to use is probably

    a. chronological order.   c. example.

    b. process.   d. listing.

_____ 2. To write a paragraph describing how to load a disk into a computer, which pattern would you most likely use?

    a. listing   c. definition

    b. process   d. example

_____ 3. Which of the following topics would most likely be developed using the chronological order pattern?

    a. the psychology of humor

    b. a comparison of personality theories

    c. stages of child development

    d. types of intimacy

_____ 4. If Carla wants to write a paragraph about her four favorite musical groups, which pattern will she probably use?

    a. listing   c. process

    b. chronological order   d. definition and example

_____ 5. Suppose you were explaining rap music to someone. If you talked about rap music's distinctive beat and how it is different from other types of music, what pattern would you be using?

    a. process   c. definition

    b. chronological order   d. listing

_____ 6. If, after giving the explanation in question 5, you also provided some examples—like the songs of Queen Latifah—what pattern would you be using?

    a. listing and example

    b. process and example

    c. chronological order and example

    d. definition and example

_____ 7. If a paragraph begins with the topic sentence "Various gestures and facial expressions play an important role in communication," which of the following patterns is the paragraph most likely to follow?

a. definition   c. example

b. chronological order   d. listing

_____ 8. If a paragraph begins with the topic sentence "Encouraging a preschool child to become interested in reading involves a specific sequence of activities," which of the following patterns is the paragraph most likely to follow?

a. example   c. definition

b. listing   d. process

_____ 9. If you were taking an essay exam in a health course and one question read "Explain the term _wellness_," what pattern would you use to organize your answer?

a. definition   c. chronological order

b. listing   d. process

_____ 10. If you were writing a paper on the important events that led up to the Civil War, what pattern would be the best to use?

a. process   c. example

b. chronological order   d. definition

RECOGNIZING PATTERNS

Directions: For each of the following statements, select the letter of the choice that best describes its particular pattern of organization.

_____ 1. Transitions are words and phrases that show relationships between ideas. For instance, time transitions such as *before, soon,* and *now* show time relationships.

　　　a. chronological order　　　c. definition and example

　　　b. process　　　d. listing

_____ 2. To borrow money, consumers can choose among several sources: banks, finance companies, and insurance companies.

　　　a. chronological order　　　c. definition and example

　　　b. process　　　d. listing

_____ 3. During a medical assessment, a nurse who notes a change in a patient's emotional or physical state notifies the attending physician. The doctor, in turn, assesses the problem and makes a diagnosis.

　　　a. chronological order　　　c. definition and example

　　　b. process　　　d. listing

_____ 4. To open, cut the box along the dotted lines. Then, remove the plastic bag and empty the cake mix into a bowl.

　　　a. definition　　　c. example

　　　b. process　　　d. listing

_____ 5. Pedro's father graduated from college in 1980. Four years later, he was running his own delivery service.

　　　a. chronological order　　　c. definition

　　　b. process　　　d. listing

_____ 6. Small cities often struggle to survive in today's economy. In the town of Camden, for instance, there is never enough money for essential services.

　　　a. chronological order　　　c. example

　　　b. process　　　d. listing

_____ 7. Hummingbirds have several distinctive features: their wings beat 50 times per second; they burn energy faster than any other animal; they can fly backwards, sideways, and upside-down.

a. chronological order   c. listing

b. process   d. example

_____ 8. Before you paint a room, follow a few simple steps. First, wash the walls and woodwork with a mild soap.

a. example   c. definition

b. process   d. listing

_____ 9. One method psychologists use is observation. Observation involves watching others and recording what occurs. For instance, psychologists often observe children through one-way mirrors.

a. chronological order   c. listing

b. process   d. definition and example

_____ 10. When Michael began his story, the children were noisy and jumping around. Soon, though, they began to listen and finally quieted down.

a. chronological order   c. example

b. process   d. listing

NAME _____   SECTION _____

DATE _____   SCORE _____

RECOGNIZING PATTERNS

Directions: After reading each of the following passages, complete the exercises that follow.

A.   Personality disorders are character traits that create difficulties in personal relationships. One type of disorder is called *antisocial personality disorder*. It is characterized by aggressive and harmful behavior that first occurs before the age of 15. Such behavior includes lying, stealing, fighting, and resisting authority. During adulthood, people with this disorder often have difficulty keeping a job or accepting other responsibilities.

Another disorder is the *paranoid personality disorder*. Individuals with this disorder are overly suspicious, cautious, and secretive. They may have delusions that people are watching them or talking about them. They often criticize others but have difficulty accepting criticism.

Finally, *compulsive personality disorder* is a type of disorder in which people attach great importance to organization. They strive for efficiency and may spend a great deal of time making lists and schedules. But they are also indecisive and seldom accomplish anything they set out to do. They often make unreasonable demands on other people and have difficulty expressing emotions.

—*World Book,* Volume 13, pp. 795–796

1. Complete the following map by writing the three types of personality disorders mentioned by the writer.

MAIN IDEA: PERSONALITY DISORDERS ARE CHARACTER TRAITS THAT CREATE DIFFICULTIES IN PERSONAL RELATIONSHIPS

a. _____

b. _____

c. _____

2. List two transitions used in the passage.

   a. _____   b. _____

3. Name the main pattern of organization used in this passage. _____

B.　　　Job opportunities for women have changed dramatically since colonial times. Unless they were employed as servants, colonial women had little occupational opportunity. Even during the early 1800s, after certain types of jobs had been opened to women, female wage earners continued to be stigmatized by inferior social status.

The first large-scale influx of female workers took place in the New England factories. Most of the workers were unmarried farm girls, some hardly more than children. They were welcomed, nevertheless, because they not only were conscientious employees but would work for low wages.

During the Civil War an increasing number of occupations were opened to women, a phenomenon that was to be repeated in the First and Second World Wars. During World War II, women were employed as welders, mechanics, machinists, taxi drivers, and streetcar operators; in fact, with the exception of heavy-duty laboring jobs, females could be found in virtually every branch of industry. Also, because of their excellent record, women were made a permanent part of the armed forces.

Today there are more than 52 million women in the workforce. Of those not in the labor force, the great majority are retired or have home responsibilities. From the sociological perspective it is important to note that currently even mothers with small children are likely to be employed outside the home. "Regardless of marital status or the presence of young children, labor force participation has become the norm for women." Since 1986, more than half of all women with children under three years of age have been in the labor force.

—Kephart and Jedlicka, *The Family, Society, and the Individual,* pp. 332–333

4. Complete the following map.

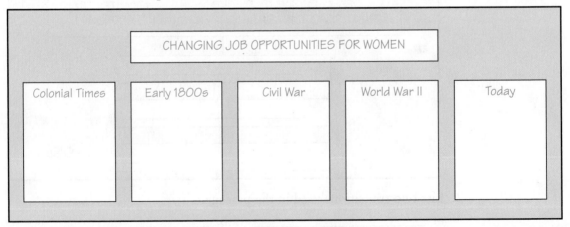

CHANGING JOB OPPORTUNITIES FOR WOMEN

| Colonial Times | Early 1800s | Civil War | World War II | Today |

5. The organizational pattern used in this passage is _____.

RECOGNIZING PATTERNS

Directions: After reading each of the passages below, select the letter of the choice that best answers each of the questions that follow.

A. The action and reaction forces make up a *pair* of forces; forces always occur in pairs. There is never a single force in any situation. For example, in walking across the floor, we push against the floor, and the floor in turn pushes against us. Likewise, the tires of a car push against the pavement, and the pavement pushes back on the tires. When we swim, we push the water backward, and the water pushes us forward. The reaction forces, those acting in the direction of our resulting movements, are what account for our motion in these cases. These forces depend on friction; a person or car on ice, for example, may not be able to exert the action force to produce the needed reaction force by the ice.

—Hewitt, *Conceptual Physics,* p. 56

_____ 1. The main idea of this paragraph appears in the
   a. first sentence.   c. fourth sentence.
   b. third sentence.   d. last sentence.

_____ 2. The main pattern of organization used in this paragraph is
   a. chronological order.   c. definition.
   b. listing.   d. example.

_____ 3. A transitional word or phrase used in this paragraph is
   a. when.   c. for example.
   b. in these cases.   d. these.

B. Horticulture, the study and cultivation of garden plants, is a large industry. Recently it has become a popular area of study. There are four areas of study in the horticulture field. First, there is pomology, the science and practice of growing and handling fruit trees. Then there is olericulture, which is concerned with growing and storing vegetables. A third field, floriculture, is the science of growing, storing, and designing flowering plants. The last category, ornamental and landscape horticulture, is concerned with using grasses, plants, and shrubs in landscaping.

_____ 4. The main idea of this paragraph is that
   a. horticulture is the study and cultivation of plants.
   b. horticulture is a large industry.
   c. horticulture has four branches of study.
   d. horticulture is a popular field of study.

_____ 5. The main pattern of organization used in this paragraph is
   a. chronological order.   c. definition.
   b. listing.   d. example.

_____ 6. The term **pomology** can best be defined as the study and care of
   a. fruit trees.   c. plants used in landscaping.
   b. flowering plants.   d. vegetables.

_____ 7. Which one of the following words or phrases is *not* used
   as a transition in this paragraph?
   a. first   c. the last category
   b. a third field   d. there are

C.   Mimosa is the name of a group of trees, shrubs, and herbs that have featherlike leaves. The mimosa grows chiefly in warm and tropical lands. The tree is similar to the acacia. The seed, or fruit, grows in flat pods. The small flowers may be white, pink, lavender, or purple. Mimosa grows throughout Asia, Africa, Mexico, and Australia. In the United States, it grows along the valley of the Rio Grande and in many states, including West Virginia, Virginia, Alabama, Kentucky, Louisiana, and Indiana.

—*World Book,* Volume 13, p. 474b

_____ 8. Which sentence states the main idea of the paragraph?
   a. first sentence   c. third sentence
   b. second sentence   d. last sentence

_____ 9. The pattern of organization used in this paragraph is
   a. process.   c. chronological order.
   b. definition.   d. example.

_____ 10. Which of the following is *not* a characteristic of mimosa?
   a. The mimosa grows in warm, tropical lands.
   b. The mimosa tree is similar to the acacia.
   c. Mimosa is the name of a group of trees, shrubs, and herbs.
   d. Mimosa seeds grow in flat pods.

RECOGNIZING PATTERNS

Directions: After reading the excerpt below, taken from a travel and tourism textbook, select the letter of the choice that best answers each of the questions that follow the passage.

HOW PEOPLE EVALUATE SERVICE

1   When you go to a water park for the first time, do you have some idea of what benefits you will receive from that particular attraction? Of course you do. And how did you develop these service expectations? You may have talked with friends who had been to the water park (word-of-mouth communications). You may be going to the water park because you believe it will be fun and provide relief from the heat (personal needs). You may have been to other water parks and therefore have a general impression of what water parks are like (past experience). And, finally, you may have seen commercials on TV giving you an impression of the park (marketing communications). These factors combine and lead to expectations about the type of experience you will have during this tourism service encounter.

2   Once you enter the park, what elements of the experience will be important in shaping your ideas about the quality of this park? People generally consider five factors when judging the quality of a service.

3   *Tangibles* are those physical aspects of the service that we can see and with which we interact—the physical appearance of the facilities, the equipment we use or which service employees use for us, the appearance and uniforms of the employees, and signs of other communications materials that are provided. For instance, in our water park example, you may be provided with a brochure that includes a map and information about support facilities such as lockers and places to buy a snack or soft drink.

4   *Reliability* refers to the ability of service personnel to perform the promised service accurately and consistently. For example, if the water park provides you with the opportunity to learn how to snorkel, do the instructors teach you well enough so that you can snorkel without drinking half of the pool?

5   *Responsiveness* involves service employees' willingness to help customers and their promptness in providing service. You expect snack bar personnel to wait on you as soon as possible and to provide your food without unnecessary delay.

6   *Assurance* is a catch-all quality that involves the faith we have in the service personnel. Do they seem well trained? Are they knowledgeable

about the park as a whole? Do they seem trustworthy? After all, the lifeguards at a water park have guests' lives in their hands.

7   Finally, *empathy* is the "warm, fuzzy" piece of service quality, the part of quality that is heartfelt. Empathy is the quality element that shows that service personnel care about you and understand your needs and frustrations. It involves setting operating hours for the convenience of guests, not management or employees. It includes caring about waiting times and fairness in waiting line systems. For example, our hypothetical water park's management realizes that many people will be waiting in lines in their bare feet on hot pavement. For guest comfort, they have located shade trees and shade umbrellas over the line areas so that you can jump from one shady area to the next while waiting your turn.

—adapted from Cook et al., *Tourism: The Business of Travel,* pp.259–260

1. What is the general subject of this passage?
   a. service expectations
   b. marketing communications
   c. evaluation of service
   d. empathy

2. Paragraph 1 is primarily concerned with
   a. the process of developing expectations.
   b. definitions and expectations.
   c. types of expectations.
   d. lists of expectations.

3. Paragraph 3 includes both
   a. definition and example.
   b. process.
   c. chronological order and example.
   d. listing.

4. The best synonym for the word **tangibles** as used in paragraph 3 is
   a. the equipment you can use.
   b. your interactions with service employees.
   c. the appearance and uniforms of employees.
   d. the physical items you see and interact with.

_____ 5. In paragraph 7, **empathy** is explained primarily by the use of
   a. example.   c. chronological order.
   b. process.   d. comparison.

_____ 6. The main point of the entire selection is that
   a. five factors are involved in evaluating service.
   b. evaluating service is very personal and time-consuming.
   c. the evaluation of service should be done by professionals, not guests.
   d. your impressions of service managers are important.

_____ 7. The example used throughout this selection is that of
   a. a theme park.   c. a water park.
   b. a guest lodge.   d. customer satisfaction.

_____ 8. The two patterns of organization used throughout this selection are
   a. definition and chronological order.
   b. definition and example.
   c. process and chronological order.
   d. listing and chronological order.

_____ 9. The term **empathy** in paragraph 7 can be defined as
   a. awareness of conveniences.
   b. sympathetic understanding and caring.
   c. concern for fairness.
   d. an emphasis on comfort.

_____ 10. In paragraph 1, what function do the words in parentheses perform?
   a. They give examples.
   b. They name what is described earlier in the sentence.
   c. They define marketing terms.
   d. They offer reasons to continue reading.

RIGHT PLACE, WRONG FACE
Alton Fitzgerald White

In this selection, the author describes what it was like to be treated as a criminal on the basis of nothing more than having the "wrong face." Read it to find out how the author became the victim of racial profiling.

Vocabulary Preview

These are some of the difficult words in this essay. The definitions here will help you if you cannot figure out the meanings from the sentence context or word parts.

ovation (para. 3) enthusiastic, prolonged applause

splurged (para. 5) indulged in a luxury

vestibule (para. 5) a small entrance hall or passage into the interior of a building

residue (para. 9) something that remains after a substance is taken away

violation (para. 14) the condition of being treated unfairly or being offended

---

1   As the youngest of five girls and two boys growing up in Cincinnati, I was raised to believe that if I worked hard, was a good person, and always told the truth, the world would be my oyster. I was raised to be a gentleman and learned that these qualities would bring me respect.

2   While one has to earn respect, consideration is something owed to every human being. On Friday, June 16, 1999, when I was wrongfully arrested at my Harlem apartment building, my perception of everything I had learned as a young man was forever changed—not only because I wasn't given even a second to use the manners my parents taught me, but mostly because the police, whom I'd always naively thought were supposed to serve and protect me, were actually hunting me.

3   I had planned a pleasant day. The night before was payday, plus I had received a standing ovation after portraying the starring role of Coalhouse Walker Jr. in the Broadway musical *Ragtime*. It is a role that requires not only talent but also an honest emotional investment of the morals and lessons I learned as a child.

4   Coalhouse Walker Jr. is a victim (an often misused word, but in this case true) of overt racism. His story is every black man's nightmare. He is hard-working, successful, talented, charismatic, friendly, and polite. Perfect prey for someone with authority and not even a fraction of those qualities. On that Friday afternoon, I became a real-life Coalhouse Walker. Nothing could have prepared me for it. Not even stories told to me by other black men who had suffered similar injustices.

5   Friday for me usually means a trip to the bank, errands, the gym, dinner, and then off to the theater. On this particular day, I decided to break my pattern of getting up and running right out of the house. Instead, I took my time, slowed my pace, and splurged by making strawberry pancakes. Before I knew it, it was 2:45; my bank closes at 3:30, leaving me less than 45 minutes to get to midtown Manhattan on the train. I was pressed for time but in a relaxed, blessed state of mind. When I walked through the lobby of my building, I noticed two light-skinned Hispanic men I'd never seen before. Not thinking much of it, I continued on to the vestibule, which is separated from the lobby by a locked door.

6   As I approached the exit, I saw people in uniforms rushing toward the door. I sped up to open it for them. I thought they might be paramedics, since many of the building's occupants are elderly. It wasn't until I had opened the door and greeted them that I recognized that they were police officers. Within seconds, I was told to "hold it"—they had received a call about young Hispanics with guns. I was told to get against the wall. I was searched, stripped of my backpack, put on my knees, handcuffed, and told to be quiet when I tried to ask questions.

7   With me were three other innocent black men who had been on their way to their U-Haul. They were moving into the apartment beneath mine, and I had bragged to them about how safe the building was. One of these gentlemen got off his knees, still handcuffed, and unlocked the door for the officers to get into the lobby where the two strangers were standing. Instead of thanking or even acknowledging us, they led us out the door past our neighbors, who were all but begging the police in our defense.

8   The four of us were put into cars with the two strangers and taken to the precinct station at 165th and Amsterdam. The police automatically linked us, with no questions and no regard for our character or our lives. No consideration was given to where we were going or why. Suppose an ailing relative was waiting upstairs, while I ran out for her medication? Or young children, who'd

been told that Daddy was running to the corner store for milk and would be right back? My new neighbors weren't even allowed to lock their apartment or check on the U-Haul.

9 After we were lined up in the station, the younger of the two Hispanic men was identified as an experienced criminal, and drug residue was found in a pocket of the other. I now realize how naive I was to think that the police would then uncuff me, apologize for their mistake, and let me go. Instead, they continued to search my backpack, questioned me, and put me in jail with the criminals.

10 The rest of the nearly five-hour ordeal was like a horrible dream. I was handcuffed, strip-searched, taken in and out for questioning. The officers told me that they knew exactly who I was, knew I was in *Ragtime*, and that in fact they already had the men they wanted.

11 How then could they keep me there, or have brought me there in the first place? I was told it was standard procedure. As if the average law-abiding citizen knows what that is and can dispute it. From what I now know, "standard procedure" is something that every citizen, black and white, needs to learn, and fast.

12 I felt completely powerless. Why, do you think? Here I was, young, pleasant, and successful, in good physical shape, dressed in clean athletic attire. I was carrying a backpack containing a substantial paycheck and a deposit slip, on my way to the bank. Yet after hours and hours I was sitting at a desk with two officers who not only couldn't tell me why I was there but seemed determined to find something on me, to the point of making me miss my performance.

13 It was because I am a black man!

14 I sat in that cell crying silent tears of disappointment and injustice with the realization of how many innocent black men are convicted for no reason. When I was handcuffed, my first instinct had been to pull away out of pure insult and violation as a human being. Thank God I was calm enough to do what they said. When I was thrown in jail with the criminals and strip-searched, I somehow knew to put my pride aside, be quiet, and do exactly what I was told, hating it but coming to terms with the fact that in this situation I was a victim. They had guns!

15 Before I was finally let go, exhausted, humiliated, embarrassed, and still in shock, I was led to a room and given a pseudo-apology. I was told that I was at the wrong place and the wrong time. My reply? "I was where I live."

16   Everything I learned growing up in Cincinnati has been shattered. Life will never be the same.

— · —

Directions: Select the letter of the choice that best completes each of the following statements.

CHECKING YOUR COMPREHENSION

_____   1. The author's main purpose in this selection is to
- a. describe his recent experience with racism.
- b. discuss the effects of racism on young people.
- c. criticize the New York police department.
- d. contrast Cincinnati with New York.

_____   2. Coalhouse Walker Jr. is the name of
- a. the author of the article.
- b. a black actor in New York.
- c. the main character in a Broadway play.
- d. a racist police officer.

_____   3. The main idea of paragraph 5 is that the author
- a. had errands to take care of.
- b. was making strawberry pancakes.
- c. lives 45 minutes from midtown Manhattan.
- d. changed his routine and was enjoying a leisurely day.

_____   4. The two strangers in the lobby of the building were
- a. friends of the author.
- b. new residents of the building.
- c. undercover police officers.
- d. suspected criminals.

_____   5. After opening the door for the police, the author was
- a. thanked by the police and released.
- b. assaulted by the criminals.
- c. handcuffed and taken away by the police.
- d. harassed by his neighbors.

USING WHAT YOU KNOW ABOUT BASIC PATTERNS

_____ 6. The main thought pattern used in this selection is
  a. definition.   c. listing.
  b. chronological order.   d. example.

_____ 7. In paragraph 2, the transitional word or phrase that indicates the chronological order thought pattern is
  a. while.   c. because.
  b. on Friday.   d. but.

_____ 8. In paragraph 5, the transitional word *instead* means that the author is about to
  a. offer an example.   c. put items in time order.
  b. add a similar point.   d. offer a different view.

_____ 9. In paragraph 9, all of the following transitional words indicate the chronological order thought pattern *except*
  a. after.   c. instead.
  b. now.   d. then.

_____ 10. In paragraph 12, the phrase "after hours and hours" is intended to show
  a. a contrast between two ideas.
  b. a change in the topic.
  c. the beginning of a list.
  d. the passage of time.

USING CONTEXT AND WORD PARTS

_____ 11. In paragraph 2, the word **naively** means
  a. negatively.   c. purposely.
  b. innocently.   d. directly.

_____ 12. In paragraph 4, the word **overt** means
  a. obvious.   c. mistaken.
  b. popular.   d. secret.

_____ 13. In paragraph 8, the word **linked** means
  a. recognized.   c. released.
  b. questioned.   d. connected.

_____ 14. In paragraph 11, the word **dispute** means
  a. obey.   c. argue/challenge.
  b. organize.   d. reveal.

_____ 15. In paragraph 12, the word **substantial** means
  a. large.   c. bulky.
  b. minor.   d. temporary.

REVIEWING DIFFICULT VOCABULARY

Directions: Complete the following sentences by inserting a word from the Vocabulary Preview on page 000 in the space provided.

16. We decided to wait in the _____ until our taxi arrived.

17. Amnesty International is dedicated to preventing the

    _____ of human rights throughout the world.

18. After her performance, the violinist received an

    _____ from the admiring audience.

19. The forest fire left a _____ of ash all over the

    surrounding area.

20. When Greta went shopping, she _____ on a

    pair of expensive leather boots.

STUDYING WORDS

_____ 21. The only meaning of the word **residue** (para. 9) that is used in
    the reading is
  a. something left over.
  b. an unusual, unexpected happening.
  c. remainder of an estate.
  d. a high pitched sound.

_____ 22. The word **naively** (para. 2) is correctly pronounced
  a. naa EVE lee.
  b. NAV ee lee.
  c. NI eve lee.
  d. naa EV e lee.

_____23. The word **humiliated** (para. 15) is derived from which of the following languages?

     a. Old English

     b. French

     c. Spanish

     d. Latin

_____ 24. The specialized meaning of the word **vestibule** (para.5) in the field of biology/anatomy is

     a. any abnormal tissue or cells.

     b. the tissue in the iris of the eye.

     c. a part of the throat.

     d. the middle cavity of the inner ear.

_____ 25. What parts of speech can the word **dispute** (para. 11) be?

     a. verb and adjective

     b. noun and verb

     c. adjective and adverb

     d. noun and adjective

QUESTIONS FOR DISCUSSION

1. Have you ever been treated unfairly on the basis of your appearance? How did your reaction compare to the author's in this selection?

2. Do you believe that racial profiling is a form of racism? Why or why not?

3. What does the author mean when he says that he was given a "pseudo-apology" (para. 15)? Do you think a different kind of apology by the police would have made a difference to the author?

WRITING ACTIVITIES

1. Write a paragraph describing an experience in which you were treated unfairly, either on the basis of either your appearance or some other factor such as age or gender.

2. Imagine that you are one of the police officers involved in the situation described in this selection. Write a letter explaining or apologizing for your actions.

3. Write a summary of paragraphs 5–10.

Chapter 9: Recognizing Basic Patterns of Organization

RECORDING YOUR PROGRESS

Test	Number Right		Score	
Practice Test 9-1	_____	× 10 =	_____	%
Practice Test 9-2	_____	× 10 =	_____	%
Practice Test 9-3	_____	× 20 =	_____	%
Mastery Test 9-1	_____	× 10 =	_____	%
Mastery Test 9-2	_____	× 10 =	_____	%
Mastery Test 9-3	_____	× 4 =	_____	%

EVALUATING YOUR PROGRESS

Based on your test performance, rate how well you have mastered the skills taught in this chapter by checking one of the boxes below or by writing your own evaluation.

☐ **Need More Improvement**
Tip: Try using the "Patterns of Organization" Module on the Reading Road Trip Web site at **http://www.ablongman.com/readingroadtrip** to fine-tune the skills that you have learned in this chapter.

☐ **Need More Practice**
Tip: Try using the "Patterns of Organization" Module on the Reading Road Trip Web site at **http://www.ablongman.com/readingroadtrip** to brush up on the skills you have learned in this chapter, or visit this textbook's companion Web site at **http://www.ablongman.com/mcwhorter** for extra practice.

☐ **Good**
Tip: To maintain your skills, quickly review this chapter by using this textbook's companion Web site by logging on to **http://www.ablongman.com/mcwhorter**.

☐ **Excellent**

YOUR EVALUATION: _____

_____

_____

_____

_____

READ ME FIRST!

The shopper in the photograph below is comparing and contrasting two different shoes. She may be comparing style, color, fit, comfort, or value. When people look at shoes in this way, they are comparing and contrasting them. Writers often use this pattern of comparison and contrast in paragraphs and in longer pieces of writing. It helps them explain how items, people , or events are alike and different.

   In Chapter 9 you learned five basic patterns of organization: example, definition, chronological order, process, and listing. In this chapter you will learn two additional patterns: comparison/contrast and cause/effect.

Comparison

A writer who is concerned only with similarities may identify the items to be compared and then list the ways they are alike. The following paragraph shows how chemistry and physics are similar.

> Although physics and chemistry are considered separate fields of study, they have much in common. First, both are physical sciences and are concerned with studying and explaining physical occurrences. Second, to study and record these occurrences, each field has developed a precise set of signs and symbols. These might be considered a specialized language. Finally, both fields are closely tied to the field of mathematics and use mathematics in predicting and explaining physical occurrences.
>
> —Hewitt, *Conceptual Physics,* 8th Ed., pp. 82–84

Such a pattern can be diagrammed as follows:

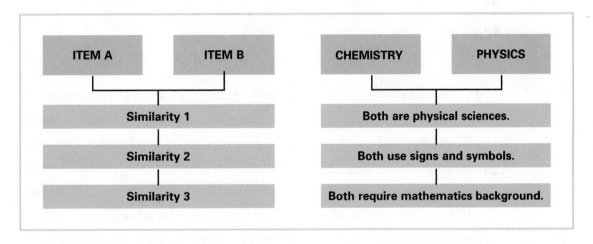

Look at the paragraph again, and notice the clues the writer provides about what kind of pattern he is following. In the first sentence—the topic sentence—the phrase *in common* tells you that the paragraph will be about the similarities between physics and chemistry. The writer also uses the words *both* and *each,* which signal that a comparison is being made. As you read, be on the lookout for words that indicate comparison or contrast.

When writers use comparison or contrast, sometimes they also include transitions to introduce each important point they are making. In the paragraph about physics and chemistry, for example, the writer uses the transitions *first, second,* and *finally* to help the reader follow the main points of the comparison. Although such transitions are not always used in comparison and contrast, you will often find them in longer selections.

Common Words in Comparison and Contrast			
To Show Similarities		**To Show Differences**	
alike	likewise	unlike	in contrast
same	both	different	despite
similar	just as	difference	nevertheless
similarity	each	on the other hand	however
like	in common	instead	but

Exercise 10-2

Directions: Select the comparison word or phrase from the box below that best completes each sentence in the paragraph that follows. Write your answer in the space provided. Use each choice only once.

same	in common	both
similarity	alike	

Although Gretchen's two brothers are ten years apart in age, they are very much _____. Andrew and Tim like to swim, they enjoy golf and jogging, and they are _____ good cooks. They also have _____ a love of playing practical jokes on their friends and relatives, especially on Gretchen. Another _____ is that while Andrew teaches physical education at a middle school, Tim coaches the high school football team. What is most important to Gretchen is that her two brothers are the _____ in one special way—they are both terrific people.

Contrast

A writer concerned only with the differences between sociology and psychology might write the following paragraph:

> Sociology and psychology, although both social sciences, are very different fields of study. Sociology is concerned with the structure, organization, and behavior of groups. Psychology, on the other hand, focuses on individual behavior. While a sociologist would study characteristics of groups of people,

a psychologist would study individual motivation and behavior. Psychology and sociology also differ in the manner in which research is conducted. Sociologists obtain data and information through observation and surveys. Psychologists, however, obtain data through carefully designed experiments.

Such a pattern can be diagrammed as follows:

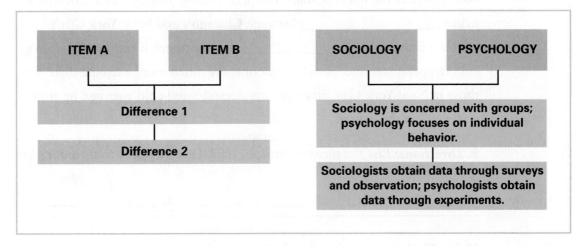

Look at the preceding paragraph again, and circle the contrast clues you can find (use the box on page 314 to help you). Did you circle the following words and phrases: *different, on the other hand, differ,* and *however?*

Exercise 10–3

A. Directions: *Select the contrast word or phrase from the box below that best completes each sentence in the paragraph. Write your answer in the space provided. Use each choice only once, but keep in mind that in some sentences, there is more than one possible right answer.*

contrast	despite	different	on the other hand
unlike	however	difference	

After visiting Chicago and New York City several times, Jeremy has decided that they are very _____ cities. First of all, Chicago's mass-transit system is _____ the one in New York. In Chicago, you need a car to reach many areas of the city. In New

York, _____, you can get to most places by subway or bus. Another _____ is Chicago's lakefront versus New York's rivers. In Chicago, you can actually live near the downtown area and walk along a beautiful sand beach. In New York, _____, there is no beach near the main business districts. Finally, Jeremy has discovered a major _____ between Chicago's and New York City's winter weather. _____ their northern locations, Chicago's cold temperatures and snowfall amounts are much more extreme than those in New York City. Since Jeremy doesn't mind cold weather, he enjoys either city in the winter.

B. Directions: *List the three transitions that the writer uses to introduce her three main points.*

1. _____   2. _____   3. _____

Using Both Comparison and Contrast

Writers often want to discuss similarities as well as differences. They might, for instance, want to compare *and* contrast the Miami Dolphins and Dallas Cowboys, presidents Franklin Roosevelt and Harry Truman, or San Francisco and Los Angeles.

When writers use comparison and contrast together, they may discuss everything about their first item (say, the Miami Dolphins) and then discuss everything about their second item (say, the Dallas Cowboys). Often, though, writers move back and forth from item to item, discussing similarities and differences as they go along. This pattern is shown in the following paragraph from a sociology textbook, which compares and contrasts primary and secondary groups.

> The term primary group, coined by Charles H. Cooley (1909), refers to small informal groups who interact in a personal, direct, and intimate way. A secondary group, on the other hand, is a group whose members interact in an impersonal manner, have few emotional ties, and come together for a specific purpose. Like primary groups, secondary groups are usually small and involve face-to-face contacts. Although the interactions may be cordial or friendly, they are more formal than primary group interactions. Secondary groups, however, are often just as important as primary groups. Most of our time is spent in secondary groups—committees, professional groups, sales-

related groups, classroom groups, or neighborhood groups. The key difference between primary and secondary groups is in the quality of the relationship and the extent of personal intimacy and involvement. Primary groups are person-oriented, whereas secondary groups tend to be goal-oriented.

—Eshleman and Cashion, *Sociology: An Introduction,* 2nd Ed., p. 88

Exercise 10–4

Directions: *After reading the preceding paragraph, choose the letter of the choice that best answers each of the following questions.*

_____ 1. Although the writer is comparing and contrasting primary and secondary groups, what other pattern (from Chapter 9) does he use in the first two sentences?

a. example   c. process

b. definition   d. listing

_____ 2. The writer uses many words to indicate similarities and differences. Which of the following is *not* used as a contrast word?

a. on the other hand   c. difference

b. whereas   d. like

3. The paragraph includes many similarities and differences between primary and secondary groups. List some of the similarities and differences below.

Primary and Secondary Groups

Similarities	*Differences*
1. _____	1. _____
2. _____	_____
_____	2. _____
3. _____	3. _____
	_____
	4. _____
	5. _____
	_____

Cause/Effect Patterns

Writers use the *cause/effect* pattern to explain why an event or action causes another event or action. For example, if you are describing an automobile accident to a friend, you would probably follow a cause/effect pattern. You would tell what caused the accident and what happened as a result.

When a single cause has multiple effects, it can be visualized as follows:

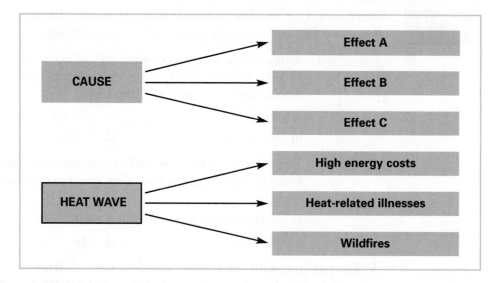

Sometimes, however, multiple causes result in a single effect. This kind of cause/effect pattern can be visualized this way:

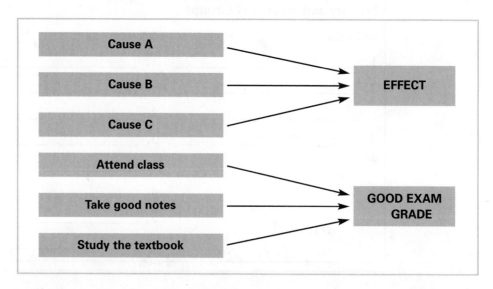

Read the following paragraph, which discusses the multiple causes of a single effect.

Research has shown that mental illnesses have various causes, but the causes are not fully understood. Some mental disorders are due to physical changes in the brain resulting from illness or injury. Chemical imbalances in the brain may cause other mental illnesses. Still other disorders are mainly due to conditions in the environment that affect a person's mental state. These conditions include unpleasant childhood experiences and severe emotional stress. In addition, many cases of mental illness probably result from a combination of two or more of these causes.

Exercise 10–5

Directions: After reading the preceding paragraph, answer the following questions.

1. What effect is the writer discussing? _____

2. The writer mentions several causes of the effect.
   List four of them.

   a. _____

   b. _____

   c. _____

   d. _____

As you worked on Exercise 10–5, did you notice that the topic sentence tells the reader that the paragraph will be about causes? Topic sentences often provide this important clue in a cause/effect paragraph, so pay close attention to them.

You also may have noticed that the writer uses specific words to show cause and effect. In addition to the word *causes,* he uses the phrases *due to* and *result from.* Writers often use such words to show why one event is caused by another. Look at the following statement:

Louis forgot to wear his glasses to the restaurant. Consequently, he couldn't read the menu.

The word *consequently* ties the cause—no glasses—to the effect—not being able to read the menu. Here is another example:

Bill couldn't wait for Nicole because he was already late for work.

In this sentence the word *because* ties the effect—Bill couldn't wait—to the cause—he was already late for work. In both of these examples, the cause and effect words help explain the relationship between two events. As you read, watch for words that show cause and effect; some common ones are listed in the box below.

Common Words in Cause and Effect			
cause	since	effect	one result is
because	due to	consequently	therefore
because of	reasons	as a result	thus

Exercise 10–6

A. Directions: *After reading the following paragraph, select the cause-and-effect word in the box below that best completes each sentence in the paragraph. Write your answer in the space provided. Not all of the words in the box will be used.*

consequently	reason	because of
result	effects	causes

The three-car accident on Route 150 had several serious

_____. First, and most tragically, two people died when

their car overturned. In addition, traffic into the city was delayed for

several hours _____ the accident. _____,

those who were headed to the fairgrounds for the Fourth of July fireworks

never got to see the colorful display. Another _____, which

occurred long afterward, was that the state legislature lowered the speed

limit in the area where the accident had occurred. After the legislation

passed, several stated that the accident was the main _____

for the change.

B. Directions: *After reading the preceding paragraph, answer the following questions.*

1. What cause is being discussed? _____

2. What four effects does the writer mention?

   a. _____

   b. _____

   c. _____

   d. _____

3. Does the topic sentence tell you that this will be a cause/effect paragraph? _____

4. Aside from the cause-and-effect words, list four transitions that the writer uses to lead the reader through the information.

   a. _____ b. _____ c. _____ d. _____

Moving Beyond Patterns

In Chapters 9 and 10 you have learned about many of the common patterns writers use—example, definition, chronological order, process, listing, comparison/contrast, and cause/effect. You have seen how these patterns help readers understand what a writer is saying and how writers may use more than one pattern in a piece of writing. In Chapter 11 you will have a chance to think about other issues involved in reading, such as whether an author is biased or is writing with a particular purpose in mind.

The Textbook Challenge

Part A: Multicultural Reader

Read "American Indian Mascots Should Go," in the Multicultural Reader on page 429, and then identify at least one paragraph that uses the following pattern of organization:

Pattern	Paragraph #
Cause/Effect _____	_____

Part B: A College Textbook

Using chapters from one of your textbooks, identify several paragraphs that use the following patterns of organization:

	Pattern	Paragraph #
Comparison/Contrast	_____	_____
Cause/Effect	_____	_____

What Have You Learned?

Directions: To check your understanding of the chapter, select the word or phrase from the box below that best completes each of the sentences that follow. Write your answer in the space provided. Not all of the choices in the box will be used and some may be used more than once.

topic sentence	process
comparison/contrast	cause/effect
definition	final statement

1. The pattern that is most concerned with relationships between events is _____.

2. Words or phrases such as *on the other hand* and *however* often suggest the _____ pattern.

3. In the _____, a writer often provides an important clue about the pattern he or she is using.

4. Words such as *consequently* and *because* often suggest the _____ pattern.

5. The pattern that is most concerned with similarities and differences is _____.

What Vocabulary Have You Learned?

Directions: The words in column A appear in exercises in this chapter. Test your mastery of these words by matching each word in column A with its meaning in column B.

	Column A		Column B
_____	1. occurrences	a.	closeness
_____	2. precise	b.	not formal; casual
_____	3. informal	c.	polite and friendly
_____	4. cordial	d.	exactly defined; specific
_____	5. intimacy	e.	events

Test-Taking Tip #10: Answering Questions About Comparison/Contrast and Cause/Effect

Paragraphs and passages written using the comparison/contrast or the cause/effect patterns commonly appear on reading comprehension tests. Expect to find questions asking you to identify these patterns. Also expect to find questions that ask you to identify what is being compared or contrasted or to identify particular causes and effects. Use the following suggestions to answer these questions correctly:

■   As with any other pattern, use transitional words to help you identify the patterns, but do not rely on them solely.

■   The topic sentence of a paragraph often reveals or suggests the pattern to be used.

Examples of Topic Sentences

a. The majority of Americans will be better off in the year 2050 than they are today. (differences)

b. Both Werner (2002) and Waible (2000) focus on genetic traces as a means of pinpointing cancer. (similarities)

c. Computer users suffer in numerous ways when spam clogs their e-mail systems. (cause and effect)

d. Acute stress may lead to the inability to think clearly and to make sensible decisions. (cause and effect)

■   If you are having difficulty sorting out causes and effects, try numbering the actions in the order in which they occurred. Your numbering will help you see the relationship.

NAME _____ SECTION _____

DATE _____ SCORE _____

RECOGNIZING PATTERNS

Directions: Each of the following statements reflects a particular pattern of organization from either Chapter 9 or Chapter 10. Select the letter of the choice that indicates the correct pattern for each passage.

_____ 1. Eleanor Roosevelt received threatening letters after her husband became president. Therefore, the Secret Service insisted she carry a pistol.

a. example   c. comparison/contrast

b. process   d. cause/effect

_____ 2. A polliwog goes through numerous stages before becoming a frog.

a. comparison/contrast   c. process

b. definition   d. cause/effect

_____ 3. Several factors, including unemployment, poverty, and decreased police protection, are responsible for the high crime rate in this city.

a. listing   c. chronological order

b. cause/effect   d. comparison/contrast

_____ 4. High school friendships are often different from newer friendships. Old friends can share memories, but new friends are more likely to share current interests.

a. chronological order   c. comparison/contrast

b. cause/effect   d. definition and example

_____ 5. Tim decided to save time by washing his dark clothes with his white ones. As a result, his white dress shirts are now an ugly graying pink.

a. process   c. listing

b. comparison/contrast   d. cause/effect

_____ 6. Carlos arrived at work at 8:30 AM, attended a meeting at 10:30, and went to lunch at noon.

a. listing   c. cause/effect

b. chronological order   d. comparison/contrast

_____ 7. Like butter, all margarine (with the exception of the low-fat versions) is 99 percent fat and contains about one hundred calories per tablespoon. Margarine, however, contains less saturated fat than butter.

    a. listing   c. comparison/contrast

    b. example   d. cause/effect

_____ 8. Julie gave her instructor several reasons why she hadn't completed her term paper, but her instructor gave her a failing grade anyway.

    a. cause/effect   c. comparison/contrast

    b. process   d. example

_____ 9. Dachshunds are reddish-brown dogs of German origin with long bodies and short legs.

    a. comparison/contrast   c. cause/effect

    b. listing   d. definition

_____ 10. The two baseball teams had a lot in common. Both had star home-run hitters, excellent managers, and good defensive players.

    a. comparison/contrast   c. cause/effect

    b. process   d. definition and example

NAME _____ SECTION _____

DATE _____ SCORE _____

RECOGNIZING PATTERNS

Directions: After reading each paragraph, complete the map or outline that follows.

A.   The differences in the lifestyles of the city and the suburbs should be thought of as differences of degree, not kind. Suburban residents tend to be more family-oriented and more concerned about the quality of education their children receive than city dwellers. On the other hand, because the suburbs consist largely of single-family homes, most young and single people prefer city life. Suburbanites are usually wealthier than city residents and more apt to have stable career or occupational patterns. As a result, they seem to be more hardworking and achievement oriented than city residents. They may also buy goods and services that offer visible evidence of their financial success.

—Eshleman and Cashion, *Sociology: An Introduction,* 2nd Ed., p. 583

Contrasting City Dwellers and Suburbanites

Difference #1 _____ tend to be more family-oriented.

Difference #2 _____ are usually more concerned with education.

Difference #3 Many young and single people prefer to live in the _____.

Difference #4 _____ are usually wealthier.

Difference #5 _____ seem to be more hardworking and achievement-oriented.

Difference #6 _____ may be more concerned with visible evidence of financial success.

B. Colors surely influence our perceptions and our behaviors. People's acceptance of a product, for example, is largely determined by its package. The very same coffee taken from a yellow can was described as weak, from a dark brown can too strong, from a red can rich, and from a blue can mild. Even our acceptance of a person may depend on the colors worn. Consider, for example, the comments of one color expert: "If you have to pick the wardrobe for your defense lawyer in court and choose anything but blue, you deserve to lose the case. . . ." Black is so powerful it could work against a lawyer with the jury. Brown lacks sufficient authority. Green would probably elicit a negative response.

—DeVito, *Messages: Building Interpersonal Communication Skills,* 3rd Ed., p. 153

I. Color—influences how we see things and how we behave.

A. _____ is determined by its wrapping or container.

    1. Example: _____

B. _____ is influenced by colors worn.

    1. Defense lawyers should wear blue.

    2. _____ is too powerful.

    3. Brown does not suggest authority.

    4. _____ might elicit a negative response.

RECOGNIZING PATTERNS

Directions: After reading each of the paragraphs below, select the choice that best answers each question that follows.

A.   France and the United States present an interesting contrast of cultural factors that affect how retailers market their products. U.S. homemakers spend more time watching television and reading magazines, and they rely more on friends and advertising before purchasing a new product. In contrast, French homemakers spend more time shopping, examining items on shelves, and listening to the opinions of retailers. Therefore, it has been easier to presell U.S. homemakers, whereas in France discounts to distributors and place of purchase displays have been more effective.

—adapted from Daniels and Radebaugh, *International Business: Environments and Operations,* 8th Ed., p. 679

_____ 1. This paragraph is concerned primarily with
  a. contrasts.
  b. a process.
  c. causes and effects.
  d. comparisons.

_____ 2. The purpose of the paragraph is to explain how the French and Americans
  a. have similar shopping habits.
  b. both rely on advertising.
  c. shop for bargains and discounts.
  d. differ in how they make purchases.

_____ 3. A transitional word or phrase that indicates the writer will shift from discussing American homemakers to French homemakers is
  a. therefore.
  b. interesting contrast.
  c. in contrast.
  d. present.

_____ 4. It is easier to influence U.S. homemakers before they enter a store because they
  a. pay more attention to advertising.
  b. look for discounts.
  c. are more educated.
  d. shop for quality.

_____ 5. Which stores should be the most concerned with in-store displays and the arrangement of merchandise?

    a. American stores

    b. French stores

    c. grocery stores

    d. retail stores

B.   Small businesses are likely to have less formal purchasing processes. A small retail grocer might, for example, purchase a computer system after visiting a few suppliers to compare prices and features, but a large grocery store chain might collect bids from a specified number of vendors and then evaluate those bids according to detailed corporate guidelines. Usually, fewer individuals are involved in the decision-making process for a small business. The owner of the small business, for example, may make all decisions, and a larger business may operate with a buying committee of several people.

—Kinnear, Bernhardt, and Krentler, *Principles of Marketing,* 4th Ed., p. 218

_____ 6. This paragraph is primarily concerned with

    a. similarities among businesses.

    b. differences among small businesses.

    c. similarities among chair retailers.

    d. differences between small and large businesses.

_____ 7. Small retail grocers and grocery store chains are

    a. mentioned as examples to illustrate differences.

    b. the topics of the paragraph.

    c. used to show similarities.

    d. the reasons why large and small stores differ.

_____ 8. According to the paragraph, one way large and small businesses differ is in how they

    a. advertise.

    b. establish criteria.

    c. make purchases.

    d. make bids.

9. Another way large and small businesses differ is in
   a. the number of people who make decisions.
   b. the types of decisions that are made.
   c. how budgets are prepared.
   d. how computer systems are installed.

10. A transitional word or phrase that suggests the overall patterns of the paragraph is
    a. likely.   c. usually.
    b. but.   d. for example.

NAME _____ SECTION _____

DATE _____ SCORE _____

RECOGNIZING PATTERNS

Directions: After reading the following passage by Rick Weiss, select the choice that best answers each question below.

ACUPUNCTURE*

1   Perhaps no other alternative therapy has received more attention in this country or gained acceptance more quickly than acupuncture. Most Americans had never even heard of it until 1971, when *New York Times* foreign correspondent James Reston wrote a startling first person account of the painkilling effects of acupuncture following his emergency appendectomy in China. Today the needling of America is in full swing. Last year alone, Americans made some 9 to 12 million visits to acupuncturists for ailments as diverse as arthritis, bladder infections, back pain, and morning sickness.

2   In a culture that is overwhelmingly shy of needles, what could account for such popularity?

3   Safety, for one thing. There is something to be said for a medical practice that's been around for 5,000 years, with billions of satisfied patients. If acupuncture were dangerous, even its stodgiest critics concede, somebody would have noticed by now.

4   Many people are also encouraged by doctors' growing willingness to refer patients for acupuncture—or to learn the ancient art themselves—despite its unconventional claims. Acupuncturists say that health is simply a matter of tweaking into balance a mysterious life force called *qi* (pronounced *chee*), which is said to move through invisible meridians in the body. That's hardly a mainstream view, yet of the 9,000 practicing acupuncturists in this country, fully a third are M.D.s.

5   Most important, there's mounting evidence that acupuncture has something important to offer, especially when it comes to pain. In one big study, acupuncture offered short-term relief to 50 to 80 percent of patients with acute or chronic pain. And in the only controlled trial that followed patients for six months or more, nearly six out of ten patients with low back pain continued to show improvement, compared to a control group that showed no improvement. Other studies have shown that acupuncture may be useful in treating nausea, asthma, and a host of other common ills.

—Weiss, "Acupuncture" from *Health*

*Acupuncture involves the use of needles to treat physical pains and illness.

_____ 1. The subject of this passage is
   a. how acupuncture works.
   b. the medical properties of acupuncture.
   c. alternative medical treatments.
   d. the popularity of acupuncture.

_____ 2. The article focuses primarily on
   a. the causes of acupuncture's popularity.
   b. why acupuncture relieves pain.
   c. the differences between acupuncture and traditional medicine.
   d. the process of acupuncture.

_____ 3. Acupuncture first became known in the United States through
   a. an article written by James Reston.
   b. reports from travelers to the Orient.
   c. the successful treatment of arthritis sufferers.
   d. Americans' fear of needles.

_____ 4. One reason acupuncture has grown in popularity is
   a. the life force called _qi_.
   b. it is easy to obtain.
   c. its safety.
   d. the low cost of treatments.

_____ 5. Acupuncture has been used to treat all of the following _except_
   a. back pain.   c. morning sickness.
   b. bladder infections.   d. bone fractures.

_____ 6. Some acupuncturists think acupuncture is effective because it
   a. divides the body into meridians.
   b. brings the life force _qi_ into balance.
   c. is an ancient medical treatment.
   d. has billions of satisfied customers.

_____ 7. In paragraph 4, the word **unconventional** means
   a. ordinary.   c. disturbing.
   b. important.   d. nontraditional.

_____ 8. At the beginning of paragraph 5, the transitional phrase *most important* suggests that the author will

   a. argue against widespread use of acupuncture.

   b. present a contrasting point of view.

   c. give his most compelling reason.

   d. summarize his ideas.

_____ 9. Which statement best describes the current position of the medical profession toward acupuncture?

   a. Doctors are becoming more willing to refer patients for acupuncture.

   b. Acupuncture is declining in popularity.

   c. Most doctors think acupuncture is risky.

   d. Acupuncture is not a legitimate form of medicine.

_____ 10. In paragraph 1, the main idea is stated in the

   a. first sentence.   c. third sentence.

   b. second sentence.   d. last sentence.

NAME _____ SECTION _____

DATE _____ SCORE _____

RECOGNIZING PATTERNS

Directions: After reading the following passage, select the letter of the choice that best answers each of the questions below.

In 1980, the Asian children far outperformed the American children on a broad battery of mathematical tests. On computation and word problems, there was virtually no overlap between schools, with the lowest-scoring Beijing schools doing better than the highest-scoring Chicago schools.

By 1990, the gap between the Asian and American children had grown ever greater. Only 4 percent of the Chinese children and 10 percent of the Japanese children had scores as low as those of the average American child. These differences could not be accounted for by educational resources: the Chinese had worse facilities and larger classes than the Americans. On the average, the American children's parents were far better-off financially and were better educated than the parents of the Chinese children. Nor could the test differences be accounted for by differences in the children's fondness for math: 85 percent of the Chinese kids said they like math, but so did almost 75 percent of the American children. Nor did it have anything to do with intellectual ability in general, because the American children were just as knowledgeable and capable as the Asian children on tests of general information.

Today, the same differences exist, and they are accentuated by the growing need for mathematical skills in the electronic age.

—adapted from Wade and Tavris, *Psychology*, 5th Ed., p. 494

_____ 1. The main subject of the passage is
   a. American children.
   b. Asian children.
   c. mathematical abilities of children.
   d. intellectual capacity of children.

_____ 2. The primary organizational pattern used throughout the passage is
   a. cause/effect.   c. definition.
   b. process.   d. comparison/contrast.

3. The main point of the passage is that

   a. Asian children score higher on mathematics tests than do American children.

   b. American children are superior in mathematics to Asian children.

   c. The gap between mathematical abilities of Asian and American children is lessening.

   d. The differences in mathematical abilities between Asian and American children can be explained by educational resources.

4. Which of the following is considered to be an educational resource?

   a. parental income   c. parental education

   b. fondness for mathematics   d. class size

5. The difference in mathematical abilities

   a. is not explained.

   b. is due to overall intellectual ability.

   c. can be attributed to educational resources.

   d. is easily explained by attitudes toward mathematics.

6. A "broad battery" of tests refers to

   a. tests repeated each year.

   b. teacher-written tests.

   c. a wide range of tests.

   d. commercially published tests.

7. By 1990, what percentage of Japanese children scored as low as the average American child?

   a. 4 percent   c. 50 percent

   b. 10 percent   d. 80 percent

8. The statistics comparing the performance of Asian and American children are arranged

   a. by test score.

   b. by the age of the children.

   c. by type of test.

   d. chronologically.

_____ 9. What word or phrase suggests the overall organizational pattern used throughout the passage?

a. In general

c. These differences

b. On the average

d. because

_____ 10. According to the passage, which of the following statements is accurate?

a. More Chinese than American children report that they like math.

b. Chinese parents are better educated than American parents.

c. The Chinese have superior educational facilities.

d. The income of American parents is the same as Chinese parents.

NAME _____ SECTION _____
DATE _____ SCORE _____

WHEN MOMMY GOES OFF TO FIGHT A WAR
Peter Madsen

This essay first appeared in *Newsweek* magazine in July 2005. Read it to find out how a family learned to cope while one of the parents was serving with the military in Iraq.

Vocabulary Preview

These are some of the difficult words in this essay. The definitions here will help you if you can't figure out the meanings from the sentence context or word parts.

fatigues (para. 4) military clothing worn for work or field duty

Kevlar (para. 4) an extremely tough synthetic material

medic (para. 5) a member of a military medical corps

deployment (para. 9) the activation of military forces in preparation for battle or work

rehabilitation (para. 16) the treatment of physical disabilities through therapy and exercise

As a sometimes bumbling single parent, I learned an invaluable lesson: girls don't go to barbershops.

1   It's funny how the hot and dry brings out the evil in men," my wife said on the phone one night last July. It was not a statement that gave a husband comfort from 6,000 miles away.

2   "Did something happen? Are you OK?"

3   "Fine," she said. "It was just a long day. Why don't you tell me about your day?" I sat in the family room and stared at the wall. "Peter?"

4   "Yes," I said quietly, "I'm here." I thought about her in the Iraqi desert, and smiled then. She looks tiny and childlike when she's buried beneath a mound of fatigues and body armor, blond wisps of hair escaping from under her Kevlar helmet.

5   I could never have imagined this beautiful waif of a girl going to war, but there she was. She is an Army medic who cared for the sick and injured in Iraq. I am a former officer and Army aviator who stayed behind to care for our son and two daughters. This was definitely a brave new world.

6   Last August, I took our 11-year-old daughter, the oldest child, to get her hair done. My wife had made me a list of all the things that I should remember while she was away. She was pressed for time and most of it was mundane— bills, vet appointments, school registration. Hair appointments were not on the list. I had been doing this for four months so I was pretty confident that I could successfully add one or two things on my own. I was wrong.

7   Tyler was starting the seventh grade. She was nervous about attending a new school, so I was determined to make it a good beginning. I suggested we go to the barbershop just off post. She answered with a resounding *"No!"* Rule No. 1: girls do not go to barbershops.

8   After some thought, I figured out how to make it right, and announced that we would go to a salon. She threw her arms around me and told me that she loved me. I was starting to realize I could do this.

9   The deployment had been hard on our family. My children have a deep connection with their mother and were mourning her absence. We were building a wonderful new relationship but I could not light them up the way their mother does. Watching my daughter smile, I began to think I might have mommy magic, too.

■ TRIAL AND ERROR: I made mistakes each day, but I would not trade that time for anything. My kids are goodness and light, and I am blessed to be with them.

10   The big day came and Tyler and I went to the mall. Rule No. 2: You must make an appointment beforehand.

11   I did not know rule No. 2, so we went blindly in search of a hairdresser who would give her a trim and some highlights. That is the cool thing to do and I wanted to help my little girl be cool. We found a salon and, after several minutes of conversation, agreed on blond and honey highlights, I set off to find a good cup of coffee. When I returned, Tyler was under the dryer, laughing with the girl next to her. After 20 more minutes she came out, twirled around and asked me what I thought.

12   My daughter has long, beautiful, naturally strawberry-blond hair with a wave that most women pay for. I did not expect the red—almost burgundy— streaks that were running through her hair. Whatever my expression was, it was enough to make her face go ashen. Then I really blew it.

13   "What on earth did you do to your hair?" I demanded. I paid the stylist, grabbed my daughter's hand and almost ran to the car. As we pulled out of the parking lot, I raged on about her hair and her mother and the trouble I was in. I did not notice Tyler's silence until we hit the first stoplight. She was lying on the back seat, crying quietly. I have never felt so small.

14   I told her that I loved her and that I was sorry for being a boob. Once her hair dried more, the highlights really did look good. We took pictures for her mom and sent them by e-mail. Surprisingly, given the eight-hour time difference, she wrote back almost immediately, saying she loved the new haircut. Tyler beamed.

15   The list my wife left me did not even begin to cover what she has done for us over the years. I made new mistakes each day, but I would not trade that time for anything in the world. My kids are goodness and light, and I am blessed to be with them.

16   My wife was sent home last September, after suffering a severe heat injury. Nine months later, she is still recovering from brain and central-nervous-system damage, and we are both trying to adjust to our changing roles. My children no longer come to me for everything. They don't need to. Mommy is home and she is the one they call out to when things go bump in the night. We are still very close, though, and because of my wife's rehabilitation, I'm deeply involved in their daily routines. We have shared a wonderful, terrible experience, and we are better for it. We always will be.

Directions: In the space provided, write the letter of the choice that best completes each of the following statements.

CHECKING YOUR COMPREHENSION

_____ 1. The author's main purpose in this selection is to

  a. explain how difficult it is for fathers and daughters to understand each other.

  b. complain about the hardships placed on his family by his wife's military career.

  c. describe his experience as a single parent during his wife's military service.

  d. discuss whether mothers typically make better parents than fathers.

_____ 2. The author can correctly be described as all of the following *except*

  a. a former officer.

  b. an Army medic.

  c. the father of three children.

  d. the husband of a war veteran.

_____ 3. The primary incident in this selection involved the author's difficulty in

  a. helping his son with homework.

  b. registering his children for school.

  c. handling the tasks on his wife's list.

  d. taking his daughter to get her hair done.

_____ 4. The main idea of paragraph 9 is that the author was

  a. anxious about his wife's safety in Iraq.

  b. glad to be forming a special relationship with his children.

  c. worried about the mistakes he was making as a single parent.

  d. jealous of the bond between his wife and their children.

_____ 5. The author's initial reaction to his daughter's new hairstyle was

  a. anger.

  b. delight.

  c. sympathy.

  d. guilt.

6. According to the author, rule No. 1 is
   a. highlights are cool.
   b. girls do not go to barbershops.
   c. you must make an appointment to get a haircut.
   d. moms know best.

USING WHAT YOU KNOW ABOUT ORGANIZATIONAL PATTERNS

6. What pattern of organization does the author follow in paragraph 5?
   a. definition
   b. chronological order
   c. comparison/contrast
   d. cause/effect

7. When the author describes taking Tyler to get her hair done, what overall pattern is he following?
   a. listing
   b. chronological order
   c. process
   d. cause/effect

8. In paragraph 11, all of the following transitions indicate the chronological order thought pattern *except*
   a. after several minutes of conversation.
   b. When I returned.
   c. After 20 more minutes.
   d. what I thought.

9. Of the following sentences from paragraph 13, which one reveals the effect that the author caused?
   a. "What on earth did you do to your hair?" I demanded.
   b. I paid the stylist, grabbed my daughter's hand and almost ran to the car.
   c. She was lying on the back seat, crying quietly.
   d. As we pulled out of the parking lot, I raged on about her hair and her mother and the trouble I was in.

_____ 10. In paragraph 16, the phrase "Nine months later" is intended to show

    a. a contrast between two ideas.

    b. a change in the topic.

    c. the passage of time.

    d. the beginning of a list.

USING CONTEXT AND WORD PARTS

_____ 11. In paragraph 4, the word **mound** means

    a. bump.

    b. hill.

    c. heap.

    d. embankment.

_____ 12. In paragraph 6, the word **mundane** means

    a. ordinary.

    b. earthy.

    c. complicated.

    d. fearful.

_____ 13. In paragraph 7, the word **resounding** means

    a. silent.

    b. hidden.

    c. famous.

    d. loud.

_____ 14. In paragraph 9, the word **mourning** means

    a. feeling sad.

    b. going away.

    c. making a low sound.

    d. wearing black clothes.

_____ 15. In paragraph 12, the word **ashen** means

    a. hot.

    b. pale.

    c. wooden.

    d. dirty.

REVIEWING DIFFICULT VOCABULARY

Directions: Complete each of the following sentences by inserting a word from the Vocabulary Preview box on page 337 in the space provided. A word should be used only once.

16. Physical or occupational therapy is essential to any _____ program.

17. In addition to helmets and body armor, _____ is used in sports equipment and yacht sails.

18. After the ceremony, many of the soldiers changed into their _____.

19. Military officials said that the _____would last between seven and fourteen months.

20. A _____cares for sick or injured people.

STUDYING WORDS

_____ 21. The etymology of the word **waif** (para. 5) is
   a. Middle English.
   b. French.
   c. Latin.
   d. German.

_____ 22. Which one of the following correctly indicates how **aviator** (para. 5) is pronounced?
   a. ay VEE ay ter
   b. AY vee ay ter
   c. ay vie AY ter
   d. ay VIE ay ter

_____ 23. The correct meaning of the word **post** (para. 7) as it is used in this reading is
   a. an announcement.
   b. a long piece of wood.
   c. mail delivery.
   d. a military base.

_____ 24. The correct meaning of the word **salon** (para. 8) as it is used in this reading is

   a. a large room.

   b. a social gathering.

   c. an art gallery.

   d. a beauty shop.

_____ 25. The correct meaning of the word **beamed** (para. 14) as it is used in this reading is

   a. shone a light onto.

   b. a squared-off log.

   c. smiled broadly.

   d. followed the right track.

QUESTIONS FOR DISCUSSION

1. How does the author look upon his role as a father? How do you know?

2. Discuss the author's statement, "We have shared a wonderful, terrible experience, and we are better for it." What do you think made it wonderful and terrible?

3. What does the author mean when he says, "This was definitely a brave new world"?

4. How do you feel about women in the military? Did this selection change your opinion?

WRITING ACTIVITIES

1. What can you tell about the Madsen family from the photograph that appears with the selection? Write a list of ten words or phrases you would use to describe this family based on the photograph and on what you know from reading the selection.

2. Create a time line of the events described in this selection.

3. Imagine that you are the author's daughter and write a paragraph describing the haircut experience from her point of view.

4. The author has written about his attempts to take on responsibilities that previously had belonged to his wife. Think of an experience in which you have had to step out of your usual role to take on different responsibilities, either temporarily or permanently. Write a paragraph describing your experience.

Chapter 10: Recognizing Comparison/Contrast and Cause/Effect Patterns

RECORDING YOUR PROGRESS

Test	Number Right			Score
Practice Test 10-1	_____	× 10	=	_____ %
Practice Test 10-2	_____	× 10	=	_____ %
Practice Test 10-3	_____	× 10	=	_____ %
Mastery Test 10-1	_____	× 10	=	_____ %
Mastery Test 10-2	_____	× 10	=	_____ %
Mastery Test 10-3	_____	× 4	=	_____ %

EVALUATING YOUR PROGRESS

Based on your test performance, rate how well you have mastered the skills taught in this chapter by checking one of the boxes below or by writing your own evaluation.

☐ **Need More Improvement**
Tip: Try using the "Patterns of Organization" Module on the Reading Road Trip Web site at **http://www.ablongman.com/readingroadtrip** to fine-tune the skills that you have learned in this chapter.

☐ **Need More Practice**
Tip: Try using the "Patterns of Organization" Module on the Reading Road Trip Web site at **http://www.ablongman.com/readingroadtrip** to brush up on the skills you have learned in this chapter, or visit this textbook's companion Web site at **http://www.ablongman.com/mcwhorter** for extra practice.

☐ **Good**
Tip: To maintain your skills, quickly review this chapter by using this textbook's companion Web site by logging on to **http://www.ablongman.com/mcwhorter**.

☐ **Excellent**

YOUR EVALUATION: _____
_____
_____
_____

Copyright © 2007 by Kathleen T. McWhorter

READ ME FIRST!

Look carefully at the photograph below. What feelings and emotions are evident? What is your overall impression of the photo? What details in the photograph contribute to that impression? What purpose do you think the photographer had in mind when he or she took the photograph?

When you ask questions like these, you are using *inference*—you are going beyond the "facts" of the photograph and thinking about what the photographer meant to convey. This chapter will show you how to use inference as you read and will discuss other important critical reading skills.

CHAPTER **11**

Reading and Thinking Critically

What Is Inference?

Just as you use inference when you study a photograph, you also use it when you try to figure out why a friend is sad or what an author's message is in a particular piece of writing. An **inference** is an educated guess or prediction about something unknown based on available facts and information. It is the logical connection that you draw between what you observe or know and what you do not know.

Here are a few everyday situations. Make an inference for each.

- You are driving on an expressway and you notice a police car with flashing red lights behind you. You check your speedometer and notice that you are going ten miles over the speed limit.

- A woman seated alone in a bar nervously glances at everyone who enters. Every few minutes she checks her watch.

In the first situation, a good inference might be that you are going to be stopped for speeding. However, it is possible that the officer only wants to pass you to get to an accident ahead or to stop someone driving faster than you. In the second situation, one inference is that the woman is waiting to meet someone who is late.

When you make inferences about what you read, you go beyond what a writer says and consider what he or she *means*. You have already done this, to some extent, in Chapters 3 and 7 as you inferred the meanings of words from context (see pages 71–83) and figured out implied main ideas (see pages 199–208). Thus, you know that writers may directly state some ideas but hint at others. It is left to the reader, then, to pick up the clues or suggestions and to figure out the writer's unstated message. This chapter will show you how to do so.

How to Make Inferences

Making an inference is a thinking process. As you read, you are following the writer's thoughts. You are also alert for ideas that are suggested but not directly stated. Because inference is a logical thought process, there is no simple, step-by-step procedure to follow. Each inference depends on the situation, the facts provided, and the reader's knowledge and experience.

However, here are a few guidelines to keep in mind as you read. These will help you get in the habit of looking beyond the factual level.

1. **Be sure you understand the literal meaning.** Before you can make inferences, you need a clear grasp of the facts, the writer's main ideas, and the supporting details.

2. **Notice details.** Often a particular detail provides a clue that will help you make an inference. When you spot a striking or unusual detail, ask yourself: Why did the writer include this piece of information? Remember that there are many kinds of details, such as descriptions, actions, and conversations.

3. **Add up the facts.** Consider all the facts taken together. Ask yourself: What is the writer trying to suggest from this set of facts? What do all these facts and ideas point toward?

4. **Look at the writer's choice of words.** A writer's word choice often suggests his or her attitude toward the subject. Notice, in particular, descriptive words, emotionally charged words, and words that are very positive or negative.

5. **Understand the writer's purpose.** An author's purpose, which is discussed in the next section, affects many aspects of a piece of writing. Ask yourself: Why did the author write this?

6. **Be sure your inference is supportable.** An inference must be based on fact. Make sure there is sufficient evidence to justify any inference you make.

Keep the preceding guidelines in mind as you read the following passage. Try to infer why Cindy Kane is standing on the corner of Sheridan and Sunnyside.

An oily midnight mist had settled on the city streets . . . asphalt mirrors from a ten-o'clock rain now past . . . a sleazy street-corner reflection of smog-smudged neon . . . the corner of Sheridan and, incongruously, Sunnyside . . . Chicago.

A lone lady lingers at the curb . . . but no bus will come.

She is Cindy Kane, twenty-eight. Twenty-eight hard years old. Her iridescent dress clings to her slender body. Her face is buried under a Technicolor avalanche of makeup.

She is Cindy Kane.

And she has a date.

With someone she has never met . . . and may never meet again.

Minutes have turned to timelessness . . . and a green Chevy four-door pulls slowly around the corner.

The driver's window rolls down. A voice comes from the shadow . . .

"Are you working?"

Cindy nods . . . regards him with vacant eyes.

He beckons.

She approaches the passenger side. Gets in. And the whole forlorn, unromantic ritual begins all over again. With another stranger.

—Paul Aurandt, *Paul Harvey's The Rest of the Story,* p. 116

If you made the right inferences, you realized that Cindy Kane is a prostitute and that she is standing on the corner waiting for a customer. Let us look at some of the clues the writer gives that lead to this inference.

- **Descriptive details:** By the way the writer describes Cindy Kane, you begin to suspect that she is a prostitute. She is wearing an iridescent, clinging dress and a lot of makeup, which convey the image of a gaudy, unconventional appearance. As the writer describes the situation, he slips in other clues. He establishes the time as around midnight ("An oily midnight mist"). His reference to a "reflection of smog-smudged neon" suggests an area of bars or nightclubs.

- **Action details:** The actions, although few, also provide clues about what is happening. The woman is lingering on the corner. When the car approaches, she gets in.

- **Conversation details:** The only piece of conversation, the question, "Are you working?" is one of the strongest clues the writer provides.

- **Word choice:** The writer has chosen words that help to convey the image and situation of a prostitute. Cindy is described as "hard," and her makeup is "a Technicolor avalanche." In the last paragraph, the phrase "forlorn, unromantic ritual" provides a final clue.

Exercise 11–1

Directions: Read each of the following passages. Using inference, determine whether the statements following each passage are true (T) or false (F). Write your answer in the space provided before each statement.

A.   Eye-to-eye contact and response are important in real-life relationships. The nature of a person's eye contact patterns, whether he or she looks another squarely in the eye or looks to the side or shifts his gaze from side to side, tells a lot about the person. These patterns also play a significant role in success or failure in human relationships. Despite its importance, eye contact is not involved in television watching. Yet children spend several hours a day in front of the television set. Certain children's programs pretend to speak directly to each individual child. (Mr. Rogers is an example, telling the child "I like you, you're special," etc.) However, this is still one-way communication and no response is required of the child. How might such a distortion of real-life relationships affect a child's development of trust, of openness, of an ability to relate well to other people?

—Weaver, *Understanding Personal Communication*, p. 291

_____   1. To develop a strong relationship with someone, you should look directly at him or her.

_____   2. The writer has a positive attitude toward television.

_____   3. The writer thinks that television helps children relate well to other people.

_____   4. The writer would probably recommend that children spend more time talking to others and playing with other children.

B.   There is little the police or other governmental agencies can't find out about you these days. For starters, the police can hire an airplane and fly over your backyard filming you sunbathing and whatever else is visible from above. A mail cover allows the post office, at the request of another government or police agency, to keep track of people sending you mail and organizations sending you literature through the mail. Police or other governmental agencies may have access to your canceled checks and deposit records to find out who is writing checks to you and to whom you are writing checks. Even the trash you discard may be examined to see what you are throwing away.

        No doubt by now you've realized that all of this information provides a fairly complete and accurate picture about a person, including his or her health, friends, lovers, political and religious activities, and even beliefs. Figure that, if the Gillette razor company knows when it's your eighteenth birthday to send you a sample razor, your government, with its super, interconnecting computers, knows much more about you.

—Lewis Katz, *Know Your Rights*, p. 54

_____   5. The writer seems to trust government agencies.

_____ 6. The writer would probably oppose forcing libraries to give the police information about the books you read.

_____ 7. The writer is in favor of strengthening citizens' rights to privacy.

C.   George Washington is remembered not for what he was but for what he should have been. It doesn't do any good to point out that he was an "inveterate landgrabber," and that as a young man he illegally had a surveyor stake out some prize territory west of the Alleghenies in an area decreed off limits to settlers. Washington is considered a saint, and nothing one says is likely to make him seem anything less. Though he was a wily businessman and accumulated a fortune speculating in frontier lands, he will always be remembered as a farmer—and a "simple farmer" at that.

Even his personal life is misremembered. While Washington admitted despising his mother and in her dying years saw her infrequently, others maintain that he remembered his mother fondly and considered himself a devoted son. While his own records show he was something of a dandy and paid close attention to the latest clothing designs, ordering "fashionable" hose, the "neatest shoes," and coats with "silver trimmings," practically no one thinks he was vain. Though he loved to drink and dance and encouraged others to join him, the first president is believed to have been something of a prude.

—Shenkman, _Legends, Lies, and Cherished Myths
of American History_, pp. 37–38

_____ 8. Washington is usually remembered as saintlike because he was one of the founding fathers and our first president.

_____ 9. The writer considers Washington dishonest and vain.

_____ 10. The writer believes that eventually Americans' attitudes toward Washington will change.

Directions: After reading the following selection, choose the letter of the choice that best answers each of the questions below.

THE MAN, THE BOY, AND THE DONKEY

A Man and his son were once going with their Donkey to market. As they were walking along by its side a countryman passed them and said: "You fools, what is a Donkey for but to ride upon?" So the Man put the Boy on the Donkey and they went on their way.

But soon they passed a group of men, one of whom said: "See that lazy youngster, he lets his father walk while he rides." So the Man ordered his Boy to get off, and got on himself.

But they hadn't gone far when they passed two women, one of whom said to the other: "Shame on that lazy lout to let his poor little son trudge along." Well, the Man didn't know what to do, but at last he took his Boy up before him on the Donkey.

By this time they had come to the town, and the passers-by began to jeer and point at them. The Man stopped and asked what they were scoffing at. The men said: "Aren't you ashamed of yourself for overloading that poor donkey of yours and your hulking son?" The Man and Boy got off and tried to think what to do. They thought and they thought, till at last they cut down a pole, tied the donkey's feet to it, and raised the pole and the donkey to their shoulders. They went along amid the laughter of all who met them till they came to Market Bridge, when the Donkey, getting one of his feet loose, kicked out and caused the Boy to drop his end of the pole. In the struggle the Donkey fell over the bridge, and his fore-feet being tied together he was drowned.

"That will teach you," said an old man who had followed them: "Please all, and you will please none."

—http://www.gutenberg.net/etext92/aesopa10.txt

_____ 1. Which of the following words or phrases suggests disapproval?

    a. teach   d. passers-by

    b. lout   e. poor little son

_____ 2. Which statement best describes the Man in the fable?

    a. The Man is ignorant and uncaring about animal rights.

    b. The Man is insensitive to the needs of his son.

    c. The Man readily accepts the opinions of others.

    d. The Man does not know how to care for a donkey.

_____ 3. Why did the Man and Boy tie the donkey to the pole?

    a. They attempted to find a solution that met all three criticisms they had received.

    b. They were unable to control the donkey by any other means.

    c. The Man thought he could save the donkey's life.

    d. The Son felt threatened by the crowd.

_____ 4. The donkey drowned because

    a. he was carrying too much weight.

    b. he was unable to swim.

    c. the boy held on to him.

    d. the Man wanted to get rid of him.

_____   5. The purpose of the story is to explain that

    a. animals should be treated with respect.

    b. you should ignore the opinions of others.

    c. public opinion is usually untrustworthy.

    d. you cannot make everyone happy.

Understanding a Writer's Purpose

Writers have many different reasons or purposes for writing. These purposes affect their style of writing, the language they use, and the details they include. Once you understand a writer's purpose, it becomes easier to make inferences about a particular piece of writing.

Read the following statements and try to decide why each was written:

1. About 14,000 ocean-going ships pass through the Panama Canal each year. This averages nearly forty ships per day.

2. *New Unsalted Dry Roasted Almonds.* Finally, a snack with a natural flavor and without salt. We simply shell the nuts and dry-roast them until they're crispy and crunchy. Try a jar this week.

3. Humans are the only animals that blush or have a need to.

4. If a choking person has fallen down, first turn him or her face up. Then knit together the fingers of both your hands and apply pressure with the heel of your bottom hand to the victim's abdomen.

The statements above were written (1) to give information, (2) to persuade you to buy almonds, (3) to amuse you and make a comment on human behavior, and (4) to give instructions.

In each of the examples, the writer's purpose was fairly clear, as it will be in most textbooks, newspaper articles, and reference books. However, in many other types of writing, authors have less obvious purposes. In these cases, an author's purpose must be inferred.

Sometimes a writer wants to express an opinion indirectly or encourage readers to think about a particular issue or problem. Writers achieve their purposes by controlling what they say and how they say it. This section will focus on the techniques writers use to achieve the results they want.

Style

Are you able to recognize a friend just by his or her voice? Can you identify family members by their footsteps? You are able to do so because each person's voice and footsteps are unique. Have you noticed that writers have unique characteristics as well? One writer may use many examples; another may use few. One may use relatively short sentences, whereas another may use long, complicated ones. The characteristics that make a writer unique are known as **style.** By changing style, writers can create different effects.

Intended Audience

Writers may vary their styles to suit their intended audiences. For example, someone writing a science article for a newspaper or general magazine, such as *Time* or *Newsweek,* would use fairly straightforward language and would be careful to explain or define any uncommon scientific or technical terms. The same person, writing for medical doctors in the *Journal of American Medicine,* could assume that readers would be familiar with the subject and thus could use more sophisticated language and details.

Depending on the group of people for whom an author is writing, he or she may change the level of language, choice of words, and method of presentation. One step toward identifying an author's purpose, then, is to ask yourself: Who is the intended audience? Your response will be your first clue to determining why the author wrote the article.

Exercise 11-3

Directions: After reading each of the following statements, choose the letter of the choice that best describes the audience for whom each was written.

_____ 1. Chances are you're going to be putting money away over the next five years or so. You are hoping for the right things in life. Right now, a smart place to put your money is in mutual funds or bonds.

  a. people who are struggling to pay for basic needs like rent and food

  b. people who are very wealthy and have been investing their money for many years

  c. people with enough income that they can think of investing some for the future

  d. people who are using their extra income to pay off credit-card debt and student loans

_____ 2. Think about all the places your drinking water has been before you drink another drop. Most likely it has been chemically treated to remove bacteria and chemical pollutants. Soon you may begin to feel the side effects of these treatments. Consider switching to filtered, distilled water today.

a. people who have no interest in environmental issues

b. chemists

c. employees of the Environmental Protection Agency

d. people who are concerned about the environment and their health

_____ 3. Introducing the new, high-powered Supertuner III, a stereo system guaranteed to keep your mother out of your car.

a. drivers who love music

b. teenagers who own cars

c. parents of teenage drivers

d. specialists in stereo equipment

_____ 4. The life cycle of many species of plants involves an alternation of generations in which individuals of the gametophyte generation produce gametes that fuse and develop into individuals of a sporophyte generation.

—adapted from Wallace, *Biology: The World of Life*, p. 271

a. biology students

b. readers of general-interest magazines

c. gardeners

d. managers of landscaping companies

_____ 5. As a driver, you're ahead of the repair game if you can learn to spot car trouble before it's too late. If you can learn the difference between the drips and squeaks that occur under normal conditions and those that mean big trouble is just down the road, then you'll be ahead of expensive repair bills and won't find yourself stranded on a lonely road.

a. mechanics

b. managers of auto-parts stores

c. car owners who do the repairs and maintenance on their own cars

d. car owners who are unfamiliar with a car's trouble signs and maintenance

Language: Denotation and Connotation

You already know that writers use different words to achieve different purposes. A reporter writing an objective newspaper account of a murder might use very different words than would a brother of the slain person. In this section you will learn more about the meanings of words and how they are clues to a writer's purpose.

Which of the following would you like to be a part of: a crowd, mob, gang, audience, congregation, or class? Each of these words has the same basic meaning: "an assembled group of people." But each has a different *shade* of meaning. *Crowd* suggests a large, disorganized group. *Audience,* on the other hand, suggests a quiet, controlled group.

This example shows that words have two levels of meaning—a literal meaning and an additional shade of meaning. These two levels of meaning are called *denotation* and *connotation*. A word's **denotation** is the meaning stated in the dictionary—its literal meaning. A word's **connotation** is the additional implied meanings that a word may take on. A word's connotation often carries either a positive or negative, favorable or unfavorable, impression. The words *mob* and *gang* have a negative connotation because they imply a disorderly, disorganized group. *Congregation, audience,* and *class* have a positive connotation because they suggest an orderly, organized group.

Here are a few more examples. Would you prefer to be described as *slim* or *skinny?* As *intelligent* or *brainy?* As *tall* or *gangly?* As *particular* or *picky?* Notice that each pair of words has a similar denotation, but each word within the pair has a different connotation.

Depending on the words they choose, writers can suggest favorable or unfavorable impressions of the person, object, or event they are describing. For example, through the writer's choice of words, the two sentences below create two entirely different impressions. As you read them, underline the words that have a positive or negative connotation.

- The unruly crowd forced its way through the restraint barriers and ruthlessly attacked the rock star.
- The enthusiastic group of fans burst through the fence and rushed toward the rock star.

It is important to pay attention to a writer's choice of words, especially when you are reading persuasive material. Often a writer may communicate subtle or hidden messages or encourage you to feel positively or negatively about the subject.

Read the following paragraph on violence in sports and, as you read, underline the words that have a strong positive or negative connotation.

So it goes. Knifings, shootings, beatings, muggings, paralysis, and death become part of our play. Women baseball fans are warned to walk with friends and avoid taking their handbags to games because of strong-arm robberies and purse snatchings at San Francisco's Candlestick Park. A professional football coach, under oath in a slander case, describes some of his own players as part of a "criminal element" in his sport. The commissioner of football proclaims that playing field outlaws and bullies will be punished, but to anybody with normal eyesight and a working television set the action looks rougher than ever. In Europe and South America—and, chillingly, for the first time in the United States—authorities turn to snarling attack dogs to control unruly mobs at athletic events.

—Yeager, *Seasons of Shame: The New Violence in Sports*, p. 6

Exercise 11–4	*Directions: For each of the following pairs of words, underline the word with the more positive connotation.*

1. request   demand

2. overlook   neglect

3. ridicule   tease

4. glance   stare

5. display   expose

6. garment   gown

7. gaudy   showy

8. clumsy   awkward

9. artificial   fake

10. take   snatch

11. jalopy   limousine

12. large   oversized

13. gobble   dine

14. inquire   interrogate

15. token   keepsake

Identifying Tone

The tone of a speaker's voice helps you interpret what he or she is saying. If a friend says to you, "Would you mind closing the door?" you can tell by her tone of voice whether she is being polite, insistent, or angry.

Writers also convey a tone, or feeling, through writing. **Tone** refers to the attitude or feeling a writer expresses about his or her subject. A writer's tone may be sentimental, angry, humorous, sympathetic, instructive, persuasive, and so forth. Here are a few examples of different tones. Note the words each writer uses to express a particular tone.

- **Instructive:** When purchasing a piece of clothing, one must be concerned with quality as well as with price. Be certain to check for the following: double-stitched seams, matched patterns, and ample linings.

- **Sympathetic:** The forlorn, frightened-looking child wandered through the streets alone, searching for someone who would show an interest in helping her find her parents.

- **Convincing:** Child abuse is a tragic occurrence in our society. Strong legislation is needed to control the abuse of innocent victims and to punish those who are insensitive to the rights and feeling of others.

In the first example, the writer offers advice in a straightforward way, using the words *must* and *be certain*. In the second example, the writer wants you to feel sorry for the child. In the third example, the writer tries to convince the reader that action must be taken to prevent child abuse. The use of such words as *tragic, innocent,* and *insensitive* establish this tone.

A writer's tone is intended to rub off on you, so to speak. A writer whose tone is humorous hopes you will be amused. A writer whose tone is persuasive hopes you will accept his or her viewpoint. Thus, tone can be important in determining an author's purpose. Tone also alerts you to a writer's possible biases about a subject. When trying to determine a writer's purpose, then, you should ask yourself certain questions: What tone does the writer use? How is the writer trying to make me feel about the subject?

To identify a writer's tone, ask yourself the following questions:

- What feelings does the author reveal toward his or her subject?
- How is the writer trying to make me feel about the subject?
- What words reveal the writer's feelings toward the subject?

It is sometimes difficult to find the right word to describe a writer's tone. Table 11-1 lists words that are often used to describe the tone of a piece of writing.

TABLE 11-1 Words Frequently Used to Describe Tone

abstract	condemning	forgiving	joyful	playful
absurd	condescending	formal	loving	reverent
amused	cynical	frustrated	malicious	righteous
angry	depressing	gentle	melancholic	sarcastic
apathetic	detached	grim	mocking	satiric
arrogant	disapproving	hateful	nostalgic	sensational
assertive	disrespectful	humorous	objective	serious
awestruck	distressed	impassioned	obsequious	solemn
bitter	docile	incredulous	optimistic	sympathetic
caustic	earnest	indignant	outraged	tragic
celebratory	excited	indirect	pathetic	uncomfortable
cheerful	fanciful	intimate	persuasive	vindictive
comic	farcical	ironic	pessimistic	worried
compassionate	flippant	irreverent		

Exercise 11-5

Directions: Read each statement listed below, choose a word that describes the tone it illustrates, and write it in the space provided.

amused	disapproving	informative
sympathetic	optimistic	ironic
apathetic	nostalgic	formal
pessimistic	incredulous	sensational

1. Why in the world did the school superintendent take an all-expenses-paid trip to Orlando when the school system was short on funds?

   _____

2. I will always remember my grandmother's unique "perfume," a lovely combination of lavender soap and fresh-baked bread.

   _____

3. People who file frivolous lawsuits should be held responsible for court costs and then fined for tying up the courts. _____

4. Every curb, every doorway, every stairwell represents a potential barrier for people in wheelchairs. _____

5. The particles that make up an atom are called protons, neutrons, and electrons. _____

6. Even if the fines for littering were tripled, some people would still insist on tossing their trash out the car window. There is no way to change humans' bad habits. _____

7. What makes us happy in the spring? All those blooming flowers! And what makes us miserable? The pollen on all those bloomin' flowers. _____

8. This contract represents a binding agreement between the seller, Mr. Thomas Hannigan, and the buyer, Ms. Ana Lopez, on this twentieth day of March, 2007. _____

9. The new system of bike trails throughout the city will let commuters leave traffic jams behind while they pedal to work and become healthier and happier people. _____

10. At the first school dance of the year, the boys line up on one side of the room with panic in their eyes. The first boy to venture to the girls' side of the room is considered a hero or a fool, depending on whom you ask. _____

Exercise 11-6

Directions: After reading each of the following passages, choose the letter of the choice that best describes the tone that the writer is expressing.

_____ 1. No one says that nuclear power is risk free. There are risks involved in all methods of producing energy. However, the scientific evidence is clear and obvious. Nuclear power is at least as safe as any other means used to generate electricity.

a. angry   c. sentimental

b. convincing   d. casual

_____ 2. Cross-country skis have heel plates of different shapes and materials. They may be made of metal, plastic, or rubber. Be sure that they are tacked on the ski right where the heel of your boot will fall. They will keep snow from collecting under your foot and offer some stability.

a. persuasive   c. instructive

b. sympathetic   d. humorous

_____ 3. The condition of our city streets is outrageous. The sidewalks are littered with paper and other garbage—you could trip while walking to the store. The streets themselves are in even worse condition. Deep potholes and crumbling curbs make it unsafe to drive. Where are our city tax dollars going if not to correct these problems?

a. angry   c. sympathetic

b. instructive   d. impersonal

_____ 4. I am a tired American. I am tired of watching criminals walk free while they wait for their day in court. I'm tired of hearing about victims getting as much hassle as criminals. I'm tired of reading about courts of law that even accept a lawsuit in which a criminal sues his or her intended victim.

a. persuasive   c. logical

b. instructive   d. disgusted

_____ 5. In July of 1986 my daughter, Lucy, was born with an underdeveloped brain. She was a beautiful little girl—at least to me and my husband—but her disabilities were severe. By the time she was two weeks old we knew that she would never walk, talk, feed herself, or even understand the concept of mother and father. It's impossible to describe the effect that her five-and-a-half-month life had on us; suffice it to say that she was the purest experience of love and pain that we will ever have, that she changed us forever, and that we will never cease to mourn her death, even though we know that for her it was a triumphant passing.

a. instructive   c. persuasive

b. emotional   d. angry

Distinguishing Fact and Opinion

The ability to distinguish between fact and opinion is an important part of reading critically. You must be able to evaluate ideas you encounter and determine whether they are objective information from a reliable source or whether they are one person's expression of a personal belief or attitude.

Facts

Facts are statements that can be verified. They can be proven true or false. Statements of fact are objective—they contain information but do not tell what the writer thinks or believes about the topic or issue. The statement "My car payments are $250 per month" is a fact. It can be proven by looking at your car loan statement. Here are a few more statements of fact:

EXAMPLES   *Facts*

1. The population of the United States in 2000 was 281,421,906. (You can check this by looking at Census figures found in various fact books and almanacs.)

2. In Washington State, drivers must stop for pedestrians and bicyclists at crosswalks and intersections. (You can check this in the Washington State Drivers' Guide.)

3. Greenpeace is an organization dedicated to protecting the environment, preserving ancient forests, sustaining the sea and its animals. (You can check this by reading its mission statement or "About Us" on its Web site.)

Opinions

Opinions are statements that express a writer's feelings, attitudes, or beliefs. They are neither true nor false. They are one person's view about a topic or issue. The statement "My car payments are too expensive" is an opinion. It expresses your feelings about the cost of your auto payments. Others may disagree with you, especially the company that sold you the car or another person paying twice as much as you are paying. As you evaluate what you read, think of opinions as one person's viewpoint that you are free to accept or reject. Here are a few more examples of opinions:

EXAMPLES   *Opinions*

1. Bill Clinton was a better president than most people realize. (Those who dislike Clinton's policies or lifestyle would disagree.)

2. The slaughter of baby seals for their pelts should be outlawed. (Hunters who make their living selling pelts would disagree.)

3. Population growth should be regulated through mandatory birth control. (People who do not believe in birth control would disagree.)

Exercise 11-7

Directions: Read the following statements and mark each one as either fact (F) or opinion (O).

_____ 1. The Atlanta Braves baseball team has won its division title twelve times in a row.

_____ 2. Alfred Hitchcock was the greatest director in the history of filmmaking.

_____ 3. Organic gardening methods produce the biggest, tastiest vegetables.

_____ 4. Female singers can be classified by pitch as soprano, mezzo-soprano, or contralto.

_____ 5. The Galapagos Islands are located on the equator, 600 miles west of mainland Ecuador.

_____ 6. Digital photography is the wave of the future.

_____ 7. A recession is characterized by low prices, high unemployment, and a slowdown in business activity.

_____ 8. Children under 13 years old should not be allowed in PG-13 movies without an adult.

_____ 9. The country that became Iran in 1935 had been known for centuries as Persia.

_____ 10. Companies should be required to offer health insurance and other benefits to their unmarried employees' partners.

Judgment Words

When a writer or speaker expresses an opinion, he or she often uses words or phrases that can tip you off that a judgment or opinion is being offered. Here are a few examples:

Professor Rodriguez is a *better* teacher than Professor Harrigan.

The word *better* suggests someone is deciding who is more skilled than someone else. Many students disagree about the qualities that make a good teacher.

My sister's behavior at the party was *disgusting.*

The word *disgusting* reveals the writer's attitude toward the sister's behavior.

Here is a list of words that often suggest that the writer is interpreting, judging or evaluating, or expressing feelings.

Judgment Words				
bad	good	worthwhile	important	frightening
worse	better	worthless	lovely	inappropriate
worst	best	valuable	shameful	magnificent

Exercise 11-8

Directions: For each of the following statements, underline the judgment word or phrase that suggests the statement is an opinion.

1. Purchasing a brand new car is a terrible waste of money.

2. Many wonderful vegetarian cookbooks are available in bookstores.

3. Of all the film versions of Victor Hugo's novel *Les Miserables,* the 1935 version starring Charles Laughton is the best.

4. The introductory biology textbook comes with an amazing CD-ROM.

5. Volunteers for Habitat for Humanity are engaged in a worthwhile activity.

Understanding More of What You Read

Now that you know about inference and about the various clues to look for in a piece of writing, you should gain a better understanding of everything you read—textbooks, newspapers, magazines, and so forth. A writer's purpose is one of the best clues to look for as you read. When you pay attention to style, audience, tone, and denotative and connotative language, and distinguish fact from opinion, you come to understand the writer's motivation and the effect he or she is trying to have on you, the reader.

The Textbook Challenge

Part A: Student Resource Guide A

1. For Textbook Excerpt 2 in Student Resource Guide A, page 403, describe the author's purpose.
2. For Textbook Excerpt 2, describe the author's tone. Then compare this tone with that of Textbook Excerpt 3 (p. 407). How do they differ?

Part B: A College Textbook

1. Using a textbook chapter that you have read for one of your other courses, describe the author's tone and purpose.

What Have You Learned?

Directions: Match each word in column A with its meaning in column B.

	Column A		Column B
_____	1. denotation	a.	an educated guess or prediction about something unknown based on available facts and information
_____	2. audience	b.	the characteristics that make a piece of writing unique
_____	3. style	c.	a word's literal meaning
_____	4. connotation	d.	the attitude or feeling a writer expresses about a subject
_____	5. tone	e.	the group of people for whom an author is writing
_____	6. inference	f.	the additional implied meanings that a word may take on

What Vocabulary Have You Learned?

Directions: The words in column A appear in exercises in this chapter. Test your mastery of these words by matching each word in column A with its meaning in column B.

	Column A	Column B
_____	1. distortion	a. combine, unite
_____	2. prude	b. someone who shows extreme modesty
_____	3. fatuous	c. be enough for somebody or something
_____	4. fuse	d. showing lack of awareness and intelligence
_____	5. suffice	e. inaccurate reporting or presentation

Test-Taking Tip #11: Critical Reading Questions

Reading comprehension tests usually ask questions that require critical reading and thinking. Answers to critical reading questions, unlike questions about details, are not directly stated in the passage. Instead, you have to reason out the answer. Use the following suggestions to answer critical reading questions correctly:

▪ Remember, all questions are answerable if you use the information contained in the passage.

▪ Some questions will require you to make inferences. To answer these, you need to add up the facts contained in the passage and come to your own conclusion. Unless you can point to some evidence in the passage to support a particular answer, do not choose it.

▪ You may also be asked questions about tone. To find the tone of a passage, ask yourself the following question: "How does the author feel toward his or her subject?" Also pay particular attention to connotative language. Words with emotional meanings often reveal tone.

▪ To answer questions about the author's purpose, answer the following question: "What does the writer intend to accomplish by writing this?" Then match your answer to the available choices.

▪ Questions about intended audience are often worded as follows: "This passage is written for . . . " or "This passage is intended to appeal to . . . " To answer this type of question, consider each choice and look for evidence in the passage that supports one of the choices.

ANALYZING TONE AND MAKING INFERENCES

A. Directions: Select the choice that best describes the tone expressed in each of the following statements.

_____ 1. The best thing to do when you feel the urge to exercise is to lie down until the feeling goes away.

    a. instructive   c. humorous

    b. persuasive   d. angry

_____ 2. Put the book back on the shelf when you are through reading it.

    a. instructive   c. humorous

    b. disapproving   d. nostalgic

_____ 3. I can remember when our house was surrounded by tall, majestic trees and furry little animals. Now when I look outside my window all I see is a highway.

    a. instructive   c. thankful

    b. persuasive   d. nostalgic

_____ 4. We need to start caring more about the rights of baby seals. They are defenseless against the ruthless hunters who kill them for their pelts.

    a. instructive   c. forceful

    b. persuasive   d. nostalgic

_____ 5. Lincoln is one of our most famous and respected presidents. His most notable and important accomplishment was the freeing of slaves in the southern United States.

    a. persuasive   c. admiring

    b. forceful   d. disapproving

B. Directions: After reading the following passage, select the letter of the choice that best answers each of the questions below. You will have to use inference in order to answer the questions.

THE LION'S SHARE

The lion, the jackal, the wolf, and the hyena had a meeting and agreed that they would hunt together in one party and share equally among them whatever game they caught.

They went out and killed an antelope. The four animals then discussed which one of them would divide the meat. The lion said, "Whoever divides the meat must know how to count."

Immediately the wolf volunteered, saying, "Indeed, I know how to count." He began to divide the meat. He cut off four pieces of equal size and placed one before each of the hunters.

The lion was angered. He said, "Is this the way to count?" And he struck the wolf across the eyes, so that his eyes swelled up and he could not see.

The jackal said, "The wolf does not know how to count. I will divide the meat." He cut three portions that were small and a fourth portion that was very large. The three small portions he placed before the hyena, the wolf, and himself. The large portion he put in front of the lion, who took his meat and went away.

"Why was it necessary to give the lion such a large piece?" the hyena said. "Our agreement was to divide and share equally. Where did you ever learn how to divide?"

"I learned from the wolf," the jackal answered.

"Wolf? How can anyone learn from the wolf? He is stupid," the hyena said.

"The jackal was right," the wolf said. "He knows how to count. Before, when my eyes were open, I did not see it. Now, though my eyes are wounded, I see it clearly."

—Harold Courlander, *The King's Drum and Other African Stories*

_____ 6. The lion was angered because

    a. he did not receive a larger share of meat.

    b. the wolf made an error in counting.

    c. the meat was not divided equally.

    d. the wolf treated him unfairly.

_____ 7. Which statement best describes the jackal's learning experience?

    a. The jackal learned from the wolf's mistake.

    b. The jackal learned not to trust the hyena.

    c. The jackal learned how to divide evenly.

    d. The jackal learned that the lion is violent.

_____ 8. What did the wolf mean when he said, "though my eyes are wounded, I see it clearly"?

    a. He dislikes the lion.

    b. He resents the way the lion treated him.

    c. He understands the mistake that he made.

    d. He realizes that all jungle animals are ruthless.

_____ 9. What lesson can be learned from this story?

    a. Don't trust your friends.

    b. Do it yourself if you want something done correctly.

    c. Sometimes it is wise to pay tribute to those who are more powerful than you are.

    d. Animals are natural enemies.

_____ 10. Which of the following was most useful in making inferences about the story?

    a. descriptions of the animals

    b. conversation by the animals

    c. unusual word meanings

    d. interesting writing style

NAME _____ SECTION _____

DATE _____ SCORE _____

READING CRITICALLY

Directions: After reading the following passage, select the choice that best answers each of the questions below.

WHAT'S BEST FOR THE CHILD?

1   In many states, there are no regulations governing the number of infants a day care staff member may care for. In those where there are, many states allow five or six. In Wisconsin, where I live, the maximum is four infants per worker. [According to the National Association for the Education of Young Children, 29 states require this four-to-one ratio, while only three—Kansas, Maryland, and Massachusetts—require a three-to-one ratio. Most of the remaining states have five-to-one ratios.]

2   Consider the amount of physical care and attention a baby needs—say 20 minutes for feeding every three hours or so, and 10 minutes for diapering every two hours or so, and time for the caregiver to wash her hands thoroughly and sanitize the area after changing each baby. In an eight-and-a-half-hour day, then, a caregiver working under the typical four-to-one ratio will have 16 diapers to change and 13 feedings to give. Four diaper changes and three feedings apiece is not an inordinate amount of care over a long day from the babies' point of view.

3   But think about the caregiver's day: Four hours to feed the babies, two hours and 40 minutes to change them. If you allow an extra two and a half minutes at each changing to put them down, clean up the area, and thoroughly wash your hands, you can get by with 40 minutes for sanitizing. (And if you think about thoroughly washing your hands 16 times a day, you may begin to understand why epidemics of diarrhea and related diseases regularly sweep through infant-care centers.)

4   That makes seven hours and 20 minutes of the day spent just on physical care—if you're lucky and the infants stay conveniently on schedule.

5   Since feeding and diaper changing are necessarily one-on-one activities, each infant is bound to be largely unattended during the five-plus hours that the other three babies are being attended to. So, if there's to be any stimulation at all for the child, the caregiver had better chat and play up a storm while she's feeding and changing.

6   Obviously, such a schedule is not realistic. In group infant care based on even this four-to-one ratio, babies will not be changed every two hours and they will probably not be held while they're fed.

7   They also will not get the kind of attention and talk that is the foundation of language development. If a child is deprived of language stimulation for eight to ten hours a day, how much compensation—how much "quality time"—can concerned parents provide in the baby's few other waking hours at home?

—Dorothy Conniff, "What's Best for the Child," *The Progressive*

_____   1. The writer's primary purpose is to

   a. explain the advantages of day care.

   b. explain the limitations of infant care in day care centers.

   c. argue for the legislation governing day care centers.

   d. explain why illnesses are common in day care centers.

_____   2. What is the author suggesting in the last sentence of paragraph 3?

   a. Caregivers do not wash their hands as frequently or carefully as they should.

   b. Washing one's hands 16 times a day is too much.

   c. Caregivers should use alternative sanitizing methods.

   d. Caregivers do not care about the spread of disease.

_____   3. In paragraph 7, the author is suggesting that

   a. language development is more important than physical care.

   b. infants in day care centers do not need stimulation.

   c. parents should talk to their infants as much as possible.

   d. parents cannot make up for the lack of stimulation of infants in a day care center.

_____   4. Based on the reading, the author is most likely to favor which of the following?

   a. legislation to decrease the number of infants a worker may care for at one time

   b. legislation to require sanitary procedures

   c. legislation to require intellectual stimulation of all infants

   d. legislation to require parents to spend quality time with their infants

_____ 5. In paragraph 2, the term **inordinate** means
  a. inadequate.   c. undefined.
  b. excessive.   d. undervalued.

_____ 6. This passage seems written primarily for which of the following audiences?
  a. day care givers   c. legislators
  b. parents   d. teachers

_____ 7. Which of the following words has a negative connotation as used in the passage?
  a. regulations   c. stimulation
  b. epidemics   d. storm

_____ 8. Which of the following terms best describes the tone of this passage?
  a. concerned   c. accepting
  b. humorous   d. angry

_____ 9. The author supports the main ideas in this passage primarily by using
  a. stories about infants.
  b. examples of infant neglect.
  c. facts and statistics about infant care.
  d. comparisons among day care centers.

_____ 10. Which statement best summarizes the author's view of infant day care?
  a. Infants should not be allowed to attend day care centers when they are ill.
  b. Day care centers are frequently unable to provide adequate language stimulation, play, and one-on-one care to infants.
  c. Infants' parents should provide language stimulation by playing tapes.
  d. Day care should not be allowed for children under age one.

NAME _____ SECTION _____
DATE _____ SCORE _____

READING CRITICALLY

A. Directions: After reading the following passage, select the choice that best answers each of the questions below.

STIFF LAWS NAIL DEADBEATS

1   The sight of deadbeat dad king Jeffrey Nichols nabbed, cuffed, and jailed in New York for ducking $580,000 in child support ought to shake up other scofflaws.

2   A few years ago, Nichols almost surely would have escaped his responsibilities. His wealth enabled him to run to Toronto, Boca Raton, Fla., and Charlotte, Vt., and he got away with it for five years. He defied three states' court orders to pay up.

3   He was finally caught because in the past few years, local, state, and federal governments have finally gotten serious about child support.

4   A law Congress passed in 1992 required the FBI to chase child-support cheats when they cross state lines. Nichols became a target, culminating in his arrest.

5   As the scale of such enforcement has grown, it has prompted occasional criticism—particularly about the use of Internal Revenue Service records to track down deadbeats. But there's no doubt it's needed.

6   There are 7 million deadbeat parents, 90% of them dads. If all paid what they are supposed to, their children would have $34 billion more—money that sometimes has to come from the taxpayers instead.

—McMiller, *USA Today*

_____ 1. In paragraph 1, the writer is suggesting that the sight of Nichols in handcuffs may

    a. encourage other deadbeat dads to pay.

    b. create legal problems.

    c. encourage more children to apply for child support.

    d. help track down other deadbeat dads.

_____ 2. In paragraph 1, the word **scofflaws** means

    a. lawyers.   c. fathers.

    b. parents.   d. lawbreakers.

_____ 3. In paragraph 2, the word **defied** means

    a. appealed.   c. reported.

    b. did not obey.   d. discouraged.

_____ 4. The author's purpose is to
   a. argue that deadbeat dads should be made to pay up.
   b. explain how Nichols got what he deserved.
   c. show that most deadbeat parents are males.
   d. explain why children deserve more money.

_____ 5. The tone of this passage could best be described as
   a. serious.   c. argumentative.
   b. casual.   d. annoying.

_____ 6. For which one of the following audiences is the article intended?
   a. deadbeat dads who escape responsibilities
   b. citizens who are concerned about how tax dollars are spent
   c. children who do not receive the support they deserve
   d. men like Jeffrey Nichols

_____ 7. Which one of the following words, as used in this passage, has a negative connotation?
   a. enforcement   c. taxpayers
   b. target   d. cheats

_____ 8. How could the use of the Internal Revenue Service records help track down deadbeat dads?
   a. The records reveal income.
   b. The records report marital status.
   c. The records report expenses.
   d. The records reveal job titles.

_____ 9. The writer uses the case of Jeffrey Nichols to
   a. give an example of a deadbeat dad.
   b. defend Nichols.
   c. show how much money taxpayers are losing each year.
   d. make deadbeat dads feel guilty.

_____ 10. Which one of the following words does _not_ usually have a negative connotation?
   a. ducking   c. deadbeat
   b. taxpayers   d. cheats

READING CRITICALLY

A. Directions: Study the photograph below and then use inference to answer the questions that follow. Write your answers in the space provided.

1. What does the photo reveal about the couple?

   They need money to buy Food.

2. What events may have brought the couple to their current circumstances?

   No jobs (unemployed)

3. What is the relationship among the individuals shown in the photo?

   A couple and a child

4. What details in the photo suggest that it was taken in an urban setting?

   the rail road and the buildings

B. Directions: After reading the following passage, select the choice that best answers each of the questions below.

WHAT YOU DON'T KNOW ABOUT NATIVE AMERICANS

1   Most Americans, even those deeply concerned about issues of justice, tend to speak of Indian issues as tragedies of the distant past. So ingrained

is this position that when the occasional non-Indian does come forward on behalf of *today's* Indian cause—Marlon Brando, William Kunstler, Robert Redford, Jane Fonda, David Brower—they are all dismissed as romantics. People are a bit embarrassed for them, as if they'd stepped over some boundary of propriety.

2   The Indian issue is *not* part of the distant past. Many of the worst anti-Indian campaigns were undertaken scarcely 80 to 100 years ago. Your great-grandparents were already alive at the time. The Model-T Ford was on the road.

3   And the assaults continue today. While the Custer period of direct military action against Indians may be over in the United States, more subtle though equally devastating "legalistic" manipulations continue to separate Indians from their land and their sovereignty.

—Mander, *In the Absence of the Sacred: The Failure of Technology and the Rise of Indian Nations*

5. The main point of the passage is that
    a. the problems of Native Americans are not just history; they continue today.
    b. Native Americans experience anti-Indian campaigns.
    c. famous people who speak out for Native Americans are considered romantics.
    d. Native Americans experienced many tragedies.

6. Paragraph 3 focuses on
    a. solutions.   c. military actions.
    b. Custer's victories.   d. legal manipulations.

7. Which phrase best describes the tone of the passage?
    a. scientific
    b. casual and informal
    c. serious and concerned
    d. light and humorous

8. For which audience was this written?
    a. Native Americans not living on a reservation
    b. lawyers who represent Native Americans
    c. history teachers
    d. Americans who do not know much about Native American issues

_____ 9. Which of these words has a strong negative connotation?

  a. issue

  b. assaults

  c. great-grandparents

  d. Model-T Fords

_____ 10. The statement "The Model-T Ford was on the road" was included in paragraph 2 to

  a. focus on the past.

  b. emphasize that the issue is an American problem.

  c. call attention to big business.

  d. emphasize that the issue is part of modern times.

READING CRITICALLY

Directions: After reading the following brief story, select the choice that best answers each of the questions below.

The caller's voice does not hold together well. I can tell he is quite old and not well. He is calling from Maryland.

"I want four boxes of the Nut Goodies," he rasps at me after giving me his credit card information in a faltering hurry.

"There are 24 bars in each box," I say in case he doesn't know the magnitude of his order. Nut Goodies are made here in St. Paul and consist of a patty of maple cream covered with milk chocolate and peanuts. Sort of a Norwegian praline.

"OK, then make it five boxes but hurry this up before my nurse gets back."

He wants the order billed to his home address but sent to a nursing home.

"I've got Parkinson's," he says. "I'm 84."

"OK sir, I think I've got it all. They're on the way." I put a rush on it.

"Right. Bye," he says, and in the pause when he is concentrating God knows how much energy on getting the receiver back in its cradle, I hear a long, dry chuckle.

One hundred and twenty Nut Goodies.

Way to go, buddy.

—Swardson, *City Pages,* p. 8

_____ 1. The caller is most likely

    a. not supposed to eat candy.

    b. angry with his nurse.

    c. unable to pay for his order.

    d. unhappy.

_____ 2. Which word best describes the tone of this passage?

    a. disgusting   c. sympathetic

    b. instructive   d. forceful

_____ 3. A praline is

    a. a Norwegian plate.   c. a type of nut.

    b. a type of candy.   d. a Norwegian tradition.

_____ 4. Why does the caller chuckle at the end of the conversation?

    a. The order-taker made a joke.

    b. The caller thought his nurse had returned.

    c. The caller thought he would get better service.

    d. The caller thinks he has gotten away with something.

_____ 5. What is the writer's purpose?

    a. to share an amusing incident

    b. to criticize nursing home care

    c. to sell Norwegian pralines

    d. to defend living conditions of the elderly

_____ 6. The concluding phrase "Way to go, buddy" suggests

    a. disapproval.   c. approval.

    b. disappointment.   d. lack of understanding.

_____ 7. The word **faltering** suggests

    a. pride.   c. assurance.

    b. importance.   d. weakness.

_____ 8. What word best describes the person taking the call?

    a. indifferent.   c. prejudiced.

    b. polite.   d. elderly.

_____ 9. The word **magnitude** means

    a. cost.   c. importance.

    b. weight.   d. size.

_____ 10. Why did the order-taker put a rush on the order?

    a. He was afraid the nurse would discover the order.

    b. He felt sorry for the caller.

    c. He disliked the company that sold the pralines.

    d. He wanted to add extra costs to the order.

NAME _____ SECTION _____

DATE _____ SCORE _____

THE BEAUTIFUL LAUGHING SISTERS
Mary Pipher

This reading is taken from Mary Pipher's book *The Middle of Every-where*, which examines the plight of refugees who have fled to America from countries where they were mistreated and abused. Read this selection to learn the story of a courageous Kurdish family.

Vocabulary Preview

These are some of the difficult words and terms in this essay. The definitions here will help you if you can't figure out the meanings from the sentence context or word parts.

refugee (para. 1) one who flees in search of protection or shelter, especially to a foreign country

cultural broker (para. 1) one who helps people from other countries learn the customs of the new country

amendment (para. 3) an additional comment or correction

makeshift (para. 10) describing a temporary and rough substitute

immigrate (para. 20) to enter and settle in a country or region to which one is not native

1   One of the best ways to understand the refugee experience is to befriend a family of new arrivals and observe their experiences in our country for the first year. That first year is the hardest. Everything is new and strange, and obstacles appear like the stars appear at dusk, in an uncountable array. This story is about a family I met during their first month in our country. I became their friend and cultural broker and in the process learned a great deal about the refugee experience, and about us Americans.

2   On a fall day I met Shireen and Meena, who had come to this country from Pakistan. The **Kurdish** sisters were slender young women with alert expressions. They wore blue jeans and clunky high-heeled shoes. Shireen was taller and bolder, Meena was smaller and more soft-spoken. Their English was limited and heavily accented. (I later learned it was their sixth language after Kurdish, Arabic, Farsi, Urdu, and Hindi.) They communicated with each other

Kurdish: The Kurds are a people of the Middle East whose homeland is in the mountainous regions of Iraq, Iran, and Turkey.

via small quick gestures and eye movements. Although they laughed easily, they watched to see that the other was okay at all times.

3   Shireen was the youngest and the only one of the six sisters who was eligible for high school. Meena, who was twenty-one, had walked the ten blocks from their apartment to meet Shireen at school on a bitterly cold day. Shireen told the family story. Meena occasionally interrupted her answers with a reminder, an amendment, or laughter.

4   Shireen was born in Baghdad in 1979, the last of ten children. Their mother, Zeenat, had been a village girl who entered an arranged marriage at fourteen. Although their father had been well educated, Zeenat couldn't read or write in any language. The family was prosperous and "Europeanized," as Shireen put it. She said, "Before our father was in trouble, we lived just like you. Baghdad was a big city. In our group of friends, men and women were treated as equals. Our older sisters went to movies and read foreign newspapers. Our father went to cocktail parties at the embassies."

5   However, their father had opposed Saddam Hussein, and from the time of Shireen's birth, his life was in danger. After Hussein came to power, terrible things happened to families like theirs. One family of eleven was taken to jail by his security forces and tortured to death. Prisoners were often fed rice mixed with glass so that they would quietly bleed to death in their cells. Girls were raped and impregnated by the security police. Afterward, they were murdered or killed themselves.

6   It was a hideous time. Schoolteachers tried to get children to betray their parents. One night the police broke into the family's house. They tore up the beds, bookcases, and the kitchen, and they took their Western clothes and tapes. After that night, all of the family except for one married sister made a daring escape into Iran.

7   Meena said, "It was a long time ago but I can see everything today." There was no legal way to go north, so they walked through Kurdistan at night and slept under bushes in the day. They found a guide who made his living escorting Kurds over the mountains. Twice they crossed rivers near flood stage. Entire families had been swept away by the waters and one of the sisters almost drowned when she fell off her horse. The trails were steep and narrow and another sister fell and broke her leg. Meena was in a bag slung

over the guide's horse for three days. She remembered how stiff she felt in the bag, and Shireen remembered screaming, "I want my mama."

8   This was in the 1980s. While this was happening I was a psychologist building my private practice and a young mother taking my kids to *Sesame Street Live* and **Vacation Village on Lake Okoboji.** I was dancing to the music of my husband's band, Sour Mash, listening to Van Morrison and Jackson Browne and reading P.D. James and Anne Tyler. Could my life have been happening on the same planet?

Vacation Village on Lake Okoboji: A family resort in northwestern Iowa.

9   The family made it to a refugee camp in Iran. It was a miserable place with smelly tents and almost no supplies. Shireen said this was rough on her older siblings who had led lives of luxury. She and Meena adjusted more quickly. The sisters studied in an Iranian school for refugees.

10   They endured this makeshift camp for one very bad year. The Iranians insisted that all the women in the camp wear heavy scarves and robes and conform to strict rules. The soldiers in the camp shouted at them if they wore even a little lipstick. Shireen once saw a young girl wearing makeup stopped by a guard who rubbed it off her face. He had put ground glass in the tissue so that her cheeks bled afterward.

11   They decided to get out of Iran and traveled the only direction they could, east into Pakistan. They walked all the way with nothing to drink except salty water that made them even thirstier. I asked how long the trip took and Shireen said three days. Meena quickly corrected her: "Ten years."

12   Once in Pakistan they were settled by a relief agency in a border town called Quetta, where strangers were not welcome. The family lived in a small house with electricity that worked only sporadically. The stress of all the moves broke the family apart. The men left the women and the family has never reunited.

13   Single women in Quetta couldn't leave home unescorted and the sisters had no men to escort them. Only their mother, Zeenat, dared go out to look for food. As Meena put it, "She took good care of us and now we will take care of her."

14   The sisters almost never left the hut, but when they did, they wore robes as thick and heavy as black carpets. Meena demonstrated how hard it was to

ask about an art course advertised on a book of matches. It promised a college degree for thirty-five dollars. I said, "Don't do it." A couple of weeks later she called again. This time she had seen an ad for models. She wondered if she should pay and enter the modeling contest. Again I advised, "Don't do it." I was embarrassed to tell her that we Americans lie to people to make money. Before I hung up, we chatted for a while.

30   I wanted to make sure they learned they learned about the good things in our city. Advertisers would direct them to the bars, the malls, and anything that cost money. I told them about what I loved: the parks and prairies, the lakes and sunsets, the sculpture garden, and the free concerts. I lent them books with Georgia O'Keeffe paintings and pictures of our national parks.

31   For a while I was so involved with the lives of the sisters that Zeenat told me that her daughters were now my daughters. I was touched that she was willing to give her daughters away so that they could advance. I tactfully suggested we could share her daughters, but that she would always be the real mother.

— ▪ —

Directions: Select the letter of the choice that best completes each of the following statements.

CHECKING YOUR COMPREHENSION

_____   1. The "beautiful laughing sisters" referred to in the title are
   a. the author's children.
   b. the author's sisters.
   c. members of a refugee family from Iraq.
   d. characters in a song about the Middle East.

_____   2. The topic of paragraph 5 is the
   a. comfortable life of the family in Baghdad.
   b. treatment of prisoners in Iraq.
   c. tactics of the security police.
   d. conditions in Iraq under Saddam Hussein.

_____ 3. The family finally decided to escape from Iraq when

    a. their father was arrested.

    b. their home was broken into.

    c. a schoolteacher tried to make the girls betray their parents.

    d. the Pakistanis tested a nuclear bomb near their home.

_____ 4. According to the reading, the person who was most responsible for the sisters' survival was

    a. their father.

    b. their brother.

    c. their mother.

    d. a relief worker at the refugee camp.

_____ 5. The final three paragraphs (29–31)

    a. describe the author's involvement in the family's life.

    b. criticize certain American businesses.

    c. draw conclusions about the girls' relationship with their mother.

    d. encourage the reader to learn more about the plight of refugees.

USING WHAT YOU KNOW ABOUT INFERENCE AND THE WRITER'S PURPOSE

_____ 6. The author's primary purpose in "The Beautiful Laughing Sisters" is to

    a. examine the official channels people must go through to immigrate.

    b. describe the experience of a refugee family.

    c. encourage people to make friends with refugees.

    d. comment on the racism that exists worldwide.

_____ 7. The author presents information about the refugee experience primarily through

    a. figurative language.

    b. historical facts.

    c. the family's personal experience.

    d. expert opinion.

_____ 8. The author's tone can best be described as

    a. persuasive.   c. grim.

    b. worried.   d. sympathetic.

_____ 9. When the author asks in paragraph 8, "Could my life have been happening on the same planet?" she means that

    a. her world was incredibly different from that of the sisters.

    b. she was not paying attention to the current events of the time.

    c. Americans do not understand the plight of refugees.

    d. everyone on Earth is unique.

_____ 10. In paragraph 24, the author states that Shireen said the word "'rights' as if it were a sacred word." Shireen felt this way because she

    a. had been taught about rights in her religion.

    b. had been without rights for a long time and believed they were important.

    c. was not able to pronounce the word correctly.

    d. was afraid that someone would hear her and take her rights away.

USING CONTEXT AND WORD PARTS

_____ 11. In paragraph 3, the word **eligible** means

    a. questionable.   c. qualified.

    b. obvious.   d. formal.

_____ 12. In paragraph 10, the word **conform** means

    a. disagree.   c. obey.

    b. change.   d. avoid.

_____ 13. In paragraph 12, the word **sporadically** means

    a. frequently.   c. consistently.

    b. reliably.   d. at irregular intervals.

_____ 14. In paragraph 15, the word **incredulously** means

    a. remarkably.   c. hopefully.

    b. disbelievingly.   d. rudely.

_____ 15. In paragraph 27, the word **resilience** means

    a. the ability to recover from a bad experience.

    b. an unwillingness to deal with bad news.

    c. irresponsible behavior.

    d. a rigid attitude toward difficulties.

REVIEWING DIFFICULT VOCABULARY

Directions: Match each word in column A with its meaning in column B. The words in column A are from the Vocabulary Preview on page 380.

Column A	Column B
_____ 16. refugee	a. an additional comment or correction
_____ 17. cultural broker	b. to enter and settle in a country or region to which one is not native
_____ 18. amendment	c. one who flees in search of protection or shelter, especially to a foreign country
_____ 19. makeshift	d. one who helps people from other countries learn the customs of the new country
_____ 20. immigrate	e. a temporary and rough substitute

STUDYING WORDS

_____ 21. The word **resilence** (para. 27) is correctly pronounced

    a. ri ZIL yence.

    b. RIZ ell ance.

    c. REE zil yance.

    d. re ZI yance.

_____ 22. The word **embassies** (para. 4) is derived from which of the following languages?

    a. Russian

    b. French

    c. Spanish

    d. Latin

_____ 23. The restrictive meaning of the word **obstacles** (para. 1) in the field of sports is

    a. something that blocks progress.

    b. a hindrance.

    c. a substance that disables the participant.

    d. a fence or hurdle.

_____ 24. What part of speech is the word **tactfully** (para. 31)?

    a. adjective

    b. verb

    c. adverb

    d. noun

_____ 25. What part of speech is the word **sporadically** (para. 12)?

    a. noun

    b. adverb

    c. verb

    d. adjective

QUESTIONS FOR DISCUSSION

1. After you have read the selection, look at a map of the Middle East and locate the places that are mentioned. What else do you know about these places, especially with regard to current events?

2. Discuss the issue of immigration. Who should be allowed to enter our country? Should our laws be stricter or more lenient?

3. Think about the main immigrant groups in your community. What services are available to help them adjust? What sort of contact, if any, do you have with new people in our country?

WRITING ACTIVITIES

1. Take a virtual tour of a refugee camp at the Web site of the organization Doctors Without Borders, http://www.doctorswithoutborders.org/index.shtml, or at http://www.refugeecamp.org/. Write a paragraph comparing the conditions depicted on the Web sites with those described in the selection.

2. The sisters in the story arrive in a place that is foreign to them. Think about a time when you visited a new place for the first time (perhaps your college campus) and write a paragraph describing your experience, your feelings, and any problems or difficulties that you faced.

3. Brainstorm a list of aspects of American life or culture that may have been unfamiliar to the sisters. (Pipher provides such a list later in the book and includes such things as what vitamins are, how to write a check, what elections are, and how to play cards.)

4. Write a letter to a real or imagined immigrant student in which you welcome the student and offer advice about adjusting to life in America.

Chapter 11: Reading and Thinking Critically

RECORDING YOUR PROGRESS

Test	Number Right			Score	
Practice Test 11-1	_____	× 10	=	_____	%
Practice Test 11-2	_____	× 10	=	_____	%
Practice Test 11-3	_____	× 10	=	_____	%
Mastery Test 11-1	_____	× 10	=	_____	%
Mastery Test 11-2	_____	× 10	=	_____	%
Mastery Test 11-3	_____	× 4	=	_____	%

EVALUATING YOUR PROGRESS

Based on your test performance, rate how well you have mastered the skills taught in this chapter by checking one of the boxes below or by writing your own evaluation.

☐ **Need More Improvement**
Try using the "Inference" Module on the Reading Road Trip Web site at **http://www. ablongman.com/readingroadtrip** to fine-tune the skills that you have learned in this chapter.

☐ **Need More Practice**
Tip: Try using the "Inference" Module on the Reading Road Trip Web site at **http://www. ablongman.com/readingroadtrip** to brush up on the skills you have learned in this chapter, or visit this textbook's companion Web site at **http://www.ablongman.com/mcwhorter** for extra practice.

☐ **Good**
Tip: To maintain your skills, quickly review this chapter by using this textbook's companion Web site by logging on to **http://www.ablongman.com/mcwhorter**.

☐ **Excellent**

YOUR EVALUATION: _____

_____

_____

_____

_____

Introduction to College Textbook Reading

Each semester, you will spend hours reading, reviewing, and studying textbooks. By learning to read and study textbooks effectively you can save hours of time and achieve higher grades. This resource guide will show you the features a textbook offers to help you learn, explain a system for reading and studying textbooks, and present suggestions for learning textbook material. It also contains three textbook excerpts for you to use in applying the skills taught in this guide.

- Textbook Excerpt 1: "Civil Liberties and the Right to Privacy," page 400
- Textbook Excerpt 2: "Food Safety: A Growing Concern," page 403
- Textbook Excerpt 3: "Legible Clothing," page 407

The Features of Your Textbooks

Textbooks are written by college teachers. Because teachers understand how students learn and are familiar with topics that students may have trouble with, they include many features in textbooks to help you learn.

Assessing Textbook Learning Aids

Using a textbook for one of your other courses, check which of the following features it contains. Place a check mark in front of each item that you find (not all texts will have all features). Then decide how you can use each feature to help you learn.

Feature	Value
☐ Chapter Objectives	_____
☐ Chapter Outline	_____
☐ Marginal Definitions or Footnotes for Key Vocabulary	_____
☐ Numbered Lists of Important Information	_____
☐ Headings	_____
☐ Boxed Inserts	_____
☐ Tables, Graphs, Charts	_____
☐ Photographs	_____
☐ Problems or Exercises	_____
☐ Discussion Questions	_____
☐ Review Questions	_____
☐ List of Key Terminology	_____
☐ Chapter Summary	_____
☐ Suggested Readings	_____
☐ Glossary	_____
☐ Appendix	_____

Examining the Preface or "To the Student"

The preface is the introduction to the book; it describes the book's organization and use.

1. Read the preface or "To the Student" in one of your other textbooks.

2. Write a list of information you learned about your textbook from reading the preface or "To the Student." Look for the answers to these questions:
   • How is the book organized?
   • What topic does the book cover?
   • What makes the book unique?
   • What learning features are included?

Examining the Table of Contents

The table of contents provides you with **a** detailed outline of the book's topics. The chapter titles are the main divisions of the book, and the titles within each chapter give the smaller subdivisions of the topics.

Exercise A–1

Directions: Complete each of the following activities.

1. Look at the table of contents of one of your textbooks for another course. Choose one chapter that you will have to read soon.

2. Examine the titles and subtitles for that one chapter. What is the main topic of the chapter? What are the major divisions of that main topic?

3. Think about what you already know about this topic, from talking to other people, watching the news, reading, or listening to the radio.

4. What do you expect to learn from reading this chapter?

The SQ3R Reading/Study System

SQ3R is a system that combines reading and study. Instead of reading a chapter one day and studying it later when a test is announced, you can do both at once using SQ3R. The SQ3R system is a model. Once you see how and why SQ3R works, you can adapt it to suit your own academic needs.

Steps in the SQ3R System

The SQ3R system involves five basic steps that integrate reading and study techniques. As you read the following steps, some of them will seem similar to the skills you have already learned.

S—Survey Try to become familiar with the organization and general content of the material you are to read.

1. Read the title.
2. Read the lead-in or introduction. (If it is extremely long, read just the first paragraph.)
3. Read each boldface heading and the first sentence that follows it.
4. Read the titles of maps, charts, or graphs.

5. Read the last paragraph or summary.

6. Read the end-of-chapter questions.

7. After you have surveyed the material, you should know generally what it is about and how it is organized.

The Survey step is the technique of prereading that you learned in Chapter 1.

Q—Question   Try to form questions that you can answer as you read. The easiest way to do this is to turn each boldface heading into a question. Think of these as similar to the guide questions discussed in Chapter 1.

R—Read   Read the material section by section. As you read each section, look for the answer to the question you formed from the heading of that section.

R—Recite   After you finish each section, stop. Check to see whether you can answer your question for the section. If you can't, look back to find the answer. Then check your recall again. Be sure to complete this step after you read each section.

R—Review   When you have finished the whole reading assignment, go back to each heading; recall your question and try to answer it. If you can't recall the answer, be sure to look back and find the answer. Then test yourself again.

Why SQ3R Works

Results of research studies overwhelmingly suggest that students who use the SQ3R system understand and remember what they read much better than students who do not use it.

If you consider for a moment how people learn, it becomes clear why reading/study systems are effective. One major way to learn is through repetition. Consider the way you learned the multiplication tables. Through repeated practice and drills, you learned $2 \times 2 = 4$, $5 \times 6 = 30$, $8 \times 9 = 72$, and so forth. The key was repetition. Reading/study systems provide some of the repetition necessary to ensure learning. Compared with the usual once-through approach to reading textbook assignments that offer one chance to learn, SQ3R provides numerous repetitions and increases the amount learned.

SQ3R also has many advantages over ordinary reading. First, surveying (prereading) gives you a mental organization or structure—you know what to expect. Second, you always feel that you are looking for something specific rather than wandering aimlessly through a printed page. Third, when you find the information you're looking for, you feel you have accomplished something. And if you can remember the information in the immediate- and long-term recall checks, it is even more rewarding.

Exercise A-2

Directions: Choose a section of a textbook chapter that you have been assigned for one of your courses. Use the SQ3R method to read and review the section. Write the questions you form on a separate sheet of paper, leaving space for the answers. Answer your questions after you have read the section.

Learning Strategies

Use the following suggestions to improve how efficiently you learn information contained in your textbooks.

Use Immediate Review

After working on a chapter for several hours (with frequent breaks) it is tempting, when you finish, to close the book and move on to something else. To quit, however, without taking five to ten minutes to review what you have read is a serious mistake. Since you have already invested several hours of time and effort, it is worthwhile to spend a few more minutes insuring that investment by rereading each chapter heading and then rereading the summary (as suggested in the SQ3R method above).

Use Periodic Review

Periodic review means returning to and quickly reviewing previously learned material on a regular basis. Suppose you have learned the material in the first three chapters of your criminology text during the first two weeks of the course. Unless you review that material, you are likely to forget it and have to relearn it by the time your final exam is given. You might establish a periodic review schedule in which you quickly review these chapters every three weeks or so.

Use Mnemonic Devices

Mnemonics are memory tricks, or aids, that you can devise to help you remember information. Mnemonics include rhymes, anagrams, words, nonsense words, sentences, and mental pictures that aid in the recall of facts. Do you remember this rhyme? "Thirty days hath September, / April, June, and November. / All the rest have thirty-one / except February, alone, / which has twenty-eight days clear / and twenty-nine in each leap year." The rhyme is an example of a mnemonic device. It is a quick and easy way of remembering the number of days in each month of the year. You may have learned to recall the colors of the rainbow by remembering the name *Roy G. Biv;* each letter in this name stands for one of the colors that make up the spectrum: *R*ed, *O*range, *Y*ellow, *G*reen, *B*lue, *I*ndigo, *V*iolet. Mnemonic devices are useful when you are trying to learn information that has no organization of its own. You will find them useful in reviewing texts and lecture notes as you prepare for exams.

Use Numerous Sensory Channels to Store Information

Many students regard reading and studying as only a visual means of taking in information. You can learn better, however, if you use sight, sound, and touch, as well. If you can incorporate writing, listening, drawing or diagramming, and recitation or discussion into your study plan, learning will be more effective.

Organize Information

Remembering a large number of individual facts or pieces of information is often a difficult, frustrating task. Organize or reduce information into groups or chunks. Instead of overloading your memory with numerous individual facts, learn organized, meaningful sets of information that you can store as one chunk. For example, instead of learning 14 individual causes of World War II, group them into political, social, and economic causes.

To organize information, keep the following suggestions in mind:

- Discover how the material you are studying is connected. Search for some organizing principle.
- Look for similarities and differences.
- Look for sequences and for obvious divisions or breaking points within the sequences.

Connect New Learning with Previous Learning

Isolated, unrelated pieces of information are difficult to store and also difficult to retrieve. If, however, you can link new learning to already stored information, it will be easier to store and retrieve since you have an established memory slot in which to hold it. For example, an economics student associated the factors influencing the supply and demand curves with practical instances from his family's retail florist business.

Use Visualization

As you read, study, and learn a body of information, try to visualize or create a mental picture of it. Your picture or image should be sufficiently detailed to include as much related information as possible. A student of anatomy and physiology found visualizations an effective way to learn the parts of the skeletal system. She would first draw the system on paper and then visualize, or mentally draw, it.

Develop Retrieval Clues

Think of your memory as having slots or compartments in which information is stored. If you can name or label what is in the slot, you will know where to look to find information that fits that slot. Think of memory slots as similar to the way kitchen cupboards are often organized, with specific items in specific places. If you need a knife to cut a pizza, you look in the silverware and utensils drawer. Similarly, if you have a memory slot labeled "environmental problems" in which you store information related to pollution and its problems, causes, and solutions, you can retrieve information on air pollution by calling up the appropriate retrieval clue. Developing retrieval clues involves selecting a word or phrase that summarizes or categorizes several pieces of information. For example, you might use the phrase "motivation theories" to organize information for a psychology course on instinct, drive, cognitive, arousal, and opponent-process theories and the major proponents of each.

Test Yourself

Practice retrieving learned information by simulating test conditions. If you are studying for a math exam, prepare by solving problems. If you know your exam in a law enforcement course will consist of three essay questions, then prepare by anticipating possible essay questions and drafting an answer to each. The form and process of practice, then, must be patterned after and modeled upon the event for which you are preparing.

Overlearn

It is tempting to stop studying as soon as you feel you have learned a given body of information. However, to ensure complete, thorough learning, it is best to conduct a few more reviews. When you learned to drive a car, you did not stop practicing parallel parking after the first time you accomplished it correctly. Similarly, for a botany course you should not stop reviewing the process of photosynthesis and its place within the carbon cycle at the moment you feel you have mastered it. Instead, use additional review to make the material stick and to prevent interference from subsequent learning.

Exercise A-3	*Directions: Discuss the strategies you would use to learn each of the following types of information most efficiently.*

1. the process of cell division for a biology course

2. vocabulary words for a Spanish I course

_____

3. the different types of white collar crimes and their cost to society for a criminology course

_____

4. the names of various bacteria forms

_____

Textbook Excerpt 1: Political Science/History

CIVIL LIBERTIES AND THE RIGHT TO PRIVACY
Edward S. Greenberg and Benjamin I. Page

Civil Liberties in the Constitution

1   **Civil liberties** are freedoms protected by constitutional provisions, laws, and practices from certain types of government interference. The framers of the Constitution were particularly concerned about establishing a society in which liberty might flourish. As embodied in the Bill of Rights, civil liberties are protected by prohibitions against government actions that threaten the enjoyment of freedom.

2   In the Preamble to the Constitution, the framers wrote that they aimed to "secure the Blessings of Liberty to ourselves and our Posterity." But in the original Constitution, they protected few liberties from the national government they were creating and almost none from state governments. Rather than listing specific prohibitions against certain kinds of actions, they believed that liberty was best protected by a constitutional design that fragmented government power, a design that included separation of powers, checks and balances, and federalism. Still, the framers singled out certain freedoms as too crucial to be left unmentioned. The Constitution prohibits Congress and the states from suspending the writ of **habeas corpus,** except when public safety demands it because of rebellion or invasion, and from passing **bills of attainder** or **ex post facto laws** (see Table A for an enumeration).

3   Many citizens found the proposed Constitution too stingy in its listing of liberties, so the Federalists were led to promise a *"bill of rights"* as a con-

habeas corpus: The legal doctrine that a person who is arrested must have a timely hearing before a judge.

bills of attainder: A governmental decree that a person is guilty of a crime that carries the death penalty, rendered without benefit of a trial.

ex post facto law: A law that retroactively declares some action illegal.

dition for passing the Constitution. The Bill of Rights was passed by the 1st Congress in 1789 and was ratified by the required number of states by 1791. Passage of the Bill of Rights made the Constitution more democratic by specifying protections of political liberty and by guaranteeing a context of free political expression that makes popular sovereignty possible.

4   Looking at the liberties specified by the text of the Constitution and its amendments, however, emphasizes how few of our most cherished liberties are to be found in a reading of the bare words of the Constitution. Decisions by government officials and changes brought about by political leaders, interest groups, social movements, and individuals remade the Constitution in the long run, so many of the freedoms we expect today are not specifically mentioned there. Some extensions of protected liberties were introduced by judges and other officials. Others have evolved as the culture has grown to accept novel and even once threatening ideas. Still other liberties have secured a place in the Republic through partisan and ideological combat. The key to understanding civil liberties in the United States is to follow their evolution during the course of our history. Let us consider first the right to privacy issue.

The Right to Privacy

5   The freedom to be left alone in our private lives—what is usually referred to as the *right to privacy*—is nowhere mentioned in the Bill of Rights. Nevertheless, most Americans consider the right to privacy one of our most precious

■ Inmates complain about their living conditions at the crowded Central Penitentiary in Tegucigalpa, Honduras. Only 10 percent of the 10,000 imprisoned inmates in Honduras were sentenced by judges. The remainder were detained and many languish in jail without a trial for years. The Honduras Congress, as a way of combating a rising crime rate, is debating the introduction of a life sentence for criminals to replace the current maximum 30-year sentence.

freedoms; most believe we ought to be spared wiretapping, e-mail snooping, and the regulation of consensual sexual activities in our own homes, for instance. Many (though not all) constitutional scholars believe, moreover, that a right to privacy is *inherent* (not explicitly stated) in the Bill of Rights; note the prohibitions against illegal searches and seizures and against the quartering of troops in our homes, as well as the right to free expression and conscience. Such scholars also point to the Ninth Amendment as evidence that the framers believed in the existence of liberties not specifically mentioned in the Bill of Rights: "The enumeration in the Constitution of certain rights, shall not be construed to deny or disparage others retained by the people." The Supreme Court agreed with this position in *Griswold v. Connecticut* (1965), in which it ruled that a constitutional right to privacy exists when it struck down laws making birth control illegal.

6   Some advocates of the right to privacy see a growing peril in the ability of the new information technology to collect and make accessible a vast amount of data about each and every American. Under a new law designed to root out "deadbeat dads"—fathers who owe child support payments—the federal government, for example, has begun to operate computerized directory showing every person newly hired by every employer in the country. Federal officials say it will be one of the largest, most up-to-date, and most detailed files of personal information kept by the government.

7   So far the Supreme Court has refused to endorse the existence of a privacy-based "right to die." Indeed, in *Vacco v. Quill* (1997), it threw out two federal circuit court decisions that had overturned two state laws banning doctor-assisted suicide (Washington and New York) as unconstitutional. The Court majority ruled that states were free to ban doctor-assisted suicide. Their ruling did not prohibit states from passing laws establishing such a right, however. Indeed, five of the justices suggested in their written opinions that they might support a claim for the existence of such a right in the future.

8   Whether there is or ought to be a constitutionally protected right to privacy, and other rights (such as the right to die) associated with privacy, remains an issue of intense debate.

▬ ▪ ▬

APPLYING YOUR TEXTBOOK READING SKILLS

1. Identify the textbook learning aids contained in this textbook excerpt and evaluate their usefulness.
2. Apply the SQ3R method to this textbook excerpt. Write your questions and answers on a separate sheet of paper.
3. What learning strategies would be useful in studying this excerpt?

Textbook Excerpt 2: Health

FOOD SAFETY: A GROWING CONCERN
Rebecca Donatelle

1   As we become increasingly worried that the food we put in our mouths may be contaminated with bacteria, insects, worms, or other substances, the food industry has come under fire. To convince us that their products are safe, some manufacturers have come up with "new and improved" ways of protecting our foods. How well do they work?

Food-Borne Illnesses

2   Are you concerned that the chicken you are buying doesn't look pleasingly pink, or that your "fresh" fish smells a little *too* fishy or has a grayish tinge? Are you *sure* that your apple juice is free of animal wastes? You may have good reason to be worried. In increasing numbers, Americans are becoming sick from what they eat, and many of these illnesses are life threatening. Scientists estimate, based on several studies conducted over the past 10 years, that food-borne pathogens sicken between 6.5 and 81 million people and cause some 9,000 deaths in the United States annually. Because most of us don't go to the doctor every time we are sick, we may not make a connection between what we eat and later symptoms.

3   Signs of food-borne illnesses vary tremendously and usually include one or several symptoms: diarrhea, nausea, cramping, and vomiting. Depending on the amount and virulence of the pathogen, symptoms may appear as early as 30 minutes after eating contaminated food, or as long as several days or weeks. Most of the time, symptoms occur five to eight hours after eating and last only a day or two. For certain populations, however, such as the very

young or very old or persons with AIDS or other severe illnesses, food-borne diseases can be fatal.

Responsible Use: Avoiding Risks in the Home

4   Part of the responsibility for preventing food-borne illness lies with con-sumers—over 30 percent of all such illnesses result from unsafe handling of food at home.

- *When shopping, pick up packaged and canned foods first, and save frozen foods and perish-ables such as meat, poultry, and fish for last.*
- *Check for cleanliness at the salad bar and meat and fish counters.*
- *When shopping for fish, buy from markets that get their supplies from state-approved sources.*
- *Most cuts of meat, fish, and poultry should be kept in the refrigerator no more than one or two days.*
- *Eat leftovers within three days.*
- *Keep hot foods hot and cold foods cold.*
- *Use a thermometer to ensure that meats are completely cooked. Beef and lamb should be cooked to at least 140°F, pork to 150°F, and poultry to 165°F. Don't eat poultry that is pink inside.*
- *Fish is done when the thickest part becomes opaque and the fish flakes easily when poked with a fork.*
- *Never leave cooked food standing on the stove or table for more than two hours.*
- *Never thaw frozen foods at room temperature.*
- *Wash your hands and countertop with soap and water when preparing food, particularly after handling meat, fish, or poultry.*
- *When freezing foods like chicken, make sure juices can't spill over into ice cubes or into other areas of the refrigerator.*

Food Irradiation: How Safe Is It?

5   Each year, thousands of people get sick from largely preventable diseases such as that caused by *E. coli* as well as other bacteria such as *Salmonella* and *Listeria*. In response to these illnesses, in February 2000 the USDA approved large-scale irradiation of beef, lamb, poultry, pork, and other raw animal foods. **Food irradiation** is a process that involves treating foods with gamma radiation from radioactive cobalt, cesium, or other sources of x-rays. When foods are irradiated, they are exposed to low doses of radiation, or ionizing

energy, which breaks chemical bonds in the DNA of harmful bacteria, destroying the pathogens and keeping them from replicating. The rays essentially pass through the food without leaving any radioactive residue.

6   Some companies use cobalt 60, a radioactive substance, for irradiation, but others are beginning to use a new kind of irradiation that dispenses with radioactive compounds and uses electricity as the energy source instead. Thus, as foods pass along a conveyor belt, the energy used to kill bacteria comes from electron beams rather than gamma rays. Irradiation lengthens food products' shelf life and prevents the spread of deadly microorganisms, particularly in high-risk foods such as ground beef and pork. Thus, the minimal costs of irradiation should result in lower overall costs to consumers, in addition to reducing the need for toxic chemicals now used to preserve foods and prevent contamination from external pathogens.

7   Food irradiation has been approved for potatoes, spices, pork carcasses, and fruits and vegetables since the mid-1980s. Some environmentalists and consumer groups have raised concerns, so irradiated products are not common fare. However, the facts appear to support the use of irradiation.

Food Additives

8   Additives generally reduce the risk of food-borne illness (i.e., nitrates added to cured meats), prevent spoilage, and enhance the ways foods look and taste. Additives can also enhance nutrient value, especially to benefit the general public. A deficiency can be a terrible public health problem, and a solution is relatively easy to administer. The fortification of milk with vitamin D serves as a perfect example. Many other such examples exist. One of the newest additives to our daily food is folate, one of the B vitamins. Produced by plants and yeasts, folate is believed to offer many health benefits, reducing the risk of neural tube defects, certain anemias, cervical dysplasia, and heart attacks. According to the FDA and the U.S. Public Health Service, folate's benefits have been proved again and again in observational and clinical trials. In 1992, the U.S. Public Health Service recommended folate for all women who might become pregnant. All women should get 180 micrograms per day, and if pregnant, 400 micrograms per day. The best sources of folate are fruits and vegetables, particularly beans, spinach, and broccoli. Many multivitamin supplements also supply this amount. Recently, the Public

Health Service took the recommendation one step further by approving the addition of folate to flour.

9   Although the FDA regulates additives according to effectiveness, safety, and ability to detect them in foods, questions have been raised about those additives put into foods intentionally and those that get in unintentionally before or after processing.

10 **Intentional Food Additives**

- *Antimicrobial agents: substances such as salt, sugar, nitrates, and others that tend to make foods less hospitable for microbes.*
- *Antioxidants: substances that preserve color and flavor by reducing loss due to exposure to oxygen. Vitamins C and E are among those antioxidants believed to play a role in reducing the risk of cancer and cardiovascular disease. BHA and BHT are additives that also are antioxidant in action.*
- *Artificial colors.*
- *Nutrient additives.*

11 **Indirect Food Additives**

- *Substances that inadvertently get into food products from packaging and/or handling.*
- *Dioxins: found in coffee filters, milk containers, and frozen foods.*
- *Methylene chloride: found in decaffeinated coffee.*
- *Hormones: bovine growth hormone (BGH) found in animal meat.*

12 Whenever such products are added, consumers should take the time to determine what the substances are and whether there are alternatives. As a general rule of thumb, the fewer chemicals, colorants, and preservatives, the better. Also, certain foods and additives have an effect on medications. Being aware of these potential dietary interactions is a key to wise consumerism.

━ ▪ ━

APPLYING YOUR TEXTBOOK READING SKILLS

1. Identify the textbook learning aids contained in this textbook excerpt and evaluate their usefulness.
2. Apply the SQ3R method to this textbook excerpt. Write your questions and answers on a separate sheet of paper.
3. What learning strategies would be useful in studying this excerpt?

Textbook Excerpt 3: Communication

LEGIBLE CLOTHING
Joseph A. DeVito

1   Legible clothing is anything that you wear which contains some verbal message; such clothing can literally be read. In some instances it says status; it tells others that you are, for example, rich or stylish or youthful. The Gucci or Louis Vuitton logos on your luggage communicate your status and financial position. In a similar way your sweatshirt saying Bulls or Pirates communicates your interest in sports and perhaps your favorite team.

2   John Molloy, in *Molloy's Live for Success,* advises you to avoid legible clothing except the kind that says rich. Legible clothing, argues Molloy, communicates lower status and lack of power. Humorist Fran Lebowitz says that legible clothes "are an unpleasant indication of the general state of things. I mean, be realistic. If people don't want to listen to you, what makes you think they want to hear from your sweater?"

3   Yet legible clothing is being bought and worn in record numbers. Many designers and manufacturers have their names integrated into the design of the clothing: DKNY, Calvin Klein, L.L. Bean, and Levi's are just a few examples. At the same time that you are paying extra to buy the brand name, you also provide free advertising for the designer and manufacturer. To paraphrase Vidal Sassoon, "As long as you look good, so does the advertiser. And, when you look bad, the advertiser looks bad." Imitators—the cheap knockoffs you see on the street—are resisted by the original manufacturers not only because these impact on their own sales. In fact, the impact is probably minimal since the person who would pay $6,000 for a Rolex would not buy a $10 imitation on the street. Rather, such knock-offs are resisted because they are perceived to be worn by the wrong people—people who would destroy the image the manufacturer wishes to communicate.

4   T-shirts and sweatshirts are especially popular as message senders. In one study, the types of t-shirt messages were classified into four main categories. The order in which these are presented reflects the shirts the subjects (600 male and female college students) considered their favorites. Thirty-three percent, for example, considered affiliation message shirts their favorites

while 17 percent considered those with personal messages their favorites. The order from most favorite down, was:

1. Affiliation messages—for example, a club or school name. It communicates that you are a part of a larger group.
2. Trophy—for example, a shirt from a high-status event such as a concert or perhaps a ski lodge. This is a way of saying that the wearer was in the right place.
3. Metaphorical expressions—for example, pictures of rock groups or famous athletes.
4. Personal message—for example, beliefs, philosophies and causes as well as satirizing current events.

5   Another important dimension of clothing, currently being debated in educational and legal circles, is the use of gang clothing. Some argue that gang clothing and gang colors contribute to violence in the schools and should therefore be prohibited. Others argue that gang clothing—or any clothing—is covered by the first amendment to the Constitution. Consider a specific case. In Harvard, Illinois, you can be arrested for wearing a Star of David in public—not because it's a religious symbol, but because certain gangs use it as a gang symbol. In 1993, Harvard passed a law that makes it illegal "for any person within the city to knowingly use, display or wear color, emblems, or insignia" that would communicate their membership in (or sympathy for) gangs.

6   Consider your own use of legible clothing. Do you wear legible clothing? What messages do you wish to communicate? Are you successful in communicating the message you want? Do labels influence your perceptions of others? How do you feel about the law in Harvard, Illinois? Would you support such a law in your own community?

APPLYING YOUR TEXTBOOK READING SKILLS

1. Identify the textbook learning aids contained in this textbook excerpt and evaluate their usefulness.
2. Apply the SQ3R method to this textbook excerpt. Write your questions and answers on a separate sheet of paper.
3. What learning strategies would be useful in studying this excerpt?

A Guide for ESL (ELL) Readers

This guide offers important tips for ESL (ELL) readers and then covers three topics in detail: sentence basics, word order, and idioms. It also contains a Glossary of Frequently Confusing Words and Phrases.

Tips for ESL Readers

Developing your skill in reading English is a worthwhile challenge. The more you read English, the easier reading English will become. Use the following suggestions to make the process as easy as possible.

Use a Two-Way Dictionary

A two-way dictionary (Spanish–English or Japanese–English, for example) is a useful tool for finding the English word for a word in your native language. However, do not rely only on a two-way dictionary. Once you have found the appropriate English word, be sure to check its meaning in an English dictionary. There you will find many more meanings of the word and learn more about its usage.

Always Keep an English Dictionary Handy

Because you never know when you will hear or read a word you do not know, keep a paperback English dictionary handy at all times. Take it with you to classes and keep it handy when you are reading and studying.

Practice, Practice, Practice

Practice is the key to learning any language. Be sure to read, write, listen to, and speak English as much as possible. While it is tempting to speak to friends and family in your native language, you will not improve your English by doing so. Likewise, while it is tempting to read books, magazines, and newspapers in your native language, you should avoid doing so. The more exposure you have to English, the faster you will learn it.

Vocabulary Is the Key to Success

Increasing your vocabulary is the key to becoming fluent in any language. As you learn new English words, keep track of them in a notebook, on a pack of index cards, or in a computer file. Review these new words frequently. Make an effort to use each new word in your speech or writing.

Take Notes in English

Be sure to take notes in English in all of your classes. Writing and reviewing your notes will give you additional practice using English. Remember, too, the tests you will take will be in English, so you will be better prepared if you have studied from English notes. Also, taking notes in English eliminates the need to translate back and forth between languages when you take a test.

Use Context

In your native language, you often use context, the words around the unknown word, to figure out its meaning. Be sure to use this skill when reading English, as well. See Chapter 3 of this book for more information on how to use context.

Sentence Basics

Sentences are among the basic building blocks of language. To understand paragraphs, articles, and textbook chapters, you first have to understand the sentences with which each is built. Some sentences are short and easy to understand (*Close the door.*); others are long, complicated, and difficult to follow. This section provides a brief review of how to understand these difficult sentences.

A **sentence** is a group of words that express at least one complete thought or idea. Every sentence, then, expresses at least one main point. The main point is a statement about someone or something.

Finding the Subject and Predicate

Every sentence is made up of at least two parts, a subject and a predicate. The **subject,** often a noun, identifies the person or object the sentence is about. The main part of the **predicate**—the verb—tells what the person or object is doing or has done. Usually a sentence contains additional information about the subject and/or the predicate.

EXAMPLE   The average <u>American</u> <u>consumed</u> six gallons of beer last year.

The key idea of this sentence is "American consumed." It is expressed by the subject and predicate. The simple subject of this sentence is American; it explains who the sentence is about. The rest of the sentence gives more information about the verb by telling what (beer) and how much (six gallons last year) was consumed. Here are a few more examples:

EXAMPLES   The <u>ship</u> <u>entered</u> the harbor early this morning.

<u>Lilacs</u> <u>bloom</u> in the spring.

Questions to Ask

In many long and complicated sentences, the key idea is not as obvious as in the preceding examples. To find the key idea, ask these questions:

1. Who or what is the sentence about?
2. What is happening in the sentence?

Here is an example of a complicated sentence that might be found in a psychology textbook:

EXAMPLE   Intelligence, as measured by IQ, depends on the kind of test given, the skill of the examiner, and the cooperation of the subject.

In this sentence, the answer to the question, "Who or what is the sentence about?" is *intelligence.* The verb is *depends,* and the remainder of the sentence explains the factors upon which intelligence depends. Let us look at a few more examples:

EXAMPLES   <u>William James</u>, often thought of as the father of American psychology, <u>tested</u> whether memory could be improved by exercising it.

<u>Violence</u> in sports, both at amateur and professional levels, <u>has increased</u> dramatically over the past ten years.

Multiple Subjects and Multiple Verbs

Some sentences may have more than one subject and/or more than one verb in the predicate.

EXAMPLES

subject   subject
Poor <u>diet</u> and <u>lack</u> of exercise can cause weight gain.

verb   verb
My brother always <u>worries</u> and <u>complains</u> about his job.

subject   subject   verb   verb
Many <u>homes</u> and <u>businesses</u> <u>are burglarized</u> or <u>vandalized</u> each year.

subject   verb   verb   verb
The angry <u>customer</u> <u>was screaming</u>, <u>cursing</u>, and <u>shouting</u>.

**Exercise
B–1**

Directions: Find the key idea in each of the following sentences. Draw a line under the subject and circle the verb.

Example: The instructor (assigned) a fifteen-page article to read.

1. Every summer my parents travel to the eastern seacoast.

2. Children learn how to behave by imitating adults.

3. William Faulkner, a popular American author, wrote about life in the South.

4. Psychologists are interested in studying human behavior in many different situations.

5. Terminally ill patients may refuse to take their prescribed medication.

6. The use of cocaine, although illegal, is apparently increasing.

7. The most accurate method we have of estimating the age of the earth is based on our knowledge of radioactivity.

8. Elements exist either as compounds or as free elements.

9. Attention may be defined as a focusing of perception.

10. The specific instructions in a computer program are written in a computer language.

Understanding Sentences with Two Main Points

Sentences that express two or more equally important ideas are called **coordinate sentences.** Coordinate sentences got their name because they coordinate, or tie together, two or more ideas. They do this for three reasons: (1) to emphasize the relationship between ideas, (2) to indicate their equal importance, and/or (3) to make the material more concise and easier to read. In the following example, notice how two related ideas can be combined.

`EXAMPLE`   **Two Related Ideas**

Marlene was in obvious danger.
Joe quickly pulled Marlene from the street.

Combined Sentence

Marlene was in obvious danger, and Joe quickly pulled her from the street.

In this case, the combined sentence establishes that the two equally important events are parts of a single incident.

As you read coordinate sentences, be sure to locate both subjects and predicates. If you do not read carefully or if you are reading too fast, you might miss the second idea. Often you can recognize a sentence that combines two or more ideas by its structure and punctuation. Coordinate ideas are combined in one of two ways:

1. With a semicolon:

`EXAMPLE`   The union members wanted to strike; the company did nothing to discourage them.

2. With a comma and one of the following joining words: *and, or, but, nor, so, for, yet.* These words are called coordinating conjunctions. See Table B-1 for the meaning clues each provides.

TABLE B-1 Coordinating Conjunctions—Words That Join Two Important Ideas		
Joining Words	**Meaning Clues**	**Example**
and	Links similar and equally important ideas	Jim is in my biology class, <u>and</u> Pierce is in my psychology class.
but, yet	Connects opposite ideas or change in thought	Professor Clark had given a homework assignment, <u>yet</u> she did not collect it.
for, so	Indicates reasons or shows that one thing is causing another	Most English majors in our college take a foreign language, <u>for</u> it is a requirement.
or, not	Suggests choice or options	We could make a fire in the fireplace, <u>or</u> we could get out some extra blankets.

EXAMPLES   Some students decided to take the final exam, and others chose to rely on their C semester average.

The students wanted the instructor to cancel the class, but the instructor decided to reschedule it.

Understanding Sentences with One Main Point and One Related Idea

Sentences that express one main point and one related idea are called **subordinate sentences.** Subordinate sentences contain one key idea and one or more less important, or subordinate, ideas that explain the key idea. These less important ideas each have their own subject and predicate, but they depend on the main sentence to complete their meaning. For example, in the following sentence you cannot understand fully the meaning of the underlined portion until you read the entire sentence.

EXAMPLE   <u>Because Stewart forgot to make a payment</u>, he had to pay a late charge on his loan.

In this sentence, the more important idea is that Stewart had to pay a late charge since that portion of the sentence could stand alone as a complete sentence. The reason for the late charge is presented as background information that amplifies and further explains the basic message.

As you read subordinate sentences, be sure to notice the relationship between the two ideas. The less important idea may provide a description or explain a condition, cause, reason, purpose, time, or place set out in the more important idea. Here are a few additional examples of sentences that relate two or more ideas. In each, the base idea is underlined and the function of the less important idea is indicated in brackets above it.

description

EXAMPLES   <u>My grandfather,</u> who is eighty years old, <u>collects stamps.</u>

time

<u>American foreign policy changed</u> when we entered the Vietnam War.

condition

<u>I'll be late for my dental appointment</u> unless my class is dismissed early.

reason

Since I failed my last history exam, <u>I decided to drop the course.</u>

TABLE B-2   Subordinating Conjunctions—Words That Join an Important Idea with a Less Important Idea

Joining Words	Meaning Clues	Example
before, after, while, during, until, when, once	Indicates time	<u>After</u> taking the test, Leon felt relieved.
because, since, so that	Gives reasons	<u>Because</u> I was working, I was unable to go bowling.
if, unless, whether, even if	Explains conditions	<u>Unless</u> I leave work early, I'll miss class.
although, as far as, in order to, however	Explains circumstance	<u>Although</u> I used a dictionary, I still did not fully understand the word.

Notice that if the subordinate idea comes first in the sentence, a comma follows it. If the key idea comes first, a comma is not used.

As you read subordinate sentences, pay attention to the connecting word used. It should signal the relationship of ideas. You must be sure to pick up the signal. You should know *why* the two ideas have been combined and *what* they have to do with each other. Table B-2 lists some common connecting words, called **subordinating conjunctions,** and tells you what each signals.

Exercise B-2

Directions: After reading each of the following sentences, in the space provided write the letter that best indicates how the underlined idea is related to the rest of the sentence. Select one of the following choices for each.

a. indicates time

b. gives a reason

c. explains a condition

d. explains a circumstance

_____ 1. <u>Although I broke my leg</u>, I am still able to drive a car.

_____ 2. Peter will become a truck driver, <u>unless he decides to go back to school for further training</u>.

_____ 3. She always picks up her mail <u>after she eats lunch</u>.

_____ 4. <u>Because violence is regularly shown on television</u>, children accept it as an ordinary part of life.

_____ 5. <u>Since comparison shopping is a necessary part of the buying process</u>, wise consumers look for differences in quality as well as price.

<table>
<tr><td>Exercise
B-3</td><td>*Directions: After reading each of the following sentences, decide whether it is a coordinate or a subordinate sentence. Write C in the space provided if the sentence is coordinate, and underline both sets of subjects and predicates. Mark S if it is subordinate, and underline the more important idea.*</td></tr>
</table>

_____ 1. The personnel office eagerly accepted my application for a job, and I expect to receive an offer next week.

_____ 2. Computers have become part of our daily lives, but their role in today's college classrooms has not yet been fully explored.

_____ 3. As far as we can tell from historical evidence, humankind has inhabited this earth for at least one million years.

_____ 4. Because sugar is Cuba's main export, the Cuban economy depends upon the worldwide demand for sugar.

_____ 5. We never learn anything in a vacuum; we are always having other experiences before and after we learn new material.

Understanding How Modifiers Change Meaning

After you have identified the key ideas, the next step in understanding a sentence is to see how the modifiers affect its meaning. **Modifiers** are words that change, describe, qualify, or limit the meaning of another word or sentence part. Most modifiers either add to or change the meaning of the key idea. Usually they answer such questions about the subject or predicate as *what, where, which, when, how,* or *why.* For example:

EXAMPLES

               where   when

Sam drove his car to Toronto last week.

  when   how   which

Last night I read with interest a magazine article on sailing.

As you read a sentence, be sure to notice how the details change, limit, or add to the meaning of the key idea. Decide, for each of the following examples, how the underlined portion affects the meaning of the key idea.

EXAMPLES

Maria took her dog to the pond <u>yesterday</u>.

Recently, I selected <u>with great care</u> a wedding gift for my sister.

The older Cadillac <u>with the convertible top</u> belongs to my husband.

In the first example, the underlined detail explains *when* Maria took her dog to the pond. In the second example, the underlined words tell *how* the gift was selected. In the last example, the underlined phrase indicates *which* Cadillac.

Copyright © 2007 by Kathleen T. McWhorter

Exercise B–4

Directions: *After reading each of the following sentences, circle the subject and predicate and decide what the underlined words tell about the key idea. Write* which, when, where, how, *or* why *in the space provided.*

1. You can relieve tension <u>through exercise.</u> _____

2. Many students <u>in computer science courses</u> can use the computer terminals only late at night. _____

3. Many shoppers clip coupons <u>to reduce their grocery bills.</u> _____

4. <u>After class</u> I am going to talk to my instructor. _____

5. The world's oil supply is concentrated <u>in only a few places around the globe.</u> _____

Expressing the Ideas in Your Own Words

The best way to be sure you have understood an author's idea is to express it in your own words. Putting an author's thoughts into your own words is called **paraphrasing.** Paraphrasing can help you sort out what is important in a sentence, and it can also help you remember what you read. Here are some tips for paraphrasing.

1. Use your own words, not the author's wording. Pretend you are telling a friend what a sentence means.

2. Use synonyms. A **synonym** is a word that has the same general meaning as another word. The following pairs of words are synonyms:

   ruin—destroy   rich—affluent
   rough—harsh   repeat—reiterate

Now, look at the following sentence from the U.S. Constitution:

EXAMPLE

The Congress shall have power to regulate commerce with foreign nations, and among the several States and with the Indian tribes.

The sentence below paraphrases the original by substituting the underlined synonyms.

EXAMPLE

Congress is <u>allowed</u> to <u>control trade</u> with foreign <u>countries</u>, among states, and with Indian tribes.

When selecting synonyms use the following guidelines.

3. Choose words close in meaning to the original.

EXAMPLE

Prehistoric people worshipped *animate* objects.

The words *living, alive,* and *vital* are synonyms for *animate,* but in the preceding sentence, *living* is closest in meaning to *animate.*

4. Split lengthy, complicated sentences into two or more shorter sentences.

EXAMPLES

Lengthy Sentence

Fads—temporary, highly imitated outbreaks of unconventional behavior—are particularly common in popular music, where the desire to be "different" continually fosters the emergence of new looks and sounds.

Split into Two Sentences

Fads are occurrences of nontraditional behavior. They are especially common in popular music because the need to set oneself apart from others encourages the development of new looks and sounds.

Exercise B-5

Directions: Using the procedures suggested in this section, paraphrase each of the following sentences.

1. There has been an increase in female sports participation since the early 1970s.

2. A distinction still exists between what are traditionally considered to be male and female sports.

3. The right of citizens of the United States, who are 18 years of age or older, to vote shall not be denied or abridged by the United States or any state on account of age. (Amendment XXIV to the U.S. Constitution)

4. In armed robberies, potential violence—violence that is rarely carried out—enables the robber to achieve his or her material goal, usually money.

_____

_____

5. In trying to identify the causes of problem drinking, some researchers have stressed the role of genetic factors, while others have viewed it as an inability to adjust to the stress of life.

_____

_____

Pay Attention to Word Order

The order of words in a sentence in English may differ from the word order used in your native language. Here are a few major differences.

Sentence Order

1. The subject comes first, followed by the verb.

EXAMPLE   Correct: The <u>professor</u> <u>is</u> late.

EXAMPLE   Incorrect: <u>Is</u> late the <u>professor</u>.

2. Groups of words that begin with relative pronouns (*who, whom, whose, that, which*) come after the noun they modify.

EXAMPLE   Correct: The student <u>who is late</u> will not be admitted to class.

EXAMPLE   Incorrect: The student will not be admitted to class <u>who is late</u>.

Adverbs

3. Adverbs come after one-word verbs.

EXAMPLE   Correct: The athlete ran <u>fast</u>.

4. Adverbs come after *to be* (is, are, was, were) verbs.

EXAMPLE   Correct: Professors are <u>usually</u> on time for class.

5. Adverbs come between two-part verbs.

EXAMPLE

Correct: The movie has <u>often</u> started late.

Adjectives

6. Adjectives usually come before nouns.

EXAMPLE

Correct: Sarah wore a <u>tattered</u>, <u>baggy dress</u>.

EXAMPLE

Incorrect: Sarah wore a dress—<u>tattered</u> and <u>baggy</u>.

Learn Idioms

An **idiom** is a phrase that has a meaning other than the common meaning of the words in the phrase. For example, the phrase "turn over a new leaf" is not about the leaves on a tree. It means *to start fresh* or *begin over again in a new way*. Idioms are particularly troublesome to ESL students because they cannot figure out idioms logically by piecing together the meaning of each word in the phrase.

You can locate idioms in a dictionary by looking under the key words in the phrase. To find the meaning of the idiom *as the crow flies*, look under the entry for *crow*. Idioms are usually identified by the label "—idiom," followed by the complete phrase and its meaning.

If you need more help figuring out idioms, consult a handbook or dictionary of American idioms, such as *Webster's New World American Idioms Handbook*. It is usually best not to use idioms in your own writing. Many are overused and do not express your ideas in a clear or concise way.

Exercise B–6

***Directions:** Explain the meaning of each of the following idioms.*

1. to keep tabs on _____

2. to steal someone's thunder _____

_____

3. in the dark _____

4. to bite the bullet _____

5. to make no bones about _____

Glossary of Frequently Confused Words and Phrases

This glossary is intended as a guide to words and phrases that often are confusing to ESL students. If the word or phrase you seek is not here, check in a dictionary.

a while, awhile   *A while* is a phrase containing an article and a noun; *awhile* is an adverb meaning "for some time." *A while* can be used following a preposition, such as for: *Wait here for <u>a while</u>. Awhile* is used to modify a verb: *We need to rest <u>awhile</u>.*

accept, except   *Accept* is a verb that means "receive": *She accepted the gift gratefully. Except* is usually a preposition meaning "other than," "but," or "excluding": *Everyone has left <u>except</u> me.*

advice, advise   *Advice* is a noun: *He gave me his best <u>advice</u> about health insurance. Advise* is a verb: *I can only <u>advise</u> you about it.*

affect, effect   *Affect* is almost always a verb meaning "influence": *Smoking <u>affects</u> one's health. Effect* can be either a verb or a noun. In its usual use, as a noun, it means "result": *The drug has several side <u>effects</u>.* When *effect* is used as a verb, it means "cause" or "bring about": *The committee was able to <u>effect</u> a change in the law.*

all ready, already   *All ready* means "completely prepared." *Already* means "by this time" or "previously."

all right, alright   Although the form *alright* is often used, most authorities regard it as a misspelling of *all right.*

all together, altogether   *All together* means "as a group" or "in unison": *The workers presented their grievance <u>all together</u> to the supervisor. Altogether* is an adverb that means "completely" or "entirely": *His answer was not <u>altogether</u> acceptable.*

allusion, illusion   An *allusion* is an indirect reference or a hint: *Her <u>allusions</u> about his weight embarrassed him.* An *illusion* is a false idea or appearance: *Cosmetic surgery is intended to create the <u>illusion</u> of youth.*

almost, most   See *most, almost.*

among, between   See *between, among.*

amount of, number of   *Amount of* refers to quantities that cannot be counted: *A large <u>amount of</u> milk had been left in the refrigerator. Number of* refers to quantities that can be counted: *A large <u>number of</u> eggs had been left in the carton.*

anybody, any body; anyone, any one   *Anybody* and *anyone* are indefinite pronouns that mean "any person at all": *Does <u>anybody (anyone)</u>*

have change for a dollar? Any body consists of a noun modified by the adjective *any*: *Is* <u>*any body*</u> *of government responsible for this injustice? Any one,* the pronoun *one* modified by *any,* refers to a certain person or thing in a group: *You may choose* <u>*any one*</u> *of the desserts with your entrée.*

bad, badly   *Bad* is an adjective; *badly* is an adverb. *Badly* is used to modify verbs: *They sang quite* <u>*badly*</u>*. Bad* can be used to modify nouns or pronouns: *The* <u>*bad*</u> *behavior irritated the child's hostess.* In addition, bad is used after linking verbs, such as *am, is, become, feel,* or *seem*: *She felt* <u>*bad*</u> *last night.*

between, among   Use *between* when referring to two things or people: *My wife and I divide the household chores* <u>*between*</u> *us.* Use *among* for three or more things or people: *The vote was evenly divided* <u>*among*</u> *the four candidates.*

bring, take   *Bring* is used to describe the movement of an object toward you: <u>*Bring*</u> *me the newspaper, please. Take* is used when the movement is away from you: *Will you* <u>*take*</u> *these letters to the mailbox?*

can, may   *Can* refers to the ability to do something: *He* <u>*can*</u> *run a mile in less than five minutes. May* indicates permission: *You* <u>*may*</u> *choose whichever CD you want.*

censor, censure   *Censor* as a verb means "edit or ban from the public for moral or political reasons": *The school board voted not to* <u>*censor*</u> *the high school reading lists but to recommend novels with literary merit.* The verb *censure* means "criticize or condemn publicly": *The member of Congress was* <u>*censured*</u> *because of questionable fundraising practices.*

complement, compliment   *Complement* is a verb meaning "complete, add to, or go with": *They make a good couple; their personalities* <u>*complement*</u> *each other. Compliment* as a verb means "praise or flatter": *I must* <u>*compliment*</u> *you on your quick wit.* As a noun it means "flattering remark": *You should not regard his* <u>*compliments*</u> *as sincere.*

conscience, conscious   *Conscience* is a noun meaning "sense of moral right or wrong": *His* <u>*conscience*</u> *required him to return the lost wallet. Conscious* is an adjective meaning "alert, aware, awake": *Were you* <u>*conscious*</u> *of the change in temperature?*

continual, continuous   *Continual* means "happening regularly": <u>*Continual*</u> *call by telemarketers are a nuisance. Continuous* means "happening for a long period of time without interruption": *The car alarm made a* <u>*continuous*</u>*, high-pitched noise.*

data   *Data,* the plural form of the Latin noun *datum,* means "facts or information." *Data* is often accepted as either a plural or a singular noun: *These data <u>are</u> conclusive. This data <u>is</u> conclusive.* Though technically correct, the singular form *datum* is rarely used.

different from, different than   *Different from* is the preferred expression: *Today is <u>different from</u> yesterday.* However, when *different from* leads to an awkward construction, *different than* is becoming acceptable: *Today Cheryl is <u>different than</u> she was last month* (avoids *<u>from what</u> she was last month*).

disinterested, uninterested   *Disinterested* means "objective or impartial": *The dispute was mediated by a <u>disinterested</u> party. Uninterested* means "not interested": *She was so <u>uninterested</u> in the football game that she nearly fell asleep.*

doesn't, don't   *Don't* is the contraction for *do not*, not for *does not*: *We <u>don't</u> want it. She <u>doesn't</u> have any.*

effect, affect   See *affect, effect.*

elicit, illicit   *Elicit* is a verb meaning "draw out" or "bring to light": *The police were unable to <u>elicit</u> any information from the accomplice. Illicit* is an adjective meaning "illegal": *The suspect had <u>illicit</u> drugs on his person.*

emigrate, immigrate   See *immigrate, emigrate.*

etc.   This is the abbreviation for the Latin *et cetera,* meaning "and so on." Ending a list with *etc.* is acceptable in informal writing and in some technical writing and business reporting. However, in formal writing it is preferable to end a list with an example or with *and so on.*

everyday, every day   *Everyday* is an adjective that means "ordinary" or "usual": *They decided to use their <u>everyday</u> dishes for the party. Every day,* an adjective and a noun, means "occurring on a daily basis": *<u>Every day</u>, he walks the dog in the morning.*

explicit, implicit   *Explicit* is an adjective that means "clearly stated": *I left <u>explicit</u> instructions for the worker. Implicit* means "indirectly stated or implied": *The fact that he didn't object indicated his <u>implicit</u> approval of the arrangement.*

farther, further   When referring to distance, use *farther: He lives <u>farther</u> from work than she does.* When you mean "additional," use *further: Upon <u>further</u> consideration, I accept the position.*

fewer, less   *Fewer* refers to items that can be counted: *There are <u>fewer</u> people here today than yesterday. Less* refers to a general amount that cannot be counted: *We have <u>less</u> orange juice than I thought.*

further, farther   See *farther, further.*

good, well   *Good* is an adjective: *I enjoy a <u>good</u> workout.* It is not to be used as an adverb. *Well* is used instead:

- *We ate <u>well</u> on our vacation. Well can also be an adjective when used with verbs expressing feeling or state of being: She feels <u>well</u> today.*

hanged, hung   *Hanged* is the past tense and past participle form of the verb *hang,* meaning "execute": *He was <u>hanged</u> as a traitor. Hung is the past tense and past participle form of the verb hang in all its other meanings: We <u>hung</u> the picture above the fireplace.*

hung, hanged   See *hanged, hung.*

if, whether   Use *if* when expressing a condition: <u>*If I leave early, I can beat the rush hour traffic. Use whether when expressing an alternative: I don't know <u>whether</u> to stay or to leave.*</u>

illicit, elicit   See *elicit, illicit.*

illusion, allusion   See *allusion, illusion.*

immigrate, emigrate   *Immigrate (to)* means "to come to a country": *They recently <u>immigrated</u> to the United States. Emigrate (from) means "leave a country": They <u>emigrated</u> from Mexico for economic reasons.*

implicit, explicit   See *explicit, implicit.*

imply, infer   Speakers or writers *imply;* they suggest or hint at something: *He <u>implied</u> that he was unhappy with my work.* Listeners or readers *infer* by drawing conclusions from what they have read, heard, or seen: *I <u>inferred</u> that I need to become more conscientious.*

in, into, in to   *In* indicates position or location: *Your book is <u>in</u> the drawer. Into shows movement: They were led <u>into</u> a winding corridor.* Sometimes *in* and *to* are used close together as separate words: *They gave <u>in to</u> our requests.*

infer, imply   See *imply, infer.*

its, it's   *Its* is the possessive case form of the pronoun *it;* no apostrophes are used to show possession with personal pronouns *(his, hers, its, theirs): The poodle scratched <u>its</u> ear. It's is the contraction for it is: <u>It's</u> time for a change.*

kind, sort, type   These words are singular and are used with singular modifiers and verbs: <u>*This*</u> *kind of book <u>is</u> expensive.* They are used in their plural forms with plural modifiers and verbs: <u>*These*</u> *types of <u>pens</u> work best.* Using *a* following *type of, kind of,* or *sort of* is incorrect.

- **What type of ~~a~~ dog is that?**

Also, omitting *of* is nonstandard:

- **I can't guess what type ^*of* car that is.**

lay, lie   *Lay* is a transitive verb meaning "put or place." Its principal forms are *lay, laid, laid:* <u>Lay</u> *your bag here. She* <u>laid</u> *her bag here. She* <u>has</u> <u>laid</u> *her bag here every day. Lie is an intransitive verb meaning "recline or be situated." Its principal forms are lie, lay, lain:* <u>Lie</u> *down for a while. He* <u>lay</u> *down for a while. He* <u>has lain</u> *down every few hours.*

leave, let   *Leave* is a verb that means "depart," "exit," or "let be": *We will* <u>leave</u> *the room so that you can be left alone. Let means "permit or allow": They would not* <u>let</u> *me go.*

less, fewer   See *fewer, less.*

loose, lose   *Loose* is an adjective meaning "not tight" or "not attached securely": *A* <u>loose</u> *brick fell into the fireplace. Lose is a verb that means "misplace" or "not win": Don't* <u>lose</u> *your way in the woods. They will* <u>lose</u> *the game unless they score soon.*

may, can   See *can, may.*

may be, maybe   *May be* is a verb phrase: *The train* <u>may be</u> *late this morning. Maybe is an adverb meaning "perhaps" or "possibly":* <u>Maybe</u> *we can have lunch together tomorrow.*

media, medium   *Media* is the plural form of *medium: Of all the broadcast* <u>media</u>, *television is the* <u>medium</u> *that reaches most households.*

most, almost   *Most* should not be used in place of *almost.* When you mean "nearly," use *almost;* when you mean "the greatest number or quantity," use *most: She gets* <u>most</u> *of her exercise by walking to work* <u>almost</u> *every day.*

number of, amount of   See *amount of, number of.*

percent (per cent), percentage   *Percent* should be used with a specific number: *Less than 40* <u>percent</u> *of the class passed the exam. Percentage is used when no number is referred to: A large* <u>percentage</u> *of adults cannot program a VCR.*

principal, principle   The noun *principal* can mean "sum of money (excluding interest)" or important person in an organization": *At any time, you can pay the* <u>principal</u> *on this loan. The high school* <u>principal</u> *distributed the awards.* As an adjective, *principal* means "most important": *His* <u>principal</u> *concern was their safety. Principal is a noun meaning "rule or standard": The* <u>principles</u> *stated in the Constitution guide our democracy.*

raise, rise   *Raise* is a transitive verb meaning "lift." Its principal forms are *raise, raised, raised:* <u>Raise</u> *the flag at sunrise. He* <u>raised</u> *the flag at sunrise. They* <u>have raised</u> *the flag at sunrise for years. Rise is an intransitive verb meaning "go higher" or "get to one's feet." Its principal forms* are *rise, rose,* and *risen: I <u>rise</u> early on weekends. The sun gradually <u>rose</u> in the sky. The bread dough <u>has</u> already <u>risen</u>.*

real, really *Real* is an adjective meaning "genuine" or "actual": *He found a <u>real</u> gold coin. Really* is an adverb meaning "very or extremely": *He is <u>really</u> proud of his discovery.*

set, sit *Set* is a transitive verb meaning "put or place." Its principal forms are *set, set, set: Please <u>set</u> the pitcher on the table. I <u>set</u> it on the counter, instead. I <u>will set</u> it on the table later. Sit* is an intransitive verb meaning "be seated." Its principal parts are *sit, sat,* and *sat: I <u>sit</u> in the front row. He <u>sat</u> behind me. They <u>have sat</u> for too long.*

sometime, some time, sometimes *Sometime* is an adverb meaning "at an unspecified point in the future": *We'll see that movie <u>sometime</u>. Some time* is an adjective *(some)* and a noun *(time),* and as a phrase it means "a period of time": *We'll find <u>some time</u> for that later. Sometimes* is an adverb meaning "now and then": *<u>Sometimes</u> recreation must be viewed as important.*

sort See *kind, sort, type.*

stationary, stationery *Stationary* is an adjective meaning "not moving": *Attach the birdhouse to a <u>stationary</u> object, such as a tree. Stationery* is a noun meaning "writing paper": *She sent a note on her personal <u>stationery</u>.*

suppose to, use to, supposed to, used to *Suppose to* and *use to* are nonstandard and unacceptable substitutes for *supposed to* and *used to.*

sure, surely *Sure* is an adjective: *She was <u>sure</u> she was correct. Surely* is an adverb: *She is <u>surely</u> correct.*

sure and, try and, sure to, try to *Sure to* and *try to* are the correct forms.

take, bring See *bring, take.*

than, then *Than* is a conjunction that is used to make a comparison: *That is larger <u>than</u> I thought. Then* is an adverb used to indicate time: *Let's finish this first and <u>then</u> have dinner.*

that, which, who Frequently, there is confusion about these relative pronouns. *That* refers to persons, animals, and things; *which* refers to animals and things; *who* and *whom* refer to persons. To keep the distinctions clear, follow these guidelines.

1. *Who (whom)* is used when referring to persons: *He is the one <u>who</u> won the contest.*

2. *Which* is used for animals and things when it introduces nonrestrictive clauses: *My Sony Walkman, <u>which</u> I bought at Wal-Mart, works perfectly.*

3. *That* is used for animals and things when introducing restrictive relative clauses: *Everything <u>that</u> I did was misunderstood.*

their, there, they're   *Their* is a possessive pronoun: *They gave <u>their</u> tickets to the usher. There is an adverb indicating place: Put the chair over <u>there</u>, please. They're is the contraction of they are: <u>They're</u> going to be disappointed.*

to, too, two   *To is either a preposition indicating direction or part of an infinitive: I'm going <u>to</u> the store <u>to</u> buy groceries. Too is an adverb meaning "also" or "more than enough": She is <u>too</u> thin to be healthy. Can I come, too? Two is a number: I'll be home in <u>two</u> hours.*

try and, try to   See *sure and, try and, sure to, try to.*

type   See *kind, sort, type.*

use to, used to   See *suppose to, use to, supposed to, used to.*

wait for, wait on   *Wait for means "await" or "pause in expectation": <u>Wait for</u> me at the bus stop. Wait on means "serve" or "act as a waiter": The restaurant owner <u>waited on</u> us.*

well, good   See *good, well.*

whether, if   See *if, whether.*

which, who, that   See *that, which, who.*

who's, whose   *Who's is the contraction of who is: <u>Who's</u> knocking on the door? Whose is the possessive form of who: <u>Whose</u> car is that? Naomi is the one <u>whose</u> mother is the famous writer.*

Multicultural Reader

THE MOST HATEFUL WORDS
Amy Tan

This reading is taken from Amy Tan's collection of autobiographical essays, *The Opposite of Fate*. Read it to learn about the author's relationship with her mother.

Vocabulary Preview

These are some of the difficult words in this essay. The definitions here will help you if you can't figure out the meanings from the sentence context or word parts.

tilted (para. 2) turned to one side

impenetrable (para. 3) not capable of being affected by sentiment or argument

frantically (para. 9) in a manner that is uncontrolled, nervous, or anxiety driven

bequeathed (para. 15) gave or handed down

---

1   The most hateful words I have ever said to another human being were to my mother. I was sixteen at the time. They rose from the storm in my chest and I let them fall in a fury of hailstones: "I hate you. I wish I were dead. . . ."

2   I waited for her to collapse, stricken by what I had just said. She was still standing upright, her chin tilted, her lips stretched in a crazy smile. "Okay, maybe I die too," she said between huffs. "Then I no longer be your mother!" We had many similar exchanges. Sometimes she actually tried to kill herself by running into the street, holding a knife to her throat. She too had storms in her chest. And what she aimed at me was as fast and deadly as a lightning bolt.

3   For days after our arguments, she would not speak to me. She tormented me, acted as if she had no feelings for me whatsoever. I was lost to her. And because of that, I lost, battle after battle, all of them: the times she criticized me, humiliated me in front of others, forbade me to do this or that without even listening to one good reason why it should be the other way. I

swore to myself I would never forget these injustices. I would store them, harden my heart, make myself as impenetrable as she was.

4   I remember this now, because I am also remembering another time, just a few years ago. I was forty-seven, had become a different person by then, had become a fiction writer, someone who uses memory and imagination. In fact, I was writing a story about a girl and her mother, when the phone rang.

5   It was my mother, and this surprised me. Had someone helped her make the call? For a few years now, she had been losing her mind through Alzheimer's disease. Early on, she forgot to lock her door. Then she forgot where she lived. She forgot who many people were and what they had meant to her. Lately, she could no longer remember many of her worries and sorrows.

6   "Amy-ah," she said, and she began to speak quickly in Chinese. "Something is wrong with my mind. I think I'm going crazy."

7   I caught my breath. Usually she could barely speak more than two words at a time. "Don't worry," I started to say.

8   "It's true," she went on. "I feel like I can't remember many things. I can't remember what I did yesterday. I can't remember what happened a long time ago, what I did to you. . . ." She spoke as a drowning person might if she had bobbed to the surface with the force of will to live, only to see how far she had already drifted, how impossibly far she was from the shore.

9   She spoke frantically: "I know I did something to hurt you."

10   "You didn't." I said. "Don't worry."

11   "I did terrible things. But now I can't remember what. . . . And I just want to tell you . . . I hope you can forget, just as I've forgotten."

12   I tried to laugh so she would not notice the cracks in my voice. "Really, don't worry."

13   "Okay. I just wanted you to know."

14   After we hung up, I cried, both happy and sad. I was again that sixteen-year-old, but the storm in my chest was gone.

15   My mother died six months later. By then she had bequeathed to me her most healing words, as open and eternal as a clear blue sky. Together we knew in our hearts what we would remember, what we can forget.

— ▪ —

Directions: In the space provided, write the letter of the choice that best completes each of the following statements. Record your score on page 487.

CHECKING YOUR COMPREHENSION

_____ 1. The author's primary purpose in this selection is to
  a. complain about the way her parents spoke to each other.
  b. explain the hardships her mother faced as a Chinese immigrant.
  c. describe her difficult relationship with her mother.
  d. compare her relationship with her mother with those of her friends.

_____ 2. What does the author mean when she refers to "storms"?
  a. bad weather
  b. unhappy emotions
  c. headaches
  d. chest pains

_____ 3. The author says she lost all of her battles with her mother because
  a. her mother threatened to kill herself.
  b. she felt sorry for her mother.
  c. her mother would stop speaking to her.
  d. her father refused to help her.

_____ 4. What pattern of organization does the author follow in paragraph 3?
  a. comparison/contrast
  b. cause/effect
  c. definition
  d. chronological order

_____ 5. All of the following transitions indicate the passage of time in paragraph 5 *except*
  a. Early on.
  b. Then.
  c. Lately.
  d. many.

_____ 6. The author was surprised that her mother called her because
   a. her mother did not have a telephone.
   b. they had already spoken that day.
   c. they had had an argument.
   d. her mother had Alzheimer's disease.

_____ 7. The main idea of paragraphs 6–8 is that the author's mother was
   a. struggling with her memories.
   b. able to speak only in Chinese.
   c. going crazy.
   d. still angry with her daughter.

_____ 8. The author supports her thesis primarily with
   a. facts and statistics.
   b. research evidence.
   c. personal experience.
   d. inferences.

_____ 9. At the beginning of paragraph 15, the transition _later_ is intended to show
   a. a contrast between two ideas.
   b. a change in the topic.
   c. the beginning of a list.
   d. the passage of time.

_____ 10. At the end of the selection, the author's tone is
   a. bitter.
   b. cheerful.
   c. forgiving.
   d. worried.

WORDS IN CONTEXT

Directions: Locate each word in the paragraph indicated and reread that paragraph. Then, based on the way the word is used, write a synonym or brief definition in the space provided. You may use a dictionary if necessary.

11. huffs (para. 2) _____

12. tormented (para. 3) _____

13. sorrows (para. 5) _____

14. drifted (para. 8) _____

15. eternal (para. 15) _____

VOCABULARY REVIEW

Directions: Complete each of the following sentences by inserting a word from the Vocabulary Preview on page 448 in the space provided.

16. She wore a diamond ring that her great aunt had _____ to her many years ago.

17. The sailboat was _____ at a dangerous angle.

18. We searched _____ for our passports after our hotel room was robbed.

19. The alpine skier was known for her cool, _____ manner both on and off the slopes.

STUDYING WORDS

_____ 20. The etymology of the word **collapse** (para. 2) is

    a. Latin.

    b. German.

    c. French.

    d. Middle English.

_____ 21. The correct meaning of the word **stricken** (para. 2) as it is used in this reading is

    a. packed up for departure.

    b. produced on a musical instrument.

    c. affected by something overwhelming.

    d. hit sharply with a hand or fist.

_____ 22. The correct meaning of the word **exchanges** (para. 2) as it is used in this reading is
   a. substitutions.
   b. markets.
   c. conversations.
   d. reversals.

_____ 23. The word **forbade** (para. 3) is the past tense of the word
   a. forbear.
   b. forbid.
   c. forbidden.
   d. forbidding.

_____ 24. Which one of the following correctly indicates how **injustices** (para. 3) is pronounced?
   a. in just EYE sis
   b. in JUST is is
   c. IN just is is
   d. in JUST eye sis

QUESTIONS FOR DISCUSSION

1. What were the "most hateful words" of the title? What were the most healing words?
2. How would you describe the author's mother, based on what you know from the selection?
3. How did the mother's memory loss affect her daughter?
4. Why do you think the author was both happy and sad after her conversation with her mother?

WRITING ACTIVITIES

1. Can you remember the most hateful words you have ever spoken to another person? Write a journal entry describing the situation and the effects your words had on the person to whom you spoke.
2. Throughout the selection, the author uses descriptive language to help the reader understand her experience. After each of the following examples of descriptive language, write a brief explanation in your own words.

a. "I let them fall in a fury of hailstones" (para. 1):

_____

b. "And what she aimed at me was as fast and deadly as a lightning bolt" (para. 2):

_____

c. "I would . . . harden my heart" (para. 3):

_____

d. "I was again that sixteen-year-old, but the storm in my chest was gone" (para. 14):

_____

e. "By then she had bequeathed to me her most healing words, as open and eternal as a clear blue sky" (para. 15):

_____

3. The author says that when her mother called her, she had "become a different person by then." Are you a different person than your teenage self? Write a paragraph describing the ways in which you have changed.

SEOUL SEARCHING
Rick Reilly

This article appeared in *Time* magazine in August 2000. The author, a professional writer, describes the search for his adopted daughter's birth mother in Korea.

Vocabulary Preview

These are some of the difficult words in this article. The definitions here will help you if you can't figure out the meanings from the sentence context or word parts.

disowned (para. 6) refused to acknowledge or accept as part of one's family

steeled (para. 9) filled with courage or determination in the face of possible disappointment

chic (para. 15) stylish

gaggle (para. 18) a group or cluster

unruffled (para. 19) calm, not upset

---

1   After 11 years and 6,000 miles, we still hadn't met our daughter's mother. We had come only this close: staked out in a van across from a tiny Seoul coffee shop, the mother inside with a Korean interpreter, afraid to come out, afraid of being discovered, afraid to meet her own flesh.

2   Inside the van, Rae, our 11-year-old Korean adopted daughter, was trying to make sense of it. How could we have flown the entire family 6,000 miles from Denver to meet a woman who was afraid to walk 20 yards across the street to meet us? Why had we come this far if she was only going to reject Rae again?

3   We were told we had an hour. There were 40 minutes left. The cell phone rang. "Drive the van to the alley behind the coffee shop," said the interpreter. "And wait."

4   When a four-month-old Rae was hand-delivered to us at Gate B-7 at Denver's Stapleton Airport, we knew someday we would be in Korea trying to find her birth mother. We just never dreamed it would be this soon. Then again, since Rae was a toddler, we've told her she was adopted, and she has

constantly asked about her birth mother. "Do you think my birth mother plays the piano like I do?" "Do you think my birth mother is pretty?" And then, at 10, after a day of too many stares: a teary "I just want to meet someone I'm related to."

5 "When they start asking that," the adoption therapist said, "you can start looking."

6 We started looking. We asked the agency that had arranged the adoption, Friends of Children of Various Nations, to begin a search. Within six months our caseworker, Kim Matsunaga, told us they had found the birth mother but she was highly reluctant to meet us. She had never told anyone about Rae. In Korea, the shame of unwed pregnancy is huge. The mother is disowned, the baby rootless. Kim guessed she had told her parents she was moving to thecity to work and had gone to a home for unwed mothers.

7 Kim told us the agency was taking a group of Colorado and New Mexico families to Korea in the summer to meet birth relatives. She said if we went, Rae's would probably show up. "The birth mothers almost always show up," she said. Almost.

8 We were unsure. And then we talked to a family who had gone the year before. They said it would be wonderful. At the very least, Rae would meet her foster mother, who had cared for her those four months. She would meet the doctor who delivered her. Hell, I had never met the doctor who delivered me. But meeting the birth mother was said to be the sweetest. A 16-year-old Korean-American girl told Rae, "I don't know, it just kinda fills a hole in your heart."

9 We risked it. Five plane tickets to Seoul for our two redheaded birth boys—Kellen, 15, and Jake, 13—Rae, me and my wife Linda. We steeled Rae for the chance that her birth mother wouldn't show up. Come to think of it, we steeled ourselves.

10 At first it was wonderful. We met Rae's foster mother, who swooped in and rushed for Rae as if she were her long-lost daughter, which she almost was. She bear-hugged her. She stroked her hair. She touched every little nick and scar on her tan arms and legs. "What's this from?" she asked in Korean. She had fostered 31 babies, but it was as if she'd known only Rae. Rae was half grossed out, half purring. Somebody had just rushed in with the missing four months of her life. The foster mother wept. We wept.

■ Rae with adoptive family.

11   All of us, all six American families, sat in one room at a home for unwed mothers outside Seoul across from 25 unwed mothers, some who had just given up their babies, some soon to. They looked into their unmet children's futures. We looked into our unmet birth mothers' pasts. A 17-year-old Korean-American girl—roughly the same age as the distraught girls in front of her—rose and choked out, "I know it's hard for you now, but I want you to know I love my American family."

12   Another 17-year-old adoptee met not only her birth father but also her four older birth sisters. They were still a family—had always been one—but they had given her up as one mouth too many to feed. Then they told her that her birth mother had died of an aneurysm two weeks earlier. So how was she supposed to feel now? Joy at finding her father and her sisters? Grief at 17 years without them? Anger at being given up? Gratitude for her American parents? Horror at coming so close to and then missing her birth mother? We heard her story that night on the tour bus, went to our hotel room and wept some more.

13   All these kids—even the three who never found their birth relatives—were piecing together the puzzle of their life at whiplash speed. This is where you were born. This is the woman who held you. This was the city, the food, the smells. For them, it was two parts home ("It's so nice," Rae said amid a

throng of Koreans on a street. "For once, people are staring at Kel and Jake instead of me") and three parts I'm-never-coming-here-again (a teenage boy ate dinner at his foster parents' home only to discover in mid-bite that they raise dogs for meat).

14   When the day came for our visit with Rae's birth mother, we were told "It has to be handled very, very carefully." She had three children by a husband she had never told about Rae, and she was terribly afraid someone would see her. And that's how we found ourselves hiding in that van like **Joe Friday**, waiting for the woman of a lifetime to show up. It is a very odd feeling to be staring holes in every Korean woman walking down a Korean street, thinking that your daughter may have sprung from her womb. All we knew about her was that she 1) might have her newborn girl with her, 2) was tiny—the birth certificate said she was 4 ft. 10 in.—and 3) would look slightly more nervous than a cat burglar.

15   First came a youngish, chic woman pushing a stroller. "That might be her!" yelled Rae—until she strolled by. Then a short, fat woman with a baby tied at her stomach. "There she is!" yelled Rae—until she got on a bus. Then a pretty, petite woman in yellow with an infant in a baby carrier. "I know that's her!" yelled Rae—and lo and behold the woman quick-stepped into the coffee shop across the street.

16   The only problem was, she didn't come out. She stayed in that coffee shop, talking to the interpreter for what seemed like six hours but was probably only 20 minutes. We stared at the dark windows of the shop. We stared at the cell phone. We stared at one another. What was this, **Panmunjom?** Finally, the interpreter called Kim: Drive down the alley and wait. We drove down the alley and waited. Nothing.

17   By this time, I could have been the centerfold for *Psychology Today*. Rae was still calm. I told her, "If she's not out here in five minutes, I want you to walk right in and introduce yourself." Rae swallowed. Suddenly, at the van window . . . and now opening the van door the woman in yellow with the baby. And just as suddenly, inside . . . sitting next to her daughter. Our daughter—all of ours. She was nervous. She wouldn't look at us, only at her baby and the interpreter. "We'll go somewhere," said the interpreter.

18   Where do you go with your deepest, darkest secret? We went to a park. Old Korean men looked up from their chess games in astonishment to see a gaggle of whites and redheads and Koreans sit down at the table next to them with cameras, gifts and notebooks. Rae presented her birth mother with a book she had made about her life—full of childhood pictures and purple-penned poems—but the woman showed no emotion as she looked at it. Rae presented her with a silver locket—a picture of herself inside but again, no eye contact, no hugs, no touches. The woman was either guarding her heart now the way she'd done 11 years ago, or she simply didn't care anymore, maybe had never cared.

19   Months before, Rae had drawn up a list of 20 questions she wanted to ask at the big moment. Now, unruffled, she pulled it out of her little purse. Some of us forgot to breathe. "Why did you give me up?" Rae asked simply. All heads turned to the woman. The interpreted answer: Too young, only 19 then, no money, great shame. "Where is my birth dad?" The answer: No idea. Only knew him for two dates. Long gone. Still no emotion. I ached for Rae. How would she handle such iciness from the woman she had dreamed of, fantasized about, held on to? Finally, this one: "When I was born, did you get to hold me?" The woman's lips parted in a small gasp. She swallowed and stared at the grass. "No," she said slowly, "they took you from me." And that's when our caseworker, Kim, said, "Well, now you can."

20   That did it. That broke her. She lurched, tears running down her cheeks, reached for Rae and pulled her close, holding her as if they might take her again. "I told myself I wouldn't cry," she said. The interpreter wept. Linda wept. I wept. Right then, right at that minute, the heavens opened up, and it poured a **monsoon** starter kit on us, just an **all-out Noah.** Yeah, even the sky wept.

21   Any sane group of people would have run for the van, but none of us wanted the moment to end. We had finally got her, and we would float to **Pusan** before we would give her up. We were all crying and laughing and trying to fit all of us under the birth mother's tiny pink umbrella. But the rain was so loud you couldn't talk. We ran for the van and sat in there, Rae holding her half sister and her birth mother holding the daughter she must have thought she would never see.

monsoon: The heavy rainfall that accompanies a seasonal wind system in southern Asia.

all-out Noah: A reference to the biblical story of Noah's ark, built during a flood.

Pusan: A city in the extreme southeast of South Korea on Korea Strait southeast of Seoul.

22   Time was so short. Little sentences contained whole lifetimes. She thanked us for raising her baby. "You are a very good family," she said, eyeing the giants around her. "Very strong and good." And how do you thank someone for giving you her daughter? Linda said, "Thank you for the gift you gave us." The birth mother smiled bittersweetly. She held Rae with one arm and the book and the locket tight with the other.

23   Then it was over. She said she had to get back. She asked the driver to pull over so she could get out. We started pleading for more time. Meet us for dinner? No. Breakfast tomorrow? No. Send you pictures? Please, no. The van stopped at a red light. Somebody opened the door. She kissed Rae on the head, stroked her hair one last time, stepped out, finally let go of her hand and closed the door. The light turned green. We drove off and watched her shrink away from us, dropped off on the corner of Nowhere and Forever.

24   I think I was still crying when I looked at Rae. She was beaming, of course, which must be how you feel when a hole in your heart finally gets filled.

—Rick Reily, (Seoul Searching,) *Time*, August 28, 2000. © 2000 Time Inc. Reprinted by permission.

CHECKING YOUR COMPREHENSION

Directions: In the space provided, write the letter of the choice that best completes each of the following statements. Record your score on page 487.

_____   1. The author's primary purpose in "Seoul Searching" is to
   a. describe his family's search for his adopted daughter's birth mother in Korea.
   b. encourage people to consider international adoption.
   c. criticize his daughter's birth mother for giving up her baby.
   d. compare the cultures of Korea and America.

_____   2. The birth mother gave her child up for adoption for all of the following reasons *except*
   a. she was ashamed of being unmarried and pregnant.
   b. she had kept her pregnancy a secret from her parents.
   c. she felt she was too young and had no money.
   d. she and her husband had too many children already.

3. The main idea of paragraph 8 is that

    a. the author and his wife were unsure about going to Korea.

    b. another family had made the same trip a year earlier.

    c. the author never met the doctor who had delivered him.

    d. the author's daughter would at least get to meet her foster mother.

4. The topic of paragraph 10 is

    a. the wonderful trip.

    b. Rae's foster mother.

    c. the language barrier between Rae's family and her Korean foster mother.

    d. the missing four months of Rae's life.

5. The main point of paragraph 13 is expressed in the

    a. first sentence.   c. third sentence.

    b. second sentence.   d. last sentence.

6. The title "Seoul Searching" refers to

    a. the author's difficult decision to begin the search for his daughter's birth mother.

    b. an American family's struggle to adopt a Korean baby.

    c. the physically stressful search for Rae's birth mother.

    d. both the physical search of Seoul for Rae's birth mother and Rae's emotional search for a missing part of herself.

7. The author supports his thesis primarily with

    a. facts and statistics.

    b. cause/effect relationships.

    c. personal experience.

    d. research evidence.

8. The most important aspect of paragraph 20 is that

    a. a monsoon had just begun.

    b. the interpreter was upset.

    c. the author and his wife were afraid they would lose their daughter.

    d. the birth mother finally allowed her emotions to show.

9. The statement "Little sentences contained whole lifetimes" (para. 22) means

    a. the birth mother knew only a little English.

    b. Rae's parents and her birth mother expressed a wealth of meaning in very few words.

    c. the interpreter had trouble translating their conversation.

    d. Rae's birth mother described her life after Rae's birth in short sentences.

10. The best description of the author's tone throughout the reading would be

    a. lighthearted and humorous.

    b. sad and unforgiving.

    c. sympathetic and anxious.

    d. bitter and angry.

WORDS IN CONTEXT

Directions: Locate each word in the paragraph indicated and reread that paragraph. Then, based on the way the word is used, write a synonym or brief definition in the space provided. You may use a dictionary if necessary.

11. reluctant (para. 6) _____

12. distraught (para. 11) _____

13. lurched (para. 20) _____

14. beaming (para. 24) _____

VOCABULARY REVIEW

Directions: Complete each of the following sentences by inserting a word from the Vocabulary Preview on page 455 in the space provided.

15. The business owner was a _____ woman in her early fifties.

16. Despite being heckled by several members of the audience, the guest speaker remained _____.

17. A _____ of young fans waited outside the theater in hopes of getting the actor's autograph.

18. After he was convicted of fraud, the criminal's family _____ him.

19. We _____ ourselves for the possibility that our team would not make the playoffs.

STUDYING WORDS

Directions: Use a dictionary to answer the following questions.

_____ 20. The word **distraught** (para. 11) originated from which of the following languages?

    a. Latin

    b. Greek

    c. Spanish

    d. French

_____ 21. Another meaning of the word **foster** (para. 8) that is not used in the reading is

    a. to cultivate.

    b. to encourage.

    c. to eliminate.

    d. to express.

_____ 22. The correct pronunciation of the word **aneurysm** (para. 12) is

    a. a ney ER ism.

    b. an ye iz EM.

    c. AN ye riz em.

    d. an yer RIZ um.

_____ 23. The slang expression **grossed out** (para. 10) means

    a. amazed.

    b. disgusted.

    c. anxious.

    d. angered.

_____ 24. What part of speech is the word **bittersweetly** (para. 22)?

    a. noun

    b. adjective

    c. adverb

    d. verb

QUESTIONS FOR DISCUSSION

1. What does the girl mean when she says that finding your birth mother "fills a hole in your heart" (para. 8)? Why did the author repeat the phrase at the end of the story?

2. How does the author illustrate the cultural differences between the visiting Americans and the Koreans?

3. Think about the questions Rae asked her birth mother. Would you have asked similar questions? What additional questions would you ask?

WRITING ACTIVITIES

1. Visit the Rainbow Kids Personal Adoption Stories Web site at http://www.rainbowkids.com/stories/. Read the stories posted there. Write a paragraph explaining how the experiences seem similar to those of the women in "Seoul Searching."

2. Rae had only a few moments to ask her birth mother questions to learn about her past. Brainstorm a list of questions that you would like to ask your parents or another family member about your family's history.

NAME _____ SECTION _____

DATE _____ SCORE _____

COMING INTO MY OWN
Ben Carson, M.D.

Ben Carson is a famous pediatric neurosurgeon. Read this selection to learn how he overcomes racial prejudice in the medical profession.

1   The nurse looked at me with disinterest as I walked toward her station. "Yes?" she asked, pausing with a pencil in her hand. "Who did you come to pick up?" From the tone of her voice I immediately knew that she thought I was an orderly. I was wearing my green scrubs, nothing to indicate I was a doctor.

2   "I didn't come to pick up anyone." I looked at her and smiled, realizing that the only black people she has seen on the floor had been orderlies. Why should she think anything else? "I'm the new intern."

3   "New intern? But you can't—I mean—I didn't mean to—" the nurse stuttered, trying to apologize without sounding prejudiced.

4   "That's OK," I said, letting her off the hook. It was a natural mistake. "I'm new, so why should you know who I am?"

5   The first time I went into the intensive care unit, I was wearing my whites (our monkey suits, as we interns called them), and a nurse signaled me. "You're here for Mr. Jordan?"

6   "No, ma'am, I'm not."

■ Dr. Ben Carson

7   "You sure?" she asked as a frown covered her forehead. "He's the only one who's scheduled for respiratory therapy today."

8   By then I had come closer and she could read my name badge and the word *intern* under my name.

9   "Oh, I'm so very sorry," she said, and I could tell she was.

10   Although I didn't say it, I would like to have told her, "It's all right because I realize most people do things based on their past experiences. You've never encountered a black intern before, so you assumed I was the only kind of black male you'd seen wearing whites, a respiratory therapist." I smiled again and went on.

11   It was inevitable that a few white patients didn't want a black doctor and they protested to Dr. Long. One woman said, "I'm sorry, but I do not want a black physician in on my case."

12   Dr. Long had a standard answer, given in a calm but firm voice. "There's the door. You're welcome to walk through it. But if you stay here, Dr. Carson will handle your case."

13   At the time people were making these objections, I didn't know about them. Only much later did Dr. Long tell me as he laughed about the prejudices of some patients. But there was no humor in his voice when he defined his position. He was adamant about his stance, allowing no prejudice because of color or ethnic background.

14   Of course, I knew how some individuals felt. I would have had to be pretty insensitive not to know. The way they behaved, their coldness, even without saying anything, made their feelings clear. Each time, however, I was able to remind myself they were individuals speaking for themselves and not representative of all whites. No matter how strongly a patient felt, as soon as he voiced his objection he learned that Dr. Long would dismiss him on the spot if he said anything more. So far as I know, none of the patients ever left!

15   I honestly felt no great pressures. When I did encounter prejudice, I could hear Mother's voice in the back of my head saying things like, "Some people are ignorant and you have to educate them."

16   The only pressure I felt during my internship, and in the years since, has been a self-imposed obligation to act as a role model for black youngsters. These young folks need to know that the way to escape their often dismal situations is contained within themselves. They can't expect other people to do it for them. Perhaps I can't do much, but I can provide one living example of someone who made it and who came from what we now call a disadvantaged background. Basically I'm no different than many of them.

17   As I think of black youth, I also want to say I believe that many of our pressing racial problems will be taken care of when we who are among the minorities will stand on our own feet and refuse to look to anybody else to save us from our situations. The culture in which we live stresses looking out for number one. Without adopting such a self-centered value system, we can demand the best of ourselves while we are extending our hands to help others.

18   I see glimmers of hope. For example, I noticed that when the Vietnamese came to the United States they often faced prejudice from everyone—white, black, and Hispanic. But they didn't beg for handouts and often took the lowest jobs offered. Even well-educated individuals didn't mind sweeping floors if it was a paying job.

19   Today many of these same Vietnamese are property owners and entrepreneurs. That's the message I try to get across to the young people. The same opportunities are there, but we can't start out as vice president of the company. Even if we landed such a position, it wouldn't do us any good anyway because we wouldn't know how to do our work. It's better to start where we can fit in and then work our way up.

— ▪ —

CHECKING YOUR COMPREHENSION

Directions: In the space provided, write the letter of the choice that best completes each of the following statements. Record your score on page 487.

_____   1. This reading demonstrates that
   a. most white patients do not want black doctors.
   b. female nurses are prejudiced against male doctors.
   c. orderlies and respiratory therapists are not treated with respect by other medical professionals.
   d. it is possible to overcome prejudice and a disadvantaged background to become a success.

_____   2. The writer's purpose in describing the conversations in paragraphs 1–9 was to
   a. expose medical professionals as racists.
   b. defend his own behavior toward nurses.
   c. illustrate the prejudice he faced as a black intern.
   d. explain the bitterness he feels toward whites in general.

_____   3. During his internship, the writer dealt with the prejudice of some of his patients by
   a. refusing to treat those patients.
   b. reminding himself that they did not represent the attitudes of all whites.
   c. quitting his internship and becoming a writer.
   d. becoming prejudiced against all whites.

_____ 4. Dr. Long handled the prejudices of some of the white patients by

    a. asking the writer to complete his internship elsewhere.

    b. agreeing to personally treat the patients who objected to a black doctor.

    c. encouraging the writer to find another profession.

    d. informing the patients that they could either leave or be treated by the black intern.

_____ 5. The statement that best expresses the main idea of paragraph 17 is that

    a. people should look to themselves rather than others to improve their situations.

    b. adopting a self-centered value system is the only way to succeed in our culture.

    c. the racial problems in our society are caused primarily by misunderstanding.

    d. extending help to others is not as important as getting ahead.

_____ 6. From the situation described in paragraphs 1–4, the writer suggests

    a. all nurses are disrespectful to orderlies.

    b. all orderlies are black males.

    c. black doctors are not typical in the hospital described.

    d. doctors should be required to wear identification.

_____ 7. From the reference to the writer's mother, you can tell that she

    a. was prejudiced against whites.

    b. thought fighting prejudice was hopeless.

    c. believed that one could change people's attitudes toward blacks.

    d. had never experienced prejudice.

_____ 8. Paragraphs 18–19 indicate that the writer seems to believe that

    a. minorities should help themselves and work to solve their own problems.

    b. immigrants are taking jobs away from blacks.

    c. blacks should be given special treatment because they must face prejudice.

    d. minorities are better off today than they were ten years ago.

_____ 9. The writer supports his ideas primarily by

    a. describing his personal experience.

    b. reporting statistics.

    c. defining medical terms.

    d. citing facts.

_____ 10. By stating in paragraph 2 that he looked at the nurse "and smiled," the writer indicates that he

    a. was being sarcastic.

    b. understood the nurse's error and forgave her.

    c. was surprised at being treated that way.

    d. did not understand the situation.

WORDS IN CONTEXT

Directions: Locate each word in the paragraph indicated and reread that paragraph. Then, based on the way the word is used, write a synonym or brief definition in the space provided. You may use a dictionary if necessary.

11. scrubs (para. 1) _____

12. adamant (para. 13) _____

13. stance (para. 13) _____

14. encounter (para. 15) _____

VOCABULARY REVIEW

Directions: Complete each of the following sentences by inserting a word from the Vocabulary Preview of page 465 in the space provided.

15. A person who assists with nonmedical work in a hospital is an

    _____.

16. People who organize and take risks for a business are called

    _____.

17. An _____ is a medical doctor who is working in a hospital for practical training.

18. After knee surgery, the patient needed several weeks of physical

    _____.

19. The elderly patient suffered from pneumonia and related

    _____ problems.

STUDYING WORDS

Directions: Use a dictionary to answer the following questions.

_____ 20. The word **entrepreneurs** (para. 19) originated from which of the following languages?

    a. Latin

    b. Greek

    c. Spanish

    d. French

_____ 21. Another meaning of the word **glimmers** (para. 18) that is not used in the reading is

    a. message.

    b. movement.

    c. distress signal.

    d. flickering light.

_____ 22. The correct pronunciation of the word **adamant** (para. 13) is

    a. AD a ment.

    b. ad A ment.

    c. a DA ment.

    d. AD am ent.

_____ 23. The word **representative** (para. 14) when used in the field of government means

    a. ruling party.

    b. decision.

    c. party in power.

    d. member of a legislature.

_____ 24. What part of speech is the word **objections** (para. 13)?

    a. noun

    b. adjective

    c. adverb

    d. verb

QUESTIONS FOR DISCUSSION

1. Describe situations in which you have experienced or observed some type of prejudice. How did you respond to the situation?

2. This article focuses on racial prejudice. What other types of prejudice exist?

3. Explain why you agree or disagree with the following statement made by Dr. Carson: "The way [for disadvantaged youth] to escape their often dismal situations is contained within themselves."

WRITING ACTIVITIES

1. Dr. Carson wants to serve as a role model for black youngsters. Are you a role model for anyone? Who has served as a role model for you? Write a paragraph answering one of these questions.

2. Dr. Carson was misidentified as an orderly by a nurse. Write a paragraph describing a situation in which someone made false assumptions about you or misidentified you.

LIVING LIFE TO THE FULLEST
Maya Angelou

Are you living life to its fullest? Read this selection to find out. Maya Angelou tells a story that will help you answer this question.

Vocabulary Preview

These are some of the difficult words in this essay. The definitions here will help you if you can't figure out the meanings from the sentence context or word parts.

sinewy (para. 1) lean and muscular

incurred (para. 1) brought on; met with

tautly (para. 2) tightly

meticulous (para. 3) extremely careful

maven (para. 6) expert

camaraderie (para. 14) friendship

founts (para. 14) sources

convivial (para. 14) agreeable; cheerful

scenarios (para. 16) plans; expected events

1   Aunt Tee was a Los Angeles member of our extended family. She was seventy-nine when I met her, sinewy, strong, and the color of old lemons. She wore her coarse, straight hair, which was slightly streaked with gray, in a long braided rope across the top of her head. With her high cheekbones, old gold skin, and almond eyes, she looked more like an Indian chief than an old black woman. (Aunt Tee described herself and any favored member of her race as Negroes. *Black* was saved for those who had incurred her disapproval.)

2   She had retired and lived alone in a neat ground-floor apartment. Wax flowers and china figurines sat on elaborately embroidered and heavily starched doilies. Sofas and chairs were tautly upholstered. The only thing at ease in Aunt Tee's apartment was Aunt Tee.

3   I used to visit her often and perch on her uncomfortable sofa just to hear her stories. She was proud that after working thirty years as a maid, she

spent the next thirty years as a live-in housekeeper, carrying the keys to rich houses and keeping meticulous accounts.

4   "Living in lets the white folks know Negroes are as neat and clean as they are, sometimes more so. And it gives the Negro maid a chance to see white folks ain't no smarter than Negroes. Just luckier. Sometimes."

5   Aunt Tee told me that once she was housekeeper for couple in Bel Air, California, lived with them in a fourteen-room ranch house. There was a day maid who cleaned, and a gardener who daily tended the lush gardens. Aunt Tee oversaw the workers. When she had begun the job, she had cooked and served a light breakfast, a good lunch, and a full three- or four-course dinner to her employers and their guests. Aunt Tee said she watched them grow older and leaner. After a few years they stopped entertaining and ate dinner hardly seeing each other at the table. Finally, they sat in a dry silence as they ate evening meals of soft scrambled eggs, melba toast, and weak tea. Aunt Tee said she saw them growing old but didn't see herself aging at all.

6   She became the social maven. She started "keeping company" (her phrase) with a chauffeur down the street. Her best friend and her friend's husband worked in service only a few blocks away.

7   On Saturdays Aunt Tee would cook a pot of pigs' feet, a pot of greens, fry chicken, make potato salad, and bake a banana pudding. Then, that evening, her friends—the chauffeur, the other housekeeper, and her husband—would come to Aunt Tee's commodious live-in quarters. There the four would eat and drink, play records and dance. As the evening wore on, they would settle down to a serious game of bid whist.

8   Naturally, during this revelry jokes were told, fingers snapped, feet were patted, and there was a great deal of laughter.

9   Aunt Tee said that what occurred during every Saturday party startled her and her friends the first time it happened. They had been playing cards, and Aunt Tee, who had just won the bid, held a handful of trumps. She felt a cool breeze on her back and sat upright and turned around. Her employers had cracked her door open and beckoned to her. Aunt Tee, a little peeved, laid down her cards and went to the door. The couple backed away and asked her to come into the hall, and there they both spoke and won Aunt Tee's sympathy forever.

10 "Theresa, we don't mean to disturb you . . ." the man whispered, "but you all seem to be having such a good time . . ."

11 The woman added, "We hear you and your friends laughing every Saturday night, and we'd just like to watch you. We don't want to bother you. We'll be quiet and just watch."

12 The man said, "If you'll just leave your door ajar, your friends don't need to know. We'll never make a sound." Aunt Tee said she saw no harm in agreeing, and she talked it over with her company. They said it was OK with them, but it was sad that the employers owned the gracious house, the swimming pool, three cars, and numberless palm trees, but had no joy. Aunt Tee told me that laughter and relaxation had left the house; she agreed it was sad.

13 That story has stayed with me for nearly thirty years, and when a tale remains fresh in my mind, it almost always contains a lesson which will benefit me.

14 My dears, I draw the picture of the wealthy couple standing in a darkened hallway, peering into a lighted room where black servants were lifting their voices in merriment and camaraderie, and I realize that living well is an art which can be developed. Of course, you will need the basic talents to build upon: They are a love of life and ability to take great pleasure from small offerings, an assurance that the world owes you nothing and that every gift is exactly that, a gift. That people who may differ from you in political stance, sexual persuasion, and racial inheritance can be founts of fun, and if you are lucky, they can become even convivial comrades.

15 Living life as art requires a readiness to forgive. I do not mean that you should suffer fools gladly, but rather remember your own shortcomings, and when you encounter another with flaws, don't be eager to righteously seal yourself away from the offender forever. Take a few breaths and imagine yourself having just committed the action which has set you at odds.

16 Because of the routines we follow, we often forget that life is an ongoing adventure. We leave our homes for work, acting and even believing that we will reach our destinations with no unusual event startling us out of our set expectations. The truth is we know nothing, not where our cars will fail or when our buses will stall, whether our places of employment will be there when we arrive, or whether, in fact, we ourselves will arrive whole and alive at the end of our journeys. Life is pure adventure, and the sooner we realize

that, the quicker we will be able to treat life as art: to bring all our energies to each encounter, to remain flexible enough to notice and admit when what we expected to happen did not happen. We need to remember that we are created creative and can invent new scenarios as frequently as they are needed.

17 Life seems to love the liver of it. Money and power can liberate only if they are used to do so. They can imprison and inhibit more finally than barred windows and iron chains.

— ∙ —

CHECKING YOUR COMPREHENSION

Directions: In the space provided, write the letter of the choice that best completes each of the following statements. Record your score on page 487.

_____ 1. One main point of the reading is that living well

a. requires money.

b. depends on other people.

c. involves taking pleasure in small things.

d. depends on one's personality.

_____ 2. Aunt Tee worked for the couple in Bel Air as a

a. chauffeur.   c. maid.

b. housekeeper.   d. gardener.

_____ 3. The couple in Bel Air won Aunt Tee's sympathy forever when they

a. asked if they could watch Aunt Tee and her friends.

b. allowed Aunt Tee to live with them.

c. allowed Aunt Tee to use the swimming pool.

d. employed Aunt Tee for thirty years.

_____ 4. The couple from Bel Air changed over the years when they

a. became richer.

b. stopped entertaining and ate dinner in silence.

c. became ill and needed nursing care.

d. became more demanding and difficult to work for.

5. The main idea of paragraph 16 is expressed in the
   a. first sentence.   c. third sentence.
   b. second sentence.   d. last sentence.

6. Which one of the following is *not* a basic talent for living well?
   a. the ability to love life
   b. awareness that the world owes you nothing
   c. recognition that people different from you can be a source of pleasure
   d. acquiring the financial means to enjoy life

7. The pattern of organization used in this reading is
   a. chronological order.   c. comparison and contrast.
   b. cause and effect.   d. process.

8. In paragraph 5, which of the following words or phrases is *not* a transition?
   a. there was   c. once
   b. hardly seeing each other   d. finally

9. The couple in Bel Air had many possessions, but had no
   a. will power.   c. joy.
   b. direction.   d. grace.

10. Aunt Tee could best be described as
    a. wise and fun loving.   c. nonjudgmental.
    b. assertive and focused.   d. opinionated.

WORDS IN CONTEXT

Directions: Locate each word in the paragraph indicated and reread that paragraph. Then, based on the way the word is used, write a synonym or brief definition in the space provided. You may use a dictionary if necessary.

11. revelry (para. 8) _____

12. beckoned (para. 9) _____

13. peering (para. 14) _____

14. stance (para. 14) _____

VOCABULARY REVIEW

Directions: Match each word in column A with its meaning in column B.

	Column A		Column B
_____	15. camaraderie	a.	tightly
_____	16. meticulous	b.	expert
_____	17. scenarios	c.	sources
_____	18. incurred	d.	friendship
_____	19. maven	e.	plans
_____	20. convivial	f.	brought on; met with
_____	21. sinewy	g.	extremely careful
_____	22. tautly	h.	agreeable; cheerful
_____	23. founts	i.	lean and muscular

STUDYING WORDS

Directions: Use a dictionary to answer the following questions.

_____ 24. The word **scenarios** (para. 16) originated from which of the following languages?

    a. French

    b. Latin

    c. Spanish

    d. Greek

_____ 25. Another meaning of the word **comrade** (para. 14) that is not used in the reading is

    a. a member of the same social group.

    b. a resident of the same country.

    c. a fellow member of the Communist Party.

    d. a member of an unpopular group.

_____ 26. The correct pronunciation of the word **camaraderie** (para. 14) is

    a. KAM rad er ee.

    b. KA mera de ree.

    c. ka me RA de ree.

    d. KA mer a ree.

_____ 27. A meaning of **liberate** (para. 17) used in the field of chemistry is

    a. release a gas.

    b. create a chemical reaction.

    c. mix elements.

    d. precipitate waste.

_____ 28. What part of speech is the word **lush** (para. 4)?

    a. adjective

    b. adverb

    c. noun

    d. preposition

QUESTIONS FOR DISCUSSION

1. Describe your "requirements for good living."

2. Choose a favorite relative or friend and explain his or her outlook on life. How does it differ from Aunt Tee's?

3. Maya Angelou says that "life is pure adventure." Do you agree with this? Why?

WRITING ACTIVITIES

1. Do you believe that money can liberate or imprison a person? Write a paragraph explaining how you regard money.

2. Angelou mentions the "ability to take great pleasure from small offerings." Write a paragraph describing a small thing that has made a positive difference in your life.

AMERICAN INDIAN MASCOTS SHOULD GO
Rich Heffern

This article first appeared in the *National Catholic Reporter* in February 2005. Read it to find out the author's views on the use of American Indian names and symbols as sports mascots.

Vocabulary Preview

These are some of the difficult words in this essay. The definitions here will help you if you can't figure out the meanings from the sentence context or word parts.

caricature (para. 1) a representation of a person that is exaggerated for comic effect

activists (para. 1) those engaged in direct action supporting or opposing a controversial issue

paraphernalia (para. 4) the equipment used in a particular activity

stereotypes (para. 4) standardized mental pictures held in common by members of a group, representing an oversimplified opinion or a prejudiced attitude

advocacy (para. 5) actively support a cause

derogatory (para. 5) disparaging or belittling; expressing a low opinion

matrilineal (para. 8) tracing ancestors through the maternal (female) line

1   A sports-page headline screams: "Cowboys scalp Redskins to maintain lead." The logo of the Cleveland "Indians" is a buck-toothed, big-nosed caricature of a Native American. The University of North Dakota bookstore sells sweatpants with the word "Sioux" stenciled across the backside. For several years, a T-shirt graphically showing a Native American having sex with a buffalo has been worn by North Dakota State University fans. Yet some sports columnists still name anti-mascot activists as "whiners" and "fusspots."

2   A little investigation reveals that people against Indian sports mascots truly aren't a tiny, whiny liberal minority. In a survey by *Indian Country Today* magazine, for example, 81 percent of respondents reported use of American

Indian names, symbols and mascots are predominantly offensive and deeply disparaging to Native Americans. In one survey done by a Stanford University psychologist, the results indicated that among Native American high school students 50 percent said they opposed Native mascots; 50 percent said they didn't mind. But overall, 90 percent said they felt it was disrespectful. When asked why they didn't mind being used as a mascot even if they felt it disrespectful, students responded: "It's better than being invisible."

3   Cornel Pewewardy, a Native American educator and professor at the University of Kansas, spells it out thusly: "Native Americans would never have associated the sacred practice of becoming a warrior with the hoopla of a high school pep rally, half-time entertainment, being a sidekick to cheerleaders, or royalty in homecoming pageants. . . . Indian mascots exhibit either idealized or comical facial features and 'native' dress, ranging from body-length feathered headdresses to more subtle fake buckskin attire or skimpy loincloths.

4   "Some teams and supporters display counterfeit Indian paraphernalia, including foam tomahawks, feathers, face paints, and symbolic drums and pipes. . . . These negative images, symbols and behaviors play a crucial role in distorting and warping Native American children's cultural perceptions of themselves as well as non-Indian children's attitudes toward Native peoples. Most of these proverbial stereotypes are manufactured racist images that prevent millions of students from understanding the past and current authentic human experience of Native Americans." Much like Holocaust deniers, mascot lovers seem to be willfully ignorant of the large body of evidence against their position.

5   Virtually every America Indian advocacy group in the country has spoken out against mascots, including the Washington-based National Congress of American Indians, the American Indian Movement, Indian Psychologists of the Americas, Native American Journalists Association, Concerned American Indian Parents, and more. The U.S. Commission on Civil Rights, chaired by Elsie Meeks, a Lakota, has officially endorsed retiring institutionalized "Indian" sports team tokens from public schools. The NAACP and the National Education Association have also weighed in against Indian sports mascots. Even the U.S. Patent and Trademark Office ruled that the "Washington Redskins" trademark is derogatory.

6   In a CBS news interview, Native American author Sherman Alexie said: "The mascot thing gets me really mad. Don't think about it in terms of race. Think in terms of religion. Those are our religious imagery up there: feather, paint, the sun. You couldn't have a Catholic priest running around the floor with a basketball throwing Communion wafers. You couldn't have a rabbi running around."

7   "I use a two-fold analysis," said Chad Smith, principal chief of the Cherokee Nation. In an interview in *Indian Country Today* magazine, he explained: "The first one is called Anaweg, who is my 8-year-old daughter. Does it teach her the truth about Indians? If the image doesn't, I have no use for it. The second is Nedsin, my deceased father. Does it honor our ancestors? If it doesn't, I have no use for it. That is how I look at all the stuff I see about Indians."

8   Barbara Munson, member of the Oneida nation, digs down to the heart of the problem: "People ask 'Aren't you proud of your warriors?' I always answer: 'Yes, and we don't want them demeaned by being "honored" in a sports activity.' Indian men are not limited to the role of warrior. In many of our cultures, a good man is learned, gentle, patient, wise and deeply spiritual. In present time as well as in the past, our men are also sons and brothers, husbands, uncles, fathers and grandfathers. Contemporary Indian men wear contemporary clothes and live and love just as men from other cultural backgrounds do. . . . What's more many Indian nations are both matrilineal and child-centered. Indian cultures identify women with the Creator, because of their ability to bear children, and with the Earth, which is mother to us all."

9   If nonbelligerent people of Irish descent were upset by Notre Dame's nickname or members of the Sons of the Vikings by the football franchise in Minneapolis, then these names should be changed as well. The fact is that few object to these names, yet a growing number of people around the country are campaigning against Native American mascots and nicknames.

■ ▪ ■

CHECKING YOUR COMPREHENSION

Directions: In the space provided, write the letter of the choice that best completes each of the following statements. Record your score on page 487.

_____ 1. The author's main purpose in this selection is to

    a. persuade sports teams to stop using Native American mascots and nicknames.

    b. explain the long and distinguished history of Native American mascots.

    c. compare the various types of mascots used in different sports.

    d. defend the use of Native American nicknames and mascots.

_____ 2. What pattern of organization does the author follow in paragraph 1?

    a. chronological order

    b. process

    c. example

    d. definition

_____ 3. The topic of paragraph 3 is

    a. *Indian Country Today* magazine.

    b. Indian sports mascots.

    c. Native American high school students.

    d. a survey by Stanford University.

_____ 4. Which answer identifies the cause/effect relationship described in paragraph 4?

    a. *cause:* sports teams
       effect: Indian paraphernalia

    b. *cause:* negative images, symbols, and behaviors
       effect: distorted perceptions of Native Americans

    c. *cause:* cultural perceptions of Native American children
       effect: attitudes toward Native peoples

    d. *cause:* mascot lovers
       effect: Native Americans

5. The main point of paragraph 4 is expressed in the
   a. first sentence.
   b. second sentence.
   c. third sentence.
   d. last sentence.

6. Native American author Sherman Alexie sees the mascot issue in terms of
   a. race.
   b. sports.
   c. symbols.
   d. religion.

7. In paragraph 7, the transitions *first* and *second* mean that
   a. two ideas are being contrasted.
   b. two related ideas are being listed.
   c. a definition and an example are being given.
   d. one event is being described as the cause of another.

8. The main point of paragraph 8 is that, according to Barbara Munson,
   a. Indian men are much more than warriors.
   b. Indian men wear contemporary clothing.
   c. Indian cultures identify women as more important than men.
   d. sports activities are demeaning to Indians.

9. The overall tone of this article could best be described as
   a. factual and objective.
   b. lighthearted and humorous.
   c. earnest and indignant.
   d. mocking and sarcastic.

10. The author supports his thesis with all of the following *except*
    a. facts and statistics.
    b. expert opinions.
    c. research evidence.
    d. personal experience.

WORDS IN CONTEXT

Directions: Locate each word in the paragraph indicated and reread that paragraph. Then, based on the way the word is used, write a synonym or brief definition in the space provided. You may use a dictionary if necessary.

11. disparaging (para. 2)_____

12. hoopla (para. 3) _____

13. counterfeit (para. 4)_____

14. crucial (para. 4) _____

15. warping (para. 4) _____

16. endorsed (para. 5)_____

17. demeaned (para. 8) _____

18. nonbelligerent (para. 9) _____

VOCABULARY REVIEW

Directions: Match each word in column A with its meaning in column B.

Column A	Column B
_____ 19. caricature	a. those engaged in direct action supporting or opposing a controversial issue
_____ 20. activists	b. standardized mental pictures held in common by members of a group, representing an oversimplified opinion or a prejudiced attitude
_____ 21. paraphernalia	c. disparaging or belittling; expressing a low opinion
_____ 22. stereotypes	d. a representation of a person that is exaggerated for comic effect
_____ 23. advocacy	e. tracing ancestors through the maternal line
_____ 24. derogatory	f. the equipment used in a particular activity
_____ 25. matrilineal	g. actively supporting a cause

STUDYING WORDS

_____ 26. In parts of speech, the word **exhibit** (para. 3) is used in this reading as

    a. a noun.

    b. a verb.

    c. an adverb.

    d. an adjective.

_____ 27. The correct meaning of the word **subtle** (para. 3) as it is used in this reading is

    a. crafty.

    b. skillful.

    c. not obvious.

    d. clever.

_____ 28. The etymology of the word **counterfeit** (para. 4) is

    a. Middle English.

    b. Greek.

    c. German.

    d. Italian.

_____ 29. Which one of the following correctly indicates how **paraphernalia** (para. 4) is pronounced?

    a. PAIR uh fur nell ya

    b. pair uh FUR nell ya

    c. pair uh fur NAIL ya

    d. pair uh FUR nail ya

_____ 30. Which one of the following correctly indicates how **proverbial** (para. 4) is pronounced?

    a. PROV erb ee all

    b. pro VERB ee all

    c. prov erb EE all

    d. PRO verb ee all

_____ 31. The prefix *matri* in **matrilineal** (para. 8) means

    a. line.

    b. mother.

    c. marriage.

    d. mature.

QUESTIONS FOR DISCUSSION

1. How do you feel about American Indian mascots? Did this article have an effect on your opinion?

2. Discuss the audience for which this article was written. What do you think the responses of Native Americans and non–Native Americans might be?

3. Discuss the statement by Native American students: "It's better than being invisible" (para. 2). Why do you think they feel this way? Do you agree that it is better to be noticed in a negative way than not to be noticed at all?

WRITING ACTIVITIES

1. Do you agree or disagree that "mascot lovers seem to be willfully ignorant" of the evidence against their position? Write an essay defending your point of view.

2. The author uses connotative language throughout this selection. List ten examples of connotative language from the article and identify whether each word carries a positive or negative impression.

3. Consider the different groups to which you belong, including racial or ethnic, religious, gender, or age. Have you ever been confronted by a stereotype associated with one of those groups? Write a paragraph describing your experience and how you responded.

4. Reread paragraph 7, in which Chad Smith describes his two-fold analysis of Indian images. What do you think of his philosophy? Can you apply it to an aspect of your own life? Write a paragraph explaining your answer.

HISPANIC USA: THE CONVEYOR-BELT LADIES
Rose del Castillo Guilbault

An important part of many jobs is getting along with coworkers as well as working with supervisors and customers. In this article, a young woman describes her experiences working in a vegetable-packing plant. Read the article to find out how she came to be respected by her older coworkers.

Vocabulary Preview

These are some of the difficult words in this essay. The definitions here will help you if you can't figure out the meanings from the sentence context or word parts.

tedious (para. 4) tiresome, dull

strenuous (para. 4) requiring great physical effort or energy

sorority (para. 5) an organization of women

irrevocably (para. 10) in a way that is impossible to change

stigmatize (para. 10) to brand or label

gregarious (para. 12) sociable

dyspeptic (para. 12) having a bad disposition, grouchy

pragmatic (para. 17) practical

melancholic (para. 18) sad, gloomy

fatalism (para. 19) the belief that events in life are determined by fate and cannot be changed

crescendo (para. 29) a steady increase in volume or force

anticlimactic (para. 30) characterizing an ordinary or commonplace event that concludes a series of important events

1   The conveyor-belt ladies were the migrant women, mostly from Texas, I worked with during the summers of my teenage years. I call them conveyor-belt ladies because our entire relationship took place while sorting tomatoes on a conveyor belt.

2   We were like a cast in a play where all the action occurs on one set. We'd return day after day to perform the same roles, only this stage was a vegetable-packing shed, and at the end of the season there was no applause.

The players could look forward only to the same uninspiring parts on a string of grim real-life stages.

3   The women and their families arrived in May for the carrot season, spent the summer in the tomato sheds and stayed through October for the bean harvest. After that, they emptied the town, some returning to their homes in Texas (cities like McAllen, Douglas, Brownsville), while others continued on the migrant trail, picking cotton in the San Joaquin Valley or grapefruits and oranges in the Imperial Valley.

4   Most of these women had started in the fields. The vegetable-packing sheds were a step up, easier than the back-breaking, grueling work the field demanded. The work was more tedious than strenuous, paid better, provided fairly steady hours and clean bathrooms. Best of all, you weren't subjected to the elements.

5   The summer I was 16, my mother got jobs for both of us as tomato sorters. That's how I came to be included in the seasonal sorority of the conveyor belt.

6   The work consisted of standing and picking flawed tomatoes off the conveyor belt before they rolled off into the shipping boxes at the end of the line. These boxes were immediately loaded onto waiting delivery trucks, so it was crucial not to let imperfect tomatoes through.

7   The work could be slow or intense, depending on the quality of the tomatoes and how many there were. Work increased when the company's deliveries got backlogged or after rainy weather had delayed picking.

8   During those times, it was not unusual to work from 7 A.M. to midnight, playing catch-up. I never heard anyone complain about the overtime. Overtime meant desperately needed extra money.

9   I was not happy to be part of the agricultural workforce. I would have preferred working in a dress shop or baby-sitting, like my friends. But I had a dream that would cost a lot of money—college. And the fact was, this was the highest-paying work I could do.

10   But it wasn't so much the work that bothered me. I was embarrassed because only Mexicans worked at packing sheds. I had heard my schoolmates joke about the "ugly, fat Mexican women" at the sheds. They ridiculed the way they dressed and laughed at the "funny way" they talked. I feared

working with them would irrevocably stigmatize me, setting me further apart from my Anglo classmates.

11   At 16 I was more American than Mexican and, with adolescent arrogance, felt superior to these "uneducated" women. I might be one of them, I reasoned, but I was not like them.

12   But it was difficult not to like the women. They were a gregarious, entertaining group, easing the long, monotonous hours with bawdy humor, spicy gossip and inventive laments. They poked fun at all the male workers and did hysterical impersonations of a dyspeptic Anglo supervisor. Although he didn't speak Spanish (other than "*Mujeres, trabajo, trabajo!*")[1], he seemed to sense he was being laughed at. That would account for the sudden rages when he would stamp his foot and forbid us to talk until break time.

13   "I bet he understands Spanish and just pretends so he can hear what we say," I whispered to Rosa.

14   "*Ay, no, hija,*[2] it's all the buzzing in his ears that alerts him that these *viejas* (old women) are bad-mouthing him!" Rosa giggled.

15   But it would have been easier to tie the women's tongues in a knot than to keep them quiet. Eventually the ladies had their way and their fun, and the men learned to ignore them.

16   We were often shifted around, another strategy to keep us quiet. This gave me ample opportunity to get to know everyone, listen to their life stories and absorb the gossip.

17   Pretty Rosa described her romances and her impending wedding to a handsome field worker. Bertha, a heavy-set, dark-skinned woman, told me that Rosa's marriage would cause nothing but headaches because the man was younger and too handsome. Maria, large, moon-faced and placid, described the births of each of her nine children, warning me about the horrors of childbirth. Pragmatic Minnie, a tiny woman who always wore printed cotton dresses, scoffed at Maria's stupidity, telling me she wouldn't have so many kids if she had ignored that good-for-nothing priest and gotten her tubes tied!

---

[1]Women, work, work.
[2]Oh, no, little one.

18   In unexpected moments, they could turn melancholic: recounting the babies who died because their mothers couldn't afford medical care; the alcoholic, abusive husbands who were their "cross to bear"; the racism they experienced in Texas, where they were branded "dirty Mexicans" or "Mexican dogs" and not allowed in certain restaurants.

19   They spoke with the detached fatalism of people with limited choices and alternatives. Their lives were as raw and brutal as ghetto streets—something they accepted with an odd grace and resignation.

20   I was appalled and deeply affected by these confidences. The injustices they endured enraged me; their personal struggles overwhelmed me. I knew I could do little but sympathize.

21   My mother, no stranger to suffering, suggested I was too impressionable when I emotionally told her the women's stories. "That's nothing," she'd say lightly. "If they were in Mexico, life would be even harder. At least there's opportunities here, you can work."

22   My icy arrogance quickly thawed, that first summer, as my respect for the conveyor-belt ladies grew.

23   I worked in the packing shed for several summers. The last season also turned out to be the last time I lived at home. It was the end of a chapter in my life, but I didn't know it then. I had just finished junior college and was transferring to the university. I was already over-educated for seasonal work, but if you counted the overtime, no other jobs came close to paying so well, so I went back one last time.

24   The ladies treated me with warmth and respect. I was a college student, deserving of special treatment.

25   Aguedia, the crew chief, moved me to softer and better-paying jobs within the plant. I went from the conveyor belt to shoving boxes down a chute and finally to weighing boxes of tomatoes on a scale—the highest-paying position for a woman.

26   When the union's dues collector showed up, the women hid me in the bathroom. They had decided it was unfair for me to have to join the union and pay dues, since I worked only during the summer.

27   "Where's the student?" the union rep would ask, opening the door to a barrage of complaints about the union's unfairness.

28   Maria (of the nine children) tried to feed me all summer, bringing extra tortillas, which were delicious. I accepted them guiltily, always wondering if I was taking food away from her children. Others would bring rental contracts or other documents for me to explain and translate.

29   The last day of work was splendidly beautiful, warm and sunny. If this had been a movie, these last scenes would have been shot in soft focus, with a crescendo of music in the background.

30   But real life is anticlimactic. As it was, nothing unusual happened. The conveyor belt's loud humming was turned off, silenced for the season. The women sighed as they removed their aprons. Some of them just walked off, calling "*Hasta la proxima!*" Until next time!

31   But most of the conveyor-belt ladies shook my hand, gave me a blessing or a big hug.

32   "Make us proud!" they said.

33   I hope I have.

CHECKING YOUR COMPREHENSION

Directions: In the space provided, write the letter of the choice that best completes each of the following statements. Record your score on page 487.

_____   1. This article focuses primarily on
        a. working conditions in vegetable-packing sheds.
        b. the life history of migrant workers.
        c. the author's experiences with the women with whom she worked.
        d. how migrant workers are treated unfairly.

_____   2. Through her experiences with the women workers, the author learns
        a. to understand and respect the women.
        b. how to avoid problems with the union.
        c. to avoid getting personally involved.
        d. how to get the best-paying job.

_____ 3. Why did the author choose to take a job at the packing shed?

    a. She wanted to get to know the women.

    b. It counted as community service.

    c. She could not get hired elsewhere.

    d. It was the highest-paying job.

_____ 4. Why was the author at first unhappy about working at the packing shed?

    a. She thought her Anglo friends would make fun of her.

    b. She thought the work would be tiring.

    c. She disliked the poor working conditions.

    d. She thought the women would treat her poorly.

_____ 5. Why did the ladies hide the author when the union's dues collector arrived?

    a. They knew she was hired illegally.

    b. They thought it was unfair for her to pay dues when she worked only in the summer.

    c. They thought the collector would fire her.

    d. They knew the collector was dishonest.

_____ 6. The events in this article are arranged

    a. chronologically.

    b. according to the place in which they occurred.

    c. according to jobs held.

    d. from most to least important.

_____ 7. Why did the author initially feel superior to the women with whom she worked?

    a. They dressed differently than she did.

    b. They gossiped.

    c. She thought of them as uneducated.

    d. They spoke Spanish.

8. Which statement best describes the women's attitude toward education?

   a. They thought it was a waste of time.

   b. They thought only men should go to college.

   c. They intended to get high school equivalency diplomas.

   d. They respected and valued education.

9. Why did the author's attitude change toward her coworkers?

   a. She became part of their families.

   b. She was touched by their humor and kindness.

   c. She had to do so in order to keep her job.

   d. She decided they were not lazy, after all.

10. Which statement best summarizes the author's last day at the packing shed?

   a. The women expressed their appreciation.

   b. Nothing unusual happened.

   c. The women offered her advice for the future.

   d. Many tearful good-byes were said.

WORDS IN CONTEXT

Directions: Locate each word in the paragraph indicated and reread that paragraph. Then, based on the way the word is used, write a synonym or brief definition in the space provided. You may use a dictionary if necessary.

11. uninspiring (para. 2) _____

12. grueling (para. 4) _____

13. impending (para. 17) _____

14. scoffed (para. 17) _____

15. recounting (para. 18) _____

VOCABULARY REVIEW

Directions: Match each word in column A with its meaning in column B.

Column A

Column B

_____ 16. gregarious

a. describe or identify in negative terms

_____ 17. dyspeptic

b. unchangeably

_____ 18. stigmatize

c. practical

_____ 19. sorority

d. sociable

_____ 20. pragmatic

e. grouchy

_____ 21. tedious

f. physically hard

_____ 22. melancholic

g. gloomy

_____ 23. irrevocably

h. belief that life is controlled by fate

_____ 24. strenuous

i. tiresome

_____ 25. fatalism

j. steady increase in volume

_____ 26. anticlimactic

k. group of women; sisterhood

_____ 27. crescendo

l. commonplace

STUDYING WORDS

Directions: Use a dictionary to answer the following questions.

_____ 28. The word **melancholic** (para. 18) originated from which of the following languages?

   a. French
   b. Latin
   c. Spanish
   d. Greek

_____ 29. Another meaning of the word **barrage** (para. 27) that is not used in the reading is

   a. a barrier against an enemy.
   b. a rapid discharge of missiles.
   c. a group of baronets.
   d. a dramatic change.

_____ 30. The correct pronunciation of the word **dyspeptic** (para. 12) is
        a. DIS pep tik
        b. dis pep TIK
        c. disp e IK
        d. dis PEP tik

_____ 31. A meaning of **transferring** (para. 23) used in the field of law is
        a. nullifying a contract.
        b. applying for a chance of residence.
        c. abandoning a cause.
        d. changing possession of legal title.

_____ 32. What part of speech is the word **laments** (para. 12)?
        a. adjective
        b. adverb
        c. noun
        d. preposition

QUESTIONS FOR DISCUSSION

1. Describe a situation or event that changed your attitude toward a person or group.
2. Working on a conveyor belt has many obvious disadvantages. Can you think of any advantages?
3. The ladies treated the author specially because she was a college student. How do people treat college students today? Compare your treatment with that of the author.

WRITING ACTIVITIES

1. Choose a person, perhaps someone who has not attended, or is not attending, college. Write a paragraph describing how he or she regards your college attendance.
2. Analyze what, if anything, you have learned from coworkers in a particular job. Summarize your findings in a brief essay.

I HAVE HAD TO LEARN TO LIVE WITH PEACE
Alephonsion Deng

This article first appeared in *Newsweek* magazine in October 2005. Read it to find out about the author's experiences both in Sudan and in the United States.

> **Vocabulary Preview**
>
> These are some of the difficult words in this essay. The definitions here will help you if you cannot figure out their meanings from the sentence context or by using word parts.
>
> **sanctuary** (para. 1) a shelter from danger and hardship
>
> **refugee camp** (para. 2) a shelter for persons displaced by war or political or religious oppression
>
> **mentors** (para. 4) teachers; counselors
>
> **vengeance** (para. 7) the act of harming someone in retaliation for something harmful he or she has done
>
> **memoir** (para. 10) an account of an author's personal experiences

How do you make a new life for yourself when you're consumed with the pain of your past?

1   In 1989, when government troops attacked my village in southern Sudan, my peaceful world fell apart. As a boy of 7 I ran barefoot and naked into the night and joined up with streams of other boys trying to escape death or slavery. We crossed a thousand miles of war-ravaged country without hope of sanctuary. Bullets replaced food, medicine, shelter and my loving parents. I lived on wild vegetables, ate mud from Mother Earth and drank urine from my own body.

2   We walked for five years, occasionally finding shelter at a refugee camp, only to have to leave again when it was attacked by Sudanese soldiers. Finally we made it to a camp in Kenya, where I lived for nearly a decade on a half cup of cornmeal a day and went to school. After several interviews with workers from the Office of the United Nations High Commissioner for

■ SURVIVAL SKILLS: I knew how to challenge a hyena, but I had never turned on a light or used a telephone.

Refugees, I was chosen, along with a few thousand other "lost boys," to go to the United States.

3   When I arrived here four years ago, I found that the skills I'd learned in order to survive in Sudan were useless. I knew how to catch a rabbit, challenge a hyena or climb a coconut palm, but I had never turned on a light, used a telephone or driven a car.

4   Luckily, the International Rescue Committee provided us with classes and mentors to teach us basics about computers, job interviews and Western social customs. Within a month I understood how to work most modern conveniences and started my first job as a courtesy clerk and stocker at a Ralph's grocery store in San Diego. Things like mangoes, chard and yams were familiar, but when customers asked about Cheerios, mayonnaise or Ajax, it was as though my years of learning English in the refugee camp were worthless.

5   Eventually I became acquainted with most things in a modern grocery store, but I still faced a much greater challenge. I'd lived with war, but I still needed to learn to live with peace. At work people joked around and although they made attempts to be friendly, I couldn't understand or connect with much of what they said. It often felt as if their jokes were about me. When one woman said, "Al, you are hot!" I didn't know what it meant and

assumed it wasn't good. I began to dread going to work, school or anywhere. Always the outsider who was ready to fight, I existed in a cloud of anger and depression.

6   It would take two more years for me to understand that these difficulties had little to do with language and cultural differences, and more with being caught up in conflict as a young boy. I could not forget the sound of guns or the cries of women and children dropping next to me like leaves shaken off a tree in a storm. For so many years, the smell and taste of death had spread within me poison.

7   I felt like I was dead when people around me laughed, and their smiles only made me feel more isolated and unhappy. I carried a weight as heavy as the earth. Anger boiled inside me and made me wonder if I was losing my mind. Sanity could not exist as long as I held onto the desire for vengeance against those who had taken my childhood. Trapped by my mental confusion, I blamed myself for what I was feeling, and lashed out at everyone around me.

8   Now I realize that the gigantic void created within me when I was young wasn't my fault. There was nothing I could have done. The emotions I held onto for so long only kept me from interacting with my new countrymen. I could not reach out in a friendly way or through humor because I lived in a fog of rage.

9   I'm finally making friends and adapting to my new country. When my friend Adam took me to a football game, the sound and smell of the halftime fireworks brought back bad memories and made me dizzy, but he understood and I managed to stay for the whole game. I drive a car, work as a medical-records clerk at Kaiser Hospital, attend college and even have a cell phone— a convenience I deeply appreciate. There was no way to call 911 years ago on that terrible walk.

10   I can't identify an exact turning point in my emotions, and I'm still struggling. However, I've found that speaking about my experiences at schools and community organizations and writing my memoir have helped. Sharing my feelings has lessened the burning inside me.

11   I do worry that when the American soldiers return from Iraq, even without cultural differences to deal with, they, too, will find that happiness in others can feel insensitive. At a time when they need it most, they may find it difficult to reconnect emotionally with their families and friends. Writer José

Narosky said, "In war, there are no unwounded soldiers." I would add that there are no women, children or animals who escaped unscathed.

12   Still, I know it is possible to move on. For all those years I lived with revenge on my mind. Now I'm a man with the seeds of love, dignity and hope in his heart.

CHECKING YOUR COMPREHENSION

Directions: In the space provided, write the letter of the choice that best completes each of the following statements. Record your score on page 487.

_____ 1. The author's main purpose in this selection is to
  a. discuss the civil war that has claimed countless lives in Sudan.
  b. comment on the differences between life in the United States and in Sudan.
  c. describe his efforts to make a new life for himself after surviving the effects of war.
  d. express his concern about soldiers returning from war.

_____ 2. After the attack on his village, the author survived by doing all of the following *except*
  a. living on wild vegetables.
  b. hunting with his parents.
  c. eating mud.
  d. drinking his own urine.

_____ 3. The main point of paragraph 3 is that the author
  a. came to the United States four years ago.
  b. did not know how to turn on a light or drive a car.
  c. knew how to catch a rabbit and climb a coconut palm.
  d. realized that his survival skills were useless in the United States.

_____ 4. The author's first job in the United States was at
  a. a grocery store in San Diego.
  b. the Office of the Commissioner for Refugees.
  c. the International Rescue Committee.
  d. Kaiser Hospital.

5. According to the author, the "greater challenge" he faced was to learn how to
   a. work modern conveniences.
   b. speak English.
   c. purchase groceries.
   d. live with peace.

6. When the author describes his difficulties in paragraph 5, what overall pattern does he follow?
   a. process
   b. comparison/contrast
   c. example
   d. definition

7. The main point of paragraphs 6–8 is that the
   a. author was having difficulties with language and cultural differences.
   b. author's past experiences were preventing him from moving on with his life.
   c. people around the author were insensitive to his feelings.
   d. author was confused by his anger and desire for revenge.

8. The author supports his thesis primarily with
   a. facts and statistics.
   b. historical evidence.
   c. personal experience.
   d. figurative language.

9. The main point of paragraph 9 is expressed in the
   a. first sentence.
   b. second sentence.
   c. third sentence.
   d. last sentence.

10. According to the author, what has helped him deal with his past?
   a. counseling
   b. having modern conveniences
   c. sharing his experiences through speaking and writing
   d. working

WORDS IN CONTEXT

Directions: Locate each word in the paragraph indicated and reread that paragraph. Then, based on the way the word is used, write a synonym or brief definition in the space provided. You may use a dictionary if necessary.

11. war-ravaged (para. 1) _____

12. challenge (para. 3) _____

13. acquainted (para. 5) _____

14. lashed out (para. 7) _____

15. void (para. 8) _____

16. interacting (para. 8) _____

VOCABULARY REVIEW

Directions: Match each word in column A with its meaning in column B.

Column A	Column B
_____ 17. sanctuary	a. the act of harming someone in retaliation for something harmful he or she has done
_____ 18. refugee camp	b. an account of an author's personal experiences
_____ 19. mentors	c. a shelter from danger or hardship
_____ 20. vengeance	d. teachers; counselors
_____ 21. memoir	e. a shelter for persons displaced by war or oppression

STUDYING WORDS

_____ 22. The correct meaning of the word **streams** (para. 1) as it is used in this reading is

a. continuously moving processions.

b. beams of light.

c. prevailing attitudes.

d. pours out.

_____ 23. Which one of the following correctly indicates how
conveniences (para. 4) is pronounced?

    a. CON veen eye ents is

    b. con VEEN ee ents is

    c. con veen EYE ents is

    d. con veen ee ENTS is

_____ 24. The etymology of the word **isolated** (para. 7) is

    a. English.

    b. Greek.

    c. French.

    d. German.

_____ 25. The French root of the word **memoir** (para. 10) means

    a. biography.

    b. writing.

    c. author.

    d. memory.

_____ 26. The best synonym for the word **unscathed** (para. 11) is

    a. unhurt.

    b. unmarked.

    c. unhappy.

    d. distressed.

QUESTIONS FOR DISCUSSION

1. Have you ever heard of the lost boys of Sudan? What did this essay teach you that you did not know?

2. What do you think about the author's concern for soldiers returning from Iraq? What does it tell you about him?

3. Discuss the title of this selection. What are some other possible titles?

4. Discuss how the author has coped with the trauma of his lost childhood. What do you think was the most important factor in his survival?

WRITING ACTIVITIES

1. The author has had to adapt to a completely different culture than his own. Have you ever visited a place or been thrust into a situation in which the customs (or the language) were foreign to you? Write a paragraph describing your experience.

2. Write an essay about the immigrant groups in your community and answer the following questions within your essay: How did your community respond to the arrival of immigrants? What services are in place to help them adapt to life in their new country? What contact do you have with people who are new to this country? What can you do to make a newcomer feel welcome?

3. The author came to understand that his desire for revenge was holding him back from making a new life. Can you think of a time when a strong emotion was blocking you from reaching a goal? How did you eventually get past your obstacle? Write a paragraph describing your experience.

4. Imagine that you are responsible for introducing the author at a speaking event. Write a short introduction based on what you know about him from the selection.

Multicultural Reader Selections

RECORDING YOUR PROGRESS

Reading	Test	Number Right	Score
1 The Most Hateful Words	Checking Your Comprehension	_____ × 10 =	_____ %
2 Seoul Searching	Checking Your Comprehension	_____ × 10 =	_____ %
3 Coming Into My Own	Checking Your Comprehension	_____ × 10 =	_____ %
4 Living Life to the Fullest	Checking Your Comprehension	_____ × 10 =	_____ %
5 American Indian Mascots Should Go	Checking Your Comprehension	_____ × 10 =	_____ %
6 Hispanic USA: The Conveyor-Belt Ladies	Checking Your Comprehension	_____ × 10 =	_____ %
7 I Have Had to Learn To Live With Peace	Checking Your Comprehension	_____ × 10 =	_____ %

EVALUATING YOUR PROGRESS

Based on your test performance, rate how well you have mastered comprehension skills by checking one of the boxes below or by writing your own evaluation.

☐ **Need More Improvement**

Tip: Try using the Reading Road Trip Web site at **http://www.ablongman.com/readingroadtrip** for extra practice with comprehension questions.

☐ **Need More Practice**

Tip: Try using the Reading Road Trip Web site at **http://www.ablongman.com/readingroadtrip** to brush up on your comprehension skills, or visit this textbook's companion Web site at **http://www.ablongman.com/mcwhorter.**

☐ **Good**

Tip: To maintain your skills, log on to this textbook's companion Web site at **http://www.ablongman .com/mcwhorter** for a quick review.

☐ **Excellent**

YOUR EVALUATION: _____

_____

_____

_____

Credits

Photo Credits

Preceding Page 1, top to bottom: Tore Bersaker/Sygma/Corbis; Ryan McVay/Getty Images; **22**: Karl Hentz/Getty Images; **26**: Omni Photo/Index Stock; **34**: © The New Yorker Collection 2000, Leo Cullum from cartoonbank.com. All Rights Reserved.; **64**: Dennis Kleiman; **70**: Patrik Giardino/Corbis; **102**: Corbis; **132**: Photofest; **157**: John McPherson/Universal Press Syndicate; **166**: Anne Domdey/Corbis; **199**: © The New Yorker Collection 1999, Arnie Levin from cartoonbank.com. All Rights Reserved.; **202**: Marilyn Root/Index Stock; **204**: Bob Daemmrich/The Image Works; **225**: Jeffrey Greenberg/Photo Researchers, Inc.; **272**: Richard Hutchings (2); **310**: Frank Herholdt/Getty Images; **338**: John Loomis/Redux; **346**: AP/Wide World Photos; **375**: Morton Beebe, S.F./Corbis; **401**: Eugene Hoshiko/AP/Wide World Photos; **437**: Jay Dickman Photography; **446**: Gail Burton/AP/Wide World Photos; **478**: Jean Bourget

Text Credits

Chapter 1

5 From Joseph A. DeVito, *Messages:Building Interpersonal Communication Skills*, 4/e, p. 146. Published by Allyn and Bacon, Boston, MA. Copyright © 1999 by Pearson Education. Adapted by permission of the publisher.

16 From Michael R. Solomon and Elnora W. Stuart, *Marketing: Real People, Real Choices*, 3/e, pp. 161-162. Copyright © 2003. Reprinted by permission of Pearson Education, Inc., Upper Saddle River, NJ.

22 From Joseph A. DeVito, *Messages:Building Interpersonal Communication Skills*, 4/e, p. 100. Published by Allyn and Bacon, Boston, MA. Copyright © 1999 by Pearson Education. Reprinted/adapted by permission of the publisher.

25 Michelle Kearns, "To Love and to Cherish," *The Buffalo News*, June 7, 2003. Reprinted by permission of The Buffalo News

Chapter 2

36 Dictionary entry "Curve" Copyright © 2000 by Houghton Mifflin Company. Reproduced by permission from *The American Heritage Dictionary of the English Language*, Fourth Edition.

38 "Sample Pronunciation Key" Copyright © 1982 by Houghton Mifflin Company. Adapted and reproduced by permission from *The American Heritage Dictionary*, Second College Edition.

41 Dictionary entry "Green" Copyright © 2000 by Houghton Mifflin Company. Reproduced by permission from *The American Heritage Dictionary of the English Language*, Fourth Edition.

42 Dictionary entry "Oblique" Copyright © 2000 by Houghton Mifflin Company. Reproduced by permission from *The American Heritage Dictionary of the English Language*, Fourth Edition.

58 Dictionary entries "Panoply," "Ventilate," "Manifest," "Besiege," "Facile." Copyright © 2000 by Houghton Mifflin Company. Reproduced by permission from *The American Heritage Dictionary of the English Language*, Fourth Edition

63 Kerrel McKay, "We Don't Have AIDS, But We Suffer, Too" from *Newsweek*, November 28, 2005. © 2005. All rights reserved. Reprinted by permission.

Chapter 3

82 From H.L. Capron, *Computers: Tools for an Information Age*, 5/e, p. 233. Copyright © 1998. Adapted by permission of Pearson Education, Inc., Upper Saddle River, NJ.

91 James Geiwitz, *Psychology: Looking at Ourselves*, 2/e, p. 189. Boston: Little, Brown, 1980.

92 Alex Thio, *Sociology*, 5/e, p. 235. New York: Longman, 1998.

93 Randy Dotinga, "Online Dating Sites Aren't Holding People's Hearts," *The Christian Science Monitor*, January 27, 2005. Reprinted by permission of the author.

Chapter 4

124 Mark S. Zelermyer, "Saved by the Kindness of a Virtual Stranger" from *Newsweek*, August 11, 2003. © 2003 Newsweek, Inc. Reprinted by permission.

Chapter 5

136 Curtis Byer and Louis Shainberg, *Living Well: Health in Your Hands*, 2/e, p. 256. New York: HarperCollins College Publishers, 1995.

136 K. Warner Schaie and James Geiwitz, *Adult Development and Aging*, pp. 371-372. Boston, Little, Brown, 1982.

137 From Richard George, *The New Consumer Survival Kit*, p. 212. Copyright © 1978. Reprinted by permission of Little, Brown and Company.

137 Warren Agee, Phillip Ault, and Edwin Emery, *Introduction to Mass Communication*, 12/e, p. 153. New York: Longman, 1997.

137 David Hicks and Margaret Gwynne, *Cultural Anthropology*, 2/e, p. 270.New York: HarperCollins College Publishers, 1996.

138 From B.E. Pruitt and Jane J. Stein, *Decisions for Healthy Living*, pp. 49-51. Copyright © 1994. Adapted by permission of Pearson Education, Inc., publishing as Benjamin Cummings.

142 Curtis Byer and Louis Shainberg, *Living Well: Health in Your Hands*, 2/e, p. 289. New York: HarperCollins College Publishers, 1995.

142 Joseph A. DeVito, *Human Communication: The Basic Course*, 7/e, p. 170. New York: Longman, 1997.

142 Bob Weinstein, *Jobs for the 21st Century*, p. 118. New York: Collier Books, 1983.

142 Dr. Joyce Brothers, from "What Dirty Words Really Mean" in *Good Housekeeping*, May 1973. Reprinted by permission of Joyce B Enterprises, Inc.

143 Jean Weirich, *Personal Financial Management*, p. 155. Boston: Little, Brown, 1983.

143 John Dorfman, *Well Being: An Introduction to Health*, p. 263. Glenview, IL: Scott, Foresman, 1980.

143 Edward Fox and Edward Wheatley, *Modern Marketing*, p. 142. Glenview, IL: Scott, Foresman, 1978.

144 Joseph A. DeVito, *Human Communication: The Basic Course*, 7/e, p. 78. New York: Longman, 1997.

150 From Roger LeRoy Miller, *Economics Today*, 8/e, p. 84. Copyright © 1994 Pearson Education, Inc. Reprinted by permission of Pearson Education, Inc. All rights reserved.

150 Christopher Anson and Robert Schwegler, *Longman Handbook for Writers and Readers*, 2/e, p. 78. New York: Longman, 2000.

151 Joseph A. DeVito, *The Elements of Public Speaking*, 6/e, p. 164. New York: Longman, 1997.

151 Spencer A. Rathus et al., *Human Sexuality in a World of Diversity*, 4/e, p. 189. Boston: Allyn and Bacon, 2000.

152 Wendy G. Lehnert, *Light on the Internet: Essentials of the Internet and the World Wide Web*, pp. 53, 55. Reading, MA: Addison Wesley Longman, 1999.

154 Spencer A. Rathus et al., *Human Sexuality in a World of Diversity*, 4/e, p. 221. Boston: Allyn and Bacon, 2000.

156 Deborah Tannen, "Don't Ask." Excerpt from *You Just Don't Understand* by Deborah Tannen. Copyright © 1990 by Deborah Tannen. Reprinted by permission of HarperCollins Publishers. William Morrow imprint.

Chapter 6

172 David Hicks and Margaret Gwynne, *Cultural Anthropology*, 2/e, p. 258. New York: HarperCollins College Publishers, 1996.

175 From Rebecca Donatelle, *Health: The Basics*, 5/e, pp. 290-291. Copyright © 2003 by Pearson Education Inc., publishing as Benjamin Cummings. Reprinted by permission of Pearson Education, Inc.

176 Michael R. Solomon, *Consumer Behavior: Buying, Having, and Being*, 5/e, pp. 92-93. Upper Saddle River, NJ: Prentice Hall, 2002.

176 George C. Edwards et al., *Government in America: People, Politics and Policy*, 10/e, pp. 654-655. New York: Longman, 2002.

177 Duane Preble and Sarah Preble, *Artforms: An Introduction to the Visual Arts*, 7/e, p. 144. Upper Saddle River, NJ: Prentice Hall, 2002.

177 Edward F. Bergman and William H. Renwick, *Introduction to Geography*, Updated 2/e, p. 106. Upper Saddle River, NJ: Prentice Hall

180 From Richard George, *The New Consumer Survival Kit*, p. 114. Copyright © 1978. Reprinted by permission of Little, Brown and Company.

182 James M. Henslin, *Essentials of Sociology*, 2/e, p. 239. Boston: Allyn and Bacon, 1998.

185 From Ricky W. Griffin and Ronald J. Ebert, *Business*, 5/e, p. 43. Copyright © 1999. Reprinted by permission of Pearson Education, Inc., Upper Saddle River, NJ.

188 Barbara Tunick, "Why Go Veg?" from *Vegetarian Times*, July 2002. Reprinted by permission of Vegetarian Times / Active Interest Media.

Chapter 7

205 From Michael R. Solomon, *Consumer Behavior: Buying, Having, and Being*, 4/e, pp. 49-50. Copyright © 1999. Reprinted by permission of Pearson Education, Inc., Upper Saddle River, NJ.

207 James Coleman and Donald Cressey, *Social Problems*, 6/e, p. 130. New York: HarperCollins College Publishers, 1996.

214 Nora Newcombe, *Child Development: Change Over Time*, 8/e, p. 354. New York: HarperCollins College Publishers, 1996.

214 Frans Gerritsen, *Theory and Practice of Color*, p. 9. New York: Van Nostrand Reinhold, 1975.

215 From "Trees Talk to One Another" by Jack Schultz and Ian Baldwin," *Science Digest*, January 1984. © 1984 by Science Digest. Reprinted by permission of Ian Baldwin

216 John Naisbitt, *Megatrends*, p. 23. New York: Warner Books, 1982.

216 From Michael R. Solomon, *Consumer Behavior: Buying, Having, and Being*, 4/e, pp. 49-50. Copyright © 1999. Reprinted by permission of Pearson Education, Inc., Upper Saddle River, NJ.

217 From Michael R. Solomon, *Consumer Behavior: Buying, Having, and Being*, 4/e, p. 48. Copyright © 1999. Reprinted by permission of Pearson Education, Inc., Upper Saddle River, NJ.

218 Wendy G. Lehnert, *Internet 101: A Beginner's Guide to the Internet and World Wide Web*, p. 95. Reading, MA: Addison Wesley Longman, 1998.

219 From Roger LeRoy Miller, *Economics Today*, 8/e, p. 185. Copyright © 1994 Pearson Education, Inc. Reprinted by permission of Pearson Education, Inc. All rights reserved.

220 From Roger LeRoy Miller, *Economics Today*, 8/e, p. 513. Copyright © 1994 Pearson Education, Inc. Reprinted by permission of Pearson Education, Inc. All rights reserved.

222 Patsy Neal, excerpt from ""My Grandmother, the Bag Lady," *Newsweek*, February 11, 1985. Written and copyrighted © by Patsy Neal. Reprinted by permission.

224 Kim McLarin, "Primary Colors," first appeared in *The New York Times Magazine*, 1998. Reprinted by permission of Inkwell Management on behalf of the author.

Chapter 8

234 MapQuest map of Austin, TX. The MapQuest logo is a registered trademark of MapQuest, Inc. Map content © 2006 by MapQuest, Inc. and Tele Atlas. The MapQuest trademarks and all content are used with permission.

236 Curtis Byer and Louis Shainberg, *Living Well: Health in Your Hands*, 2/e, pp. 78-79. New York: HarperCollins College Publishers, 1995.

238 From Thomas C. Kinnear, Kenneth L. Bernhardt, and Kathleen A. Krentler, *Principles of Marketing*, 4/e, p. 132. Copyright © 1995. Reprinted by permission of Pearson Education, Inc., Upper Saddle River, NJ.

238 From Thomas C. Kinnear, Kenneth L. Bernhardt, and Kathleen A. Krentler, *Principles of Marketing*, 4/e, p. 132. Copyright © 1995. Reprinted by permission of Pearson Education, Inc., Upper Saddle River, NJ.

240 Alex Thio, *Sociology*, 5/e, p. 534. New York: Longman, 1998.

241 From Thomas C. Kinnear, Kenneth L. Bernhardt, and Kathleen A. Krentler, *Principles of Marketing*, 4/e, pp. 39-40. Copyright © 1995. Reprinted by permission of Pearson Education, Inc., Upper Saddle River, NJ.

245 Neil A. Campbell et al., *Biology: Concepts and Connections*, 3/e, p. 430. San Francisco: Benjamin / Cummings, 2000.

248 Bruce E. Gronbeck et al., *Principles of Speech Communication*, 12th Brief ed., p. 302. New York: Harpercollins College Publishers, 1995.

248 From Laura Uba and Karen Huang, *Psychology*, p. 148. Copyright © 1999. Reprinted by permission of Laura Uba.

252 From Michael R. Solomon, *Consumer Behavior: Buying, Having, and Being*, 6/e, pp. 480-481. Copyright © 2004. Adapted by permission of Pearson Education, Inc., Upper Saddle River, NJ.

255 From Michael R. Solomon, *Consumer Behavior: Buying, Having and Being*, 4/e, pp. 252-253. Copyright © 1999. Reprinted by permission of Pearson Education, Inc., Upper Saddle River, NJ.

258 From Rebecca Donatelle, *Health: The Basics*, 4/e, p. 213. Copyright © 2001 Allyn and Bacon. Reprinted by permission of Pearson Education, Inc.

260 From Rebecca Donatelle, *Health: The Basics*, 4/e, p. 99. Copyright © 2001 Allyn and Bacon. Reprinted by permission of Pearson Education, Inc.

262 Joseph A. DeVito, *The Interpersonal Communication Book*, 8/e, p. 141. New York: Longman, 1998.

264 From Rebecca Donatelle, *Access to Health*, 7/e, pp. 470-471. Copyright © 2002 by Pearson Education, Inc., publishing as Benjamin Cummings. Reprinted by permission of Pearson Education, Inc.

Chapter 9

274 Sydney B. Newell, *Chemistry: An Introduction*, p. 11. Boston: Little, Brown and Co., 1980.

279 From Laura Uba and Karen Huang, *Psychology*, p. 483. Copyright © 1999. Reprinted by permission of Laura Uba.

279 Hal B. Pickle and Royce Abrahamson, *Introduction to Business*, 6/e, p. 40. Glenview, IL: Scott, Foresman, 1986.

280 Hal B. Pickle and Royce Abrahamson, *Introduction to Business*, 6/e, p. 119. Glenview, IL: Scott, Foresman, 1986.

281 From Carole Wade and Carol Tavris, *Psychology*, 5/e, p. 499. Copyright © 1998. Reprinted by permission of Pearson Education, Inc., Upper Saddle River, NJ.

282 Hugh D. Barlow, *Criminal Justice in America*, p. 332. Upper Saddle River, NJ: Prentice Hall, 2000.

283 From William Kephart and Davor Jedlicka, *The Family, Society, and the Individual*, 7/e, p. 332. Copyright © 1991. Reprinted by permission of Pearson Education, Inc., Upper Saddle River, NJ.

284 Richard L. Weaver II, *Understanding Interpersonal Communication*, 4/e, p. 123. Glenview, IL: Scott, Foresman, 1987.

284 Robert A. Wallace, *Biology: The World of Life*, 7/e, p. 572. Menlo Park, CA: Benjamin / Cummings, 1997.

284 James M. Henslin, *Essentials of Sociology*, 2/e, p. 272. Boston: Allyn and Bacon, 1998.

285 From John A. Thill and Courtland Bovee, *Excellence in Business Communication*, 4/e, p. 79. Copyright © 1999. Reprinted by permission of Pearson Education, Upper Saddle River, NJ.

286 Joseph A. DeVito, *The Elements of Public Speaking*, 7/e, p. 164. New York: Longman, 2000.

286 From Ricky Griffin and Ronald Ebert, *Business*, 5/e, p. 83. Copyright © 1999. Reprinted by permission of Pearson Education, Inc., Upper Saddle River, NJ.

295 From "Personality Disorders." Excerpted from *The World Book Encyclopedia*. © 2006 World Book, Inc. By permission of the publisher. http://www.worldbook.com.

296 From William Kephart and Davor Jedlicka, *The Family, Society, and the Individual*, 7/e, p. 332-333. Copyright © 1991. Reprinted by permission of Pearson Education, Inc., Upper Saddle River, NJ.

297 Paul G. Hewitt, *Conceptual Physics*, 8/e, p. 56. Reading, MA: Addison Wesley, 1998.

298 From "Mimosa." Excerpted from *The World Book Encyclopedia*. © 2006 World Book, Inc. By permission of the publisher. http://www.worldbook.com.

299 From Cook/Yale/Marqua, *Tourism: The Business of Travel*, 2/e, pp. 259- 260. Copyright © 2002. Reprinted by permission of Pearson Education, Inc., Upper Saddle River, NJ.

302 Alton Fitzgerald White, "Right Place, Wrong Face." Original title: "Ragtime, My Time." Reprinted with permission from the October 11, 1999 issue of *The Nation*. For subscription information, call 1-800-333-8536. Portions of each week's *Nation* magazine can be accessed at http://www.thenation.com.

Chapter 10

313 Paul G. Hewitt, *Conceptual Physics*, 8/e, pp. 82, 84. Reading, MA: Addison Wesley, 1998.

317 J. Ross Eshleman and Barbara Cashion, *Sociology: An Introduction*, 2/e, p. 88. Boston: Little, Brown, 1985.

326 J. Ross Eshleman and Barbara Cashion, *Sociology: An Introduction*, 2/e, p. 583. Boston: Little, Brown, 1985.

327 Joseph A. DeVito, *Messages: Building Interpersonal Communication Skills*, 3/e, p. 153. New York: HarperCollins College Publishers, 1996.

328 John D. Daniels and Lee H. Radebaugh, *International Business: Environments and Operations*, 8/e, p. 679. Reading, MA: Addison-Wesley, 1998.

329 From Thomas C. Kinnear, Kenneth L. Bernhardt, and Kathleen A. Krentler, *Principles of Marketing*, 4/e, p. 218.Copyright © 1995. Reprinted by permission of Pearson Education, Inc., Upper Saddle River, NJ.

331 Rick Weiss, "Acupuncture" excerpted from "Medicine's Latest Miracle" by Rick Weiss in *Health Magazine*, January/February 1995. Copyright © 1995 by The Health Publishing Group. Used by permission of the author.

334 From Carole Wade and Carol Tavris, *Psychology*, 5/e, p. 494. Copyright © 1998. Reprinted by permission of Pearson Education, Inc., Upper Saddle River, NJ.

337 Peter Madsen, "When Mommy Goes Off to Fight a War" from *Newsweek*, July 18, 2005. © 2005 Newsweek, Inc. Reprinted by permission.

Chapter 11

349 Paul Aurandt, *Paul Harvey's The Rest of the Story*, edited and compiled by Lynne Harvey, p. 116. Garden City, NY: Doubleday, 1977.

350 Richard L. Weaver II, *Understanding Interpersonal Communication*, 4/e, p. 291. Glenview, IL: Scott, Foresman, 1987.

350 From Lewis Katz, *Know Your Rights*. Copyright © 1993. Reprinted by permission of West, a division of Thomson Publishing.

351 Richard Shenkman, *Legends, Lies and Cherished Myths of American History*, pp. 37-38. New York: Morrow, 1988.

351 Aesop, "The Man, The Boy, and the Donkey" from *Aesop's Fables*

355 Robert A. Wallace, *Biology: The World of Life*, 4/e, p. 271. Glenview, IL: Scott, Foresman, 1987.

357 Robert C. Yeager, *Seasons of Shame: The New Violence in Sports*, p. 6. New York: McGraw-Hill, 1979.

367 "The Lion's Share" from *The King's Drum and Other African Stories* by Harold Courlander. Copyright © 1962, 1990 by Harold Courlander. Reprinted by permission of Michael Courlander.

370 Dorothy Conniff, "What's Best for the Child?" from *The Progressive*, November 1988. Reprinted with permission from The Progressive. http://www.theprogressive.org.

373 "Stiff Laws Nab Deadbeats" from *USA Today*, August 16, 1995. © USA TODAY, 1995. Reprinted with permission.

375 Jerry Mander, *In the Absence of the Sacred: The Failure of Technology and the Survival of the Indian Nations*. San Francisco: Sierra Club Books, 1991.

378 Richard Swardson, excerpt from "Long Days and Short Keystrokes on the Electronic Plantation," *City Pages*, October 21, 1992, p. 8. Reprinted by permission of the author's daughter, Rachel Swardson Wenham.

380 Mary Pipher, excerpts from "The Beautiful Laughing Sisters— An Arrival Story" in *The Middle of Everywhere: The World's Refugees Come to Our Town*. Copyright © 2002 by Mary Piper. Reprinted by permission of Harcourt, Inc.

Student Resource Guide A

400 From Edward Greenberg and Benjamin Page, *The Struggle for Democracy*, Brief Version 2/e, pp. 336-338, 347-348. Copyright © 1999 Addison Wesley Educational Publishers. Reprinted by permission of Pearson Education, Inc.

403 From Rebecca Donatelle, *Health: The Basics*, 5/e, pp. 245-247. Copyright © 2003 by Pearson Education Inc., publishing as Benjamin Cummings. Reprinted by permission of Pearson Education, Inc.

407 From Joseph A DeVito, *Human Communication*, 8/e, pp. 139-140. Published by Allyn and Bacon, Boston, MA. Copyright © 2000 by Pearson Education. Reprinted by permission of the publisher.

Multicultural Reader

Amy Tan, "The Most Hateful Words" from *The Opposite of Fate: A Book of Musings*. Copyright © 2003 by Amy Tan. First appeared in *The New Yorker*. Reprinted by permission of the author and the Sandra Dijkstra Literary Agency.

Rick Reilly, "Seoul Searching," *Time*, August 28, 2000. ©2000 Time Inc. Reprinted by permission.

Benjamin Carson, "Coming into My Own." Taken from *Gifted Hands* by Dr. Benjamin Carson. Copyright © 1990 by Review and Herald ® Publishing Association. Used by permission of Zondervan.

From *Wouldn't Take Nothing for My Journey Now* by Maya Angelou. Copyright © 1993 by Maya Angelou. Used by permission of Random House, Inc.

Rich Heffern, "American Indian Mascots Should Go," *National Catholic Reporter*, February 25, 2005, p. 18. Reprinted by permission.

Rose del Castillo Guilbault, "Hispanic USA: The Conveyor Belt Ladies" as appeared in *The San Francisco Chronicle*, April 15, 1990. Reprinted by permission of the author.

Alephonsion Deng, "I Have Had to Learn to Live with Peace" from *Newsweek*, October 31, 2005. © 2005 Newsweek, Inc. Reprinted by permission.

Index